'I absolutely LOVE [this] book. It is absolutely fabulous and I enjoyed every single page. What an incredible undertaking!! I thought I knew much of women at sea but I have learned so much more from reading [this] book. Thank you for writing it!!'
— Tracy Edwards MBE

'*Stars To Steer By* is an entertaining and inspiring cruise through the lives of women sailors: adventurers, racers, travellers, workers, pootlers, rich and poor, happy and sad. It's a lovely portrait gallery as much as a history, and deserves a place on every sea-lover's bookcase, whether you're a real sailor or an arch fantasist.'
— Louisa Young, author of *My Dear I Wanted to Tell You*

'*Stars to Steer By* is a long overdue celebration of the spirit of women's independence through sailing, shining a spotlight on achievements which, all too often, have been wiped from the sailing record; it advocates what all women sailors want - normalisation and a sense of fairness on the water. Julia's writing brings each of her subjects vividly to life, giving a voice to many pioneers whose success and trailblazing have been overshadowed by the achievements of men, just on the basis of gender. This book is the start of the correction of the record.'
— Katy Stickland, *PBO* Editor

'A tour de force that details the fascinating stories, mostly untold, of the lives of women sailors throughout the 20th century. Julia gathers the stories of pioneering women sailors from all classes, describes the important roles of the WRNS in two World Wars and looks at the changing attitudes of society to the present day. Informative, thought-provoking and a tremendously enjoyable read.'
— Heather Prentice, *Yachting Monthly* Deputy Editor

For Dolly and Ada, my youngest granddaughters, in case they need to answer this question for themselves:

'What is it makes a man follow the sea?
Ask me another!' says Billy Magee:
'Maybe its liquor and maybe it's love –
Maybe it's likin' to be on the move –
Maybe the salt drop that runs in his blood
Won't let his killick lie snug in the mud:
What is it makes such poor idjits as me
Follow the sea – follow the sea?...
Jiggered if I know!' says Billy Magee.

Cicely Fox Smith, 'Follow the Sea' (1922)

STARS TO STEER BY

Celebrating the 20th Century
Women who went to Sea

JULIA JONES

ADLARD COLES

LONDON • OXFORD • NEW YORK • NEW DELHI • SYDNEY

ADLARD COLES
Bloomsbury Publishing Plc
50 Bedford Square, London, WC1B 3DP, UK
Bloomsbury Publishing Ireland Limited
29 Earlsfort Terrace, Dublin 2, Ireland

BLOOMSBURY, ADLARD COLES and the Adlard Coles logo are trademarks of Bloomsbury Publishing Plc

First published in Great Britain 2025

Copyright © Julia Jones, 2025

Julia Jones has asserted her right under the Copyright, Designs and Patents Act, 1988, to be identified as Author of this work

For legal purposes the Acknowledgements constitute an extension of this copyright page

Note: Every effort has been made to trace the copyright holders and obtain permission to reproduce this material. Please do get in touch with any enquiries or any information relating to images or the rights holders

All rights reserved. No part of this publication may be: i) reproduced or transmitted in any form, electronic or mechanical, including photocopying, recording or by means of any information storage or retrieval system without prior permission in writing from the publishers; or ii) used or reproduced in any way for the training, development or operation of artificial intelligence (AI) technologies, including generative AI technologies. The rights holders expressly reserve this publication from the text and data mining exception as per Article 4(3) of the Digital Single Market Directive (EU) 2019/790

A catalogue record for this book is available from the British Library

Library of Congress Cataloguing-in-Publication data has been applied for

ISBN: HB: 978-1-3994-1546-0; ePDF: 978-1-3994-1548-4; ePub: 978-1-3994-1549-1; audio: 978-1-3994-15453

2 4 6 8 10 9 7 5 3 1

Typeset in Bell MT Std by Deanta Global Publishing Services, Chennai, India
Printed and bound in Great Britain by Clays Ltd, Elcograf S.p.A.

To find out more about our authors and books visit www.bloomsbury.com and sign up for our newsletters

For product safety related questions contact productsafety@bloomsbury.com

Front cover images, clockwise from top left: Gladys Newell sailing *Fortis* (John Newell), Ellen MacArthur (Getty Images), Nicolette Milnes-Walker sailing *Aziz* (Nicolette Coward), Clare Francis (Alamy)

Back cover, from top to bottom: 'Mr. W.L. Wyllie, A.R.A., in his yawl *Ladybird*, crossing the North Sea' (Lionel Smythe), Abbey 'Boat Builder' Molyneux, (Abbey Molyneux), crew sailing *Maiden* (Maiden Factor Foundation)

CONTENTS

Acknowledgements	vii
Introduction: Pink Shorts: Women overlooked	1
1 *In the shade of one's own hat brim* Circumnavigating for pleasure	9
2 *My mother sewed constantly* Invisible women at sea	19
3 *Blue gauze veils are useful but not ornamental* New designs for 'New Women'	28
4 *The coiffure harks back to primitive simplicity* Outdoor women	38
5 *My red skirt was to be the signal* Independent Irish women	51
6 *We don't want any petticoats here* Pioneering women in the First World War	61
7 *Winter Shoes in Springtime* Overcoming trauma	71
8 *Fed up with this skirt nonsense* Post-war pioneers and fickle yacht owners	84
9 *Clothes not fit for a girl to wear* Sailing on the last of the grain ships	98
10 *Elastic-waisted blue serge skirts* Pleasure sailors between the wars	106
11 *I only joined for the hat* Women sailors in the Second World War	116
12 *Things will never be the same again* Women's lives disrupted by the war	131

13 *I wore the right shoes and didn't interfere*
Unexpected jobs in wartime   144

14 *I handed him a bundle of garments for a flare*
Discovering courage   154

15 *With my best suspender belt*
Adapting to the post-war world   163

16 *No experience necessary*
Mixed-sex sailing, 1950s to 1970s   178

17 *If I'm coming, I'm coming in my duffle coat*
Women in offshore racing   190

18 *Heather at the stemhead*
Sailing from the Clyde   199

19 *Nobody can find you*
Families at sea   209

20 *Enormous biceps, baggy jeans and a jolly, yo-ho manner*
Femininity and determination   224

21 *Hiring leaky oilskins from the charter company*
Women making their own way   238

22 *Who wore the pants?*
The role of skipper   251

23 *Trouser suits*
Married teamwork   262

24 *I pinned a smile on my face*
Winners   273

25 *Dressed like I wanted it*
Changing priorities   284

    Bibliography   301
    Endnotes   307
    Index   321

ACKNOWLEDGEMENTS

This has been the most collaborative book I have ever written. So many people have helped so generously, either telling their own or their relatives' stories or introducing me to other people who they believed I should meet. For this I would like to thank Jo Adey, Clare Allcard, Charles and Liz Bazeley, Di Beach, Anne Billard, Janet Bradley, Richard Bridges, Elaine Bunting, Alison Chadwick, Katie Christie, Nicolette Coward (Milnes-Walker), Miranda Delmar-Morgan, Ann Eaton, Tracy Edwards, Clare Francis, Janet Grosvenor, Anne and Liz Hammick, Janet Harber, Peter Harvey, Suzanne Heywood, Annie Hill, Elspeth Iskander, Vuyisile Jaca, Naomi James, Rob Kemp, Jill Kernick, Simon Kiln, Sam Llewellyn and his cousins, Astrid Dixon Llewellyn, Cathy MacAleavey, Lesley Marsh, Rowan and Janet McFerran, Robin Minney, Abbey Molyneux, Claudia Myatt, John Newell, Anthony Osler, Merfyn Owen, Ian Palmer, Elaine Penhaul, Ashley Perrin, Jojo Pickering, Heather Prentice, Julia Ramos, Clive Reeves, Seonaid Reid, Jane Russell, Jane Shaddick, Clio Smeeton, Ewen Southby-Tailyour, Carla Stanley, Katy Stickland, Theo Stocker, Heather Thomas, Christopher Thornhill, Penny and Naomi Vera-Sanso, Natalie Wheen, Richard Woodman.

Others have shared their own research or reading. I wish I could have used even more of it. Thank you Chris Andreae, Jeremy Batch, Michael Clarke, Rose Collis, Richard Crockatt, Sarah Curtis, Vincent Delany, Charles J Doane, Jane Flower, Kate Lance, Ben Lowings, Bruce Moss, WM Nixon, Chris O'Flaherty, Ned Phillips, David Swinstead, Tim Trafford, Chris Thompson. I'm also grateful to archivists at Bembridge Sailing Club, Charterhouse School, St Leonards School, the Clyde Cruising Club, Hastings Museum, Royal Harwich Yacht Club and the Royal Cruising Club; to Jackie de Fin (Sail Africa), Libby Muddit (The Maiden Factor), Anne Hammick (Ocean Cruising Club) for answering my questions; to the Cruising Association for their excellent library facilities; to the Clyde Corinthian YC, the King and Queen pub (Hamble), the Little Ship Club, the Royal Cruising Club and the Water Wag Club for their welcome and hospitality.

Everyone who I interviewed has read what I wrote about them (or their friend or relative), has checked its accuracy and given me their permission to quote from their writing or use their photographs. I'm additionally grateful to the following people, publishers, photographers and institutions: Ted Alexander (*Ransome in Russia*), Rob Cowan (Yachting Images Ltd, photo of Seonaid and Millicent Reid), Nick Grainger (*A Voyage of the Aegre*), Julie Grainger, Charlie Ipcar and Jim Saville (Cicely Fox Smith), Christina Hardyment (quote from Evgenia Ransome Journal on behalf of the Arthur Ransome Literary Executors), The British Library (Barbara Hughes engraving, i7917. b.48), Claire Isbester, Simon Kiln (Ann Davison), Leeds University Library special collections (Evgenia Ransome quote, p86) reproduced with the permission of Special Collection Leeds University Library BC MS 20c Ransome/3/13, Craig Leweck (*Scuttlebutt*), Sam Llewellyn (*Marine Quarterly*), Mardle Books, an imprint of Gemini (Beyond the Sea), Barrie Martin (*Little Ship Club Journal*), Mark AT McNeill (Classic Boat Museum, Blanche Thornycroft photo), the Morgan Giles Heritage Project, Margaret Radcliffe (*No Holds Barred*), Theo Stocker (*Yachting Monthly*), James Tew, University of Nebraska (*Pacific Lady*), Chris Thompson (SailCraft blog), Linus Wilson (*Sailing the Ogre*), Hugh Matheson and Thoresby Settlement Trustees (Rozelle Raynes).

I can't leave this section without thanking someone I have never corresponded with nor met – professional football player and sports presenter – Alex Scott. Her post-match comments when the England women's football team beat Germany on 31 July 2022, opened my eyes to the struggle and prejudice endured by 20th-century women footballers and inspired this book.

I owe special debts of thanks to my co-grandmother, Eileen Bamford, for her outstanding skill and conscientiousness as a birthdates detective and family researcher and to my daughter-in-law, Alice Thorogood, for her insights into the experience of young girls sailing now, particularly my older granddaughters Gwen and Hettie Thorogood, who welcome me so warmly to their events. Matt Lis and the Woodbridge Boatyard team help me care for *Peter Duck* through my failing attempts to maintain a work/life balance. Bertie Wheen's kindness and skill is indispensable bringing old photos up to standard and old books back into circulation. My husband, Francis Wheen, has given unwavering support and newspaper cuttings on demand. He is the person who enables me to be more myself than I could ever be otherwise. I can't thank him enough.

INTRODUCTION: PINK SHORTS

Women overlooked

One early evening in August 2023 I looked across St Katherine's Dock in London at the yacht *Maiden*, lying calm and elegant in the gentle sunlight. This was the yacht that had carried 12 women round the world in the 1989/90 Whitbread Race. *Maiden* had shown what women could achieve together. She was about to do it again.

Tracy Edwards, *Maiden*'s owner and the skipper on that first voyage, opened the pontoon gate to the small queue of visitors. I had thought there would be more of us. This was a chance to go on board the yacht, meet the new skipper and her crew, talk to Tracy and offer our support to the only British entry in the forthcoming Ocean Globe Race. They would also be the only all-female team. Who were these younger women? Why did *Maiden* need to race round the world again? I was too shy to speak to Tracy as she led us along the sloping gangway, down into the small marquee. There was *Maiden*, moored alongside the pontoon. Suddenly I felt the prickle of tears in my eyes and my breathing came a little faster. Two young women in red polo shirts stepped forward to welcome me. They were Payal Gupta, from the Indian Navy, and Vuyisile Jaca, from Durban in South Africa, members of *Maiden*'s 21st-century crew. They understood my moment of emotion. They told me they had felt the same the previous day when Tower Bridge had opened, for them.

Later, as I learned more about the vision that had put young women from every inhabited continent on board this iconic yacht, I asked Tracy why I hadn't read about it in the newspapers. A chance fragment on BBC Radio 4's *Today* programme had alerted me to *Maiden*'s visit to London. I had expected the pontoon to be heaving with visitors, but it was not. 'Because the British press just don't care?' she answered, unguardedly. At that point only *Agence France-Presse* had shown any interest in writing about *Maiden*'s entry to the Ocean Globe Race. I grew up in the age of Francis Chichester and Robin Knox-Johnston:

I still feel surprised that the centre of enthusiasm for global yacht racing is now in France, not Britain.

The concept of this new race was as a 50th-anniversary retrospective for the 1973 Whitbread Round the World Race. That had been a British idea, competitors following the clipper route round the three great capes, which still capture imaginations long after the square-rigged sail trading ships disappeared. Even the Royal Navy (RN) was involved back in those 20th-century days, through its sailing association. But the oceans are international: water offers a freeway, an escape from the land, as even the smallest river seems to do. *Maiden*'s 21st-century race entry was intended to speak to people of different countries, particularly women who might not normally consider setting out on such an adventure or have the opportunity to do so. The new crew, some of whom I would meet that evening, included Najiba Noori, a 28-year-old Afghan woman who had fled the Taliban two years previously. Najiba is a photographer, recently introduced to sailing, who says that it gives her 'the freedom and peace that I have not had in most of my life'. If *Maiden*'s new venture were to succeed, other members of her crew might become the first Black women to race round the world.

This wasn't mere tokenism or a PR exercise, however; it was a competition. Heather Thomas, *Maiden*'s 25-year-old skipper, told us they were 'In it to win it!' I was impressed by Heather. She'd grown up in Otley, West Yorkshire, not obviously a seafaring centre, but had made the most of all available opportunities, learning to sail in a Mirror dinghy on a former quarry, becoming a watch leader on a sail training ship, winning a bursary to cross the Pacific in the Clipper 2015/16 Race when she was just 18. Heather is a professional, earning her living at sea – a person with whom you'd feel safe sailing round the world. Tracy says that Heather is also a brilliant navigator.

In the summer of 2022, the England women's national football team, the Lionesses, won the UEFA European Championship. It was the best international result for England since the men's World Cup victory in 1966. Whether or not one loves football, the post-match discussion gave a shocking insight into the way 20th-century British women who wanted to play this 'beautiful game' had been treated by the (male) authorities ever since 1922 when the Football Association banned women's teams from their grounds. Sports commentator and former professional footballer, Alex Scott's unforgiving comments made me

INTRODUCTION: PINK SHORTS

aware of the long struggle endured by earlier women footballers for the right to use their energies, their bodies and their talents in this way. She honoured them for never giving up. It encouraged me to think about another group of women from the same time, who had wanted to sail for their own pleasure and fulfilment, and who persisted against all discouragement. Like that first *Maiden* team who had competed in the 1989/90 Whitbread race.

The history of British women in sailing includes petty prohibitions, gratuitous insults and wonderful triumphs of determination and courage. Sailing perhaps does not have the public profile of football, but it's infinitely more varied. For some people it's a sport, a pastime, an activity; for others it's a way to live or a means to earn a living, a way to explore the world or to discover oneself. None of these things should be gender-dependent. The sea is not a men-only space. Only our social and cultural perceptions make it so. Women have travelled by sea, and lived and worked on ships, for centuries, though in tiny numbers and almost invisibly. One of my favourite characters in all fiction is Mrs Croft, the Admiral's wife in Jane Austen's *Persuasion* (1817). Austen captures the mutual incomprehension existing between her and the land-based Mrs Musgrove.

> *'What a great traveller you must have been ma'am,'* said Mrs Musgrove to Mrs Croft.
> *'Pretty well ma'am, in the 15 years of my marriage, though many women have done more. I have crossed the Atlantic four times and have been once to the East Indies and back again and only once; besides being in different places about home: Cork, and Lisbon, and Gibraltar but I never went beyond the Straits and was never in the West Indies. We do not call Bermuda or Bahama, you know, the West Indies.'*
> Mrs Musgrove had not a word to say in dissent. She could not accuse herself of having ever called them anything in the whole course of her life.[1]

Exploration under sail would seem to have a rich literature. Yet when I search the shelves in a sailing library, skim through book reviews in a yachting magazine or check the contents in cruising club annuals, only about one book in 40 records such experience through a woman's eyes. And that may be a wild over-estimate. Recently I stood in front of a specialist book corner run by an antiquarian bookseller in Cowes. There were between 300 and 350 books on the shelves. I checked their spines as carefully as time allowed. Three were by women authors and two more by men and women writing together. This absence of books by women sailors of the past is a matter for regret. I would love to have read a memoir by the American Virginia Slocum, who sailed with Joshua from 1871 to 1884 and had seven children, all born at sea or in foreign ports. Slocum's second wife, Henrietta, experienced a hurricane, attack by pirates, a smallpox outbreak, shipwreck and stranding. After all this, she stayed at home, enabling Joshua to achieve lasting fame through (as described by the name of his book) *Sailing Alone Around the World* (1900). Historically, women's educational opportunities and literacy rates have lagged behind men's. Globally, they still do – girls' education is one of the causes for which today's *Maiden* was sailing – but such extreme under-representation by women writers about the sea is not because 19th-century and 20th-century women seafarers couldn't write, or even that they were few in number, but that publishers didn't think anyone would be interested in what they had to say.

Fortunately, this is a book of celebration, not complaint, so where better to start than with the first undeniable sailing bestseller written by a woman – Anna Brassey's *A Voyage in the Sunbeam*, published in 1878. Eight years previously, the first Married Women's Property Act (1870) had come to pass. In England, Wales, Ireland and various overseas territories (though not yet Scotland), the Act provided that the wages a wife earned through her own work or the property she inherited would remain hers, rather than being automatically transferred to her husband. (If you have no right to your own money, you can't buy yourself a boat!) It also ensured that married women writers kept the copyright to their works. This might not have been a matter of great financial importance to Anna Brassey but the success of her book spurred her to continue to explore in *Sunbeam* and to write, not only for herself but so other people might vicariously enjoy the world across the seas.

I've chosen to focus this study on the 20th century, mainly because it feels like 'my' century. The passion and determination of the women (and men) who fought the incremental, decades-long battle for equal rights has affected my everyday life. That spirit of independence that inspired women sailors to take the helm into their own hands from the late 19th century onwards has made it possible for me to sail unobtrusively on my own, making my own decisions, now, without feeling like an oddity. Beginning in the 1870s rather than on the dot of 1900 seems quite naturally to align observations of British women in sailing with

INTRODUCTION: PINK SHORTS

the position of British women generally. After 1867, when the Second Reform Act enfranchised a wider section of the male population, the question of women's right to vote was debated almost yearly in Parliament. People in Anna Brassey's social circle were increasingly aware of the anomalies and injustices in women's position at home. As she visits the different countries of the world, her interest in women's as well as men's experience is obvious. Occasionally, it's possible to see a legal change having a direct impact on the maritime opportunities available to women – the Sex Disqualification (Removal) Act 1919 and the Sex Discrimination Act 1975 forced some institutions to open their doors. But more usually it's the general mood of the time, as well as an individual's talents and circumstances, that shapes people's perceptions and conversations and the likelihood that they will be able to realise their dreams. Different generations often have subtly different attitudes from their parents or grandparents so, wherever possible, I've included dates of birth to bring some sailing women together as contemporaries. It's not a narrative of consistent progress. There are decades when some women seem more willing to, as it were, hand over the helm to men, and others when they assert their right to take their own chances. Major national crises, such as wars, have an immediate impact on opportunities and relationships, then, afterwards, a more complex ripple effect.

The phrase that has most inspired me was supplied by an 1890s Solent racer, Barbara Hughes. She didn't have much money or property of her own but seems to embody the assertive attitudes of the New Woman, much discussed in middle- and upper-class circles at the time, along with heated arguments as to the relative impropriety or liberation of riding a bicycle or wearing a divided skirt. Barbara wanted to be in charge of her own boat, competing on equal terms with men: 'you should have it all in your own hands, with no one to say you "nay", otherwise that spirit of independence (so rarely enjoyed by our sex) is lost.'[2]

I've amused myself by choosing mainly clothing-related chapter titles. Clothes can liberate or constrain, can send messages of defiance or conformity – or simply the wearer can assert some common sense by choosing utility over fashion. For much of this period, in yachting circles men tended to adopt a pseudo-naval uniformity: reefer jacket, brass buttons, club tie, yachting cap or an open-collared shirt with either flannel trousers or khaki shorts. Women had more opportunity to develop their own style. Tracy Edwards and the first *Maiden* crew sported pink shorts, then made the most obviously outrageous sartorial statement when they distracted attention from a poor result by wearing swimsuits to sail into Fort Lauderdale. The 21st-century inclusion of Najiba Noori, however, might remind us of the dark truth that while she has been sailing round the world, wearing whatever clothing has been appropriate for the weather or her need to move around freely and safely, women and girls in her native Afghanistan and neighbouring Iran have been 're-educated', whipped and possibly even killed for not wearing the hijab.

The 20th century in Britain brought legal, medical and social changes that affected women in all areas of their lives, including their opportunities to achieve 'that spirit of independence' through sailing. Family planning made an immediate difference; it's a lot easier to sail with one or two children than with nine, though Marian Wyllie managed this (and one of them seriously disabled). It has also, gradually, dissuaded overprotective men from treating all women as if we might inadvertently be pregnant all of the time – therefore seriously restricting our freedom of action. Technical changes, such as efficient winches, lighter-weight materials, Bermudan rig and self-steering systems, have also made a difference to women's enjoyment of sailing – though the newly developed punts and 1/2-raters sailed by talented women helms in the 1880s and 1890s made it obvious that if there was a will to build boats that women could sail, designers could quite well manage this.

Though the current century, so far, seems to be full of women winners and headline-grabbing female firsts, Tracy Edwards doesn't believe that the battle for true equality is won yet, even in Britain, either at sea or on land. She recommended that I read *Hags* (2023) by Victoria Smith, an angry book about the double discrimination of age and gender. I'm 70 as I finish writing this and don't find that my experience coincides with Victoria's. But she is only in her forties and it may feel different there. The strong and relevant point that she makes is that it's all too easy to pit generations of women against each other, thus risking the experience of one generation being dismissed or simply forgotten by the next. I am shocked by the ease with which some women's achievements have been wiped from the sailing record. The 20th-century publishing industry, whether producing books or magazines, must bear some responsibility for this. Caroline Criado-Perez's book *Invisible Women* (2020) has nothing to do with seafaring but everything to do with the way our society has been organised. Women's triumphs go unrecorded (or are credited to men), our statues are absent from public spaces, our shapes and sizes are forgotten when safety equipment is being designed. Yachting is no different. Towards the end of the period being considered here, 5ft 2in-tall Ellen MacArthur could not reach the cleats on the main mast of the racing yacht she had chartered because it had been designed for a 6ft-tall man. Many men do have greater height, more powerful hand grip and greater upper body strength than many women, but by no means all of them. More thoughtful design makes sailing more accessible for smaller, weaker but still adventurous men – as well as for women. Once Ellen became a 21st-century star, the enormous trimaran *B&Q/Castorama* was designed for her needs, to enable her to set a new world record for single-handed, non-stop circumnavigation – and was equally available to be sailed by a man when Ellen retired from competition.

Invisibility can, however, be a blessing if all that one truly wants from sailing is self-reliance and solitude. Arguably this was easier to achieve in the 20th century than in the 21st. Automatic identification systems (AIS), sophisticated communication equipment and pressure to behave responsibly by lodging a passage plan with an onshore contact or to use an app that will generate an alarm if one fails to turn up on time can make one feel safely enclosed in a goldfish bowl. The 'retro' Ocean Globe Race required all competitors to put away their 21st-century phones for the duration and I didn't speak to anyone who was not actively looking forward to that moment. As Peter Gerard decided in the 1920s, 'too frequent bulletins was a habit to be discouraged, and dear ones ashore must learn not to worry unduly over empty letter boxes'.[3]

Through the 20th century, and still today, women in sailing are almost always aware of being in a minority. This can bring an unwelcome visibility to some. In 2018 Susie Goodall, aged 28, was the only female competitor in the reincarnation of the 1968 Golden Globe single-handed 'race for madmen'. Her gender and age made her a gift to the event organisers, who needed to attract media interest and sponsors. 'Pretty girl sailing round the world [...] I made the most of it,' said yachting journalist Barry Pickthall. Susie recalls feeling 'dangled like a puppet'[4] for the media. What made her acutely uncomfortable was the feeling that she was being presented as a feminist icon, an ambassador for all women – so her failure would be a failure for all. Most of the women in this book did not see themselves as campaigners: they merely wanted the personal freedom to develop their talent or follow their dreams.

The outstanding help that I've received from other people who sail (both women and men) may primarily be because we are glad to see 20th-century women's achievements celebrated – it appeals to our sense of fairness – but also because it may help to normalise female involvement. As well as the 'stars to steer by' who inspire others directly on the water, I have also written about just a few women who provided the 'surround-sound' of sailing: a magazine editor, a photographer, a pundit, a cartoonist, a judge, some wives, a naval officer. They too were pioneers. As my daughter-in-law Alice pointed out when we talked about my grandchildren's experience of 21st-century dinghy sailing, an equal mix of girls and boys on the water has been achieved, but if the overwhelming majority of adults in positions of authority – the judges, official measurers, coaches, safety boat drivers and sailing club commodores – are still men, the girls must wonder where their longer-term future lies.

Finally, I'm aware that most of the women I've written about here are those who achieve 'firsts', win prizes or write books. There are others, I'm sure you've seen them, who simply go down the river and out to sea independently – just as men do.

Tracy Edwards becomes the first woman in its 34-year history to be awarded the Yachtsman of the Year Trophy (Tracy Edwards)

1

'In the shade of one's own hat brim'[1]
Circumnavigating for pleasure

Anna Brassey (b. 1839)

'AT MIDDAY THE SUN was so exactly vertical over our heads that it was literally possible to stand in the shade of one's own hat brim and be sheltered all round.'[2] On 6 July 1876, Anna and Tom Brassey, their four children, two naval officers, an artist, a doctor, a 29-strong crew, a nurse, a lady's maid, a stewardess and an ever-changing array of plants, pets and other livestock had left Cowes on their steam-yacht *Sunbeam*. By 29 July they had reached the Cape Verde Islands, where Anna made this observation.

To a fanciful 21st-century reader, standing on a yacht in an exotic location, completely sheltered 'in the shade of one's own hat brim', might seem to symbolise the position of a wealthy British traveller in the 1870s – protected, confident, sure of their position in the world. To Anna (aged 36) and Tom (aged 40), just three weeks into their pioneering voyage, their situation may have felt less securely fixed. 'Our navigators experienced considerable difficulty in taking their noon tide observations as the sun appeared to dodge about in every direction.'[3] Anna needed to replenish their provisions. She had responsibility for domestic organisation and, as she remarked several months later when leaving Honolulu for Yokohama in 1877, 'the departure of a small vessel with 40 people on board for a voyage of a month's duration is a matter requiring considerable preparation'.[4] In total, they would be away for 11 months and would travel 36,000 miles.

Sunbeam had left England rolling under the weight of an extra 30 tons of spare sails, spars and provisions, 15 tons of water and

84 tons of coal. The additional fruit and vegetables loaded in Madeira had rotted almost before they could be consumed. They'd then spent three days anchored in La Orotava Harbour off Tenerife. Part of that time had been spent on a thrilling but exhausting expedition up to the Peak and the rest in entertaining visitors. *Sunbeam*, their 'home on the ocean', was already becoming famous and people wanted to see her. She was an iron-framed, three-masted topsail schooner, 159ft long, 27.5ft wide and displaced 532 tons. She was both unique and (for some) conceptually puzzling. When she reached Kobe, Japan in February 1877 the authorities found her bewildering; she was neither a man-of-war nor a merchant ship: she was a yacht. 'But what can be the object of a ship without guns is quite beyond their comprehension.'[5]

Sunbeam's building and fitting out had been a big project in which Anna had been fully involved. When they reached Singapore the Maharajah of Johor came on board and inspected her 'with the utmost minuteness and interest'. Anna noted that 'his Mohammedan ideas about women were considerably troubled when he was told I had a great deal to do with the arrangement and designing of the interior.'[6] Anna's husband Tom rated Anna's contribution more highly still: 'The voyage would not have been undertaken, and assuredly it would never have been completed, without the impulse derived from her perseverance and determination.'[7] It had been her idea, and she made the arrangements for their reception, entertainment and sightseeing across the world.

Tom was the MP for Hastings, though he apparently had no scruples about leaving his constituency for months to go travelling. Anna was fully involved in his political career, and in a range of good causes. She was an enthusiastic early photographer and had set herself to keep a record of their voyage, with the idea of enabling others to share their experience. I'm sure she would have enjoyed publishing a blog or vlog. She installed a darkroom on their boat and kept up a busy correspondence from every port. Her subsequent record of the voyage, published as *A Voyage in the Sunbeam*, became a bestseller. It was translated into several languages, used as a schoolbook and an exam text, and remained continuously in print for many years.

Though *Sunbeam* was primarily a sailing vessel (7,525 sq m of canvas) she had a 70hp auxiliary steam engine that could push her along at a top speed of just over 10 knots, consuming about 4 tons of coal a day when steaming continuously. However, Tom almost always preferred to sail. Among his many achievements, he was the first British yachtsman to gain a Board of Trade Masters' Certificate. He loved his yacht and loved to navigate, frequently turning away the services of a pilot and taking sole responsibility for *Sunbeam* even in complex, unfamiliar harbour entrances or situations as challenging as the Magellan Straits. Anna wrote:

> *I cannot help admiring the manner in which Tom has piloted his yacht through the Straits for it would do credit not only to any amateur but to a professional seaman. He has never hesitated or been at a loss for a moment, however intricate the part or complicated the directions; but having thoroughly studied and mastered the subject beforehand, he has been able to go steadily on at full speed the whole way.*[8]

All their writings and actions show that Tom and Anna were devoted to each other and to their family and were deeply respectful of each other's qualities. They were also generous hosts, able to rely on the professionalism of their crew even when they themselves were absent. On Sunday 23 July in La Orotava, for instance, they decided to have a lie-in as they only returned from their expedition to the Peak at 03.30 that morning. It was 10.30 before they woke and midday before they went on deck, with Anna writing:

> *Long before this the* Sunbeam *had been inundated with visitors from the shore. From breakfast-time until prayers at three o'clock, when the yacht was closed for an hour, there was a constant stream of them [...] Many of the poor people had come from villages far away over the mountains. We could not help feeling a certain respect for the determined way in which physical infirmity was mastered by curiosity for, though many experienced very serious inconvenience from the motion of the vessel, they still persevered in examination.*[9]

One group of Spanish ladies, beautifully dressed in black with lace mantillas, caused some private amusement as each arrived on board accompanied by a young man carrying her individual sick bowl. Even when Anna, Tom and their family went ashore, the visitors kept coming.

On Monday morning the yacht was steaming up and down, attempting to leave, before the final sightseers could be persuaded to depart.

As they passed the Cape Verde islands of Sao Antonio and São Vicente six days later, they began looking out for a suitable supply stop. The next likely anchorage, off Tarrafal Bay, seemed unpromising. 'High, rocky mountains, sandy slopes and a black volcanic beach comprised a scene of arid desolation, in the midst of which was situated one small white house with four windows and a thatched roof, surrounded by a little green patch of sugar canes and cocoa-nut palms.'[10] They dropped anchor anyway. Mr Martinez, the son of the house, came out to the yacht and assured the Brasseys that all sorts of fresh food could be provided, if they were able to wait. They went ashore, where Mr Bingham (the artist) sketched, Anna took photographs, the children played, and the crew of *Sunbeam* filled water breakers and transported the provisions as they were delivered. Anna's description uses language that we wouldn't choose today.

> *Every five minutes a negro arrived with a portion of our supplies. One brought a sheep, another a milch-goat for baby while the rest contributed severally a couple of coconuts, a papaya, three mangoes, a few watercresses, a sack of sweet potatoes, a bottle of milk, three or four quinces, a bunch of bananas, a little honey, half a dozen cabbages, some veal and pork and so on; until it appeared as if every little garden on either side of the three leagues of stream, must have yielded up its entire produce [...] They were brought in by people varying in colour from dark yellow to the blackest ebony and ranging in size from fine stalwart men over 6 feet in height to tiny little blackies of about 3 foot 6 with curly hair, snowy teeth and mischievous beady eyes.*[11]

She saw her first cocoa-nut palm growing and tasted her first mango. The food seemed cheap; the water expensive. 'However, as ours is the only yacht, with one exception, that has ever visited this island there was nothing for it but to pay the bill without demur.' Evidently, she didn't know about the severe droughts that regularly afflict these islands. Water was indeed a precious commodity. As the *Sunbeam* sails away down the coast of Africa, the 21st-century reader may be left worrying about the language used and the wider implications of the scene. Were these cheerful people emptying their gardens willingly or

'IN THE SHADE OF ONE'S OWN HAT BRIM'

under duress? Would they go hungry as a result? Was Mr Martinez an enslaver? Were the Brasseys guilty of looting?

The Cape Verde islands had been worked by slave labour since the 15th century and, although the trade had been prohibited in the northern hemisphere since 1815, it was not finally banned in the islands until 1878, more than a year after *Sunbeam*'s visit. It was then replaced by a system of share-cropping (paying the landlord in produce), which may have been what was already in operation here. The Brasseys observed only cheerfulness and generosity, as people arriving by boat frequently do.

When *Sunbeam* reached Brazil, the situation was more difficult and describing it was more complex. Though Britain had passed both the Slave Trade Act 1807 and the Slavery Abolition Act 1833, Brazil's economy depended heavily on slave labour and it would be the last nation in the world to abolish it. Tom was a businessman as well as a politician and in addition to being on a family holiday, he was on an unobtrusive fact-finding mission. He and Anna were invited to spend a day on an estate called a *fazenda*. It was a day off for the workforce – the equivalent of a Sunday, though this was Thursday. Anna noted that all the neighbouring *fazenda*s chose different days to give enslaved people time off 'to prevent them meeting and getting into mischief'. The party from *Sunbeam* attended Mass and admired the singing. Anna was relieved to see that the children looked well-fed and not afraid of the enslaver or the overseers. They were shown the school and the hospital, the new water-powered machinery for cleaning coffee, and the light work done by the mothers with babies. Anna was glad to leave at the end of the day. But what did she think?

Very often, when reading *A Voyage in the Sunbeam* there's a sense that the author is deliberately not commenting. That she is observing but not imposing her own view. Occasionally she breaks out, as when she sees the crippled feet of a Chinese needlewoman, a monkey being tormented for visitor amusement or mares, separated from their foals, being flogged round and round in tight circles, trampling clay into bricks. Very rarely she allows herself a moment of sarcasm, as in Hong Kong when she describes the way of life for families on sampans.

> *The young mother of the small family generally rows with the smallest baby strapped under her back and the next sized one in her arms who she*

13

is also teaching to row. The children begin to row by themselves when they are about two years old. The boys have a gourd intended for a life preserver tied around their necks as soon as they are born. The girls are left to their fate, a Chinese man thinking it rather an advantage to lose a daughter or two occasionally.[12]

Does she generally avoid value judgements because it would be discourteous to people in whose countries she is a visitor or is she complacent and abhorrent? Anna was living at the height of the feathers-in-hats craze (as well as the stuffing-for-science) and her attitude to seabirds, for instance, will shock the modern reader. When steaming through the Gulf of Penas in south-western Chile, she describes the Cape pigeons as so tame that they can be caught in butterfly nets. 'Their plumage is not unlike grebe, and I mean to have some muffs and trimmings for the children made out of it.'

Everything elsewhere in her life suggests that she had clear personal values – philanthropy, communication, personal kindness, love. She was strongly independent. When Tom was unable to explore new places with her, either because he had business commitments or he didn't want to leave *Sunbeam*, she went alone. Though 'alone' for Anna was a relative term. There were usually other members of the party wishing to travel inland and both she and Tom also took their older daughters, Maybelle (11) and Muriel (5), with them as frequently as they could.

When I visited an exhibition of Anna's photographs in Hastings Museum, notices warned me about their 'cultural sensitivity' (meaning insensitivity). Captions invited me to consider the extent to which the people portrayed were being used as 'a model for Imperial eyes'. Elsewhere, I read that 'Brassey's bestselling books describe the places she visited and the people she encountered from a perspective of assumed Western superiority.' Apparently, she 'often' commented on the British colonial mission and the *Sunbeam* has been described by historian James Ryan as 'without doubt a vehicle of empire'.[13]

Sometimes one feels that a little more doubt wouldn't be a bad thing. Though *Sunbeam*'s circumnavigation took place in the same year that Disraeli raised the imperial idea to a new level by declaring Queen Victoria as 'Empress of India', the Brasseys were Gladstonian Liberals, thus unlikely to have endorsed such aggrandisement. Anna was sharply interested in trade, its details and contradictions, not imperial colonisation. Her readers learn that the best ponchos are made in Argentina; the cheaper, less waterproof ones come from Manchester. She notices fake Birmingham jewels for sale in Ceylon, says American tinned meat is better that British and points out that the Hawaiian islanders are wearing machine-made English cotton. She doesn't try to reconcile her view that British manufacturing is something to be proud of (and therefore its quality matters) with her frequently expressed opinion that people of other nations would be wiser to stick to their own cultural traditions rather than follow European fashion. She's in the anomalous, but not unfamiliar, position of a world traveller deploring globalisation.

When Anna and Tom reach their first Pacific island, they are greeted with courtesy but some bewilderment as to why they had visited at all. "'No sell brandy?' 'No.' 'No stealy men?' 'No.' 'No do what then?' Their knowledge of English was too limited for us to make them understand that we were only making a voyage of circumnavigation in a yacht.'[14] Without being rude to her hosts, she makes it clear to her readers that the princess who has stayed in her own Tahitian costume looks better than the queen who has stuffed herself into court dress. She also doesn't hesitate to suggest that missionaries who attempt to supress the island people's natural love of colour and flowers are making a bad mistake. She thinks it's a pity that the Japanese are being persuaded to abandon their traditional crafts in favour of mass-produced articles for the British and American market though she is glad that the country has recently opened up sufficiently for her to be able to visit. There is an atmospheric moment in Simono-Seki on the island of Honshu when she and five-year-old Muriel are walking through the muddy streets being stared at and followed by a timid crowd who shrink back if she turns round. She learns that no European lady or child has ever visited this place before and as she walks, she feels her serge dress and sealskin jacket being gently touched and stroked.

Despite their wealth, Anna and Tom were not cocooned from the problems that would become familiar to 20th-century cruising families before quick flights home were an option. Tom's mother died while they were away. Their oldest child, Thomas Allnutt, aged 13, had to leave the yacht at Rio to return to school. It would be nine months before they saw him again. There were dangers, too. Their oldest daughter, Mabelle, was washed overboard only nine days into the voyage but was saved by one of the RN officers. The children's kitten went the same way and was not saved. There was a scare when one of the crew developed smallpox and had to be hospitalised on shore. Everyone was offered a vaccination. Some refused it, to Anna's surprise. Their youngest daughter, Marie, was only a year old when they left England and became so ill during the rough passage from Honolulu to Yokohama that her mother believed she was going to die. An older daughter, Constance, nicknamed 'Sunbeam', had died from scarlet fever. Their yacht was named after her and her likeness provided its figurehead.

Anna was alert and knowledgeable about sailing but not hands-on. Tom said:

She made yachting with all its drawbacks a source of pleasure [...] She enjoyed the fair breezes and took deep pleasure in estimating the daily run, in which she was always wonderfully exact. She had a great faculty for seamanship and knew as well as anyone what was being done and what should be done on deck.[15]

As they approached the coral island of Tatakotoroa, he arranged for her to be hauled up the foretop masthead in the bosun's chair, with her petticoats tied under her, so she could get a better view of the surrounding reef. She loved it; 'I was so happy up aloft that I did not care to descend.'[16]

Anna enjoyed the relative informality of life at sea – though, on board *Sunbeam*, it was only relative.

Nothing could be more luxurious and delightful than our present mode of existence. With perfect weather, plenty of books to read and writing to do, no possibility of interruptions one can map out one's day and dispose of one's time exactly as one pleases until the 6:30 dressing bell – which always seems to come long before it's wanted – recalls one to the duties and necessities of life.[17]

Later in the voyage, as they pass through the Strait of Malacca and experience the heat of the Indian Ocean, they relax even further.

I fear our toilets would hardly pass muster in civilised society. Tom sets the example of leaving off collars, coats and waistcoats so shirts and trousers are now the order of the day. The children wear grasscloth pinafores and very little else, no shoes or stockings, Manila or Chinese slippers being worn by those who dislike bare feet. I find my Tahitian and Hawaiian dresses invaluable; they are really cool, loose, and comfortable, and I scarcely ever wear anything else.[18]

This would have been a rare experience in the days of corsets, buttons, stays and bustles. A portrait of Anna, drawn on the voyage, shows her in a neatly waisted sailor-style dress, still with a choker and cameo round her neck, long earrings and a ruched skirt over her petticoats, gazing intently out to sea with her hat off and the wind blowing through her short curls. Her life had not been without its difficulties. Her mother had died when she was very young. She was an only child, brought up in her grandfather's house and largely self-educated from his library, while also loving riding, the country life and studying botany. In her late teens she was very badly burned and spent six months lying wrapped in cotton wool, unable to feed herself. She suffered from bronchitis and had contracted malaria in 1869 when travelling in Syria. It recurred regularly and would finally kill her.

Tom describes her as someone who loved life. Voteless herself, she had supported him throughout the 1860s when he was struggling to find a Parliamentary seat. 'I have put her love for me as the primary motive for her interest in politics, but she had too much intelligence not to form an opinion of her own on public issues. Her sympathies were instinctively on the side of the people, in opposition to old-fashioned Toryism.'[19] Hastings, where Tom was finally successful, was a constituency that positively welcomed female involvement. Activist Barbara Bodichon, who led the successful campaign for the Married Women's Property Acts, was a constituent of Tom's and he took her petitions to Parliament. Anna's daughters joined Suffrage Societies when they were older but Anna herself chose to campaign on behalf of working men's clubs, first aid, the ambulance service and the Royal Navy Artillery Volunteers (RNAV). Tom's political responsibilities had increased steadily, particularly when he worked at the Admiralty, which meant that Anna's did too. When he finally lost his Hastings seat in 1886, following the defeat of Gladstone's Government of Ireland

Bill, he was glad they would be able to spend more time together and travel further.

> *She set out on her last journey full of hope and enterprise. In India, in Borneo, in Australia she was resolved to leave no place unvisited which could by any possibility be reached and where she was led to believe that objects of interest could be found. [...] In northern India her health was better than it had been for years but she fell away after leaving Bombay. Rangoon and Borneo told on her. She did not become really ill until the day after leaving Borneo when she was attacked by the malarial fever which infests the river up which she had travelled to visit the famous birds nest caves.*[20]

Anna died at sea on 14 September 1887 and was committed to the deep later that same day. She was 47 years old.

Anna Brassey, by George Bingham

2

'My mother sewed constantly'[1]
Invisible women at sea

Fanny Austen (b. 1790); Elizabeth Young (b. 1868); Susie Isbester (b. 1864)

Anna Brassey chose to sail – or at least she chose to explore the world by sea for her own pleasure. The children and the maids on board *Sunbeam* didn't have that choice. The daughters were put at risk on occasion but enjoyed experiences far removed from other children and more 'quality time' in the company of their parents than might have been the case if they'd been at home. The eldest son, sent home on his own to Eton, away from his parents and sisters and their exciting experiences for nine of the 11 months would seem to have had the worst deal. But what about the maids? They were there as part of their jobs – to look after Anna, to care for and teach her daughters, to wash and press their clothing and keep the cabins clean. One might assume that the male crew on *Sunbeam* had signed up expecting long periods away from home, but would the women have chosen to do so? Anna believed there was a pleasant communal atmosphere on the *Sunbeam* but we have only her word for it. There are glimpses of the maids getting splashed in the boats going ashore, feeling nervous or excited but, regrettably, no direct evidence of what they thought of their experiences.

Other British women went to sea during the 19th century as maids, cooks, stewardesses and as the employees of travelling families. Jo Stanley, descendant of May Quin, a ship's stewardess, has researched the subject of women employed at sea, particularly from 1850, when the coming of steam marginally decreased the objection to women on board as being too weak to handle sails. In 1875 the Merchant

Shipping Act stipulated that there must be a matron on all ships taking mixed groups of emigrants overseas. The numbers are very small: the 1851 census lists 76 'seawomen', increasing to 420 in 1901 – though presumably these were only the women who were ashore at the time.[2] Women had gone to sea earlier with the Royal Navy, though with minimal recognition. Suzanne Stark has written about the wives of warrant officers (the non-commissioned officers assigned permanently to a ship) who accompanied their husbands as a matter of course, despite the superstitions about women bringing ill luck to a ship, or the fact that they were neither paid, fed nor recognised as part of the ship's company. The ladies – wives or daughters of the ship's most senior officers (usually only the captain) – who also sailed with their male relative would only have had the degree of private choice negotiated between the relations themselves.

Jane Austen had two brothers in the Royal Navy. Both of them married and achieved sufficient rank for their wives to be officially permitted to sail with them. Both couples made different decisions. Francis, the older of the brothers married first Mary Gibson, with whom he had 11 children, then Martha Lloyd, with whom he had none. Neither is known to have sailed with him. Charles married Fanny Palmer, 17-year-old daughter of the Governor of Bermuda, in 1807. She sailed with him for the rest of her short life. It was four years before she met the rest of her husband's family, by which time she had two children. Then Charles was posted to HMS *Namur* at Sheerness, on patrol duty in the English Channel, where he and Fanny had another daughter. Aunts Jane and Cassandra were anxious about the children's health and inclined to be critical of their upbringing. The oldest child, Cassy (b. 1808), suffered badly from seasickness so was very thin. There's a glimpse of her, tired and bewildered, arriving at one of the family houses late at night after a long journey. She was also shy when in company with her more boisterous, land-based cousins. Her mother, Fanny, wondered whether it would be better for her to remain ashore with relatives. Jane and Cassandra offered to have her to stay with them.

> *Papa and Mama have not yet made up their mind as to parting with her or not – the chief, indeed the only difficulty with Mama – is a very reasonable one, the child's being very unwilling to leave them. When it was mentioned*

to her, she did not like the idea at all. All the same she has been suffering so much from seasickness that her Mama cannot bear to have her too much on board this winter. Charles is less inclined to part with her. I do not know how it will end or what is to determine it.[3]

A compromise seems to have been reached whereby Cassy and her younger sister Harriet spent extended time ashore with their aunts and also with their maternal grandparents, who returned to London from Bermuda. Fanny continued to live on the *Namur* with Charles and died in Sheerness, aged 24, giving birth to their fourth daughter, who also died. The three surviving children then made their home in London with their grandparents, while also spending lengthy periods with their aunts. Charles subsequently married Fanny's sister and had more children, though my impression is that they remained ashore.

Had Fanny Austen been given this choice? When she married Charles, he was on duty in the West Indies and a life afloat might have seemed the only way to spend time together. He was clearly devoted to her and their children. Their next phase of life living on the *Namur* may have been an economy measure – Charles was not as successful as his older brother Frank. It was clearly tough and forced Fanny to make choices for her children, whatever she decided for herself. Did she like living at sea or did she endure it out of duty? We will never know. It's arguable that the wives who stayed at home, managing their own lives and households, exercised more independent power than those who went to sea, where they were merely passengers. Yet Austen's fictional Mrs Croft (who had no children to worry about) presents shore life alone as a miserable, nerve-wracked existence:

The only time that I ever really suffered in body and mind, the only time I ever fancied myself unwell, or had any ideas of danger, was the winter that I passed by myself in Deal when the Admiral (Captain Croft then) was in the North Sea. I lived in perpetual fright at that time and had all manner of imaginary complaints from not knowing what to do with myself, or when I should hear from him next.[4]

When Admiral Charles Austen did die, he was far up the Irrawaddy River, away from his family. One of his last acts was to write a letter to his then wife, Fanny's sister, who was living ashore. Neither Cassy nor

Harriet married but both seem to have stayed close to the sea as adults, retaining their links with the navy.

* * *

Elizabeth Young (later Linklater) was about the right age to have been one of Anna Brassey's daughters but her life at sea was very different to theirs. Her father, James Eric Young, was the Swedish-born captain of the 345-ton barque *Parajero*. Elizabeth's seagoing experience began in 1872 at the age of four when she and her 29-year-old mother, Sarah, travelled from Greenock on the Clyde to Grays in Essex to join him. *Parajero* then loaded a cargo of chalk and sailed for Boston, Massachusetts.

This was work, not pleasure. Opportunities for exploring foreign ports were strictly subordinated to the needs of the ship, though whenever there was an opportunity to enjoy some social life with other captain's families, or to go ashore and shop or sightsee, it was welcomed. On their first voyage, Sarah was almost completely incapacitated by seasickness, which meant little Elizabeth had to stay below much of the time, sharing their cabin because there was no one else to look after her. Writing as an adult, Elizabeth can see how hard it must have been for her mother having the perfectly healthy child 'sitting up, playing in bed and shrieking with delight when the waves dashed up over the porthole'.[5]

It must have been hard for the child, too. Occasionally her father used to put some old clothes on her and 'take her for a run' and at other times he wrapped her mother in blankets and carried her out into the fresh air. Her mother later said she'd been so miserable that if it had been decided she should have been thrown overboard in those early days of the first voyage, she would not have asked for the suggestion to be reconsidered. Charles Darwin once wrote to his father 'If it were not for sea sickness, the whole world would be sailors.' Statistically, women are more likely than men to suffer from seasickness, though individual susceptibility remains a mystery. Young children often become sick more quickly than adults, though Elizabeth did not suffer badly. She enjoyed that first voyage. The first mate fed her cakes and jam and when they reached Boston the second mate and the carpenter took her ashore to drink sarsaparilla. It was hard to return home to Greenock and be sent to school.

Elizabeth remembered her mother sewing constantly to keep her husband clothed against the cold. 'She knitted thick stockings, reaching well above the knee, vests and drawers and mufflers, gloves and mittens and cuffs.'[6] This was woman's work then, whether at home or at sea. After that first experience, Sarah wouldn't travel in the North Atlantic again but when her husband was promoted to the clipper *Norval* and sailed from Liverpool to Calcutta in 1875, she and Elizabeth went too. There was space for the seven-year-old to run around – in good weather at least. The carpenter welcomed her into his shop, the sailmaker taught her to sew, and her father showed her how to use his sextant. When they were in port Elizabeth's mother, as the captain's wife, entertained other captains and their wives and perhaps gave a feeling of normal family life to those many other men voyaging alone.

In rough weather, Elizabeth was made to stay below decks, do lessons with her mother, learn to knit and crochet or simply endure. In times of tension and danger she knew that their presence was superfluous, even a nuisance. 'Women on board a merchant ship were there on sufferance. They had no part in the work of the ship and as far as she was concerned, they were non-existent. It behoved them to keep their thoughts to themselves and conceal their feelings.'[7] She remembered a particularly stormy passage off the Falklands Islands on the iron clipper ship *Orpheus*, when the ship was pooped while she and her mother were battened down below. They put on their rubber boots and swept the water out of their cabin, then refastened belongings that had been floating about. She wondered whether anyone understood what this was like for them:

> *How can one describe the feelings of women battened down in a ship's cabin in circumstances such as these? I don't mean the water coming into the cabins. That was a diversion that relieved the tension after the first shock was over but the awful suspense till we knew that the three men on the poop – the captain, the officer on watch and the man at the wheel – had not been swept away by the terrific force of the incoming wave.*[8]

Sarah and Elizabeth's lives settled into a pattern where they would stay at home for a year or two so that Elizabeth could attend school, then go away again. They sailed to Calcutta, New Zealand, Java, Rio de

Janeiro, Montevideo and round Cape Horn east–west for Oregon. By the time Elizabeth was 21, in 1889, she had already rounded the Horn twice, and she found herself dreading the next long trip:

> *My interests and ideas had changed and I hated the thought of going to sea again. Had I been born 20 years later I might have been taught some way of earning my own living and when my mother went to sea, I could have spent the time at home pleasantly enough. But unfortunately for me, I lived in the days when girls were considered lucky who were not compelled to work so, belonging to this fortunate class, I had to endure the loneliness and discomfort of life at sea, away from my friends and all the pleasures of youth.*[9]

After this last long voyage it seems that she 'coiled up her ropes'. When she married Orkney-born master mariner Robert Linklater in 1897, she didn't sail with him. That may or may not have been her choice – not all companies allowed wives to accompany their husbands In 1916 Robert Linklater died suddenly from nephritis, 5,000 miles away in Colombo. Elizabeth's father, James Young, had died some years earlier and Elizabeth felt that her connection with the maritime world had been shattered. Her life as a child at sea, such an odd mixture of freedom and confinement, had marked her forever. Her son, writer Eric Linklater, explains: 'The sailor and the sailor's wife belonged to a mystery, in the old sense of an activity that was reserved for initiates. They were a people apart and they knew it.'[10] Elizabeth wished she could have retired and lived in a set of sailors' alms-houses, yarning her life away with fellow-seafarers, but she had her family to think of. They 'filled part of the gap left by my entire severance from all pertaining to the sea'. But only a part.

* * *

Throughout the 19th century the Shetland islands had a population imbalance greater than any other area in the British Isles.[11] The 1901 census showed 127 women to every 100 men, whereas it had been 143 to 100 in 1861. When the men left to go fishing and the women remained running the crofts, the visibility of women was so great that even casual visitors remarked on it. There was also a culture of loss with so many men in such a dangerous occupation. Many Shetland women were used to hard manual labour on their smallholdings. They were strong and independent, supplementing their earnings by craftwork, such as spinning, knitting and weaving. There was also a good deal of female mutual support within families.

Susie Irvine was her parents' only surviving child after her brother Arthur had been lost at sea in 1870. She was a 'very personable, lively young lady'[12] who had been well educated and had not had to drudge for her living. Her father was a farmer, ploughing with oxen, but her mother's family included professional men and she'd inherited several small crofts. Then, Susie fell in love with the illegitimate sailor John (Jack) Isbester when he had returned from sea in 1884 with a Masters' Certificate. They married a month after their first meeting. Susie was soon pregnant, and Jack ensured that his next job only took him to the Baltic so he wouldn't be too far away when their child was born. This first baby died soon after birth, as did three more of their nine children (it's possible that the well on Susie's parent's farm, their home while Jack was away, was contaminated with liver fluke). Their second child also died but their daughter, Kathleen, survived and so did the next child, Arthur. In 1890 Susie left both Kathleen and Arthur with her parents so she could sail from Liverpool to San Francisco with Jack. She would be gone 11 months.

Susie's letters home represent a rare survival from a merchant seaman's wife in these latter days of sail. She's enthusiastic and excited. She sets up her sewing machine in the deck house and her husband is sweet to her, doctoring her with wine and beef tea when she's unwell. With all sails set and a favourable breeze, their ship, the *Centaur*, makes 200 miles a day. One of the Cape Verde islands reminds her of Foula (most western of the Shetlands). She plays the organ even when she's almost rolling off her seat. She knows what a difference her company makes to Jack and tells her parents to have no fear for them. She also reminds them not to let Jack's employers know that she's written as she's officially invisible. Attitudes of shipowners to masters' wives sailing with them varied: some forbade it, others permitted it, others turned a blind eye.

Back in Shetland in 1892, another baby was born and died. Then, in 1894, when Susie had gone to sea once again, news of her mother's death reached her in San Francisco. She left the ship and hurried home alone, crossing America by rail, then taking a steamer from New York to Liverpool. Her father's health was also failing. He died in 1896, by which time Susie had had yet another child, who lived. Jack, meanwhile, survived the loss of his ship by fire. He and all his crew had to take to the ship's boats and sail eight days for Hilo in the Sandwich Islands (Hawaii). He too eventually returned part of the way home by rail. After a brief visit to Shetland, Jack was away to Zanzibar, then on to New South Wales, leaving Susie looking after their three surviving children, running the farm after the death of her father, and managing the crofts her mother had owned. She was clearly a very competent woman.

Jack was away for 15 months, arriving back in Falmouth in November 1897. Susie must have joined him there and possibly spent some time on his current ship, the barque *Rossdhu*, as it discharged one cargo and was towed round the Lizard into the Bristol Channel to load once again for Melbourne. In August 1898 Susie had another baby. On its return voyage from New South Wales, *Rossdhu* was wrecked while attempting to anchor off Gatico Bay, northern Chile to discharge a cargo of coal. It hit a rock and turned over, giving the crew just enough time to take to the boats again and for Jack to grab the ship's papers. Subsequently he worked to salvage whatever he could – mainly sails – but he was then out of work until March 1900, when he was appointed to his final ship. At some time in this period the family left Shetland and moved to live at Ilford in Essex, Another child, Allan, was conceived and born; little Thyra died aged two; and Jack and his new ship *Dalgomar* went round the world again, finally being towed into Hamburg.

There he persuaded the shipowners to allow Susie and the youngest children to sail with him again – unofficially of course. Susie had a new piano delivered and Allan, carried on board as a baby, took his first toddler steps in the Botanical Gardens, Sydney, New South Wales (NSW). They shipped a fresh cargo and sailed for home, rounding Cape Horn yet again. It almost leaves one breathless to learn that once they reached Liverpool Jack was almost immediately required to take on a new cargo and return to Australia. Susie, Eric and Allan remained on board and the two older children, Kathleen and Arthur, now young teenagers, joined them. Susie was once again in the early stages of pregnancy. They would all remain with the ship for a further 18 months.

'MY MOTHER SEWED CONSTANTLY'

Susie's ninth and last child, Norman, was born on board *Dalgomar* in Newcastle, NSW. Flags were flown, a short article was published in the local paper and a nurse was engaged to sail with the family to their next port of call, San Francisco. Twenty years later, Norman discovered he had no birth certificate. Jack by then was dead, lost on yet another voyage home from NSW when *Dalgomar* broached in a gale off the coast of Peru. Susie wrote a letter to the Board of Trade explaining the circumstances of Norman's birth and asking for him to be given British citizenship since Jack had hoisted the British flag on this British ship at the time her child was born. The official reply stated that she must be mistaken, as there were no women on board *Dalgomar* then. Susie had forgotten that she was invisible.

Susie Isbester knitting on Dalgomar *(Claire Isbester)*

3

'Blue gauze veils are useful but not ornamental'[1]

New designs for 'New Women'

Barbara Hughes (b. 1872); Grace Schenley (b. 1867); Maud Sutton (b. 1869); Winnie Sutton (b. 1871); Dorothy Levitt (b. 1882)

'WHAT AN EXCITING GAME it is, how enthralling, how interesting and more important still, how wholesome. How much better than the London drawing room's close atmosphere is the fresh sea air.'[2] Barbara Hughes was in love with speed on the water. 'Anything so boring as a long sea voyage in a lumbering old schooner can scarcely be imagined.' In 1888 her father, Captain John St John Hughes, had hired a 40-year-old yawl called the *Fox* to take his family cruising. Evidently it had not been a success as far as Barbara was concerned. 'The fact of being taken in nine cases out of ten where one would not, without having a hand in the matter, with a large crew of slow men to do all the work and take all the fun off one's hands, is for me nothing but an aggravation.' Almost everything seems to have irritated her: 'the deliberate cut and dried way in which everything is done; the foresail being lowered and the peak eased when about two miles from the moorings, fidgets me to death.' She concludes that 'you must be of a very leisurely disposition and a great lover of Nature to appreciate stereotyped cruising. This kind of thing is about as different from our Solent yachting as the Derby is from a Margate donkey ride.'[3]

Barbara speaks in the accents of a 'New Woman', whether or not she would have aligned herself with the movement. This was a term coined by feminist Sarah Grand (b. 1854) in 1894 but the mindset had been developing for some time. During the 1870s a few women had achieved the right to study at university; the National Society for Women's

'BLUE GAUZE VEILS ARE USEFUL BUT NOT ORNAMENTAL'

Suffrage had been established; the Married Women's Property Acts passed; access to divorce had been achieved. Women's participation in public life was becoming more acceptable, discreet advertisements concerning contraception and abortion might be found in the popular press, and the female age of consent was raised from 13 to 16. The 'New Woman' aimed for an independent lifestyle, adopting freer styles of clothes, and more involvement with education and sport, all with or without marriage. Unsurprisingly, money helped, as did social position and personal confidence. Not all were campaigners; many simply enjoyed the sense of freedom and activity. As Barbara wrote, 'Yacht racing is in every respect a sport suited to our sex... No unseemly gymnastics, no overstraining or overtiring; no cruelty can be laid to its charge, in fact nothing to offend the most exacting upholder of the feminine.'

Barbara's recommendation of yacht racing as a female sport is based on its potential for independence and equality as well as being a healthy activity. Despite her grumbles at the slowness of yacht cruising, she retained happy memories of day-sailing in an old Itchen ferry, while protesting at the tyranny of her brothers who insisted that she and her sisters used a 'ladies' cabin' – 'a kind of dog-hole place' with a smelly paraffin lamp.

> *When we were caught out on our way home from some long expedition the unfortunate women of the party used to be thrust into this salubrious resort ostensibly for their own comfort really and truly to get them out of the way. [...] If one of us ventured so much as to open a chink of door it was instantly shut again with such exclamations from our male tyrants as 'whatever you want to come out for, into all this wet and cold, when you can be warm and cosy in there I can't think' upon which the browbeaten female crawled back disconsolate into her lair, muttering rebelliously. And yet we were nothing daunted. Out we would be again with the dawn to go through all the same thing without a dissenting thought.*[4]

Barbara was the fifth child in a family of six. Her mother had died when she was about eight years old, at the time of the birth of her youngest sister Evangeline. This had been in Paris – why, isn't known. The other children, including Barbara, had been born at various locations on the Isle of Wight and one brother in Guernsey. At the time of the 1891 census they were living in Ferryside House, Hamble-le-Rice.

The records don't give the impression of a very settled family life. Her father, Captain John St John Hughes, was the son of a Suffolk vicar, descended from a family of baronets, their title earned for services to the 18th-century Navy. John, the eighth child in his family, had served in the Army, then retired. He didn't remarry until 20 years after the death of his first wife and it appears that his method of bringing up his children was to include them in his own pleasures, specifically yachting. The whole family went fishing together. 'We had not even the luxury of a paid hand in those days, my brother and my sisters and myself doing all the work, which was a splendid education in more ways than one.' Even when Barbara and her sisters had been asleep, she didn't mind being woken to help bring the net aboard. 'We scrimmaged into our clothes and rushed on deck ready to claw the great net on board. A waterproof overall and India rubber boots were essential for this performance and old gauntlet gloves were a precaution against the stinging fish.'[5]

Barbara doesn't seem particularly interested in sailing gear, though her official photo is neat and pretty. When required to make recommendations concerning clothes she writes 'really it is not a subject on which I am an authority, that is to say if one is supposed to practice what one preaches'. All she really manages to say is that 'brown in any form is to be avoided on the water, it is unspeakably ugly [...] Nothing looks so well as white and red, or dark blue but not black. Blue gauze veils are useful but not ornamental though a broad brimmed sailor hat embraces both these virtues.'[6] Presumably it would also help to maintain a ladylike pale complexion. Most people looking at Victorian and Edwardian women racing in their straw boaters wonder how they stayed on. The answer, of course, was hatpins. Opportunistic early advertisers were a good deal more imaginative than Barbara, offering yachting costumes with matching caps in *drap de soie*, special fabric finishes for waterproofing, face creams to guard against freckles and false fringes stitched on to hair nets to be worn after a blowy day on the water. Women sailors with short hair could supplement this by buying long matching tresses to pin on.[7]

From the mid-1880s Captain St John Hughes and his family had become obsessed with yacht racing. 'It is the most delightful education in the world, the most interesting and healthful. It becomes so engrossing that you will not rest until you understand the whole thing and know the why and wherefore of all the different moves,'[8]

'BLUE GAUZE VEILS ARE USEFUL BUT NOT ORNAMENTAL'

wrote Barbara. She sailed with her father or her brothers, then, in 1885, she and her older sisters participated in their first ladies' race (possibly *the* first ladies' race) against the Misses Cox and the Misses Hammersley. Barbara's father had bought a pleasure boat called *Fairy* and had it modified for competition. Barbara was then 13 years old and said that 'I was always being taken racing in one boat or another.' She praises her father's good judgement; with some slight alterations to the keel and with the addition of a large jib, little *Fairy*, built to carry day trippers, amazed the sailing community in 1886 by beating *Bird of Freedom*, one of the greatest 'flyers' of the day. This success focussed local attention on small boats – more were put forward and the Royal Southampton and Portsmouth Corinthian Yacht Clubs (YCs) began organising fortnightly races. 'Then the fun grew fast and furious for small boat racing having been given the necessary fillip, the designers put their best foot forward and the sport was fairly started.'[9]

The year 1886 was also when the Yacht Racing Association (YRA) changed its rules. When Barbara and her sisters arrived with *Fairy* on these fortnightly Saturday afternoons, she describes their competitors as 'a motley crew' and most of their boats as 'nice little cruisers, slow as a country dinner party'. Under the old Tonnage rules, boats were judged by their hull dimensions only. All that could usually be done to make them go faster was to add more sails. Under the new rules – known as the Rating rules – a formula was applied that took both sail area and waterline length into account. Classes were then run for 'raters' of different sizes: 1/2, 1, 2 1/2, 5, 10, 20 and 40 raters. Women's light bodyweight was an advantage for the smaller raters and suddenly their skills at the helm were discovered. This seems to have been a pivotal moment in the history of female participation.

The Hughes children had been educated at home by a governess. Grace, five years older than Barbara, was the first to marry. Her husband George Schenley was one of the sons of an astoundingly wealthy Pittsburgh heiress, Mary Croghan. He had the money to commission top designers to produce ultra-fast racing machines as presents for his young wife. Barbara criticised her sister's boats relentlessly but had to admit she learned from sailing them. As the sisters became better known, boats were loaned to them to race on behalf of their owners. Barbara's oldest sister, Edith, had particular success in a boat named *Viva*, lent to her by a Mr Wood. Barbara herself won a string of flags in the 1/2-rater *Coquette*, sailing on behalf of *Coquette*'s owner, Mr Jessop. There were some lady owners sailing their own boats (not least Barbara's sister Grace) but they were few compared with the men. I'm indebted to Vincent Delany, historian of the Shannon YCs in Ireland, for the observation that women's success in racing is likely to have been seriously underestimated in these early days because it was the owner's rather than the helm's name engraved on the cups and in the record books. Many more men than women had the money necessary to commission successful boats from professional designers, but they might ask a 'hired assassin' like Barbara to take the helm and win.

* * *

Yacht racing had previously focussed on a few very large yachts racing for large prizes. Fortunes were spent contesting the America's Cup. Now that smaller-sized yachts were competitive and exciting, the social range and income levels of participants widened, slightly. New sailing clubs were formed. One of these, Bembridge Sailing Club (SC) on the Isle of Wight, founded to offer a local alternative to golf, became especially well-known as 'a hotbed of fast women sailors'.[10] The club was founded in 1886 and women were admitted as members from 1891. They paid the same subscription as men but were allowed no participation in the running of the club. The relevant rule states 'Ladies are eligible for membership without voice or vote in the management of the Club or the election of its members.' One negative vote in seven meant that a person was rejected. So only the men could choose the women in their club and only the men could make or change the rules. This remained in force until the 1970s. Many of the oldest yacht and sailing clubs today are marked by this early reluctance to involve women fully or give them the right to propose other women for membership.

Despite this, Bembridge SC nurtured many outstanding women sailors from its early days. David Swinstead, historian of the Bembridge Redwing class, writes: 'These were all women from relatively wealthy families, and it seems to have been accepted at that level of society that it was perfectly natural for women to be good horsewomen, good sailors, good tennis players etc.'[11] Large families probably helped support individual opportunities and confidence – as long as there was sufficient money. There were 12 children in Sir Richard Sutton's family, eight of them girls. Mary married Blair Cochrane from Darlington, County Durham. He was the son of a wealthy land and coal mine owner but, like many men in this later Victorian generation, felt he had plenty of time to take his leisure seriously. The Solent area (Hampshire and the Isle of Wight) offered a benign climate, fashionable sport and congenial company. Blair, became the first captain of the Bembridge SC, founded by his brothers-in-law, Colonel MacDonald Moreton and Captain Ernest Du Boulay, who were married to Anna and Helen Sutton respectively. When Blair won gold in the 1908 Olympics he was sailing with two other brothers-in-law, Lionel Sutton and John Rhodes, Beatrice Sutton's husband. The only British female competitor in 1908 was Constance Cornwallis-West, then the Duchess of Westminster, who bought her own 26.2ft yacht and sailed it with the Swiss team as an extra crew member.[12]

Sisters Maud and Winnie Sutton were successful sailors in their own right. In 1892 Blair Cochrane commissioned Nathanael Herreshoff to build *Wee Win* for Winnie. This was the first Herreshoff design to race in this country and for a few years she proved almost unbeatable – even Barbara, proud of her success in *Coquette* during 1893, was honest enough to attribute part of this to the relative absence of *Wee Win*. Following *Wee Win*'s success, Winnie's older sister Maud commissioned the 1-rater *Morwena* (also American) and had great success sailing on the Clyde. She and Barbara Hughes became famous for racing in weather so bad that the male competitors were reluctant to start. *The Field* magazine dubbed such conditions 'lady's weather'.[13]

The Hughes family did not have the same financial resources as the Suttons. The boats raced by Barbara Hughes were owned by her father, her brothers, her sponsors or her married sister, never herself. The family's most successful racer was *Hummingbird*, which swept the board in 1889. Barbara sailed 'the Hummer' with her father, admiring his tactics. 'I said less and learned more', she asserted. This may not always have been the case. Dinner-time arguments at the end of a race day could become so acrimonious that a family decision was made not to sail against one another. Barbara describes a 'deadly encounter' with her sister Grace, 'jostling each other round and round and tacking and filling in a remarkable manner known only to ourselves'.[14] More often the sisters conspired against common enemies. One season it was 'war to the knife' with a Mr Percival who had brought a 5-rater from the same designer, Arthur Edward Payne, as Grace's latest boat, *Windfall*.

Chris Thompson's excellent *SailCraft* blog, which led me to much of this material, makes the point that this was a rare period when women's requirements actually influenced design – though only for those who had the money to commission a boat of their own (or a husband or father to pay for one). Barbara cared passionately about design and makes many shrewd comments that she would never be able to put into practice. She's recklessly outspoken, describing the GL Watson-designed 5-rater *Valentine*, one of her sister's expensive gifts from her husband, as 'almost as great a disaster' as Grace's previous boat *The Thief*. Barbara grumbled about *The Thief* but presented that season as a significant step on her racing career, her 'lifetime passion':[15]

> *Where it stands alone is that a woman can compete on equal terms with a man [...] To enjoy racing to the full, you should have it all in your own hands, with no one to say you 'nay', otherwise that spirit of independence – so rarely enjoyed by our sex – is lost. The sensation of being master of your own vessel, with the helm in your hand and a willing crew to do your commands unquestionably, these are elements that should be experienced to be enjoyed.*[16]

In the mid-1890s small boat racing grew so fashionable in the Solent/Isle of Wight area that it became harder for those without big money to compete, especially when a new boat was needed almost every year. Barbara fantasised about her ideal racing lifestyle: she'd like a new 2 1/2-rater whenever the old one was worsted and perhaps a 5-rater now and then to vary the monotony. 'A fifty-ton steamer, or perhaps one a little smaller' would be 'essential' as well as 'a little house in Cowes that could be rented for a season'. The raters would cost £300 each to build and £100 a year to run; the steam-yacht £3,500 to build and £300 a year to run; the little house in Cowes £100–£200 for the season – plus all the extras, such as club subscriptions. 'Racing is not a cheap amusement, but nothing nice ever is,' she wrote sadly.

The Hughes family had owned 16 racing yachts in a period of just over ten years and Captain Hughes' money was running out. His most recent purchase had been one of the new Solent One Designs, built in 1895/96, costing 'only' £200 and with running costs proportionately lower. Barbara describes this as the 'poor man's class'. (For all her charm and vivacity, she's a shocking snob.) The idea behind One

Designs, adopted by an increasing number of clubs across the country from this time, was that if everyone had identical boats, then contests would be decided on skill, not money, and the expense of constantly replacing 'worsted' boats would be prevented. In 1896 members of the Bembridge SC commissioned the designer Charles Nicholson to produce the Bembridge Redwing, a fast keelboat to be sailed by a crew of two. The first 15 boats were all purchased by men, but they were equally suitable to be sailed by women and there were long periods during which Redwing women consistently out-sailed their male competitors, one such woman being Jeannie Cochrane, daughter of Blair and Mary.

When the Redwings formed their own association there was no restriction on female management of the club. Anna Sutton's daughter, Evelyn Moreton, was club commodore from 1933 to 1960. She and her sister Margaret sailed and raced Redwings through the 1920s and 1930s, Evelyn always helming and Margaret crewing. They were affectionately known as 'The Old Soldiers' or 'The Tiller Girls' though when Margaret's son Norman joined them in 1934 he re-christened them 'Agony and Bloody Sweat', describing their progress round the course during a race.[17] David Swinstead points to consistently good and many outstanding results for women sailors throughout the earlier part of the 20th century and suggests that this is an example of what can be achieved when women are able to bring an ethos of equality and determination to a class that has been shaped and managed in a gender-free way from its earliest beginnings.

* * *

Barbara Hughes never married. Neither did Maud Sutton. Winnie Sutton married and divorced with a single child (she later married again) and there was a single child too for Grace Schenley. Were these women making their own independent choices or did they not fit easily into stable domestic relationships? Muriel Brassey, second daughter of Tom and Anna, divorced her husband Gilbert De La Warr in 1902 due to his adultery and abandonment. She felt no need to continue an unsatisfactory relationship for the sake of respectability. After her divorce Muriel joined the Labour Party, supported theosophy and lived for many years with American heiress and fellow suffragist Mary Dodge. Muriel, her stepmother Sybil, and her half-sister Helen were all active suffragettes, as were many other upper-class women of their time.

The divorced Gilbert De La Warr, meanwhile, was putting their hometown of Bexhill-on-Sea on the map by hosting Britain's first automobile races. At the second such event, in September 1903, Rudyard and Carrie Kipling were among the crowd who watched Dorothy Levitt 'the fastest girl on earth' compete. She was fast on the water, too. In July 1903 Dorothy had become the first person – not just first woman – to win the inaugural British International Harmsworth Trophy for motorboats. This was sponsored by the *Daily Mail* and held at the Royal Cork YC in Ireland. Levitt set the world's Water Speed Record when she achieved 19.3mph in a 40ft steel-hulled, 75hp Napier speedboat.

Dorothy Levitt had been born Elizabeth Levi to a Jewish family in Hackney who later anglicised their name. She seems to have had horse racing experience in addition to becoming a secretary at the British engineering company Napier & Son.[18] Dorothy was beautiful as well as courageous and there's a penny paper story that she had run away when her mother tried to arrange a marriage for her with someone she disliked. However it happened, she attracted the attention of Selwyn Edge, a partner at Napier's, who saw her potential to attract publicity for the company. Dorothy was sent on a six-month car building apprenticeship in Paris, then tasked with teaching other high-profile women, such as Queen Alexandra, to drive.

The Harmsworth Trophy for speed on the water had been instigated to encourage the building of new, fast motorised craft for the Royal Navy – as well as publicity for the *Daily Mail*. Edge developed the Napier engine as a high-performance marine model, entered the boat under his own name, with both Dorothy and Campbell Muir, a friend of Lord Northcliffe's, as drivers. The crowds lining Cork Harbour saw Dorothy at the wheel, but Selwyn's name was on the cup. She competed again at Cowes the following month, then won the Gaston Menier Cup in Trouville and the Championship of the Seas two months later.

For the first decade of the 20th century Dorothy had a high-profile lifestyle as an independent 'bachelor girl' with her own West End address and servants. She wrote a 'chatty guide' to driving as well as her newspaper column, undertook her own mechanical work and championed the cause of women motorists. 'If a woman wants to learn how to drive and to understand a motor-car, she can and will learn as quickly as a man. There are many women whose keen eyes can detect and whose deft fingers can remedy, a loose nut or a faulty electrical connection in half the time that a professional chauffeur would spend upon the work.'[19] She set new speed and endurance records, then, in 1909, went to France to try to learn to fly a monoplane. Napier pulled out of motor racing at the time and it seems likely that her relationship with Selwyn Edge had also ended. Her attempt to learn to fly may not have been successful (though she wrote an article about it) and, somehow, her career came to an end around 1912. In 1922, aged 40, she was found dead in her bed from morphine poisoning and heart failure. The coroner's verdict was misadventure.

Barbara Hughes from The Sportswoman's Library *(British Library Collection)*

4

'The coiffure harks back to primitive simplicity'[1]
Outdoor women

Charlotte Dorrien-Smith (b. 1886) and her sisters; Maude Speed (b. 1856); Marian Wyllie (b. 1861); Ivy Carus-Wilson (b. 1886)

THERE WERE GIRLS IN the late Victorian and Edwardian era who were positively encouraged to become tough and self-reliant and love outdoor adventure. Living on an island probably helped. Thomas Algernon Smith-Dorrien inherited the title Lord Proprietor of the Isles of Scilly (and an additional -Smith to his name) in 1872 and moved to Tresco from Hertfordshire. In 1875 he married Edith Tower, with whom he had seven children. While the two boys were sent away to school, the girls – Mary, Innis, Cicely, Gwendolin and Charlotte – were educated at home, not only by governesses but also by David Smith the gamekeeper, Horatio Jenkins the boatman and by the topography of the islands themselves. Whole days were spent fishing, sailing and rock climbing. When the youngest daughter Charlotte (known as 'Babs') talked to Molly Mortimer about her childhood, she described Jenkins as 'like a second father'.

> Sometimes if we said, 'Let's take a reef out,' he would answer, 'Courage without conduct is like pudding without fat. The devil,' he added, 'might make a fine sailor if he'd only look aloft.' We were not allowed the steam launch, but on Wednesday and Saturday – half-holidays – we sailed with Horatio to St Mary's to get the mail and had a good many squalls and learned how to lay to, reef and drop the peak.[2]

'THE COIFFURE HARKS BACK TO PRIMITIVE SIMPLICITY'

Their mother, Edith, had died in a flu outbreak when Babs was six years old. An aunt came to help look after the five girls without, it seems, curtailing their freedom much.

> *We had school from 9.30–12.00 and from 2.30–4.00, and then we were free. Our governess had nothing to do with us outside school. We had our workshop where we learned to carve wood, turn metal and model boats; we gardened and set eel lines. Officially, we were not allowed to sail until we could swim but on the freshwater pool we had an old mahogany dugout canoe that came in from a wreck. We took it in turns to sit in the canoe with a bath towel and mop handle. Then we tied sheets to our bootlaces, stuck our feet over the side and sailed across the pond. Guests at the Abbey said, 'Fancy letting your daughters go in that canoe!' Our father said, 'It's two foot water and four foot mud. If they fall in, more fools they!'*[3]

Grand visitors arrived – and often stayed to play: the King enjoyed being saluted by their model fleet; the Duchess of Wellington used hock in a shearwater egg to launch a battleship they'd built; Admiral Sir Michael Seymour was sick in Cicely's punt; when the Navy came, they were taken out on manoeuvres. 'Life was always at extremes,' said Babs.

Only Mary, oldest of the sisters, married and had children. All the girls sailed and raced at Cowes, and Innis (b. 1881) went on to become a pioneer of offshore racing. She skippered her own yacht, *Karin III*, in the 1930 Santander Race, then became the first lady member of the Royal Ocean Racing Club. Cicely caught measles and died in France in 1915 when she and Babs were helping run canteens for the troops. Gwen (b. 1883) also worked in France as a Red Cross nurse during the war then explored the Canadian Arctic with her friend the travel writer Clara Coltman Rogers Vyvyan. She was the first woman to cross the Great Divide in the Arctic Circle by the Rat River Route, canoeing down the Mackenzie, across the Yukon, and through Alaska to the Pacific. She paid her way by selling her watercolours, sent nearly 300 types of flowers to Kew and collected butterflies.

Gwen and her younger sister Babs made their home together on the Isle of Wight and cruised as far as the Baltic in their converted naval pinnace *Forge I*. Their niece Teona Dorrien-Smith remembers their house as having a gallery like a ship's bridge and they themselves dressed in blue serge skirts and sailor hats and equipped with telescopes to act as amateur coastguards. 'Auntie Babs swore by the sea, wore navy blue & smoked a pipe,' writes another niece, Miranda Phillimore. 'I recall a train journey to Italy when from Paris we travelled third class with hammocks suspended from the luggage racks & how appalled the ticket collector was to see Aunt Babs in a hammock smoking!'[4] Their great-nephew, Sam Llewellyn, remembers them giving him sailing lessons on Scillonian holidays in the 1950s when he was about eight years old. They were gruff and intolerant of weakness.

* * *

Maude Maturin was the daughter of the vicar of Lymington and had no previous sailing background when she met and married barrister Henry Speed, former president of the Oxford Canoe Club. From 1883 she joined him on his 2 1/2 sailing canoe *Viper*, where her bed was a canvas mattress stuffed with corks. Henry considered this a good idea as it would also act as a lifebuoy in case of disaster. The jib in its sail bag made her pillow. 'I thought the awful discomfort and sleeplessness I went through was inseparable from small boat cruising.'[5]

Henry changed career and was ordained, eventually becoming rector of Yarmouth, Isle of Wight. They continued cruising, often for weeks at a time. Maude proved herself a thorough 'Corinthian', certain that 'the real true flavour of the sport is reserved for those who cruise in small boats and do all their own work.'[6] She's fairly contemptuous of other women's efforts, accusing them of becoming helpless and useless, unable to make a rope fast properly or keep a boat accurately on a compass course. She says she finds this failure odd when many women of her generation can hunt, fish, shoot or climb with the best of the men. She admits that there are plenty of women to be found at regattas 'and some ladies even steer a racing yacht from start to finish with great ability and skill' but, somewhat uncharitably, she puts this down to a love of prizes and applause.

Maude holds little back as she spells out the drawbacks for women in cruising. It's almost as if this is part of her enjoyment. There are no hot baths at the end of the day and no chance of looking pretty. Smart blouses and elegant hats have to be left at home, hair reverts to 'primitive simplicity', complexion becomes 'like a haymaker' and one's hands 'don't exactly look as if they've come straight from a manicure!' All she is 'allowed' is a single straw boater for Sunday best, a cloth peaked cap for practical work, a sou'wester and a sunbonnet. (Sunscreen was not invented until 1938.) Cooking on board sometimes seemed incessant and washing up was a 'penance' – especially when she wanted to get out her sketch pad or her watercolour paints.

Though Maude presented herself as agreeably tyrannised by her husband, 'who I will call the skipper', she clearly derived her own independent pleasure from the whole experience. She loved the glorious lift of the yacht's bows over green rollers and relished the opportunity to explore new places, whether along the English coast or abroad. She sold articles to magazines and generally developed herself as a travel writer and artist. Queen Victoria bought one of her watercolours in 1898. Her first book was published in 1911.

After *Viper*, Henry and Maude owned slightly larger and more comfortable yachts – a 4-ton cutter capable of crossing the Channel (*Lerna*) and then the *Beaver*, a deep-keeled boat of 6 tons in which they cruised the Dutch canals. In Holland, she was tormented by being followed around by rude and noisy children who were amused by a woman wearing a yachting cap. One lad attempted to snatch a back button from her coat 'which I thought going a bit far, so I turned round and smashed the handle of my umbrella over his head.'[7]

In 1903 they commissioned a 11-ton steam-yacht, the *Pipefish*, in which the Rev Henry had to become engineer and stoker while Maude remained 'the humble deckhand, steward and cook'. She doesn't sound 'humble' at all, asserting in the introduction to her book that 'in my love of the sea and my interest in all that pertains to it I am second to none of you'.[8] She believes her practical experience of yachting makes her part of the 'brotherhood' and insists that her relationship with her husband is that of 'equality and partnership'.[9] As she grew older, her appetite for travel at sea led her to take additional cruises on small passenger liners, sometimes with Henry, sometimes with a relative or friend, sometimes alone. She wrote up and illustrated her voyages and published articles in magazines such as *The Field*, *Country Life* and *The Badminton Magazine of Sports and Pastimes*. She travelled through the French canals, to Scandinavia, Morocco, Lisbon, Sicily, South Africa and Rhodesia and spent three months in Levant Palestine and the Near East with Henry. In 1925 they were together on board *Pipefish* in Yarmouth when she rowed ashore for provisions and returned to find him dead from a heart attack. In 1926 she revised and republished his 1883 book on sailing canoes, with illustrations from his brother Launcelot. In 1933 she married retired lecturer David Marsh and died in 1958 aged 102.

* * *

If Maude had not had the confidence and talent to write, paint and publish, she would have been forgotten, together with so many other intrepid and resourceful women who sailed with their families in the years before the First World War. The early years of the Cruising Club (later Royal Cruising Club or RCC), founded in 1880, offer tantalising glimpses of women who did not write for publication and were rarely named other than as 'my wife', 'my daughter' or (more rarely) 'my mother'. They were not proposed for club membership.

It was, however, something of a change for men to choose to sail with their female relatives rather than with other men or paid professionals. The founder of the club, solicitor Arthur Underhill, admitted that there had been many 'evil prognostications' when he had announced he was spending his seven-week sailing holiday with his wife and daughter, but they had all thoroughly enjoyed it and became 'constant companions'.[10] While on holiday they met Admiral Algernon de Horsey, who was cruising alone with his daughter, Louisa. She had thoroughly mastered semaphore and was also proficient in Morse code. Louisa later married and sailed with RCC member Colonel Vaughan Phillips and was the mother of Admiral Tom Phillips, who went down with his flagship HMS *Prince of Wales* on 10 December 1941. Club member Colonel Barrington Barker preferred to save space and money by not employing paid hands but sailing with his three daughters, 'who were quite up to his nautical standard'. When he was taken ill in Holland at the outbreak of the Great War, his daughters left him in hospital there and brought their steam-yacht back across the North Sea to Yarmouth.

By 1884 the Cruising Club had changed its membership qualification to admit 'amateurs of either sex', though references on the printed candidate forms were always to 'gentlemen'. Still only a handful of women were elected – at least until the 1920s. In 1907–1908

'THE COIFFURE HARKS BACK TO PRIMITIVE SIMPLICITY'

Miss Kennedy and Miss Napier, who owned a 106-ton yawl, were recommended thus: 'These ladies are very keen cruisers and take a great practical interest in ship management and navigation and are in every way eligible for membership.'[11] They must also have been unusually well off. Generally, women were not elected unless they were either owners or skippers. An exception seems to have been made for the wife of club vice-commodore Claud Worth, Janet Worth, who was made a full member in 1915. Miss Beryl Carson, whose 1919 application was seconded by author Erskine Childers, is described as acting as a 'man' to her brother for two seasons on *Lone Wolf*, covering some 3,000 miles.

* * *

Small boat sailing and racing continued to provide more opportunities for hands-on involvement and, occasionally, recognition. Marian Carew was born in 1861. She felt fortunate that her weak eyesight meant she was often excused lessons, 'open air and exercise being the prescription'.[12] As a teenager, however, she became stubborn and rebellious until she was able to marry the man she loved. She'd met Bill Wyllie on a family holiday to Boulogne. The Wyllies had a house a little further up the coast at Wimereux. Ten-year-old Marian had been sent with her governess to invite the 19-year-old Bill to supper at their house, when some previous social arrangement had broken down. She was seated next to him and a friendship developed in which he would ask her to come with him while he was sketching, or sail with him in his small yacht *Ladybird*. Some people on a passing yacht once called out to Bill to enquire whether he had a boy or a girl on board as they were taking bets on her gender.

Marian, her mother and sisters helped decorate the cabin of Bill's yacht but were forbidden to sail with him. Marian hid in the cabin and went to sea anyway. That was the first time Bill kissed her. They became secretly engaged when she was 15, though it took several months for him to find the courage to ask for permission. Marian's parents didn't take the engagement seriously and sent her to school in Switzerland. In 1879 they told her to join them in India, where her father had been posted. She refused and eventually they gave in and wired their consent to the marriage. Marian and Bill were married from her school, then made their way back to the Wyllie's old house in Wimereux where there was a 14ft centreboard boat, *Marion*. They broke in, retrieved the boat and sailed across to Folkestone.

Bill was working as an illustrator for the *Daily Graphic* as well as sketching constantly and struggling to get his larger paintings accepted into the annual exhibitions at the Royal Academy. Marian was invaluable in practical terms, running blocks and messages to the newspaper, cossetting Bill when he was exhausted and helping him keep cheerful through setbacks. She steered their barge *Four Brothers* through the fleet at the Royal Naval Review at Spithead in 1887 while Bill sketched. Between 1880 and 1904 they had nine children, seven of whom survived childhood. There is no doubt that they were loving parents, involving their children in their lives as fully as possible. Yet there was a separateness between the lives of parents and children, which felt normal for that time when nannies and nursemaids were an accepted part of professional-class households. And, like any childcare system today, it freed Marian and Bill to work, create, innovate.

From their first home in London, they moved out to Hoo House, Gillingham in Kent. Initially the local rumour was that Mr Wyllie had married his model, so no one came to call on them. Marian was not unduly worried by this. Bill sketched whatever he saw, obsessively. This included observations of working people and working craft. Later, Marian would do the same in words, leaving the children in the care of her sister or her household staff so that she could explore the history and personalities of the area Bill was drawing. In their book *London to the Nore* (1905) we can see the crowded, vital River Thames at the centre of a worldwide trading empire through her eyes as well as his.

In 1880s Kent they hoped to open the sport of punt-racing to working people. In a chapter for *The Sportswoman's Library*, Marian described how these utilitarian craft, mainly used by 'muddies and watermen', could be adapted for pleasure sailing. The first, most basic punts cost about £4–5 each. They could be home-built by a working man and the sail sewed by his wife 'if she felt so disposed'.[13] A club was formed with an entry fee of 1s and annual subscription of 2s 6d. Bill was appointed commodore. The punts were so low in the water that in any sort of sea, all that could be seen was a man and a mast. They also leaked. They promised one to their oldest son, Harold, as soon as he could swim. It too leaked, so Bill set about improving the design. More punts were built in the local area, then the decision was made to upgrade to YRA 1/2-rater status (meaning it could be measured and raced within the Rules) and build one for Marian to sail.

As she spent hour after hour in a draughty stable loft holding the hammer for riveting, Marian began querying the design – where was she supposed to put her feet? All she was given to sit on was something resembling a butcher's tray. Apparently, she was to perch on this with her knees under her chin. Quite a problem when she would be sailing in a heavy dress. 'The Commodore' would not listen so she agreed to reserve her objections until the punt, *Sea Maiden*, was on the water. Exactly as she had predicted, there was nothing for her to hold on to other than the tiller. She almost went backwards into the river several times, until Bill relented and cut a neat little well for her feet. 'Then my real joy in sailing began. The feeling of being run away with in a boat is glorious and a good punt is hard to beat at this. The excitement keeps you in a glow even when the water breaks all round and over you.'[14]

She won the first race she sailed in and kept on winning until it became almost embarrassing. She sailed against top East Coast designer and punt specialist Linton Hope on equal terms. Locals were proud of her, calling her 'The Timoneer of the Thames'. Marian and Bill loaded *Sea Maiden* on to a truck and took her down to the Solent, where the success continued. They also raced together in *Marion*, which they had sailed back from France on their honeymoon. After the birth of their fifth child, Robert, in 1888, Marian begged the doctor to allow her back on to the water in just four weeks so she could race to Sheerness with Bill. They capsized. 'My frock, which had something like five yards of heavy blue serge in the skirt, seemed to weigh a ton.'[15] Despite this she managed to swim to a nearby rowing boat, row ashore, run up the hill to their house to change and get back in time for the start. Their gardener, who had been watching, rushed to the kitchen and demanded a whisky to steady his nerves.

Mark Foy, an Australian sailing the heavily built *Irex* with a 14-man crew, challenged English yachtsmen to a race. The Wyllies accepted and built *Maid of Kent*, 'a skimming dish', to take him on. Foy and a boatbuilder came to inspect the yacht. There was an awkward conversation.

> *'I suppose Mr Wyllie you will be helmsman?'*
> *Bill answered holding his hand out to me. 'No, my wife always steers.'*
> *Mr Foy turned quickly towards me saying 'WHAT?'*
> *And the boatbuilder said with a jeer, 'Why if you win, they will say in Sydney "He only beat a Woman!" and if she wins they will say "Beaten by a woman!" and you won't be able to hold your head up.' We finished dinner rather silently and soon after they took their leave.*[16]

Over the series of three races, *Maid of Kent*, with Marian helming, beat *Irex* decisively, winning the challenge shield for England. The two boats were towed together up Chatham Reach to Sun Pier. 'A great ovation awaited us from every vessel that could toot, whistle or scream besides the cheering crowd upon the pier. I don't know what effect it had on the crew, but it made a creepy feeling run up my spine.'[17]

Eva (b. 1885) was Marian and Bill's third child. A dreadful day came when her slightly older brother Dick was noticed to have unexplained scratches and Eva screamed in pain whenever she was turned on to her back. Her left arm also wasn't functioning. Marian rushed her to a doctor, who diagnosed tuberculosis at the base of the brain and said she would be dead in six weeks. An old nurse suggested rubbing. Gently, Marian began and, gradually Eva's arm became less stiff and the pain in her neck eased and she didn't die. When Marian took her back to the doctor at the end of the year, he expressed amazement. Eventually the truth emerged. Dick's scratches and Eva's injury had been caused by their pram being left unattended by the nurses. It had run into a ditch and overturned. Eva's pain was not tuberculosis but an irreparable spinal injury.

The whole family's priorities changed. Marian wrote, 'Till then I had never allowed myself to think of the children before Bill; but with Eva it was now different and for him too, Eva always came first.'[18] Yet, in the catch-22 of childcare, Eva's long-term and increasing needs meant that Bill and Marian needed to work harder and earn more to pay for continual high-quality exclusive attention for her.

Eva became their 'Princess' and – with her dedicated attendant – was kept at the centre of their family life. Later, when Eva was almost entirely paralysed and they were living in Portsmouth, they discovered how much pleasure she could still receive if they laid her stretcher in the bottom of a boat and sailed her around the harbour. When she died in 1912 Marian described the blank at the centre of their house as dreadful. 'But the effect of the Great War would have been worse – she would have died of grief at the loss of the brothers she had loved.'[19] Soon all Marian and Bill's five sons would be on active service and two would never return.

* * *

Ivy's Journal is a remarkably direct testimony from a young dinghy sailor desperate to succeed. It's preserved and published by her family. She was born Ivy Carus-Wilson in Devon in 1886. Her father abandoned the family when she was two years old. Her mother, Fanny, was granted a divorce and took her children to live with her own family. Ivy's life changed again in 1904 when Fanny moved to a house of her own in Shaldon, near the mouth of the River Teign. Ivy learned to row and discovered how strong and fast she was. Even with the tide against her and the wind howling off Dartmoor, she could get upriver through old Shaldon bridge. She entered the rowing race in the Teignmouth Regatta and won. She won again in the Shaldon Regatta – not necessarily making herself very popular among the established competitors. Two women ganged up to foul her, but the local people took her to their hearts, dubbing her 'The Pride of Shaldon' and yelling their support. The following year no one wanted to row against her in the local event but she found fierce competition in nearby regattas. At Exmouth, she won against a Mrs Brutton. 'She certainly is a hard woman,' commented Ivy. At Torquay, there were eight women from Dittisham, 'all screaming like parrots'. The weather was so bad that a motorboat was sent to follow the competitors round the course in case any of them were swamped. Such attention to safety would be expected these days but certainly wasn't then. Ivy won by a distance, leaving the Dittisham women wild with rage 'because they always share up and no-one goes to row against them'.[20]

Cash prizes mattered to Ivy, as she struggled to finance her growing passion for rowing and sailing. It wasn't long before she realised that she needed her own rowing boat, since she wouldn't be allocated any good ones from the general pool. This was *Solitaire*, a 13ft 6in boat built by a pilot. The materials cost £2 and his workmanship £4. The committee at Teignmouth Regatta discovered *Solitaire*'s length, so imposed a 12ft regulation. Ivy rowed and won. They asked to measure the boat. Shrewdly, Ivy had had 46cm (18in) cut off the night before so kept her £1 prize. This 'kept me floating for weeks as I was stoney broke before that.'[21]

By 1908 she had also fallen in love with sailing and had bought an 18ft open working boat called *Two Sisters*, which she'd renamed *Suastica*, historically a symbol of good fortune and well-being. She needed to employ Jim Symons, a waterman, to look after the boat and sail with her, but hadn't any money to pay him. They made an arrangement that he could use *Suastica* to earn money taking trippers out when Ivy wasn't sailing her and also that he could have the cash part of any prizes they won together. Ivy hoped that the Torquay Regatta secretary, a pawnbroker, wouldn't recognise her as 'the breathless female who comes in and clamours for 10/- on her watch'.[22]

She knew how much money mattered. When she beat Mrs Waldron, 'an ancient cocklescraper from Kingsteignton', into second place at the Teignmouth regatta, she went with her to collect the prize, which was given by a photographer called Denny. It turned out that all he was offering Mrs Waldron was to take her photograph. Ivy was furious: 'She had tramped from Kingsteignton thinking to earn a little money and was going to tramp back and she might have her photograph taken. How could a man even though he might be an overfed and prosperous snob be such a mean cad as to behave in such a way?'

Ivy was a fighter, passionately against injustice and always ready to go into battle – particularly against the protest committees. Once she had moved into sailing, she was competing against men and knew she would make enemies. 'I knew my fate as soon as I saw that committee – Burden, Croyden and all that bloated lot.'[23] She also made friends. Her diary shows her as being as scrupulous at recording acts of kindness from others as she is quick to suspect underhandedness. The key figure who inspires and supports her – and wins her heart – is 'Mr Giles'.

The first part of *Ivy's Journal* is written retrospectively from 1909. The earlier sections focus on her personal thrilled discovery of her own talent, and her struggles to overcome competitor hostility and to finance her sport. On one occasion, she describes the shameless subterfuge needed to escape the scrutiny of a great-aunt – Arthur Ransome's Nancy

'THE COIFFURE HARKS BACK TO PRIMITIVE SIMPLICITY'

Blackett would have been proud of her! She often arrived home late, wet and tired but says nothing of any domestic trouble. Her mother appears to have been understanding and supportive throughout.

Ivy was 21 in 1907 and inherited a small private income of her own. She was still sailing the former workboat *Suastica*, which was steadily earning back the £24 paid for her, but in 1908 'Mr Giles' – Frank Morgan Giles – brought a new dinghy, *Imp*, to the Shaldon Regatta 'and from then on we could think of nothing else but having one like her'.[24] Her mother, Fanny, supported the idea and the local boatbuilder, Mr Gann (of Gann and Palmer, Teignmouth) pressed hard to build them one. But Frank, by this time, was a partner in his own business Morgan Giles and May: Naval Architects and Yacht Builders, with an office in the Strand and boatbuilding premises in Hammersmith. Ivy and Fanny were among the first customers.

Their dinghy *Myosotis* was delivered in June. Fanny was the official owner until 1910, when Ivy passed *Suastica* over to Jim and 'bought out' her mother. Initially she found the change from the heavy waterman's boat to the dinghy difficult and seems to have had a crisis of confidence over her own temerity in competing against men like 'Vallance of Sidmouth who has sailed there for 18 years and Gann for 13 years and Mr Giles who knows everything there is to know about dinghies and small boat sailing.'[25] She saw Vallance as her enemy and Gann as an angry rival but Frank Giles as someone who was prepared to teach her and give her confidence. When she had her first good win with *Myosotis* and experienced the dinghy's startling ability to plane with the wind behind her, she wondered whether he'd let her pass him out of charity. He assured her that he'd had no option but to let her by and had fully intended to catch her on the run. 'From that day,' wrote Ivy, 'I recovered and began to try again.'[26]

Ivy's Journal breaks off in 1911, a year full of activity, variety, success and new friendships. She began to feel accepted in the wider yachting world. 'How often had I dreamed of being and longed to be one of those yachting people whose summer lives are so marvellous and unlike anything else. How I had felt that deep and wonderful fascination and now I am one to an extent beyond my wildest dreams.'[27]

In 1912 she was profiled in *Yachting Monthly* and was described as 'the cleverest of lady sailors' and 'the equal of most sailormen'. She and Frank married in 1913 and she had their first baby, the future Rear

Admiral Sir Morgan Morgan-Giles, in June 1914. Ivy had five children and continued to compete until her untimely death in 1937, aged 51.

Ivy Carus-Wilson racing Myosotis *above Shaldon bridge, 1909 (Morgan Giles Archive)*

Ivy's opponents (Morgan Giles Archive)

5

'My red skirt was to be the signal'[1]
Independent Irish women

Mamie Doyle (b. *c.*1880); Cathy MacAleavey (b. 1958);
Kitty O'Brien (b. pre-1880?); Molly Osgood (b. 1875);
Mary Spring Rice (b. 1914)

MARIAN WYLLIE, WINNIE SUTTON, Barbara Hughes and Anna Brassey all had experience-based opinions concerning the design, layout and build of the yachts they sailed, and even some hands-on involvement in Marian's case. However, finding any directly acknowledged British woman yacht designer has proved hard. WM Nixon's suggestion of the Irish boatbuilder's daughter Mamie (Mary Jane) Doyle, and the wealth of information provided by historian Vincent Delany, inspired me to take a trip to Lough Key in County Roscommon to join the end-of-season gathering of the Water Wags. These quick and pretty 14ft clinker-built dinghies form the oldest One Design dinghy class in the world. They have been sailing for more than 130 years and have spread far beyond their original location.

The first boats were built as double-enders for the Shankill Corinthian SC and were launched in 1887, the year of Queen Victoria's Golden Jubilee. They were the brainchild of Thomas Middleton, a Dublin lawyer, and were advertised to 'gentlemen'. The young Erskine Childers had one and so did Robert Baden-Powell, founder of the Scout movement. The first club event was a picnic cruise at Easter 1887. Then they began to race. A photograph of the second picnic in August 1888, shows two women in crisp white dresses and decorative hats sitting on the somewhat bleak slopes of Dalkey Island, south of Dún

Laoghaire harbour. Did they too sail during these informal events? In 1890 there was an amendment to the club's racing rules: 'The rule that boats shall only be steered by Members, shall not apply to Ladies' – which meant that women could also join the racing (though they couldn't be members).

As the club grew and enthusiasm for racing took over from cruising or beach sailing, members felt some dissatisfaction with the initial design. In 1900 they consulted local boatbuilder JE Doyle about modifications. James Doyle was married to Anne, a schoolteacher who had encouraged him to qualify as a marine architect. Their oldest daughter, Mamie, worked in a draper's shop but had already had a design for a 16ft open dinghy published in *The Yachtsman* magazine. The revised Water Wag design was officially credited to JE Doyle, but it's widely believed that the lines for the new transom-sterned dinghy were Mamie's. Some people like to believe she also designed the 22ft Colleen class (1896) for the Dublin Bay SC, though she was surely too young. The racing yacht *Granauile*, however, was certainly hers. Then, sadly for Dublin Bay, Mamie married an accountant and went to live in Galway. Six of the Water Wags built in the first decade of the 20th century are still sailing and new ones are being built to the same design.

Vincent Delany is more cautious than WM Nixon about the attribution to Mamie but agrees that the publication of her design in *The Yachtsman* proves that she *could* have done it. It's also possible that she would have possessed the personal confidence to have put herself forward. This was a period when many Irishwomen were active in political, educational or cultural causes outside their home lives and Mamie and her mother are said to have been committed nationalists. The Water Wag class today sees itself as one that takes female participation as normal and expects a 50:50 gender balance. There's no longer any need for ladies' races, though in 1896 these were a positive innovation. Races with women as crew became a regular weekly event in Dún Laoghaire, though no spinnakers were allowed when women were on board. When women were racing, they were 'Hon. Members', though they were not able to become full voting members and official Water Wag owners until the 1930s. And it was a long time indeed before some of the more conservative Irish yacht clubs could cope with this change. Sheelagh Armstrong, one of the first women owners (*Vega*, 1938) was class captain 1957–1959 yet still had to come in by the back entrance in the National YC.

Yacht clubs throughout the British Isles have varied widely in their welcome to female members, though most have erred on the side of exclusion. Generally, the older and grander the yacht club, the less welcoming it is to women – and Ireland has some of the oldest. Historian Vincent Delany's father Alf sailed in the 1948 and 1952 Olympics and became friendly with Danish sailor Eyvin Schiøttz. After the games he invited Schiøttz to visit Dún Laoghaire and race with him in the family Water Wag (number 3, *Pansy*, built 1906). When they visited the Royal St George YC, Eyvin was surprised to see a thick red rope running down the length of the balcony, which women were forbidden to cross. He commented that this seemed 'rather discourteous'.

Being excluded from a top yacht club also means exclusion from their facilities and training. Cathy MacAleavey (Water Wag class captain 2011–2012) didn't come to sailing until the mid-1970s, when her sister married the owner of a leaky Dublin Bay 21-footer and she was recruited to pump. Before that Cathy had seen horses as her career. She had competed in show jumping and driving classes, worked for two years in a racing yard and gained her jockey licence. But once she started helping her sister and new brother-in-law on their boat, her mother sent her on a sailing course; she was given an old 420 to sail and was immediately hooked. She needed opportunities to make progress, but she was too young for full membership and neither the Royal Irish YC nor the Royal St George YC would accept her widowed mother as a member, which would have given Cathy access. Eventually the National YC in Dublin Bay allowed her to join as a cadet.

Cathy's sailing improved rapidly. She was lucky, she says, that she bought a Laser at the same time as a number of talented male sailors. 'Because I was fast, they let me train with them and I got better and better. We were on the International circuit doing first British Nationals and then European and world events in the 1980s. Ryanair didn't really get going until 1987 so Ireland was a very expensive country to get out of.'[2] It was also, still, a country where female sailors could arouse an extreme misogynistic response. Entering the Royal Irish YC bar one day, Cathy was alarmed to see an elderly male member puce in the face and gasping for breath. She assumed he was having a heart attack, rushed downstairs and called an ambulance. By the time the emergency crew arrived the man had recovered himself sufficiently to convince them he was not in cardiac arrest. He pointed to a line on the floor. It was a male/female boundary. Cathy had crossed it.

In 1985 Cathy married Con Murphy, another of that generation of talented Laser sailors. They had their first baby in 1986, just after the double-handed 470 (a larger version of the 420) had been selected for the women's discipline for the 1988 Summer Olympics in Seoul. This would be the first Olympics where there would be an event open only to women. Cathy had been trying out some crews in this dinghy but when she found she was pregnant she assumed that was no longer a possibility. Mick Wallace, the Olympic sailing manager, thought otherwise. When he rang to ask Cathy what she was planning to do about securing her place in the team, she replied that she'd just had a baby. 'So?' he said. A great answer. Cathy found her crew member, Aisling Byrne, and went to Seoul (Busan) to sail a 470 for Ireland. When I met her in County Roscommon, I learned about her more recent career as apprentice to the traditional boatbuilder Jimmy Furey, who taught her to build her own Water Wags and Shannon One Design dinghies in the woods beside Lough Ree.[3]

* * *

Following the course of the River Shannon from the port of Foynes to Lough Key in County Roscommon (nearest town Boyle) was an eye-opening journey. The Shannon is the longest river in the British Isles but is only tidal for a relatively small proportion of its length (from the sea to Limerick). Beyond that the river continues to comprise an important part of the country's inland water transport system, though it is often relatively shallow. Periodically it opens into a series of beautiful loughs of which Lough Derg, Lough Ree and Lough Allen are the largest. Through much of the 19th century these were the locations for annual regattas, such as Lough Allen Regatta (1851–1870), Lough Key Regatta (1858–1862) and Giley Bay Regattas on west side of Lough Ree (1872–1912). These were big events in an impoverished countryside ruled by the wealthy Anglo-Irish Ascendancy families. They were a transplanted elite depending on each other for the administration of law and order, social life and entertainment, if they lived on their estates (many did not). Regattas offered a chance to meet, compete (for trophies and cash prizes), dine and dance together. For the working people of the land and towns surrounding Shannon, they were a rare day of pleasure.

Vincent Delany includes the colourful fact that the poorer people of Athlone might take the doors off their houses to provide a platform beside Lough Ree for their daughters to dance on. The richer young women might be watching from the Shannon steam-yachts and looking forward to the regatta ball. The role of the patron was to manage the organisation and publicity and provide prizes. The wealthy Tenison family of Kilronan Castle paid for special race boats to be built for the 1856 Lough Allen Regatta. Lady Louisa Tenison, regatta patron, was an artist and traveller; her husband, Edward King-Tenison, a pioneering photographer, as well as the former MP for Leitrim. Both were Anglo-Irish.

Looking back through the sharper telescope of history, it may seem bizarre that money was being spent on racing boats when the country was still traumatised by the effects of the Great Hunger. Edward King-Tenison's account books for 1847 show that he had also given what appears to be effective practical support in food and cash payments for tenants, while assisting them to emigrate. But in other areas there was a shocking disconnect between the gaiety and conspicuous consumption at the early yacht club regattas – at Cork (the oldest yacht club in the world), for instance, the starving supplicants at the local famine relief works were instructed to stay out of sight lest they upset the upper-class visitors. Jeremiah O'Callaghan, correspondent for the *Examiner*, sought them out and wrote afterwards 'during the recital of [their] distressing narrative, I was completely unmanned. I shuddered to see two hundred human beings in so deplorable a condition.'[4]

The early Shannon Regattas included competitions for working men and women – rowing races for working women were instituted several decades earlier than rowing or sailing for 'ladies'. In 1834 at Athlone Yacht Club Regatta, on Lough Ree, a race was organised for women pulling a two oared boat on both the Tuesday (first day of the regatta) and Thursday (third day of the regatta). Newspaper reports noted that these races excited considerable interest. This was appropriate as the waterways of the Shannon were the means of transport for vital supplies such as peat and coal. Vincent Delany describes the particular rowing method used by the bog men and women – combining an oar and a pole: 'The woman would pull one oar which was located on the side of the boat furthest from the bank, while her husband would steer and control the positioning of the boat, to maintain it close to the edge of the reeds where the speed of water flow was less fast.'[5] In *Some Experiences of an Irish RM* (1899) the Anglo-Irish cousins, suffragettes and lifelong companions Edith Somerville and Violet Martin (pen name Martin Ross) give a wild account of 'stalwart country girls' rowing in a fictional regatta:

> *The tumult was still at its height when out of its very heart two four-oared boats broke forth, and a pistol shot proclaimed that another race had begun, the public interest in which was especially keen, owing to the fact that the rowers were stalwart country girls, who made up in energy what they lacked in skill. It was a short race, once round the mark boat only, and, like a successful farce, it 'went with a roar' from start to finish. Foul after foul, each followed by a healing interval of calm, during which the crews, who had all caught crabs, were recovering themselves and their oars, marked its progress; and when the two boats, locked in an inextricable embrace, at length passed the winning flag, and the crews, oblivious of judges and public, fell to untrammelled personal abuse and to doing up their hair.*[6]

The first event offering a specific prize for ladies appears to have been in 1872 when Captain Smithwick of Youghal Lodge (County Tipperary) presented a gold bracelet to be won by a lady sailing on a yacht. Three women were to sail on each yacht in a race, and the three from the winning yacht were then to have a 'row off'. However, any lady who did not wish to row could nominate a gentleman to row in her place – which the winner of the bracelet duly did. The clubs on the Shannon loughs were among the earliest to admit lady members and the first recorded sailing race with lady helms was run by Lough Derg YC in 1896. The six women who took part were all from the 'Big House' strata of society. It would be surprising if some of these Ascendency women, used to an outdoor social lifestyle of hunting, fishing, picnicking and horse racing, did not assert themselves to use family-owned boats to row and sail on the loughs that were almost always on their doorstep. Further north, in County Fermanagh, women were full members of the Lough Erne YC from 1895 and aristocratic wives and daughters were soon racing the new Colleens, designed by either James or Mamie Doyle. Unfortunately, the social status of the club members was such that when *Maeve* capsized in a squall in 1905, with Lady Mabel Crichton at the helm and the Earl of Dudley, Lord Lieutenant of Ireland, among the crew, everyone blamed the boat. The eight Colleens were soon sold away.

Too much emphasis on regattas and clubs obscures the truth that not all sailing is undertaken to race – or even to cruise. Some is simply for the pleasure of the movement through the water or to have time by oneself in the fresh air. Erskine Childers' fictional character Clara in *The Riddle of the Sands* (1903) breathes this spirit. She's dressed in a jersey and skirt, using her small dinghy to escape her stepmother and the oppressive atmosphere of her father's yacht. Childers is said to have found inspiration for her when on holiday in Galway.[7] He later wrote grudgingly that he 'spatchcocked' her into the story. Media historian Alan O'Connor wonders whether she's there to prevent readers thinking that Carruthers and Davies are gay. Personally, I welcome Clara with her sensitivity and quiet competence.

When the young Childers family – two brothers and three sisters – were forced to make new lives at their uncle Robert Barton's house at Glendalough, County Wicklow, the brothers acquired a small boat on Lough Dan. They, and their Barton cousins, enjoyed an outdoor childhood, in which it's highly likely that the brothers and sisters sailed together for pleasure. Upper- and upper-middle-class sisters and brothers, when not separated by the usual segregated education, might have a special role in each other's lives. Kitty O'Brien, educated at home, with her younger sister Margaret, loved books and longed to study logic and algebra. Older brother Conor, studying architecture at Trinity College Cambridge, was able to help her on his return. All the family had enjoyed skiing and mountain walking together and when Conor began barefoot climbing, Kitty often came with him, usually to help him remain calm. She supported his sailing too – including the last lap of his 1923–1925 circumnavigation in *Saoirse*.

After their parents' deaths the O'Brien siblings bought a house in Dublin together. (The girls had been left some money of their own.) Both Kitty and Margaret were willing to help Conor when he began sailing – first in a West Kerry rowing boat with a makeshift sail, then in an open ex-coastguard whaler, the *Mary Brigid*, which they could use to fish and explore, and occasionally race. Finally, when Conor sold his share of their house and bought the 17-ton racing yacht *Kelpie*, the sisters could still be relied on.

Although Kitty, Margaret and Conor had spent a large part of their childhoods in England, their Irish roots were deep, including a much-loved Aunt Charlotte, who campaigned for better conditions for female emigrants and a revival of the Irish language. Their older half-sister Nellie O'Brien joined Charlotte in her enthusiasm for the Irish language and culture, the Gaelic League – and independence. In turn, she inspired their mutual cousin Mary Spring Rice of Mount Trenchard, near Foynes at the mouth of the Shannon. From that complex network of culture, cousinage, female initiative and national longing for independence came the Howth 'gun-running' episode. Once Irish nationalist leaders learned that 25,000 rifles and between 3 and 5 million rounds of ammunition had been landed in Larne, Donaghadee and Bangor in April 1914 and whisked away to equip the Ulster Volunteer Force (UVF), they were convinced that their own Irish Volunteers needed to make some gesture of defiance. Mary Spring Rice, Molly and Erskine Childers, Conor and Kitty O'Brien made it happen.

Molly Childers had been born Molly Osgood in Boston, Massachusetts. She had been disabled from childhood as the result of a skating accident, could only walk with sticks and had undergone a painful and complex operation to make childbearing possible. She was clever and courageous. Once she had met Erskine in 1903 and discovered sailing, she became a talented helmswoman. To celebrate their marriage, and to make long-distance cruising as comfortable as possible for her, her father had commissioned the 51ft yacht *Asgard* from Norwegian designer Colin Archer. The design included adaptions to help keep her safe on deck and enable her to move freely down below.

In the spring of 1914 Molly in London and Mary in Ireland worked with others to raise funds to purchase arms and ammunition from the same German sources who had provided them to the UVF. Then they faced the question of transport. The Larne gun-runners had chartered steamships and motorcars. Mary suggested private yachts, though her family's fishing smack, the *Santa Cruz*, was judged unsuitable for such a potentially challenging task. Molly and Erskine agreed that *Asgard* might be used to meet the tug that would bring the consignment from Hamburg out into the North Sea. They would take the guns on board, then sail down the Channel, round Land's End and up the Irish Sea towards Dublin.

Asgard was sturdy but the load would be too much for her alone, so Mary persuaded Kitty and Conor to join with *Kelpie*. She herself was not an experienced sailor so volunteered as cook and general help on *Asgard*, trying particularly to reduce some of the burden on Molly. The Childers' friend, Army officer Gordon Shepherd, would sail with them, as well as two fishermen and a lad from the Irish Volunteer office. Mary kept a diary of their voyage, detailing the worries and setbacks, awkward personal relationships, small injuries and practical challenges. She enjoyed the sailing, initially treating it as a summer cruise (when the weather allowed), eating well and buying herself an expensive yachting cap when *Asgard* rendezvoused with *Kelpie* in Cowes. Once they had met the German tug off the Ruytigen lightvessel, however, they had 900 guns and 29,000 rounds of ammunition to stow. They'd cut up the saloon berths to make space and moved their personal possessions out. It took all night to stow the guns:

> *It was fearfully hot work. They were fairly heavy and thick with grease, which made them horrible to handle. Gradually, however, the pile grew and presently the saloon was half full, level with the table, and we went up on deck to help strip straw off as they could hardly hand them down fast enough. Then when we had undone a certain number, we went below again to pack them in.*
>
> *So it went on through the night. Still, bale after bale of rifles were passed down from the tug, and every now and again we shouted to the German crew to know how many more were still to come. And the saloon got full, and the cabin and the passage, and then we began to put on another layer, and to pile them at the foot of the companion hatch.*
>
> *Meanwhile, the ammunition had been coming down in fearfully heavy boxes, which were stowed with infinite labour aft under the cockpit, a very difficult place to get at, at the foot of the companion, in the sail lockers, and a couple in the fo'castle.[...]*
>
> *Molly put pieces of chocolate literally into our mouths as we worked and that kept us going, till, about 2am, the last box was heaved on to the deck and the last rifle shoved down the companion.*[8]

The German tug towed *Asgard* as far as Dover, then the heavy-laden yacht sailed on down the Channel. There was a frightening moment off Devonport when they found themselves in the midst of a Royal Navy fleet, out on night manoeuvres. They put in at Milford Haven for Gordon Shepherd to catch a train back to London and spent three days in Holyhead sheltering from the weather and trying to get their timing right for the final entrance into Howth. Then, on Sunday 26 July, Mary hauled up the Cruising Club burgee and stood on *Asgard*'s foredeck wearing her red skirt as the signal to the waiting Volunteers; Molly took the helm and sailed the yacht in.

Mary Spring Rice and Molly Childers with an ammunition box (Wikimedia Commons)

6

'We don't want any petticoats here.'[1]
Pioneering women in the First World War

Vera Laughton (b. 1888); Cicely Fox Smith (b.1882);
Blanche Coules Thornycroft (b. 1873); Eily Keary (b. 1892),
Rachel Parsons (b. 1885)

LITTLE MORE THAN A week after *Asgard* sailed into Howth with her load of German-purchased weapons, Britain declared war on Germany. Molly and Erskine were sitting in the tearoom in the House of Commons on 3 August when Foreign Secretary Sir Edward Grey made the speech that announced the government's decision. When they heard loud cheering Molly said to Erskine, 'Thank God, that means there will not be a war.' He replied, 'Darling, when men cheer like that, it means war.'[2]

The men who had sailed on *Asgard* and *Kelpie* were soon in uniform; the role for the women was less clear. Molly Childers immediately became involved in organising support for Belgian refugees. There were 250,000 in 1914 – the largest number ever in British history. In Ireland, the war was presented as fighting for the rights of small nations, which did not convince everyone. Kitty O'Brien's sister, Margaret, is photographed wearing what is said to be a Royal Navy Reserve (RNR) uniform.[3] It's more likely to be the uniform of the Women's Volunteer Reserve, an organisation derived from the Women's Emergency Corps, founded in 1914 to train women doctors, nurses and motorcycle messengers. This was initially set up by former members of the Women's Social and Political Union (WSPU) after the (controversial) decision to suspend their campaign for the vote.

Many women attest to the effect that campaigning for a cause beyond home and family has on their personal confidence and skill.

Others say this after the experience of being in one of the uniformed services. This seems counter-intuitive when a main aim of service life is to inculcate obedience to orders and to suppress individuality through the system of ranks, service numbers, the wearing of uniform and marching while being shouted at. Vera Laughton, a former WSPU member and principal officer in the Women's Royal Naval Service (WRNS, commonly called the 'Wrens') from 1917, insisted that putting her young recruits through this system gave them pride in themselves and more chance of success in a male-dominated environment. 'Drill, in some mysterious way, is a great inculcator of esprit de corps and a real part of service life. You belong; you are no longer merely an individual but a unit in something greater than yourself and you hold your head a little higher.' Too often women were put into naval offices with no training, no experience and no help, and if they struggled to cope the sweeping verdict was 'Women are no good.'[4]

Vera had called at the Admiralty in 1914, offering her services as any sort of clerical civil servant. She was a journalist with a well-paid job on *The Ladies' Field*, a 6d magazine that ran from 1898 to 1922. It was a fashion, arts and sport magazine that used outdoor activity as part of its selling appeal. As well as furs, frills, corsets and patent medicines, it promoted clothing for country sporting, golf, riding, walking, cycling, archery and yachting, and motoring and steamer wear. Vera had a university education (King's College, London) plus professional organisational and writing skills but the Admiralty turned her away. 'We don't want any petticoats here,' she was told.

As sailors died in unprecedented numbers (6,000 at the Battle of Jutland in May 1916) the Admiralty had to change its attitude. On 29 November 1917, Vera, who was about to join the Women's Army Auxiliary Corps (WAAC), read this announcement in *The Times*.

WOMEN FOR THE NAVY
NEW SHORE SERVICE TO BE FORMED

The Admiralty announce that they have approved of the employment of women on various duties on shore hitherto performed by naval ratings and have decided to establish a Women's Royal Naval Service for this purpose.

The members of this service will wear a distinctive uniform and the service will be confined to women employed on definite duties directly connected with the Royal Navy [...] *A further announcement will be made shortly in regard to the mode of recruitment for the Women's Royal Naval Service and to the branches for which immediate entries are required and no applications or enquiries should be made until this announcement has been issued.*[5]

Vera took no notice of the final instruction, sought out the first temporary recruiting office she could find, and presented herself. 'I was not looking for a job, I wanted to do war work.' Initially she tried explaining that she'd been active in the suffrage movement but when that made no impression, she mentioned that her brother was a lieutenant in the Royal Navy. She received some cool remarks about the need to be very circumspect in her friendships if she was accepted into this new service and began to worry that the interviewers assumed she was joining to meet boyfriends. Nevertheless she was thrilled when she was accepted on to the first officers' training course and felt correspondingly grateful to the editor of *The Ladies' Field* for letting her leave immediately.

Vera could have told her interviewers that her father, Professor Sir John Laughton, had been famous as an instructor in the Royal Navy and that most of the admirals of that time had either been taught by him directly or had learned from his textbooks. However, her passionate involvement in the WSPU had been difficult for her family to accept. They had 'taken it badly' when she wrote a letter to their local newspaper protesting over the treatment of a suffragette, then, when she became volunteer sub-editor of the weekly *Suffragette* newspaper, edited by Christabel Pankhurst, she had needed to distance herself from them, 'spiritually' at least. It had been a tough apprenticeship. Years later, Vera was sitting next to Prime Minister Clement Attlee, who had been a 'Votes for Women' supporter. 'When, at the age of twenty, you have stood in the gutter selling the *Suffragette* while passersby spat at you, at the age of fifty you can face anything,'[6] she said. Atlee agreed that he had felt the same as a young man when required to sing 'The Red Flag' on the streets of Limehouse to collect a crowd for a Labour meeting.

Vera's first job with the WRNS was to recruit and train Wren ratings at the RNVR training depot at Crystal Palace. None of the established RN ports were willing to try this experiment but Crystal Palace (HMS *Victory VI*) was run by reservists and volunteers who were more open-minded.

One day in the middle of January 1918 I presented myself at the Commander's office, attired in a bottle green coat and skirt and a beige felt Breton sailor hat, for there was no uniform as yet. The Commander had a very fierce exterior, with a gruff voice and a steely eye, but he was a first-rate administrator and, what was more, possessed a really progressive mind. He was all out to do everything possible to help the new organisation and make it a success. Me he treated from the start as an officer and not as a young lady. In a booming voice, 'Well, Miss Laughton, you and I are both in the same Service and there are certain things which have to be discussed. Now regarding this matter of lavatories...'[7]

Women were not directly conscripted in the First World War, but labour exchanges ran energetic campaigns to persuade women to fill the places left empty by men. Vera's recruits were usually aged 18 and were required for clerical duties, waitressing, storekeeping, delivering post and carrying messages. She was determined they should become much more than that: they were to be part of His Majesty's Navy. They arrived in fortnightly groups of 12 to 20 until eventually she had 300 young women under her command. The first fortnight was spent in squad drill, physical training and lectures about the Royal Navy and its customs. Then they were issued with a uniform and set to work. Later, Vera realised she was probably the only officer insisting on such formal training for 'immobile' auxiliary workers, but she felt certain that it mattered. 'Immobile' workers were those who would not be posted beyond their home area, often due to family responsibilities. She could see that her system made a difference. 'Whatever the reason they originally joined, they were very soon inordinately proud of being Wrens; they developed a magnificent esprit de corps and I'm afraid considered Crystal Palace the heart and soul of the Royal Navy.'[8]

They were also the first to be dispensed with. Immediately after the Armistice, Crystal Palace was transferred to the Army as a demobilisation centre and the Wrens were told to leave. They were given a week's pay, in lieu of notice, and some of them felt very bitter about it. Vera was transferred to Immingham, where she was ill with influenza and grief at the death of her closest brother, then she was sent to an office in Edinburgh. In 1919 the WRNS, which had comprised 7,000 women at its height, was closed down with no structure or reserve retained. Vera kept some link to her wartime experience – and enabled others to do the same – by becoming part of the Association of Wrens (founded in 1920) and editing their magazine, *The Wren*, as well as becoming the first editor of Lady Rhondda's new feminist magazine *Time and Tide*. Women over the age of 30, with minimum property qualifications, had been enfranchised in 1918. Equal suffrage was achieved in 1928. Many pre-war campaigners, like Vera, now turned their attention to educating their sisters to make the most of these new opportunities.

The Association of Wrens offered formal support to the Girl Guides movement and began to train girls as Sea Guides (later Sea Rangers) for potential service afloat. Vera had command of the second company – though she says she felt like the chosen leader of a band of friends rather than any sort of captain. After she married in 1924 and went to live in Japan for four years, she retained her links with Guiding as best she could. On returning to London, she took over the first company of Sea Rangers. 'My new crew were all young London working girls, the greater number being shop assistants. They grew to be first rate Sea Rangers and became really skilful at handling boats, even though their first lessons were on Regent's Park Lake before their day's work began.'[9] Later, when they were sufficiently proficient to attend more formal Sea Rangers training courses at Portsmouth, they were taught by 'that master in the art of sailing', Marian Wyllie's oldest son, Harold.

Once Vera was also a mother, she took the approach that the best way to maintain some balance between family and working was to involve her family as fully as possible. She and her husband Gordon had amalgamated their surnames to Laughton Mathews; he became 'ship's carpenter' to her group of Sea Rangers, teaching woodworking skills. He and their three children also joined the annual expeditions and camping holidays. She, meanwhile, found further causes to champion in her fight for the equal partnership of men and women. These included the abolition of forced marriage in Africa, the equal responsibility of men and women for sexual hygiene (the movement begun in the previous century by Josephine Baker), votes for women in France (not achieved until 1946) and attendance at the League of Nations Assembly at the time of the Abyssinia Crisis. She also witnessed the speed at which women's movements in Germany were obliterated. In 1929 Germany had the highest number of women parliamentarians of any country in the world (still only 17) yet within four years they were gone, and women were described by Hitler as 'mothers of soldiers and relaxation for the tired warrior.'[10]

In Ireland, sadly, the generation of women who had campaigned for their country's independence and the restoration of its culture were also largely gone by the later 1930s. Mary Spring Rice had reluctantly returned to activism after the Easter Rising and supported republican fighters during the War of Independence. She offered the shelter of Mount Trenchard, her family home overlooking the Shannon, to men on the run and undertook to have a boat ready at any time if they needed to make contact with fighters on the other side of the river.

Mary contracted tuberculosis in 1923 and died the following year. The formation of the Irish Free State in 1922 had initially included a number of women in its legislature. Countess Markievicz, who had canoed at Crom Castle on Lough Erne and whose father, Sir Henry Gore-Booth, sailed to the Arctic, became the first woman elected to the English Parliament, though she didn't take her seat. In Ireland she was Minister for Labour in the Dáil Éireann, the second ever female cabinet minister in Europe. She died in 1927 so didn't witness the subsequent steady erosion of women's rights and disappearance from public life. When the Republic was proclaimed in 1937, the new constitution, drawn up entirely by men and influenced strongly by the Roman Catholic Church, contained clauses that emphasised women's 'special duties' within the home and curtailed their right to work. Property ownership by women, rights to their own bodies and public involvement were noticeably more restricted in the Republic then they had been under the Free State or even before. Women could – and did – still sail, and some owned boats, but their relative exclusion from the public arena (and the more traditional yacht clubs) would endure to at least the 1970s, and beyond.

* * *

The poet Cicely Fox Smith, voiced the hope that the immediate readiness of many Irish men to volunteer to fight for Britain would bring their country peace and independence. Home Rule was finally on the statute book via the Government of Ireland Act 1914, enacted in September but postponed due to the outbreak of war. Cicely's brief lilting poem 'Clare's Brigade', promises that 'the old trouble's ended now, its grey ghost is laid on the fair green hills of holy Ireland.' All too soon she would be proved wrong, but that doesn't necessarily alter the interest in seeing her as a poet of the national mood. 'Clare's Brigade' was published in 1915 by Elkin Mathews in *The Naval*

Crown: Ballads and songs of the war, the first of her almost annual collections during the war years. Her poems were also published in national magazines such as *Blackwoods*, *The Spectator*, the *TLS*, *Pall Mall Gazette* and *Punch*, to which she contributed for over 40 years. Her work was also published regularly in the United States, Canada, Australia and New Zealand.

Punch was selling 100,000–148,000 copies a week in those days, which meant that a lot of people were reading Cicely's poetry. She usually wrote in a man's voice, and so many of her readers will have assumed she was male, especially as poems in magazines were usually signed only with initials. The first editions of most of her published works give her name as C Fox Smith. Dust jackets, however, were more informative and usually included her full name. Until the 1920s, however, dust jackets (or 'wrappers') were considered vulgar and were often thrown away. One reviewer, writing in *The Bookman* in 1919, explains:

> *Most readers affect to be very scornful of the jacket which swathes a new book. Indignantly they tear off the gaudily illuminated sheet, declaring its scarehead encomiums to be one more deadly affront offered their intelligence by the money-motivated publisher. But if I had thrown away unread the covers of* Sailor Town *and* Small Craft. *I should missed half my pleasure in reading these books. For I should never have suspected C Fox Smith was a woman.*[11]

Cicely appears untroubled by questions of gender. She was professional and prolific. Her first poems had begun appearing in national magazines when she was still a schoolgirl in Manchester, and she had four volumes published and well received before she was 22. Though they are scarcely readable today, it's impossible not to sympathise with a longing for colour, adventure and wide-open spaces, denied to so many people leading drab urban lives; doubly denied to a member of the English bourgeoisie who was also female:

> *I'm weary of the weary winds that mazed from off the main*
> *Go gasping down the stifling street and up the wooded lane:*
> *I'm longing for the smell and sound of sea and salt and spray*
> *And the winds on the way my boys, the winds on the way.*[12]

Cicely herself yearned to explore Africa but eventually she, her sister and mother spent two years in Canada where one of her brothers had emigrated. Crucially for her, from 1912–1913 they lived in Victoria, at the southern tip of Vancouver Island. There she worked as a typist in a law firm and discovered the joy of 'dock-walloping', spending all her free time hanging around the Docks and nearby Chinatown. She couldn't go to sea in person – other than travelling by ocean liner – but she could watch the ships, talk to seamen, listen to their tales and the rhythms of their speech. When she returned to England in 1913, she continued this habit at Limehouse and Millwall Docks.

The language of her poetry strengthens and changes, frequently using dialect speech in a manner reminiscent of Kipling. It served her well in the war poems she wrote between 1914–1918, expressing her admiration for the bravery of fighting men, particularly the grim endurance of merchant seamen as they ran the U-boat blockade. She often chose ballad form, such as 'The Ballad of the Resurrection Packet' (*Punch*, 3 November 1915), or 'The Boats of the *Albacore*' (*Punch*, 11 September 1918) in which 'Bristol Tim' tells a grim tale of slow death in the five boats of a sunken steamer, ending:

'Seven men in an open boat, an' the fifth day, dawning red –
When a drifter picked her up at last, due South o' Lizard 'ead.
Seven men in an open boat, two livin' an' five dead.
An' the two that was livin', they'd signed again afore a month was through,
They'd signed and sailed for to take their chance as a seaman's bound to do;
And one went West when the Runnymede *was mined with all her crew...*
An' God help Fritz when we meet,' says Tim. 'For I was one of the two!'[13]

Her dock-walloping ensured that the detail of her work is correct and her voices authentic. Was it enough? Did her imagination, empathy and shill with words enable her to tell maritime truths, despite her lack of direct experience? Joseph Conrad said yes. Reviewing her work for the *Daily Mail* in 1924 he wrote: 'In her I verily believe that the quintessence of the collective soul of the latter-day seaman has found its last resting place and a poignant voice before taking its flight forever from the earth.'[14]

* * *

Although the First World War Wrens had the slightly odd strapline 'Never at Sea' and were usually employed in clerical or domestic jobs, they had felt like pioneers. Other women, not in uniform, had also began working shoreside. Fairfield shipyard in Govan took on women 'dilution' workers for the duration and gained a lasting legacy of the canteens and lavatories which the women insisted should be introduced. A handful of pioneering naval architects also made a discernible difference to the vessels that waged the war at sea. One of them was Blanche Coules Thornycroft at Bembridge on the Isle of Wight.

Blanche was the third child of Blanche Coules and John Isaac Thornycroft, shipbuilder and naval architect. Her father was an innovator, intensely interested in researching the relationship of different hull forms to both speed and stability. When he extended his business to Southampton and moved their family away from Hammersmith to Bembridge, he used part of the extra space in their new home to install a testing tank, known as the 'lily pond'. He began experiments there in 1904, with Blanche increasingly involved from about 1907. She was home-educated, working independently but in close partnership with her father and later her brother. An additional enclosed tank, with workshops, was built in 1910. These were Blanche's primary workspaces, where she would conduct experiments for more than 20 years. She also took part in official tests of the Thornycroft company's products. During the First World War she was asked by the Admiralty to calculate the resistance of mooring ropes to currents. She also tested hull shapes for racing motorboats, Acasta and Acheron class destroyers, motor torpedo boats, RAF rescue launches, high-speed RNLI lifeboats and the famous coastal motorboats (CMBs), which had to be sufficiently light as well as fast to skim over moored minefields when necessary. A replica of CMB 4, the boat used by Augustus Agar in the Kronstadt raid in 1919, is currently being completed from Blanche's test model in Cowes.

Eily Keary (b. 1892) had graduated from Cambridge with a degree in mechanical sciences and began working on the hydrodynamic properties of seaplane hulls and testing other naval hulls in the National Experimental Tank at Teddington from 1915. She was one of a team of researchers working on a variety of key naval systems, including speed and stability. Describing a new, super-fast destroyer, Sir Alfred Yarrow announced to The Institution of Naval Architects (INA) that 'the lines of that ship were determined partly by a lady, Miss Keary, and I think that is a very fine recommendation in favour of ladies'. She was also the first woman to present a paper to the INA.[15] Eily did not give up work at the end of the war or on marriage. She was known for travelling alone on ships to test her theories and working directly as an engineer and in shipyards.

In late 1918 the INA conducted a referendum among its members to make the necessary rule changes to admit women. The honorary vice president recalled making such a suggestion 25 years earlier 'but I got such a volley of abuse that I felt quite fortunate in getting out of the room with my life.'[16] This time the vote was overwhelmingly in favour. Blanche Thornycroft, Eily Keary and Rachel Parsons all became Associate members and Rachel's mother Katherine a full member. Katherine had worked with her husband Charles to invent and manufacture steam turbines. She had overseen women working in Tyneside armament factories during the war and was strongly opposed to them all being made redundant after the Armistice. The problem was close to home as Rachel, a qualified engineer and master mariner, had been overseeing the Parsons factory in the absence of her brother Charles. Charles was killed in April 1918, but Rachel's father refused to let her continue in the business. She and her mother were co-founders of the Women's Engineering Society, where Rachel was first president. She stood several times, unsuccessfully, for Parliament. Blanche Thornycroft, however, seemed uninterested in public involvement. She continued testing prototype vessels, gardened, played golf and sailed a Bembridge Redwing.

Blanche Thornycroft testing a model (Classic Boat Museum)

7

'Winter Shoes in Springtime'[1]
Overcoming trauma

Bunny Collins (b. 1884); Celia Farrar (b. 1871); Ethel Dalzel-Job (b. 1882); Beryl Boxer (b. 1905); Mary Turner/Dixon (b. 1905)

'NO-ONE EVER TOLD THE war widows that they couldn't bring up children on their own,' said my GP (herself a single mother) rather tartly. It was a good thing to say. It told me that I was going to have to put up with my newly single situation and get on with my life. It reassured me that my three young children were not necessarily destined to become delinquents just because their father had decided he didn't want to live with us anymore. I'd like to think I immediately made the decision that I was going to buy a boat for the children and I to sail together but there may have been a few months' gap.

Bembridge sailor Bunny Collins was a First World War widow. Born Elspeth Marian Towers-Clark, Bunny had been married less than 20 months when her husband's ship was lost with all hands at the Battle of Coronel on 1 November 1914. Her only brother was killed at the Battle of the Somme. She was single for over 50 years, bringing up her daughter in the same place she'd grown up, teaching and encouraging young people to sail. She owned a succession of Bembridge Redwings and Solent Sunbeams, was secretary, class captain and commodore of the Club at various times, and her racing record was such that *The Times* newspaper dubbed her the most successful helmswoman in the British Isles. 'Her prowess and fairness at the helm will never be forgotten by those who raced against her, and the waters of East Wight will seem empty without the sonorous tone of her voice ringing from boat to boat.'[2]

Celia Farrar had grown up on the River Orwell in Suffolk. She was one of 12 children born to Edward and Ellen Packard and had loved sailing since childhood. When she was young Celia accompanied her father following the regatta circuit round Britain on his professionally crewed 40-ton schooner, *Britannia*. Whereas other members of the family came for parts of the cruise or stayed in the rented holiday house on the Clyde, Celia was on board throughout, painting and keeping her log.

Celia's father Edward was a wealthy Ipswich businessman and scientist whose family firm was based on the discovery of coprolite (dinosaur dung) as a fertiliser. He was a philanthropist who did a great deal to support the pioneering female archaeologist and prehistorian Nina Layard in her excavations. He was also one of the founders of the breakaway Orwell Corinthian YC, which included female members and sought to champion the values of small boat sailing and hands-on owner involvement, differentiating themselves from their parent club, the Royal Harwich YC, which was heavily invested in big boat racing. For a while Edward had owned Grace Schenley's former 5-rater, *Valentine*, with which he won several prizes.

The Orwell Corinthians decided to commission their own One Design class, aiming for races that were dependent on skill rather than wealth. Six half-decked 18ft keel boats were commissioned from the designer H Smith of Burnham-on-Crouch and offered to club members in 1899. More than six people wanted them, so a ballot was organised. Female members were not permitted to enter. Celia and her sister Nina were so disappointed that one of their brothers, not the least interested in sailing, put his name forward, won the right to purchase a boat, named it *June* and gave it to his sisters. During the life of the club (until 1928) Celia and Nina won 67 first prizes, 66 second prizes and 45 third prizes. They were helped by Bill Read, a crane driver in Edward Packard's factory, who maintained the boat and sailed with the two young women as their paid hand. Racing was news in the days before the First World War and Celia often found her picture in the national press.

Celia had met her future husband Alfred Farrar when she was living in Sierra Leone, keeping house for her oldest brother. Celia and Alfred married in 1905 and had their first child, Norman, in 1907 and the second, Austin, in 1913. Alfred continued working as a colonial administrator in Sierra Leone while Celia and their children settled back in Suffolk. He was returning to England to visit them in 1916 when his ship was torpedoed and he was killed. Celia continued bringing up her two sons alone. She took them sailing and on cycling holidays and travelled abroad to meet members of their father's family, who lived scattered across the West Indies. She continued travelling and sailing all her life.

* * *

After Ethel Dalzel-Job's husband Ernest was killed on 11 July 1916, during the Battle of the Somme, she found it hard to manage on her war widow's pension. Her husband, a chartered accountant, had been a volunteer with the Artists Rifles. They were both keen hockey players, both good shots and had been living a contented middle-class life in London with their baby son, Patrick. Ernest volunteered for overseas service and rose to command a company in the Machine Gun Corps (MGC) – occasionally known as the 'Suicide Club'. When he was sent to France, Ethel and Patrick moved to live in lodgings in Hastings so that she could hear the guns and thus feel closer to him. On 11 July she and her younger sister were together, praying, when Ethel stood up suddenly. 'Something has happened to Ernest,' she said.

Ernest was dead and Ethel's financial problems had begun. Patrick remembered his mother as being too proud to accept 'charity' from her family. He also remembered that every meal became 'a matter of careful thought' and the prunes were counted out individually before being given to their landlady to make pudding. When he was older, Ethel struggled to pay the fees for him to attend Berkhamsted School. Patrick was often ill, and when he was 13 she took a decision to move them out of England and live more cheaply and healthily beside a lake in the Jura mountains. Patrick learned the local patois and began experimenting with the flat-bottomed boats on the lake. Ethel borrowed a sewing machine and made him a sail. When he was 18 it seems that he may have inherited a little money. They returned to England and bought an ancient converted lifeboat as their new home.

It's easy to think of this as Patrick's story but it's equally Ethel's, and he gives her full tribute for the 'gallantry' with which she embraced their new life. After two years learning to sail the lifeboat round the coast of Britain, mother and son spent a year in Tarbert while Patrick worked with boatbuilders and sailmakers to build the 15-ton schooner *Mary Fortune*.

> *My mother had not been young when I, the only son, was born, and she was an elderly little woman with tight silver curls and a taste for pretty clothes of a frilly kind when my schooner was ready for sea. Mother was much troubled with rheumatism and was habitually seasick even in the largest ships and the calmest seas; but she had a liking for going to foreign parts and she was easily persuaded to join me as my only 'hand' in the schooner.*[3]

With the help of a friend, Ethel and Patrick crossed the North Sea to Skudeneshavn in Norway in July 1937 and began exploring the country they came to love. Many of the anchorages had never before been visited by a British yacht – or by any yacht for that matter – but they were welcomed with hospitality and friendship wherever they went. The following year they sailed beyond the Arctic Circle and wintered at Tromsø, where they met the Bangsund family – a lifechanging encounter. When they sailed the following summer, rounding the northernmost point of Arctic Europe to reach Petsamo, 13-year-old Bjørg, eighth of ten children, came with them to help Ethel in the galley and Patrick on deck. 'It must have puzzled the Finnmark fisher-folk, in their unfrequented harbours, to see the strange schooner come sailing out of the West, "manned" by a lanky foreign youth, a long-legged schoolgirl and a neatly-dressed little old woman.'[4]

The outbreak of the Second World War brought a hasty end to these explorations. *Mary Fortune* was laid up and Bjørg returned home to her family. Ethel and Patrick hurried back to England, where Ethel would have to say another farewell to a man she loved.

* * *

Beryl Boxer came from a family who could scarcely remember a single male member who had died in his bed. Her great-great-grandfather had died of cholera at Balaclava, her grandfather had drowned off Cape Finisterre and her father, Hugh, was killed in action at Hooge on 16 June 1915. Initially the War Office telegram said only that he was reported wounded and missing. Beryl's mother, Jeannie, then endured months of desperate hope, placing advertisements and seeking information from his fellow servicemen before his body was discovered in January 1916. In *High Endeavours* (1991), his biography of Miles and Beryl Smeeton, based on many family interviews, Miles Clark reports that Hugh's two sons Myles and Charles had found their father intimidating, whereas Beryl, who was only nine when he died, hadn't been afraid at all. Charles Boxer believed that his sister had resented being female. Perhaps he had found her challenging? 'Her motto was, "Anything you can do, I can do better." She had this tremendous urge to surpass... She was quite fearless and would never rest or relax.'[5]

This did not make for an easy relationship with her mother. While both her brothers duly joined the Army, Beryl attended finishing school and was presented at court. She told her brother that she found life at home so intolerable that she intended to marry the first good-looking man who proposed to her – which, in 1927, she did. Tom Peddie was also in the Royal Lincolnshire Regiment – as both her brothers were, and her father had been. Jeannie's mental and emotional health declined until, in 1929, she committed suicide. Tom was posted to another regiment, the Green Howards, and Beryl went with him to India. There he introduced her to a fellow officer and brilliant horseman, Miles Smeeton, and asked him to teach Beryl to ride. This was a great success. Beryl and Miles also discovered intense pleasure swimming and climbing together. Tom Peddie seems to have been a particularly kind and good man, but he had a job to occupy him and Beryl did not. Her extreme energy was mental as well as physical; she needed new experiences, new understandings. She was soon bored with the static existence of an Army wife and travelled as frequently as she was able, characteristically choosing the cheapest means of transport to see as much of India as she could afford.

When the time came for the Green Howards to return to England, Beryl persuaded Miles that he and she should travel back overland, using local transport and hitch-hiking instead of her travelling by sea with Tom. It was a memorable journey, undertaken for less than £40 each, and for Beryl an escape from a marriage and a way of life that had become stifling. They fell in love but parted at the end of the journey, promising not to see each other for a year. Beryl returned to India with Tom and the regiment but when the year was up, she told her husband that she couldn't live with him any longer. Then she went travelling on her own.

> *I had married young and had moved straight from living with a widowed mother to living with a husband who was 14 years older than I was. My mother had died soon after I was married, and now for the first time I found myself independent and accountable to no-one.*[6]

Beryl described travel as acting on her 'like a tranquilliser'. This first solitary journey took her from India, across Persia, then across the Araxes River into Russia, north into the Caucasus then across the Black Sea to the Crimea and via Kharkov and Kiev, through Poland and Czechoslovakia to Vienna, where she found a letter from Miles suggesting they went climbing together – an activity that nearly cost them their lives. Then Miles needed to return to India and leave the regiment that he had shared with Tom. Two unexpected deaths in Beryl's family provided her with the commodity she needed most: money. This ensured her independence. 'I could now satisfy my craving to see the world and I now knew that I could do so for far less than it would cost me to live in England – which I thought was a dreadful idea anyway.'[7]

It took time to sort out her relatives' estates and go through the 'horrid sordid business' of divorce. She learned German, spent more time in Austria, then set out again across Russia into Japan, then China, Burma (now Myanmar) and finally to the Himalayas, where she met Miles. Once again, they enjoyed climbing together and survived another near-death experience canoeing down the Beas River. But when Miles proposed marriage, Beryl said that she didn't feel in the marrying mood just yet. She set off to ride 1,000 miles through the Patagonian Andes on horseback.

The title of this chapter comes from Beryl's account of the journeys she took immediately after separating from Tom. When she was travelling across China, she made herself more comfortable by buying pairs of cheap sandals. She was aware her feet didn't fit the tiny shoes made for Chinese women in that period but hadn't realised that the sandals she chose were distinctively masculine. Her fellow passengers on the Yangtze steamer used them as the clue to develop a convincing back story for her:

> *She has been rich and has lost all her money. All she has left are the camera and the alarm clock. She probably had a rich husband who grew tired of her as she had no children, or perhaps he died and now she is very poor – so poor that she has to wear men's winter shoes in springtime.*[8]

Beryl also wore a big tent-like kimono under which she could get changed or go to the lavatory with some privacy. Sir Philip Brocklehurst, an explorer who had travelled with Shackleton, took her under his protection for a dangerous stretch of journey between China and Burma. She found his solicitude intensely irritating until she realised that he had assumed she was hiding an illegitimate baby underneath its folds.

In *Winter Shoes in Springtime* (1961) Beryl takes her reader into the minute detail of her travelling life, telling her tales in a distinctively amused, observant tone. Her daughter Clio says:

> *She wrote just as she spoke, with little or no concern about 'writing' as an art form. She was also very, very funny, witty, and fascinating. At a crowded cocktail party, for example, she was always easy to find because so many people would crowd around her to chat. Some of them might also be slightly deaf too because her voice was very distinctive and easy to hear for anyone who was hard of hearing. I don't know why this was, her voice just carried, so she never shouted or had to shout.*[9]

Winter Shoes in Springtime describes solitary travels from India through Persia, Turkey across the Black Sea to the Crimea into present day Ukraine, then home through Poland, Czechoslovakia to Vienna. Her second trip took her back through Russia to Manchuria, then Korea, Japan, China and Burma. She relished hardship if it brought her closer to people living unselfconscious lives in their own countries. On more than one occasion, however, she found herself in situations of real danger:

> *The crowd did not make much noise but only murmured to each other and there was not a smile on any face. A kind of hostility seemed to be in the air and the murmuring turned into a menacing sort of a hum, broken suddenly*

> by a voice from outside the scrum which seemed to be asking a question, The answer given by those nearest me came as an appalling shock:
>
> 'Japanese!' they shouted back.
>
> For a second I couldn't really believe that they had taken me for a Japanese, but it was imperative that they shouldn't think so for long.[10]

She persuades them that she is English and hates the Japanese; she is 'rescued' by an unknown woman; then, later, she is exhibited to the crowd. Her enormous feet and hands are displayed as people file past, repelled and fascinated by her 'blind man's' blue eyes and extraordinary fair hair.

Beryl had been frightened but was undeterred. Her attitude was that of her friend and inspiration, Ella Maillart, who wrote the introduction to *Winter Shoes in Springtime*: 'We strongly agreed about the importance of travelling alone in order to travel well, as light and as cheaply as possible and, of course, unarmed. One has to be accepted by the local inhabitants whenever it is possible.'[11] Ella (b. 1903) was a Swiss national who had learned to sail on Lake Geneva and had represented her country in the monotype dinghy class at the 1924 Olympics. She had sailed as crew on a Thames barge, experimented with tunny fishing off the Breton coast and sailed to Corsica then to Crete with her friend 'Miette' (Hermine de Saussure) and an all-female crew. Ella was also an international hockey player, Olympic skier and indefatigable traveller, whose books *Turkestan Solo* (1934) and *Forbidden Journey* (1937) had thrilled Beryl.

Beryl did eventually marry Miles in 1938 and is remembered as half of one of sailing's most inspirational couples. Their daughter Clio sees her mother as the catalyst who made their partnership special. Ella Maillart considered that Beryl and Miles shared a vital attitude to life: 'Ever since they met, they have chosen the life of youth, out of doors, a life of exertion in the mountains or the jungle or at sea. With their eyes wide open, they knew the dangers they ran, and they took them in their stride'.[12]

* * *

As well as the husbands, sons and fathers who died in the Great War, there were men who survived, witnesses to barely imaginable trauma.

This might not make life easy for their families. Mary Turner was teaching herself to sail on the Norfolk Broads when she met her future husband, Douglas Dixon. She was then the principal of the Economic Intelligence Department at Barclays Bank. Initially educated at home by governesses and private tutors, Mary had studied Modern History at Lady Margaret Hall, Oxford and had gained First Class Honours in her special research subjects of Banking and Public Finance. In 1928 the college had awarded her a travelling exhibition to study municipal finance in Germany. Mary approached sailing seriously, setting out with an instruction book in one hand, tiller in the other. On this occasion she also had her father with her. She had run them aground, and he was furious. It seemed a wonderful piece of luck that a good-looking ex-naval officer should not only get them floating again but completely mollify her father.

Douglas Dixon had been just 15 years old in August 1914. He had entered the Royal Naval College at Osborne aged 12 and that summer of 1914 he and his fellow 'Blake term' cadets had moved across to Britannia Royal Naval College at Dartmouth. When the order came to mobilise for war the cadets were sent at once to ships of the reserve fleet. The young boys marched away through the streets of Dartmouth, watched by crowds of people, many of whom wept. Douglas was ordered to join HMS *Bacchante* and sent to patrol the 'Broad Fourteens' off the coast of Holland. He was there for the Battle of Heligoland Bight on 28 August when *Bacchante* was used to carry the wounded and dying men from both the British and German fleets back to Sheerness before returning to patrol. On 17 September *Bacchante* was sent back to Chatham for a brief refit – which meant that it escaped the fate of the three other cruisers of the reserve fleet, HMSs *Aboukir*, *Cressy* and *Hogue*, which were torpedoed and sunk on 22 September by the German U-boat *U-9*. About half of Douglas' classmates died then.

The remainder were promoted to midshipmen and the Broad Fourteen patrols discontinued. HMS *Bacchante* was put on escort duty for convoys running between Plymouth and Gibraltar. Then in mid-April 1915 it arrived at Moudros, on the Greek island of Lemnos, to begin transporting ANZAC troops for the invasion of the Gallipoli peninsula. Fifteen-year-old Douglas was in charge of a steam pinnace, towing two other vessels, with responsibility for landing 125 troops at a time, together with animals and supplies – and taking off the dead and wounded. The details are horrifying. More of his former classmates were killed and the carnage among shore troops was both massive and obvious. Later that summer he took part in the more successful landings at Suvla Bay. Subsequently, he was transferred to the destroyer HMS *Colne*, which assisted in the evacuation of the peninsula in January 1916. He was still only 16.

By the time Mary met Douglas on the Norfolk Broads his naval career was over. Despite being twice mentioned in dispatches and awarded the Distinguished Service Cross for his service at Gallipoli, then serving throughout the war in a variety of roles, he had not survived the difficult transition into peacetime service. In 1922, during the period of intense naval cutbacks, he had been placed on the retired list in return for a gratuity. He'd married Marjorie Brown in 1921; they'd had a baby, Shirley, and Marjorie wasn't well. Douglas probably needed the voluntary retirement money. There are also suggestions that he had not got on well with fellow officers during some of his postings. By 1928, when he met Mary, he and Marjorie were divorced. She and her daughter were living in France and Douglas was attempting to make a new career as a lecturer, teacher of navigation and yachtsman. He placed advertisements in the *Journal*s of the Little Ship Club, offering to join any crew or take any yacht anywhere.

In Mary's first novel, *Seagull and Sea-Power* (1937), the heroine, Linnet Hardcastle, is sure that marriage is not for her. She has been working as a researcher in Berlin, which she loves; has been courted by the good-looking Baron von Falkenheim, whom she likes and respects; and is told quite clearly by an amicable man in a train that a *'hübsches mädel'* ('pretty girl') like her ought to marry and make some good man happy. Linnet responds that she wants to continue academic research and 'I thought it would be more fun to make myself happy.'[13] She is persuaded to break her journey in Holland, hires a dinghy for a day and meets the ex-RN officer Nicholas Curry, who has been selling refrigerators in London and who she diagnoses as suffering from 'nervenbankrot' (her word for a nervous breakdown). The characterisations and attitudes seem likely to have been drawn from Mary's own life.

Mary and Douglas got engaged in 1932. They brought the Brightlingsea oyster smack *Daisy* (1884) as their floating home. Mary's money purchased the vessel and Douglas paid for her conversion to a yacht. After a registry office wedding ashore, they were married on board their new home by Mary's father, Rev. Henry Turner. It was midsummer 1933. The newly registered yacht was moored off the Royal Naval College Greenwich across the line of the Prime Meridian, where Mary's mother renamed her *Dusmarie* – a combination of Douglas and Mary. They were given a three-month-old terrier puppy named Rodney.

Their beautifully conceived event went sadly wrong as *Dusmarie* rolled uncontrollably in the heavy river traffic, the rain came down and the guests demanded to be taken ashore, while Mary's father determinedly continued to read the marriage service. That night – their wedding night – the anchors dragged in the sluicing Thames ebb. The wind failed as they took the tide downriver; they lost steerage way and *Dusmarie* was caught under the bow of a swimhead lighter. There seemed imminent danger that she would break up under the strain. 'I'll look after the puppy and you can look after yourself,' Douglas told Mary. A police launch appeared just in time to tow them clear and help them to a safer anchorage in the muddy mouth of a creek.

Mary had to resign her job on marriage. She then joined the lecture staff of both London County Council and Conservative Central Office. Douglas was lecturing for the Navy League. Their 1933 honeymoon was 1,671 miles spent racing and cruising their new home. This included an exploration of the Friesian Islands. With none of today's conveniences, cruising the 43ft, 10-ton gaff yawl *Dusmarie* with her 10ft 6in beam and 6ft draft was a heavy undertaking, especially as Mary suffered continually from seasickness. She therefore took main responsibility for steering at sea – often ten hours at a time – and for cooking when in harbour, while Douglas cooked at sea and was the navigator. He was skipper and she was mate. In his writings he never refers to Mary by her name, only by her title.

They returned home fired up with the idea of making a film of *Riddle of the Sands* using *Dusmarie* as *Dulcibella*. However, Molly Childers was not keen on parting with the film rights so they decided to write their own version. Though both their names are on the cover, *Seagull and Sea-Power* is very clearly Mary's book. Linnet, the heroine, takes the Carruthers role in the *Riddle* story and hero Nicholas Curry is a version of Erskine Childers' Davies but also a complex, damaged Great War survivor. Written in the mid-1930s it's a fascinating reflection on the rise of Nazism and Hitler as it appeared then. It's also eloquent and exciting and doesn't deserve to have been so completely forgotten.

In Douglas' first book, *A Sail to Lapland* (1938), he expresses some bizarrely fundamentalist ideas about women, comparing us, unfavourably, to boats:

Most ships are superior to most women for, while the elements must enter into both of them, one is fashioned by men entirely. With the manufacture of women, though admittedly men must start the business and lay the keelson, it is rarely indeed that women will allow man to finish or perfect the job that he has started.[14]

He laments that 'poor Adam' never had a chance to finish off the job of his odd rib but he also criticises Noah for failing to realise that the Ark mattered more than the two-by-twos. For theirs was a ménage à trois; in Douglas' view *Dusmarie* matters more than either himself or Mary. He has a vision of a world filled by families 'united in devotion to their ship' and 'her Master must allow her sea room'.

This word 'master' has a specific resonance when used in a naval context as it refers to the person responsible for the navigation, the sailing decisions and the trim of the ship rather than the imposition of discipline. It's also the language of the ship's papers. When *Dusmarie*'s status changed from smack to yacht she was re-registered and issued with the necessary certificate (blue book). However, it too easily slips into a male-preening attitude: 'a ship makes her master-owner completely cock of his own roost' wrote Douglas, perhaps forgetting whose money had actually paid for the yacht. Early entries in Lloyd's Register show *Dusmarie* as joint property of Douglas and Mary; later she is just entered as his.

It's a very common assumption, in sailing, that the man owns the yacht. Often it's true: a yacht is property and men have historically held more of this than women. But what of the labour and everything else that's needed to enable and maintain a functioning ship? Mary and Douglas' daughter Astrid (b. 1940) insists that her parents' management of *Dusmarie* was 'a true partnership'. She also says that it was her mother who made the whole venture possible – no one else would have 'put up with' her father.

Mary wrote only one more novel, the charming *Soft Falls the Snow* (1955), but would later develop a pioneering approach to girls' education. Meanwhile, it's hard to get away from the dedication of *Seagull and Sea-Power*: 'In memory of those who lost their lives in *Aboukir, Cressy*

'WINTER SHOES IN SPRINGTIME'

and *Hogue'* – those First World War cruisers aboard which over half of Douglas' 14- and 15-year-old classmates had been killed.

Mary Dixon sailing home from Lapland on Dusmarie (Astrid Dixon Llewellyn)

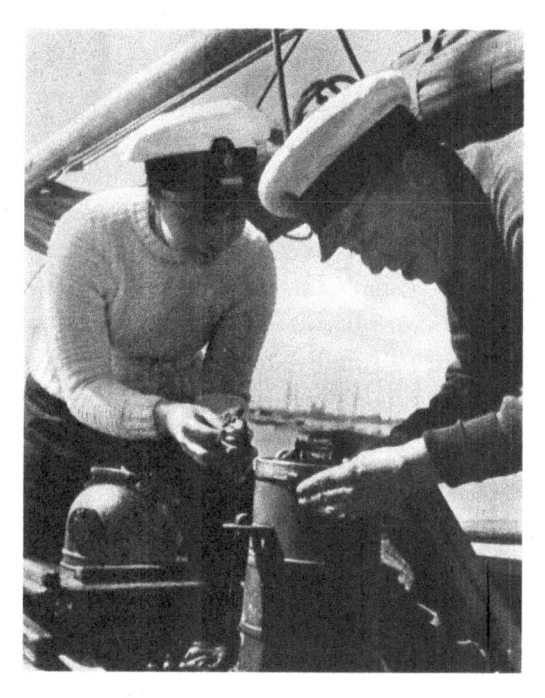

Mary and Douglas Dixon Compass Adjustment (Astrid Dixon Llewellyn)

8

'Fed up with this skirt nonsense!'[1]
Post-war pioneers and fickle yacht owners

Mabel Stock (b. 1874); Evgenia Shelepina (b. 1894);
Dulcie Kennard/Peter Gerard (b. 1900)

RALPH STOCK, CROUCHED IN his dugout during the First World War, had spent much of his spare time dreaming of exploring the South Sea Islands in a ship of his own. He was wounded sufficiently seriously to be discharged and began the search at once. But when the yacht, a sturdy 47ft Norwegian-built former lifeboat called the *Ogre*, was discovered, he needed to think about crew. 'Well, I have a sister and a sister is an uncommonly handy thing to have, provided she is of the right variety.'[2]

Mabel Stock was certainly of the right variety. The brother and sister duo had already travelled together, by emigrant ship to Australia in February 1914, with another friend known as 'The Nut'. According to Ralph's account in *The Chequered Cruise* (1916) they had lurched from one disaster to another, including the shipwreck of their unsuitable yacht, *Wanderlust*, on Norfolk Island, until news of the declaration of war had reached them on Fiji. Return to Australia saw a continuation of their difficulties as no money could be cabled from England and they were already travelling on tight budgets. The Nut joined the Australian army; Ralph ('Freckles' in the story) went north to Queensland, where he had an interest in a pineapple farm; and Mabel ('The Spinster') went to work as a live-in hotel waitress, working from 6am every day for £1 a week. 'You know I am no slacker,' she wrote, 'But this is appalling.'[3] Eventually Ralph found the money for their passage home and his account ends as they leave burning Papeete by steamer bound for England and he begins to show her his plans for *Wanderlust II*.

'FED UP WITH THIS SKIRT NONSENSE!'

Mabel was the only daughter in a middle-class London publishing family. Ralph was the youngest of her brothers and was able to supplement his small private income by writing short stories and travel accounts. He was able to earn enough to buy a sturdy Norwegian double-ender, designed by Colin Archer and named the *Ogre*. Mabel had lived at home with her parents and never married. As a child she had loved gymnastics, mountain climbing and riding and did some sort of manual work during the war. She too had a tiny income of her own. She was physically strong, level-headed, knew her limitations and wasn't easily shocked. She was convinced that this mattered on a small ship, where living together entailed 'very intimate – some would say immodest – associations with the other sex.' The specific issue was male nudity – not as a habit, but likely to occur in an emergency:

> *For example, more than once, if 'All hands on deck was shouted', it was my job to dash to the tiller and keep the ship on her course. Whoever had been below was probably clothed in nothing but a towel, owing to the great heat, and when rushing on deck to help, his exertions might deprive him even of that.*[4]

Mabel knew that there were many other women like herself, who had worked hard during the war and were feeling rootless and dissatisfied. Some of them would have paid a significant premium to have joined her and her brother on their voyage. He would have liked their money; she would have enjoyed their company, yet she vetoed the idea. She couldn't think of any of her friends who she could ask and thought it too risky to take a stranger. This was partly on the grounds of responsibility: if the woman passenger didn't enjoy it, they couldn't just drop her off anywhere as they might a man. It was also a matter of manners and expected behaviour between the sexes.

> *The least exacting woman expects certain little courtesies which it would be impossible to accord under the circumstances; that is why I made a stipulation with the boys that they should treat me as a man while on board, and that we should all work exactly alike as regarded the daily routine.*[5]

On board the *Ogre*, Mabel was called 'Peter'. Steve, another recently demobilised soldier, who had very little money but a great capacity for hard work, joined as the third member of their 'dream merchants' team. He and Ralph did the most strenuous work fitting out the *Ogre* while Mabel, who knew that moving pig-iron and raising masts was beyond her, took a job as a nurse-companion so that she could save on board and lodging as well as earning a modest wage. She put as much money as she could into the communal costs of provisioning the ship, undertook all the interior decoration – painting, upholstering and embroidering – and bought suitable clothes for the voyage. These included seven or eight pairs of 'serviceable pyjamas', which would be her daily wear on board in hot weather, and two or three skirts made in the same material 'that could be quickly slipped on when making land'.[6] On board *Wanderlust*, she had discarded her skirt for stockinette bloomers, which her brother said became baggy with exertion. She took charge of ordering and storing all the provisions but then, once they were away, cooking was shared equally, everyone doing a week at a time.

Mabel kept a diary for their voyage from Brixham to Tongatapu, which Ralph used, selectively, when he came to present their adventures as *The Cruise of the Dream Ship* (1921). Then, almost uniquely, Mabel wrote her own account, published two years later, *The Log of a Woman Wanderer* (1923). They make a fascinating comparison. Ralph's is more polished, more amusing, more consciously literary. He likes to describe and philosophise and shapes his material to suit the narrative. For instance, he never mentions that they took a paying passenger, an older yachtsman who remained with them from the Canaries to Papeete, a significant stretch. Ralph perhaps felt that this detracted from the presentation of his trio of impecunious 'dream merchants'. Mabel describes herself as 'no good at description' though, for me, her insight into the human relationships of the people they met makes far more interesting reading. She is certainly more truthful. Arthur Ransome described Ralph's book as 'very bad' but said he envied him his boat. There's no evidence that he read Mabel's account.

Abruptly, Ralph ended their dreams by selling the *Ogre*, when he was offered a high price by a gentleman he met in a club in Nuku'alofa, the capital of Tongatapu. He didn't warn or consult; instead, he merely told Mabel and Steve that he had sold 'the old girl' and that they had three hours to pack and catch the island steamer. They would travel as passengers to Australia, where he promised to buy a 'more magnificent' vessel in which they would continue their circumnavigation of the world. Mabel described it as a 'shattering blow' and didn't speak to him for the rest of the day. This was unsurprising really, as she needed to hurry to find baskets to pack her house-linen, plate and cutlery and personal possessions, to throw away all the presents and souvenirs she'd collected on their voyage so far, and then find a new home for her pet tortoise. She said goodbye to all the cushions and curtains she'd embroidered, the pretty tea set, coffee service, liqueur glasses that she'd treasured, and her Broadwood piano. As they steamed out of the harbour, bound for Samoa, she gazed at the *Ogre*, lying deserted at anchor, and could only hope that her brother felt as broken-hearted as she did.

* * *

At the age of 39, Arthur Ransome, not long escaped from the complications of the Russian Revolution and civil war, gloried in his status as 'Master and Owner of the *Racundra*'. He had owned and discarded two vessels already and there would be five more (excluding dinghies) to follow. Meanwhile, in the late summer of 1922, he had sufficient good sense to give his lover, Evgenia Shelepina, top billing as the person responsible for 'the ease and pleasantness' of their first voyage in her role as cook. '[...] the Primuses roared continuously like the blast furnaces in northern England [...] of the three of us the Cook, without a doubt, was the one who worked her passage.'[7]

In Latvia, Evgenia is remembered as sleeping with snakes around her breasts.[8] Few British writers on Ransome would see her as a tragic Cleopatra putting the asp to her breast in semi-erotic suicide; more might cast her as Medusa, the snaky-haired gorgon with a gaze that could turn lesser mortals to stone. Her direct speech, delivered in a strong Russian accent, frequently had that effect on the politely equivocal English. John Berry, who slipped through Evgenia's defences by appealing to her love of gardening, initially assumed she was the housekeeper. 'I'm afraid Mr Ransome is not at home and seldom receives visitors. I'm so sorry I cannot help you – and please will you be sure to shut the gate!'[9] Commentators mention her relentless criticism of Arthur's books, her dislike of some of his boats, her contribution to his inveterate restlessness. Was she a malign star? My mother, June, tells of rowing out to the yacht *Barnacle Goose*, chartered by the Ransomes for a Suffolk holiday in 1951. She thought it would be a generous gesture to offer Mrs Ransome some of the saucepans she'd been given as wedding presents, rather than whatever was normally used on the boat. This was a bad mistake. The pans were aluminium and Evgenia had now (probably correctly) associated them with Arthur's stomach ulcers. She didn't manage the classic British 'thanks-but-no-thanks', but rebuffed Mum furiously, almost accusing her of wishing to poison her husband.

When I lie in what was Evgenia's bunk on their post-war yacht *Peter Duck*, condemned by her as 'ridiculous', I struggle to be fair to her. The scrappy entries in her surviving 1927–1933 diaries are unrevealing. She cherished the small flowers and the birds in their garden, fished and sailed with some enthusiasm, particularly on the Norfolk Broads, and only rarely offers the slightest insights as to what it felt like to be a Russian woman in Britain then.

Evgenia Petrovna Shelepina had trained as a stenographer. Both she and her closest sister, Iroida, were working in government jobs and had just moved into a flat in St Petersburg together when the 1917 October Revolution broke out. They had become Bolsheviks sometime during 1916–1917. Evgenia later recalled her journey back to her mother's house on that first day of revolution:

> *I was never under fire. I have always had bad luck. I have never once been under fire all throughout the Revolution. Of course I heard firing all the time. Sometimes it was in the next street. Sometimes it was far away but I got the whole way to the station without being in any danger at all. I was pleased to see the workmen and sailors and excited and happy because I wanted them to win.*[10]

Travel difficulties lost Evgenia her job and brought her famous appointment as Trotsky's secretary in the Smolny Institute, where she would eventually meet Arthur. Arthur described Evgenia and Iroida as 'fierce revolutionaries, as tall as guardsmen preferring revolvers to powder puffs.' The surviving photograph of the two sisters, however, shows pleasant-faced young women in sailor blouses – with their pet snake. Arthur includes the snake (a grass snake) as part of *Racundra*'s complement for her second voyage in July 1923. He describes it as being 'over a yard long with a passion for frogs' and at its happiest 'curled round and round in the bottom of the teapot'.[11] (*Not* his lover's breasts.)

Both Evgenia and Iroida were friends with Arthur's friend Karl Radek and his wife Rosa. Evgenia also knew Lenin and Stalin but,

'FED UP WITH THIS SKIRT NONSENSE!'

as her relationship with Ransome deepened and his position became more precarious, she began to feel vulnerable. In 1918 she was glad to leave Room 67 and accept a job at the Russian Legation in Sweden. It was a blow to both her and Arthur when the Legation was expelled from Stockholm, and she was ordered back to Russia. Later in the year, complicated diplomacy ensured she was given permission to leave Moscow and accompany Arthur to Estonia as his wife – though he was not yet divorced from his first wife, Ivy. Part of the hidden deal with the Russian leadership was that she would smuggle 35 diamonds and three strings of pearls out of the country. These were intended to help finance revolution in England.

This was probably the beginning and end of her activity as a Soviet agent. Arthur made her sign an affidavit promising 'on my word of honour that I will undertake no political commissions in England from the Bolsheviks or any other political party, and further that I will engage in no conspiratorial work whatsoever without expressly informing you that I consider this promise no longer binding.'[12] While Arthur continued to travel in and out of Russia during the next few difficult years of political realignment and conflict, Evgenia settled herself to a domestic existence of cooking, cleaning and outbursts of tempestuous rage or utter obstinacy. She also sailed with him on their first boats, *Slug* and *Kittiwake*.

In May 1924 Arthur was finally free to marry. In August they enjoyed their final cruise on *Racundra*, a gentle exploration along the Aa River in Latvia; fishing, eating, Arthur writing and observing the dilapidation of the countryside in the wake of civil war. In September Evgenia found a mouse on board and left the yacht in a fury. Eventually she did return, traps were installed, and the cruise survived the few more necessary days to return *Racundra* to the Stint Lake, where she was laid up and eventually sold to Adlard and Mamie Coles. Evgenia accompanied Arthur back to England and applied her abundant energy to renovating their first home in Low Ludderburn, Windermere, where *Swallows and Amazons* would be written. Who can doubt that Evgenia's personality – and Arthur's love for her – helped inspire its strong female characters? And this is why she matters. She might even have worn a red knitted hat with a tassel, trademark of the fictional Amazons. Many Ransome-lovers, however, blame her for his decision to sell his 'best little ship' *Nancy Blackett* because she complained that the galley was too small. Once *Peter Duck* had been condemned by Evgenia as looking 'ridiculous' her fate was also sealed.

Arthur could be grumpy and difficult but as he became more famous and a National Treasure, it was easiest to deflect his more unattractive features on to his direct-speaking Russian wife and disregard his insistence that he owed her the happiest moments of his life. Perhaps she was not always as confident as she seemed to others. Once she made a mistake selecting a mooring on the Broads and had also misjudged the weather: 'I was very cross with myself [...] and being cross with myself always makes me cross with Arthur especially when I am very cold and wet as I am now and our neighbours very numerous and noisy.'[13] There's also the tiniest hint that she may have suffered from medical problems that she didn't feel able to discuss. 'Went to see Dr Atkinson. I am inclined to think that she may be a good doctor but I am afraid she is so indiscreet that I can't talk to her about the things that bother me somewhat.'[14]

* * *

Arthur and Evgenia had no children, whether from choice or inability. From the 1920s those large late Victorian and Edwardian families seem to have been a thing of the past, at least among the middle and upper classes. The publication of Marie Stopes' *Married Love* in 1918 may have been a contributory factor. It encouraged discussion of mutual pleasure in sex, the benefits of planned parenthood, and understanding the natural cycles of fertility as well as attempting to reduce the guilt of using barrier contraceptives.

Many women of the 1920s did not marry, perhaps because the men they might have loved were gone. Some chose not to marry but to pursue independent careers. After the Representation of the People Act February 1918 had granted British women over the age of 30 the right to vote, the Sex Disqualification (Removal) Act 1919 officially opened access to universities, the professions and public bodies, though it was frequently ignored. Many men would still assume it was their right to legislate for women, both publicly and privately, yet during the 1920s some progress was made as women attempted to build on their new (limited) rights. Female members of Parliament were elected in ones and twos, the laws of property were further overhauled, and the word 'obey' was dropped from the Church of England Marriage service in 1928 – though many women continued to feel required to make this promise.

Such legislative advances helped change social attitudes as well as responding to the campaigns for equality that had been becoming steadily more powerful since the 1870s. Though the financial depression meant misery for millions, for others the 1920s brought a slightly shorter working week and more opportunity for organised leisure activities. There was also the powerful desire to keep busy, to live in the moment and not to look back. Many new sailing clubs were formed, usually less expensive and socially exclusive than the older established yacht clubs. Women were not always automatically excluded though it was rare that they were encouraged to take any part in club management, other than to help organise social events or as minute-takers.

The Little Ship Club (LSC), founded in 1926, has always prided itself on its welcome to women members, though initially there had been some doubts about extending the membership beyond the 'happy band of sailing brothers'. Fortunately the club was on an outreach mission: 'In a country such as England amateur sailors should be numbered by the hundred thousand. There can be no real or lasting prosperity in the shipbuilding industry while the builders scramble for the patronage of a few wealthy yachtsmen.' The secretary of its Maldon branch observed that he was quite ready to 'accept a lady's seven-and-six, sell her a Journal and a burgee and, regarding the money, say with the Roman Emperor "Does it stink?"'[15] For a while he made his position even clearer by adding '(includes women)' whenever he wrote the word yachtsmen.

One of the founders of the LSC was eager journalist and salesman Maurice Griffiths, very recently appointed editor of *Yachting Monthly* following his success with the cheap sheet *Yacht Sales and Charters* and his first book *Yachting on a Small Income* (1930). One of the first female contributors to the *LSC Journal* was his then wife, writing under the pen name 'Peter Gerard'. She even volunteered as a speaker, which was extremely unusual.

'Peter' had been born Dulcie Hazel Kennard near Bloemfontein, South Africa, in 1900. As an Army daughter her first memories were of the open veld, which later translated into a love of the open sea – or if not the sea per se, then the boats that sail on it. Ponies, a short skirt and a friendly old jersey brought happiness as a child, but a return to Europe and a demand for greater conformity was hard. Her Eton- and

Sandhurst-educated father was a colonel in the 5th Dragoon Guards and commanded the Dublin garrison from 1915 to 1918; her mother, Nancy Poyser, was an Army daughter herself but of a more conformist type. Her older brother was killed in 1918.

Years later, when Peter (her male pseudonym that became her name of choice) looked back at her early life, she felt she had been born uncomfortably out of her time. She described her younger self as an introvert, more interested in things and theories than people, and failing to fit in with her mother's hopes for social life and a suitable marriage. 'You can't help the way you're made. Don't think there's something wrong with you – one often does in early adult life,'[16] she wrote then, perhaps recalling old pain. Rather like Elizabeth Young (Linklater) she believed that her life would have been easier if she'd been born at a time when she could have trained for a career. Elizabeth had been born in 1868 so was looking with envy at the 1890s New Women. Dulcie reached young adulthood in the 1920s. Perhaps it's not such an uncommon experience to feel somehow out of step with one's time – or with one's gender? Dulcie saw that the emancipation of women was getting into its stride but felt that her upbringing had left her less able to benefit from the new opportunities. Or was it her personality? She had little formal education and was no good at doing anything in which she was not interested. Boats and sailing came to fascinate her and she educated herself as a journalist by subscribing to a yachting magazine and getting involved in its correspondence column under her male pseudonym, which became her preferred name, even when she achieved a sub-editor's job on a yachting weekly. 'I wish you were more of a man,' sighed the editor.[17]

Peter had her first experience of sailing on holiday in the Isle of Wight. Soon, hiring a dinghy for a daysail wasn't enough and she wanted the experience of going away on a small yacht, managing for herself, realising that she wasn't going to be constantly checking in to reassure her mother that she was all right. She was demanding her independence: 'The shore would have no claim on me. My associates would be my own selection whatever their social status.'[18] She needed to escape her mother's 'fastidious' upbringing. The wearing of shorts became a crucial means of asserting herself in this new life. She did her best to persuade other female sailors to wear them too. When the husband of a friend came to collect his wife 'Mike' from a weekend sailing with Peter and found her wearing shorts, he refused to let her step ashore until she had dressed herself 'properly'.

Trousers regularly caused outrage when women cruised abroad. When Peter went ashore in Holland from a summer cruise in 1931 wearing 'beautifully creased flannels, a reefer jacket and a cheese cutter pressed over at the jaunty angle' (as described by Maurice Griffiths in *The Magic of the Swatchways*, 1932) she was pursued by 'shrieking hordes'. LSC member Muriel Wiles recounted a similar, unnerving, experience when she took her yacht *Coquette* to Holland. She'd gone ashore to change some money in Boskoop (between Gouda and Amsterdam) when she found herself being pursued by a large crowd of children. Seeing the crowd, the bank manager refused to let her inside, and the children began pulling at her legs and the big bell bottoms of her trousers. She was becoming quite frightened when a policeman appeared and brandished his truncheon to protect her. A kindly gentleman changed her money for her and accompanied her as she fled back to her boat, still followed by a great crowd.

'Whatever is the matter?' asked some of the crew.

'Well, they never before have seen a lady in trousers,' Muriel's rescuer explained.[19]

Trousers or bloomers under tunics had become almost commonplace for British women industrial workers in the First World War, women footballers played in bloomers and boots, female cyclists had divided opinion with their divided skirts, riding habits were also made with divided skirts (or a *devantière* – a split up the back), and jodhpurs (developed in India) were becoming fashionable. But what was acceptable in certain areas continued to cause outrage elsewhere. Cecily Gould and Winifred Brown were among other women sailors who evoked hostile reactions when they went ashore on the Continent. It's an interesting insight into later assumptions that the costume designer responsible for the 1973 *Swallows and Amazons* film forced Sophie Neville (playing Titty Walker) into thin cotton dresses and navy blue gym knickers. Sophie remembers:

> *The crew took great delight in the sight of my navy-blue passion killers. Claude had me tuck my dress up into them. Apparently the Altounyan girls had done this as they usually wore dresses in the 1930s rather than shorts. I was never allowed to untuck mine for fear of spoiling continuity. It made me feel I was wearing much less and haunts me still.*[20]

The Altounyan children were the 1928 inspirations for the Walker children in *Swallows and Amazons*. Contemporary photographs show them wearing utilitarian shorts and shirts, certainly not skimpy cotton dresses.[21] Ransome's drawings of Titty give her and her sister Susan unremarkable knee-length skirts while more emancipated Amazons wear shorts. There's more than a whiff of the waif-like super model Twiggy in the film presentation of Titty. Today Sophie is left feeling slightly uncomfortable about the exposure 'of my long white skinny legs'.

Peter Gerard had met Maurice Griffiths (who she usually refers to as 'Bungo') in 1925. His lucky break with *Yacht Sales and Charters* enabled them to purchase the deep-keeled 31ft *Puffin II* in which they sailed together to Maurice's native East Coast, within easy reach of London by train. Once Maurice really got to work making the sales sheet a success Peter had many adventures sailing *Puffin II* alone. This was a 'joyous period' despite frequent groundings and the general discomfort of *Puffin II*'s cramped accommodation. Eventually Peter's family were persuaded to accept her marriage to Maurice, *Puffin II* was sold, and the more substantial *Afrin* was purchased as their first home. Peter had to give up work and support Maurice in his daily commute to London from the Walton Backwaters in Essex. She lived in trousers, sweaters and sandshoes, scarcely went up to town, enjoyed a semi-feral lifestyle and worked hard. 'My own existence as wife, cook, caterer, freelance journalist, boatswain, valet and shipwright could hardly be called idle.'[22] They had no children.

In the stormy summer of 1927 Peter and Maurice joined Conor and Kate O'Brien on board *Saoirse* for the third Fastnet Race. It had been organised by the newly formed Ocean Racing Club or ORC (later the Royal Ocean Racing Club or RORC) – an organisation that didn't appear to have given much thought to female participation. There were no women entrants in the first year and no women members of the club. In 1926 Mrs Aitken Dick entered her 14-ton cutter *Altair* but didn't become a member of the club. She almost lost one of her crew in heavy weather and retired. By the following year she had sold *Altair* but joined Mr and Mrs Hunt on their cutter, *Spica*. There were still no female members of the ORC. When Peter and Kate arrived with the crew of *Saoirse* for the pre-race dinner at the Island YC, 'the officers were quite unable gracefully to swallow their surprise at the presence among the crews of two women; and through a very transparent veil of courtesy pleaded, after a feverish consultation in the passage beyond, that there was no room for us.'[23]

The other two women in the race, evidently wiser in the ways of Cowes clubs, had not attempted to attend. Kate O'Brien took it calmly; Peter was furious:

> *Such treatment was difficult to forget in the postwar era of revised values and contributed largely to a certain bitterness and contempt I felt thereafter for the average yacht club as an institution. Especially as on a later similar occasion on the East Coast at the start of a Whitsun rally [...] I found myself, although in command of my own vessel, herded into the club annex with a 'yachtsmen's harem', there to be regaled with nothing more exciting than plates of sandwiches and soft drinks.*[24]

Too many clubs had separate spaces of this sort. The Royal Yacht Squadron kept women in a sort of shed in the garden; the Royal Norfolk and Suffolk insisted that they use a separate entrance; Maurice described the ladies' room at the Walton and Frinton YC as 'a poultry run where a terrier has been let loose' – as opposed to 'the congenial club house with its crowded rooms and laughter and smoke-filled bar'.[25] He noted 'the kind of laughter men make when they wish to goodness the ladies would go home and leave them to yarn among themselves.'[26] Even the Little Ship Club thought it acceptable to run events where 'ladies will not be invited'.

Peter Gerard described her first four years of partnership (her word) with Maurice Griffiths as 'ideally happy' – perhaps especially those first tough seven months living on *Afrin* while he commuted. Both his and her writing during this period reveals mutual affection, respect and a sincere aspiration to equal partnership. He calls her 'The Shipmate' and frequently expresses his admiration for her toughness, strength and courage. It was a sincere and touching attempt at marital and maritime equality, but it didn't succeed.

Peter was not unaware of the differences between them: 'Bungo' had a much more sociable nature than she did. He also loved the swatchways and creeks of the East Coast whereas she yearned for the space and depth of the open sea – however sick it made her. He also became impatient with each successive yacht he owned, needing to move on and try new challenges of hull shape, sail plan or cabin layout. Peter felt differently. She invested emotion in each boat, endowing them with human characteristics. From her first years of chartering and borrowing boats she had expressed strong views about the quality of the living space. 'I see no reason why following the adventurous path in small ships should be synonymous with living like a pig. There's quite enough he-man stuff to put up with on deck without having it down below as well.'[27] When Maurice was so often in London, she grew restless living up a creek. She wanted a yacht she could sail by herself, in which she could try new ideas 'without going into conference'. *Afrin* was not that vessel.

In 1928 *Afrin* was sold and Peter bought *Juanita*. She expressed amazement at the criticism this provoked:

> *No one is surprised if a modern wife flies her own light aeroplane, rides her own horse, or has a separate car; yet because a boat with a lid on it at once acquires some of the characteristics of a shore residence they regard it with the same concern that might be shown on learning that a happily married pair lived in separate flats.*[28]

For Peter, *Juanita* would be a lifelong love. She was also a practical means of earning money once Peter began taking other women out as cadets, teaching them to sail.

Maurice also bought a seagoing yacht, *Wilful*, and both did their best to defer to the other when they were on the other person's boat – reversing the titles of skipper and mate. Peter was as confident a sailor as her husband, though she got colder and sicker. There are moments in Maurice's writing when one can sense that he likes the moments when she leans against his knees for warmth, or he can carry her over the mud at Horsey Island.[29] He calls her 'my poor little skipper' when she is incapacitated by seasickness and struggles to pay tributes to *Juanita*'s fine qualities. But even to me as a child, reading *The Magic of the Swatchways* and *Ten Small Yachts* (1949) in the 1960s, his underlying discomfort is obvious, as is his disappointment at her apparent rejection of his favourite cruising ground. He had an affair. Then, as Peter tried to sort out her own 'mangled emotions', she fell in love with the artist Charles Pears.

'FED UP WITH THIS SKIRT NONSENSE!'

In Peter's account the dissolution of her marriage with Maurice was 'orderly and honourable [...] and presided over by our collective respect for each other.' In 1933 she remarried. Charles, her second husband, was considerably older than she was and had been married before. He was quite happy to cruise in company on separate yachts, his *Wanderer* or her *Juanita*. He was a highly respected marine artist; she continued to offer training courses to her cadets. In yachtie tittle-tattle there was often an underlying implication that 'trouser-wearing characters' who liked to sail with other women were probably lesbian. Peter kept her pseudonym but also began calling herself 'Mrs Charles Pears', even when writing an article for the *LSC Journal*. She goes out of her way to make clear that she and Charlie enjoyed an active and satisfying sex life, even if they did sail separate yachts. 'You never ought to have been a woman, chappie,' she quotes him as saying, 'but I'm darn glad that you are.'[30]

Mabel Stock checking the log on Ogre

9

'Clothes not fit for a girl to wear'[1]
Sailing on the last of the grain ships

Herzogin Cecilie (built 1902); Jeanne Day (b. 1904); Betty Jacobsen (b. 1913); Pamela Bourne (b. c.1908)

'THERE WAS A TIME, not so long ago, when true adventure still existed – but you need to be a man like Alan Villiers to take advantage of it'[2] writes Sir Robin Knox-Johnston in his foreword to Kate Lance's biography *Alan Villiers: Voyager of the Winds* (2009). If it was hard for men to 'voyage the winds' in the 1920s and 1930s, it was harder still for women. In 1928 Villiers was sailing on the four-masted steel barque *Herzogin Cecilie* when 23-year-old stowaway Jeanne Day was discovered on board.

Herzogin Cecilie had been built in Bremerhaven in 1902 as a cadet training ship for the Norddeutscher line. Her accommodation was good, her saloon luxurious. Her nickname was the 'Duchess'. She'd been caught in Chile in the early years of the war, interned and then transferred to French ownership as a part of German reparations. Already the great cargo-carrying sailing vessels were being superseded by steamships. The French sold her on to Gustaf Erikson of Mariehamn in the Åland Islands. 'Gusta' had become expert at buying clipper ships at scrappage prices, running them at lowest possible cost, carrying timber to Australia, then wheat to Europe, and boosting his profit by filling the crews with premium-paying apprentices. He would carry passengers as well, if they could afford the fare. Many young men and occasionally young women did choose to pay Erikson's fees, as they recognised that this was a way of life that was dying. However, if you didn't have money and you weren't male, you couldn't go. Or could you?

Jeanne was a music teacher from Adelaide. She'd attended a dance on the ship in the previous year and had been laughed at when she asked to be taken on the voyage. This year she'd attempted to board dressed as a boy but had been recognised and escorted ashore. After that she'd bribed a fisherman to row her out to the ship, then had hidden in the hold with the grain. 'Don't you think it was wrong, very wrong for a young girl to come alone to such a ship with only the clothes she stood up in and those not fit for a girl to wear?' the first mate asked her. Alan Villiers was sailing with *Herzogin Cecilie*, writing *Falmouth for Orders* (1952), and Kate Lance is able to quote the shorthand transcripts he took of these initial interviews. Eventually Jeanne bursts out, 'What could a girl like me do? I said I wanted to go to sea. I did not want to go in a steamer, I wanted to go in a ship like this.'[3]

Lance compares the transcripts with Villiers' diary entries and his highly coloured, journalistic accounts of Jeanne on the voyage round Cape Horn to Cardiff. She highlights Villiers' misogynistic comments about Jeanne's appearance and personality as well as his opportunism in making the most of this scoop to gain publicity for his book. She recognises the resigned kindliness of *Herzogin Cecilie*'s then captain Ruben de Cloux (who had a teenage daughter himself) and the entrenched, illogical attitudes of the crew. When Jeanne was given material to make herself a dress, everyone relaxed. 'We forget how dislocating the sight of women in men's clothing once was,' writes Lance. Jeanne was put to work cleaning the ship's accommodation, though she also went up into the rigging and assisted with other tasks on deck. When *Herzogin Cecilie* arrived in Cardiff, Jeanne was examined by two women doctors, who confirmed she was still a virgin. She had achieved her sea voyage and chose to not to return to Australia.

* * *

The publicity surrounding Jeanne Day's 1928 voyage benefitted Gustaf Erikson as well as Alan Villiers. Even more potential passengers applied to sail on his ships and there were applications from women crew members too, though Kate Lance can only find three who were fully signed on as crew members on Erikson's four-masted square-riggers, as opposed to female passengers doing some 'sailorising'. Villiers, meanwhile, went into business with Ruben de Cloux, who had broken with Erikson, and formed a syndicate to buy the barque *Parma*. On their first voyage together, Villiers took his wife Daphne with him and gleaned sufficient material for *Grain Race* (1933). The 'last of the sailing ships' strapline was good for selling books as well as attracting passengers. As a woman on board, Daphne was expected to be 'quiet and retiring' and 'very reserved while still possessing a happy disposition'. She had to eat salt horse and pea soup with relish, sleep on a hard shelf and go without all the trappings of 'civilisation', such as cinemas and hairdressers.[4] There were no jobs for her to do and, it seems, a barrage of misogynistic comments to which she needed to turn a deaf ear. She kept herself busy 'sewing and mending and washing and reading' and appears to have enjoyed the experience, not expecting that it would mark the end of their marriage.

While Alan was in New York having *Grain Race* typed up for publication, he fell in love with Betty Jacobsen, the stenographer, and she may have fallen in love with the idea of going to sea:

> *I loved to read the story of those gallant old ships fighting their way against wind and weather on the longest, stormiest voyage it was possible to make. Every word I typed created a vivid picture in my mind and I felt almost as if I was there myself. How I would love to go!*[5]

The subsequent book, *A Girl Before the Mast*, which was published under Betty's name in 1934, shows that – if this was indeed her wish – she achieved it. She too sailed on *Parma* with Captain Ruben de Cloux, his daughter Ruby and the ship's part-owner Alan Villiers. But Kate Lance reveals that this was not a straightforward account of a young girl's wish-fulfilment. It was a commercial plan arranged between George Putnam and Alan Villiers under which Betty would indeed go to sea and would be filmed for a documentary, *Apprentice Girl*. She would appear as a Norwegian actress, under the name Sonia Lind, would be paid $25 a week and Villiers would ghost-write her book. Until I read Kate Lance's biography I had accepted *A Girl Before the Mast* as a first-hand account. Although it's psychologically interesting to observe the generally misogynistic Villiers needing to present life at sea through the eyes of a young woman with whom he had fallen in love, it would have been so much more valuable if the reader could ever be confident that they were hearing Betty's own voice. 'I wondered if they really thought women at sea were bad luck, and if they did, I wondered how they got that way. This was 1933, and I thought that all such superstitious notions were gone.'[6]

* * *

In 1934 South African-born journalist Pamela Bourne, paid to travel as a working passenger on *Herzogin Cecilie*, now captained by Ålander, Sven Eriksson. It was a life-changing experience. Looking back, in her memoir *The Life and Death of the Duchess* (1959), she wrote:

> *To watch the world lighten and the sun heave up slowly above the horizon of the cold sea, to keep lookout on the fo'c'sle head with dolphins scudding under her heel, their white bellies turned in frolic to the dawn light, to stand in the icy draught underneath the billowing crojick, safe in that narrow black shadow from the flooding moonlight. These are the things worth living for.*[7]

Pamela was 25 when she first sailed on *Herzogin Cecilie*. She knew that standing in 'the icy draught underneath the billowing crojick' was 'a queer substitute for a man, a home and babies' but she didn't care. Her English family were landed gentry; her father, Sir Henry Roland Murray Bourne, had been the defence minister for South Africa, until her parents divorced in 1922. Her father married an actress, was divorced again and committed suicide on the eve of his third wedding. (The cause was given as depression following flu.) She'd been presented at court, educated at Oxford, worked as a gossip columnist and for two years she had been a freelance journalist specialising in maritime subjects. It was the seafaring life that she loved, not the opportunities for articles, though she needed the money. She would come to believe that words were inadequate to express the experience of being at sea. Only music might come close.

Pamela had already sailed in outriggers, banana boats, a bug-infested copra boat, a clean Norwegian motor vessel and a freighter called the *Thermopylae*. Here she learned to chip rust and mix paint and explore the low-life areas of Sydney under the supervision of the bosun, Anders, 'who treated me as an equal – as no Englishman whatever his class and education ever treated a female.'[8] She also began to develop a seagoing alter ego as 'Nils', a male crew member in a female body. She didn't pretend to be a man, but dressed and worked as one and hoped to be treated the same way. She joined the *Herzogin Cecilie* in Wallaroo, Southern Australia, for her 120-day grain-carrying voyage to Belfast

– paying 10s a day for her passage. When she got back to England she would have run out of money and must produce a book to recoup her investment: 'This beautiful, magic world must somehow be got on paper – but I felt it was a sacrilege.'⁹

She describes Sven Eriksson meeting her with icy politeness, obviously struggling to conceal his distaste for passengers in general and female passengers in particular. Pamela had just had a wisdom tooth extracted and was feeling miserable:

> *'Nils, Nils,' she said to herself, 'You are tramping down this jetty, horribly handicapped by your sex, your short-sightedness, and the tenets of your education. But your infinite curiosity about the sea and seafarers is unappeased. Surely now, if you voyage in this ship, which is the culmination of man's mastery of wind, water, and himself, you will get to know the men and the ship and their way of thinking, and you will be content. It would all be so simple if you were a man. You would be a sailor yourself and that would be the end of it.*¹⁰

She did all she could to be one of the crew. The basic skills she had learned as 'Nils' were soon utilised and more were added, such as working with the sailmaker.

> *Heaving up stinking water out of the forepeak. Long splicing in the forehold. With the sailmaker under the poop. My knife soon blunt with ripping the twine stitches and my shirt wet with sweat. The work in the half light is exhausting. And the canvas, even when old, cruel on the fingers. At the windlass, all day, chipping. It is a work of art that seems to fill my whole life.*¹¹

I remember rust-chipping three days a week one summer when I was working in a barge yard. It's a tangible, gritty memory of sore eyes, stained fingers, aching muscles and unending, unrewarding toil. But I could ride my 49cc moped home and have a bath. Pamela stayed grubby. Her longing for 'a magic potion' that would turn her into 'a man and a sailor' was so intense that she was actually pleased when the second mate cuffed and kicked her along with the rest of the boys fumbling with the halyards in the dark of a stormy night. She felt it was an initiation: 'But I could never get out of him afterwards whether he knew it was me or not. His eyes sparkled, he smiled enigmatically and he blushed.'¹²

Sven, the captain, ruled his crew by a combination of outstanding seamanship, instinctive feeling for sea state and wind changes, passionate love of his ship, attention to detail – and violence. When an apprentice was insolent and slow to answer an order, he laid into him; when Felix the steward stole Pamela's private whisky supply, he was fiercely beaten and locked into his cabin. When Pamela had first arrived, Felix's wife, Elna, was in her bunk recovering from the drunken beating her husband had given her. No one took her part and she seems to have had no active role within the ship's company. Pamela remembers Elna spending much of her time with the hens, 'the only other female company on board'.

Except for the Duchess herself. Pamela holds nothing back as she tries to express the feminine identity and personality of the *Herzogin Cecilie*. Rationally she knows that 'she was just a merchant vessel plying her trade [...] an artefact the result of co-operation between man's brain and man's hands' but she is equally certain that there are intangible components 'that made her herself, like no other ship'. They may have been built into her during construction; they may developed as she became a repository of the emotions and experience of the people who had sailed in her over 30 years; 'Strong and bold and beautiful she seemed to know that her song was the swansong of her race.'[13]

Pamela learned to hear the different music from every different area of rigging and hull. She persuaded the first mate to hang a plank platform beneath the ship's bow and stood there for hours chiselling off the layers of thoughtlessly applied paint that obscured the beauty of the wooden figurehead. She felt angry with the men who had slapped these coats of paint over the carving as if it was any other utilitarian piece of wood. She talked to the figurehead, joked with her – woman to woman – as she laid bare the delicacy of the workmanship. Then she repainted it as carefully as if she was preparing a society beauty for a ball. This is an episode of ultra femininity, ridiculously exaggerated and yet emotionally sincere.

She felt sick with misgiving when she finally invited Sven to see the newly costumed and maquillaged effigy. He approved. So did the first mate who 'stayed to flirt with her for half an hour'. When Pamela was invited into the captain's saloon for a celebratory drink, she expected praise. Then he turned on her. 'But look at yourself! Nils, what seems to give you real joy is to be as feelthy dirty as a *skogs Finn*. Your legs, your arms, your ter-r-ible short hair, all covered with muck and paint.'

Pamela did not take this well: '"It's dry and it's not coming off on your blasted sofa," I said. "And what the hell do you want me to be anyway? Greta Garbo, specially materialised for your entertainment when you feel like company?"'[14]

Her femininity was a sensitive subject. She described herself stamping around the cabin for a while longer, shouting at him before she stormed out. The first mate tried to calm things by handing her a scraper and setting her to work again, but when she glanced down through the open skylight of the captain's saloon and saw Sven sitting reading a book upside down, her temper flared. She picked up a bucket of dirty water and threw it over him. Then she fled 'like a hunted rabbit'. When Sven caught her, he didn't beat her like a crew member; instead, he spanked her. She yelled. Apparently it was romance from then on.

Many years later, when Sven had died and the 'Duchess' was long gone, Pamela structured her memoir to follow this incident with her new, sympathetic understanding of Sven's cruelly hard early life and all that possession of the beautiful saloon on *Herzogin Cecilie* represented for him. (The saloon is now in the Åland Islands museum). They married and the next section of her memoir would open with their sailing from the Baltic to Port Lincoln in Australia in 1935, with herself as *kaptenska*, 'the captain's wife'. Or the captain's 'second best wife', as she described herself, acknowledging that the Duchess would always come first in Sven's affection, at least when they were at sea.

As *kaptenska*, Pamela still went 'for a walk' in the rigging when she felt like it, but dressed with more decorum and gave up the deck work that the 'feelthy' Nils had used to undertake. Instead, she typed lists, helped with the cooking and home-making, supported Sven and felt grateful to Gusta for 'allowing' her to live on board for the whole world trip. She applied herself to being the right sort of wife, one who accepted a glass of Madeira as her due and listened with intelligent attention to visiting captains' and officers' tales of their seafaring lives, no matter how many times she'd heard them before. She didn't sit glowering at the base of the ladder, refusing to get out of the motorboat and poisoning the atmosphere for everyone because her husband didn't take her straight to the Copenhagen shops.

It had been a culture shock for both sides when Pamela met Sven's matriarchal, Swedish-speaking family as his fiancée. The family found it hard to understand why she wanted to continue sailing rather than remain at home, managing a farm, cooking and weaving. She spoke only a few rough words of deckhand Swedish, so couldn't explain.

As it turned out, the voyage to Australia (Copenhagen to Port Lincoln in 83 days) then racing back to England with 4,295 tons of wheat

(Port Lincoln to Falmouth in 86 days) was Pamela's only trip as captain's wife. The *Herzogin Cecilie* was sent on from Falmouth to Ipswich, still fully loaded, and struck the Ham Stone rock off the South Devon coast on 25 April 1936 in thick fog. Pamela and Sven lived on board the dying ship for an agonising five months, hoping for effective assistance. This was mostly denied on grounds of cost by the ship's owner, or by Salcombe local authority on the grounds of possible contamination. 'If one knew and loved the Duchess, it was hard not to talk about her as a living being, hard not to think of her as a creature whose life blood was draining away on their rocky shelf.'[15] Crowds came to gawp at their disaster; hopes rose and were dashed; the final attempt at salvage – towing her into Starehole Bay – proved the final catastrophe.

Pamela was six months pregnant when they were finally forced to abandon the Duchess and return home to Lemland. Their first child was born just after Christmas, too quickly for any midwife to arrive. '"Hang on," said Sven, who had done the master mariners' childbirth course, "But heave away. Remember it's something like pulling braces."' Pamela heaved successfully and named their first child Sven-Cecilie, 'Because he's a boy with three parents.'[16]

Pamela Bourne Eriksson restoring The Duchess

10

'Elastic-waisted blue serge skirts'[1]
Pleasure sailors between the wars

Margaret Llewellyn (b. 1900s?); Elizabeth Fairholme and Pamela Powell (b. 1910s?); Phyllis Richardson (b. 1892); Winifred Brown (b. 1899); Muriel Wiles (b. 1908)

As the great sailing ships vanished from the seas, lakes and rivers filled with dayboats and dinghies. Smaller, relatively inexpensive, low-maintenance vessels offering outdoor exercise in short, accessible bursts suited the work and leisure patterns of a wider range of people. The newly developing, less elitist sailing clubs offered social life as well. Sisters Margaret and Betty Llewellyn were among the first female members of the Little Ship Club in 1927. They were ready to help, taking notes at lectures and contributing to the *Journal*.

Margaret, like many working-aged people of the generation, had only weekends available for sailing. In a *Journal* article she described a burning-hot June Saturday and her dissatisfaction with 'streets and houses and humanity'.[2] She invited a non-sailing friend to go adventuring with her on the Lower Thames. Margaret's boat was a 17ft half-decked Mersey canoe; difficult to sail well and with few comforts – 'no cockpit cover or bedding and very little food'. Even the 'two-hour drift' from Gravesend to Hole Haven on Canvey Island was full of incident, near disasters and narrow escapes. There was almost no wind, the tide turned against them, and it seemed as if they'd never reach the famous Lobster Smack Inn. When they finally arrived in Hole Haven creek, the anchor dragged, and they almost broke their mainmast on the 14ft bowsprit of a bawley. A gentlemanly stranger helped free them. He 'offered no advice, asked no questions but spoke to me as if I was most sane and sensible, which is a refreshing change,' wrote Margaret.

The other men they encountered were not as obliging. Two 'splendidly dressed' young men on a steam-yacht refused them a tow, were rude about Margaret's boat and did their best to lure her and her friend on board and into their cabin, with obvious unwelcome intentions. The two young women also spent six hours of adverse tide hanging on to the side of a barge in the rain when their anchor had dragged again off Gravesend. The bargee made it clear that he considered them lunatics; his wife and children came on deck at intervals to stare at them without speaking. He hit his children at the slightest provocation. The girls' cigarettes turned to pulp in the rain and their tea tasted of paraffin – 'nothing about that day was a success'. Then, when they arrived back at Gravesend, a stranger had taken their mooring, and they could find no other. Margaret finally sailed her boat on to the mud and left it there, needing to get home for work the next day. She apologised to fellow LSC members for her adventure being 'frightfully tame' compared with the exploits of luckier people in the North Sea and the Channel but headed her article with a quotation from Robert Louis Stevenson: 'For who can say that business is more entertaining than fooling about in boats? He has never seen a boat or been inside an office.'

A decade later, 'Liz and Poo' – Elizabeth Fairholme and Pamela Powell – wrote *A Dinghy on the London River* (1937) describing their first experiences owning and sailing a 14ft dinghy from Chiswick. They were both young and at work, responsible for their own finances though living at home in affluent families. This meant they could afford three-way shares in the £22 dinghy and to kit themselves out appropriately: 'Both Liz and Poo, when they graced the yachts of their rich friends, sported trousers, elegantly cut; but these they did not feel suitable for wear on the London River whose banks abound always with ribald youths and whose waters must be approached by sober bus or underground.'[3] Instead, they bought elastic-waisted blue serge skirts, which reached 'barely to the knee' for 1s 11d, boys' cotton shirts for 2s 11d and boys' white canvas gym shoes for half a crown (2s 6d).

They didn't want to race or join a club, merely to potter and explore. Their friend, George, found them a dinghy in Lymington, contributed the extra money they couldn't quite afford, transported it to London and taught them to sail it. Their book is charming and funny – perhaps slightly overplaying their daffiness but explaining clearly all that they learned about endurance, adventure, fun, initiative and self-reliance. 'When a jibe threatened, or water poured in over the gunwale there was no time to turn to anyone else and say, "What should I do now?" Whatever had to be done had to be done instinctively or all was lost.'[4]

They slept on bare boards, cooked on a Primus stove, spent hours stranded on sandbanks or mud and made humiliating mistakes. They learned about friendship as well as respect for the tide – Poo was habitually unpunctual and many others will know how severely missing a tide while waiting for a friend can test the relationship. Their overall approach to Thames sailing can hardly be bettered: 'Look upon every man as your friend and every bridge as your enemy.'[5] They were amazed by 'the essential kindliness of the riverman ... and the generosity and courtesy of the bargees.' The only bad language they heard came from the 'gentleman coxes' of the rowing teams. They learned to cope with ribald remarks and waved cheerfully at all the other vessels on the river.

* * *

Phyllis Richardson was a high-profile and impressive dinghy sailor who didn't have to work for her living. She was a third generation member of the Lough Erne YC in County Fermanagh and lived at the Big House, Rossfad, near Enniskillen. She had lost both her parents in the First World War. Her father, Henry Gartside-Tipping, a retired naval officer, had returned to sea service in his mid-sixties and had been given command of an armed yacht, HMS *Sanda*, which was shelled and sunk off the coast of Belgium in September 1915. Her mother, Mary, then volunteered for the Women's Emergency Corps and went to France to help run canteens for soldiers. She was shot and killed by a mentally ill French soldier who then tried to kill himself but failed. Mary was buried with full military honours and the Croix de Guerre laid on her coffin. Phyllis married her first cousin Colonel Henry Richardson who was also a keen and locally successful sailor. This brought her back to her family's roots. She was probably too grand to take a job; competitive sailing gave an outlet for her energy and determined personality.

During the late 1920s and 1930s Phyllis became a notable figure in the International 14 class. This was a highly competitive class, dominated by sailors such as Stewart Morris, Peter Scott and Uffa Fox, where the best (and most expensive) designers could pit their skills and innovative ideas against each other. The climax of each season was the Prince of Wales Cup, sailed at different venues about the UK. Among her stable of racing dinghies, Phyllis had a 14ft dinghy, *Filibuster*, designed for her by Uffa Fox. Every year she had it crated up, recruited her husband as her crew, and arrived to compete against young men half her age. They nicknamed her 'Aunt Phyllis'. Peter Scott remembered how imperious she could be. In 1936 the Prince of Wales Cup had been sailed on the Clyde. Phyllis had come fourth in an exceptionally strenuous race and was in a hurry to catch the night train back to London.

Leaving her husband to pack up the dinghy, she was driven to Glasgow by Michael (Bratby). They arrived at the barrier just as the guard was waving his green flag. The wheels had already begun to move when Aunt Phyllis, drawing herself up to her full six feet, shouted in an imperious voice 'Stop the train – I'm Mrs Henry Richardson.' The name could have meant nothing to the guard, but the tone of voice was not to be denied; he blew a shrill blast on his whistle and waved his red flag. The signal was repeated further up the platform and the train stopped.[6]

Phyllis raced in North America as well as in Britain. Michael Clarke, historian of Lough Erne racing, states that at the time of writing (his book was published in 2005) the record she set on her home waters 'has not yet been matched by any other LEYC sailor'. He too has an anecdote: 'Irwin Catherwood was her crew in 1947. They capsized. He, the 19-year-old, floundered, while his tall, tough, grey-haired helmswoman, a granny in her sixties, quickly righted the boat, baled it out with a bucket, and they were back in the race.'[7]

* * *

Winifred Brown appears to have gone her own way since childhood – or at least from the age of 14 when she was expelled from school. She had been President of the Swearers' and Smokers' Club, which met in a disused potting shed in the schoolground. While some of the girls could hardly puff at a cigarette without feeling sick, Winifred could blow smoke rings. Her parents were an inharmonious couple who appear to have lived apart for more time than they lived together. She was their only child and may have benefitted materially from parental indulgence on both sides. Her mother Elsie turned a blind eye to wild behaviour and love affairs but her father was able to seek her affection with lavish gifts (including a supply of cigarettes when she confessed that she had been stealing his). He was both a motoring and sailing enthusiast, and a member of the Manchester Cruising Association (founded 1913). Winifred would later become its first lady member.

In her racy accounts of her own life – and in the biography by Geoff Meggitt – Winifred presents herself as plump and promiscuous: a Bessie Bunter before the character was even invented. In fact she was a truly impressive all-round sportswoman and courageous adventurer. She represented Lancashire in tennis, golf and hockey, gained her private pilot's licence from the Lancashire Aero Club in April 1927, then in May she joined the England Ladies Hockey team to tour Australia as goalkeeper. England won all their matches by wide margins, and when they returned, Winifred's father offered to buy her a plane.

In this plane in 1930, supported by her faithful boyfriend, Ron Adams, Winifred caused a sensation by winning the prestigious King's Cup, flying 750 miles at an average speed of 102mph and beating 88 fellow starters, including four other women. There's a delightful clip on British Pathé where the Mayor of Salford welcomes her back to Lancashire and tells her that 'the whole of England delights to know that a Lady has carried off this very valuable trophy.' Winifred, tall, smiling and slightly shy, responds that it's 'awfully good of him and she's awfully glad to be back in Lancashire'.[8] This was gracious of her as Lancashire Aero Club had just banned women from its bar, and Hanworth Club, where the race began, had refused to allow her accommodation the night before.

Winfred took up ice hockey in 1931 and went to Chamonix with the Manchester Merlins. Then in 1933 she and Ron spent two months exploring the Amazon, partly by canoe. Gradually, however, sailing became her overriding interest. She had bought a yacht in 1935, was elected to the Royal Mersey YC in 1936 and was exploring the Irish Sea, Wales, Scotland and Ireland by the end of that year. In 1937 she and Ron set out for Norway.

In the bar parlour of the Gazelle, skippers sadly shook their heads. One night I arrived to hear a large gentleman exclaim: 'Women are no bloody good! Thinks because she can fly an aeroplane she can handle a boat – says to 'er myself, t'ain't the same up there as it is down 'ere ... Oh! Good evening, Miss Brown. Thanks, don't mind if I do – mine's a mild.'

At least I knew where I stood. They were good lads at heart, though, always ready to give me a helping hand.[9]

Winifred wrote her first book in 1939. She's an amusing writer who doesn't mind sending herself up. She had scant patience with any mystique about sailing and took little notice of potential hostility towards herself as a lady owner (aka 'bloody woman') who wasn't intending to hand over command to a paid crew. She already had a working knowledge of navigation and weather systems and possessed outstanding resilience and readiness to learn. In her first full season she and Ron sailed *Perula* from the Menai Straits to Bergen, where they spent several weeks exploring the Norwegian fjords, covering 2,500 miles in two months before returning home to Glyn Garth. 'Yes, it certainly had been hard work, but given a sound ship, a faith in weather reports, the odd spot of common sense and a large sense of humour ... It is not as difficult as it seems!'[10] The following year she and Ron sailed via the Shetland islands and the Norwegian coast to North Cape and then via Bear Island to Svalbard. When they returned home, she discovered that the local paper had her obituary ready prepared for publication as soon as the news would arrive that she had perished at sea.

* * *

Winifred and other women sailors of the 1920s and 1930s attracted notice and were felt to be making a difference. Sometimes this was resented, possibly as a backlash to the legal changes that had strengthened women's rights. When a photo was published showing women's attendance at a Little Ship Club seamanship class it sparked an angry letter to the *LSC Journal* from a male member. 'One woman doing a splice is "news". Five hundred men doing 500 (possibly much better) splices is not news. Let this sort of thing be cut out.' The committee (all male) added a note to say they agreed with him.

> *I should like to assure Mr Liddle that the recent outburst of press publicity had not escaped the notice of the committee who are in complete sympathy with his views on the subject and are taking what steps they can to avoid a repetition of it. They will, I am sure, have the support of Members in this. Publicity, valuable as it may be for a growing organisation, can come too dear.*[11]

Perhaps this masculine feeling that women sailors should be kept out of the public eye contributes to the pages of all-male news and photos throughout the yachting press, which may make 20th-century sailing appear even more monocultural than it actually was. National papers, however, were keener for a 'story' so might pick up on a female pioneer with more enthusiasm. But otherwise, women were absent from positions of official responsibility. When one looks hard at a *Little Ship Club Journal* photo of the audience at a lecture, for instance, women are there (often wearing their neat cloche hats) but they are entirely absent from the committee lists – except to take the minutes or help organise a dinner dance. I've just been looking at a 1930s' photograph of Waldringfield SC (founded 1921) in which the boys sit cross-legged at the front, men stand in the middle, and at the back, just peeping over their shoulders, are three smiling female faces. Everyone in the photo looks happy and it's proved an enduringly successful club – but it's not, I think, the way such a photo would be arranged today.

There were winning female sailors on the Suffolk rivers then, and anyone who has read E Arnot Robertson's novel *Ordinary Families* (1933), set in early 1930s Pin Mill on the River Orwell, will sense the extent to which female sailing at a local level was almost normalised. On the morning of the regatta, the heroine, Lallie, discovers she has her period. She has a sick headache and the prospect of standing about all day in the cold wind, between bouts of energetic exertion, fills her with dread. 'But the idea of getting out of it because I was so unwell did not occur to me: nor would it to any girl in our family, or, I suppose, in any of the hundreds of similar families in England.'[12]

Lallie's father is an opportunistic yacht broker. In the last year before the Second World War, *Yachting Monthly*'s editor Maurice Griffiths (who had started his own broking career on the Orwell) commissioned an article titled 'Little Ships for the Woman Owner'. It begins confidently:

> *Before the Great War only a handful of women cared about the great sport of boat sailing and those few were either ornamental passengers of large yachts or were part of a small but enthusiastic and skilful band who put up a good fight for the racing honours amongst the various small one-design and restricted classes that sailed on the Solent and the Clyde.*

The author links the increased interest from women for independent sailing in larger vessels with 'the general emancipation of women that the war years brought about' and also the availability of opportunities to learn offered by clubs such as the Little Ship Club and the initiative of women such as Mrs Charles Pears. 'No brotherless, boy-friendless, shy girl today need fret and yearn helplessly to learn how to sail: there are several ways open to her if she will take the trouble to find out.'[13] The sums of money involved in inter-war yacht ownership were on a different scale than Liz and Poo had spent on their simple dinghy – though possibly not so far removed from the cost of an International 14-footer designed for the Prince of Wales Cup. The article assumes that the woman owner, or pair of friends buying together, may be able to spend up to £300 (about £25,000 today).

Muriel Wiles was an LSC member who achieved yacht ownership at around this level. She was from Wanstead, her father a 'clerk', later a county valuer, and her mother's father a 'gentleman'. Her brother was a dentist and her stated occupation at the time of her marriage in 1946 was 'dental assistant'. Through the 1930s Muriel had owned a 9-ton, 35ft auxiliary cutter named *Coquette* and seemed able to take sufficient time off in the summer to cruise or to race. She was regularly one of the first club members to take part in a new venture, such as the first North Sea Race or the Whitsun rally to Ostend. She based her sailing at Pin Mill, where she was friend of Arthur Ransome and took a lead in organising fun 'meets' for other LSC sailors, with dinner in The Butt & Oyster and plans for a smuggling game, but 'whatever happened, the gentlemen were to be gentlemanly and the ladies ladylike.'[14] She also advertised in the LSC Crew columns:

Lady owner wishes to meet all lady members capable of:

(a) *Taking a watch*
(b) *Steering a compass course*
(c) *Helping to handle sails*[15]

She offered sailing most weekends, and an extended cruise from 14 May to 5 June, and 30 July to 14 August. Her occasional articles or photographs give a cheerful impression of young people, mainly but not entirely female, enjoying themselves sailing together. In 1938 she had cruised to the Zuyderzee and the Friesian islands and had taken part in several long-distance races, including the RORC Maas race. When she put *Coquette* up for sale, she asked £325 for her.

Muriel had opinions about yacht design and could be persuaded to air them. Her new yacht *Keryl* was being built at Pin Mill, alongside Ransome's *Serena King*, and would be 30ft long with no bowsprit; the best size, in her view, to conform to RORC regulations and give the maximum amount of fun. She wanted clear, non-slip decks, space for sail changing and the ability to reef with the wind behind her. She wanted accessibility for sail lockers, a place for wet gear, a coal fire and comfortable bunks. 'Ocean racing in a small ship is the grandest of sports but in the heat of our enthusiasm, it is well for us all sometimes to remember that the elements are a great power and that speed is not

'ELASTIC-WAISTED BLUE SERGE SKIRTS'

the only requirement of a small ocean racer.'[16] This new yacht, *Keryl* (14 tons), was larger and more strongly built than *Coquette* and Muriel's revised crew advertisement suggested she was taking her sport more seriously. She asks for young, physically fit, exceptionally enthusiastic volunteers with a good sense of humour (no gender specified) to join her for a shakedown cruise to give experience for future ocean racing. In 1939 she seems to be planning to sail all summer but, like her male companions in the Little Ship Club, she would be sailing under the shadow of approaching war. All their lives were about to change.

'The Skipper', Muriel Wiles (Yachting Monthly)

11

'I only joined for the hat'[1]
Women sailors in the Second World War

Vera Laughton Mathews (b. 1888); Hilda Buckmaster (b. 1897); Christian Oldham (b. 1920); Violetta Thurstan (b. 1879); Nancy Spain (b. 1917); Madeleine Bayard (b. 1911); Rozelle Pierrepont (b. 1925)

SOME 7,000 WOMEN HAD served in the WRNS in the First World War: numbers in the Second World War would peak at over 74,000. It would still be the smallest of the women's uniformed services, although it was the one many more women would have chosen to join. Vera Laughton Mathews, who had built on her First World War experience with an energetic range of national and international activity during 'the long weekend', believed this was because of British women's innate feeling for the sea; other people have suggested that the senior service offered additional social cachet – or perhaps potential recruits just liked the uniform?

After her service in the First World War, Vera had been called back to the Admiralty early in 1939, appointed temporary director with no formal interview, introduced to her deputy director, given a back room and (eventually) a typist, then left to get on with resurrecting the organisation. Meanwhile, a government booklet setting out future options for national service had stated that there would be spaces for about 1,500 women 'to take the place of Naval and Marine ranks and serve in Naval Establishments'.[2] In all, about 15,000 letters arrived for Vera to deal with. A later, poorly co-ordinated press announcement that the King had agreed that the WRNS was to be re-formed brought thousands more – as well as enquiries from the first batch as to why their letters hadn't been answered. One of the messages Vera found immediately touching came from a London girl who wrote, 'If you had longed all your life to be a boy so that you could join the Navy, you would understand my feelings.' Clearly Vera did. The young woman was recruited as a messenger. 'The first day she bought me a cup of tea as if she was delivering a vital signal to the Bridge. I said to her "I expect it is a great thrill to be in the Navy at last?" "Thrill, Ma'am?" she replied, 'It's life's blood."'[3]

In fact, for the first two years of the war, the Wrens were not part of the Navy's administrative organisation (as they had been in the First World War) but were part of its Civil Establishment. Vera objected to this. She believed that it situated women as helpers in traditionally female roles (clerical and domestic) instead of a distinctive service within the Navy. She was now a wife and the mother of three children, comfortable with gender difference but just as determined to achieve equality as she had been in her suffragette days. An equal-but-different uniform would be a beginning. She wanted a uniform that was flattering and smart as well as practical, so she commissioned fashion designer Edward Molyneux to give it a couture look. Perhaps she was remembering her pre-First World War days as assistant editor on *The Ladies Field*. Molyneux designed for royalty and leading international actresses and was known for the refined simplicity of his tailoring. His Wren officers' tricorn hat was considered a particular success.

It was probably a good thing that Vera was left so unsupported by the Admiralty, as it meant that she was free to act as she thought best. She looked at the piles of old paper left from the first conflict, which had been stacked in her new office, felt close to despair, then decided they were no use. She had been a Wren in the First World War; now she needed to rely on her own abilities and the wider outlook she had gained since. Above all she knew she could trust the ability of other women. 'I believed wholeheartedly that there was nothing that could be asked of women that they were not capable of carrying through with success. This was not the general idea in the Admiralty in the early days.'[4] She was determined to ensure that her Wrens had proper jobs to go to in the main ports and that they would be welcomed, accommodated, treated with respect and trained appropriately. As a naval daughter and sister, Vera knew that they would not only need uniform but also correct insignia. She insisted that Wren officers must have the same number of rings on their sleeves as their male counterparts of equivalent rank – even if they were blue instead of gold. Her rings eventually marked her as a rear admiral, though she and all Wren officers only ever got two-thirds of men's equivalent pay.

It was one of Vera's principles that future Wren officers must be appointed from within the ranks. Initially, however, other former First World War Wrens were headhunted and reappointed to senior posts. They too brought valuable inter-war experience with them. Hilda Buckmaster, for instance, was an academic whose initial period of service had been as a motor mechanic. She had then returned to the London School of Economics. She was a founder member of the National Union of Students, a Liberal party activist and in 1925/26 had spent a year on SS *Panope*, one of Gustaf Erikson's grain ships. During the 1930s she had represented Essex at the League of Nations, had unsuccessfully contested Essex Parliamentary seats and had assisted the assimilation of Jewish refugee children. In 1939 she was appointed a first officer and put in charge of training the first batches of Wren writers and coders in HMS *Pembroke I*, a hostel in Campden Hill Road.

When 19-year-old Christian Oldham (Lamb) arrived at HMS *Pembroke I* for training as a coder, she was unimpressed. Chief Officer Buckmaster greeted her heartily: 'How nice to welcome a breath of sea air!' As an admiral's daughter, Christian (who originally titled her memoir *I Only Joined for the Hat*) had spent much of her childhood following the fleet and had been hoping for a job in a naval port, not a London hostel with stricter rules than school. She had already turned down a job at Wren headquarters because she didn't want to work with 'elderly ladies'. Hilda seemed as statuesque as a ship's figurehead and HMS *Pembroke I* dreary and uncongenial. Christian hurriedly transferred back to Wren HQ, where she worked in the next-door office to giggly Diana Sandys (Winston Churchill's eldest daughter) and dealt with applications that she didn't much like by sending them on to 'big Queen Bee' Buckmaster. Wren writers and coders were a key part of the new service and would eventually travel all over the world, as would their sisters in the newly formed Women's Auxiliary Air Force (WAAF).

Violetta Thurstan was another First World War veteran who joined the Wrens as an officer in the early months of the Second World War. She had served as a nurse in the First World War. Before that she had gained an external Modern Languages degree from St Andrews University while working at Bristol Royal Infirmary. Her First World War service had taken her to Belgium (alongside Edith Cavell), then north into Russia, where she worked with refugees. In the last years of the first war, she had served with the RAF. Between the wars Violetta had become a weaver and was employed by the Egyptian government to work with Bedouin women helping them develop and market their skills. It was said that she had been further into the desert than any European woman. In 1937 she'd become involved in the Spanish Civil War and prisoner release – until she had been expelled from the country. Vera described her as 'covered with medals' and 'speaking every known tongue'.[5]

Violetta was 60 when she joined the Wrens in 1939, but no one looked too closely at her age. She was appointed a first officer and became invaluable to the Contraband Control service in Falmouth and also to the Naval Intelligence Department (NID). She accompanied the naval boarding officers on their inspections and used her charm and language skills to pick up information that the captains of the foreign merchant ships might have preferred to keep private. Later, Violetta was posted to the Wren Officer Training Centre at the Royal Naval College, Greenwich and younger women working as boarding officers became a regular phenomenon within the Naval Control Service. This was one of the jobs that took the Second World War Wrens out to sea.

The Control Service was responsible for boarding merchant ships, checking their papers and searching for 'contraband' (goods carried by neutral ships that should not be allowed to reach Germany or her allies). Wrens also assisted with the organisation of the Atlantic and Arctic convoys, working out of major ports such as Liverpool and Belfast. They went out in harbour launches or drifters to deliver the sailing orders; explained any alterations of route or convoy special instructions and checked or amended the ship's confidential books. They needed to be able to answer whatever questions were put to them by the masters of merchant ships. Wren visual signallers accompanied them to communicate with the harbour office by Morse code or semaphore if further information was needed or the orders had been changed. This work was highly skilled and carefully regulated. From 1943 boarding officers were required to pass an examination covering Routeing (chart work and elementary navigation), Convoy (preparation of orders and convoy conferences) and Secretarial (naval control of shipping office requirements, Confidential Books and signal work). If the Wren was a defensively equipped merchant ship (DEMS) officer she would also be boarding to check the ship's guns, ammunition and other armament. These could be serviced ashore by Ordnance Wrens. Wren mechanics, electricians and shipwrights worked alongside their male counterparts to keep the vessels seaworthy. This wasn't only at the convoy ports. Motor torpedo boat (MTB) officer Ian Trelawny, remembering the high level of organisation achieved at HMS *Beehive*, his Coastal Forces base at Felixstowe in Suffolk, wrote: 'Everywhere ashore that there were jobs to be done, there were Wrens there to do them.'[6]

Climbing on and off steep-sided merchant ships in all weathers and sea states required agility, good sense and courage. Initially the masters were not used to being given their instructions by a woman. Even today the arrival of a female pilot on board ship may occasion surprise. Jane Stone, currently taking ships into the Port of Felixstowe, and one of only two female commercially qualified pilots in the UK says, 'One of the most critical moments of the job is that first initial meeting on the bridge with the captain, they all being men ... so far. He has to have that trust in you right from the start, trust that you're going to steer his ship safely into port without any problems, he needs to believe that I know what I'm doing and I'm comfortable handling ships of a certain size. You also have to be fairly confident within yourself, almost to the point of arrogance.'[7]

The first Wrens to serve abroad were led by Second Officer Betty Archdale (b. 1907), daughter of suffragette Helen Archdale, who had succeeded Vera at *Time and Tide*. Betty was Emmeline Pankhurst's goddaughter and a qualified barrister. She was also England's first woman test cricket captain. In January 1941 Betty took 20 Wren wireless telegraphists to serve in Singapore, Britain's crucial Southeast Asia base. More joined later in the year. They worked from the RN wireless station at Kranji, Singapore and were there on 7 December when the Japanese attacked Pearl Harbor. They were part of the welcome for HMS *Prince of Wales* and HMS *Repulse* (led by Louisa de Horsey's son Admiral Tom Phillips) and shared in the mourning when these ships were sunk on 10 December. On 21 December the Wrens were evacuated to Ceylon.

Other groups of Wrens had followed on foreign service. Third Officer Florence MacPherson (b. 1906) had joined the WRNS after her husband Lieutenant Hugh Macpherson RNR had been one of the first casualties of the sea war, torpedoed in October 1939 when on patrol duty 100 miles west of Shetland. Florence, widowed, was one of a group of volunteer cypher officers and wireless telegraphist (W/T) Wrens travelling to Gibraltar in August 1941. The commanding officer there hadn't wanted women but was told there was no one else. The Wrens were on board SS *Aguila*, part of slow-moving and inadequately protected convoy OG 71 that was devasted by the first successful German wolfpack attack.[8] All the Wrens and the naval nurse travelling with them died. A second group of volunteers was hastily collected. They travelled on a destroyer for greater speed and safety and were unofficially allowed to get involved in watch-keeping duties. When they finally arrived in Gibraltar their service was appreciated. When the base was declared a fortress and all women were to be moved out later in the year, the Wrens stayed. 'They are all volunteers and we will probably all be blown up together, but they don't mind,' wrote Admiral Sir Dudley North.

Becoming a Wren did heighten the level of risk for individuals – though everyone experienced increased risk during the Second World War. Port areas and airfields were inherently dangerous because they were heavily bombed but so were many other cities where people lived and worked. The first group of Wrens to die during an air attack were at HMS *Daedalus* at Lee-on-Solent, Hampshire in November 1940 when a stray British anti-aircraft shell exploded in their dining room. Wrens were also on board the troopship SS *Khedive Ishmael* when it was torpedoed in the Indian Ocean in February 1944, causing the biggest single loss of life among British servicewomen (77 women died, the majority of them nurses).

The initial lack of uniform may just have been a sartorial inconvenience to the Wrens working in administrative jobs: to those already working out of doors in the freezing winter of 1939/40 it was a more direct challenge. Nancy Spain, serving as a Wren delivery driver in the North Tyneside docks, was grateful to one of the trawlermen for a fisherman's jersey that hung beneath her knees. She was given a white balaclava helmet said to have been knitted by Princess Mary and was eventually allowed to wear jodhpurs on duty.[9] It would be many months before Wrens were issued with the same warm duffle coats that men wore to work out of doors in winter. Nancy was a Roedean-educated journalist, actress and sportswoman who'd recently discovered her lesbian sexual identity. Now, like so many other people, she was tipped out of her normal social milieu. She learned to know and like the trawlermen and understand some of the disasters that could not be talked about. In one particularly gruesome incident she was sent to collect 'the meat' and discovered this was the half-frozen remains of a dead trawlerman to be taken to the mortuary.

Nancy's biographer, Rose Collis, points out that service life may also have helped women deal more effectively with problems such as menstruation. Civilian advertisers of female products were quick to take advantage of the new situation. Advertisements for period pain relief, for instance, stressed that servicewomen needed their product because they couldn't take time off; advertisements for the very recently imported Tampax, popular with Canadian and American servicewomen, were more controversial. A 1941 advertisement in the *British Medical Journal* recommending Tampax as 'safe, simple and reliable' for women engaged on national service caused controversy but prompted the Royal College of Obstetricians and Gynaecologists to survey its members for evidence of undesirable side-effects 'either on medical or ethical' grounds. The product continued to be sold but with additional safety warnings. Over the years tampons would make a huge difference to the lives of active outdoor women but this would be a long time coming.

For many non-boarding-school, non-college-educated women, war service might be the first time they had lived away from home. What about sexual protection? Vera attempted to veto the practice of surrounding Wren's quarters with barbed wire. She believed in expecting high standards of behaviour and trusting people. Not everyone agreed with her. The archivist at Felixstowe Museum remembered that when he was assembling the WRNS section of the Second World War HMS *Beehive* collection he discovered that they used regularly to get messages from people in the town accusing the Wrens of being irresponsible marriage wreckers. Ian Trelawny reported that there was indeed barbed wire ostensibly blocking illicit access to the Wrens' quarters – 'but no one had thought of the fire escape.'[10] Ian (aged 25 and separated from his first wife) fell in love with 17-year-old Wren June Wilkinson when he had been badly wounded and she was directed to run his messages for him. He also took great (and he says innocent) delight in looking at the Boat Crew Wrens in their bell-bottom seaman's trousers, which had been cut for men and sometimes fitted rather tightly.

In 1942 there was a Government Committee of Enquiry into the living conditions and welfare of the women's services generally. Vera's view was that naturally there would be some 'loose behaviour' but that this was 'a human problem, not a service one.' She believed that 'discipline, work and good comradeship tends to put the relations of men and women on a healthy and normal basis and acts as a corrective to laxity rather than an incitement.'[11] Generally, experience would show that she was right; men learned more respect for women within the shared working environment and women's confidence grew. As a Catholic, Vera was uncomfortable with the routine distribution of contraceptives to young servicemen when about to attend a dance where there would be Wrens present but she didn't (or couldn't?) interfere. Instead, she ensured that Wrens who contracted a sexually transmitted disease would not be automatically discharged but were treated within the service – just as men would be. If they became pregnant, they would need to leave but could be considered for re-entry when they'd had their baby, unless there were any further disciplinary issues. She regretted this differential treatment – men would not be sacked – but reasoned that they couldn't really afford to lose anyone at all from the war effort.[12] Many of the girls who joined the service – and indeed many of the Wren officers responsible for them – were startlingly innocent about sex.

Vera believed that the WRNS should be under the Naval Discipline Act, as this would give individual women better protection from the whims of individual men in authority. 'It always seemed wrong to me that important matters of policy which are the responsibility of the Admiralty, should be practically decided by the opinions of individual Commanders-in-Chief, especially in a matter concerning the status of women where so many men have personal prejudices.'[13] The Act would give women official Commissions. Desertion (leaving without permission) would be forbidden. She understood that soft-hearted Admirals might flinch from the prospect of court-martialling a pretty little Wren, but in her view, this merely revealed that they didn't take the work of the Women's Services seriously. It infuriated her that men could demand that their wives resign from the service when they wished. No one was troubled when servicemen were ordered away from home: 'That was just life, and these things happen; but it was quite another thing when it was the wife who went off: a husband was entitled to have his wife with him.'[14]

She did her best to practise compassionate drafting – trying to ensure, for instance, that women with caring responsibilities were enabled to carry them out.

> *No one is going to pretend that compassionate drafting is not a continuous headache for the drafting staff, nevertheless I am sure it had good results for the Service. Women are brought up to feel home ties and responsibilities weighing heavily on them and cannot shake them off in a moment even if they should.*

Vera herself knew a great deal about work–life balance. She had been persuaded to send her three children (the youngest aged seven in 1939) to stay with her cousin in Canada in the grim days after the fall of France when invasion of Britain seemed imminent and the requirements of her job overwhelming. Initially she'd been taking them into the office with her and was 'appalled' by this separation, which went against all her beliefs. Her daughter Elvira (her oldest child) returned in the summer of 1941 and joined the Wrens the following year at the minimum age of 17 1/2. Her two boys only came home in time to say goodbye to their father when he fell ill and died in 1943. Emotionally, Vera was poleaxed. 'I had often worried about the children; I worried about the Service and my work. But Gordon and I were so much part of one another that the thought of being cut off from him to go on alone had never occurred to me.'[15] Nevertheless, it's what she did.

When Christian Lamb (Oldham) was 101, she published a book detailing some more of the varied jobs her generation had undertaken: wireless telegraphy, intelligence work, listening stations, experimental work, translation, code-breaking, cooking and cleaning, and attack teachers for the submarine 'Perisher' course. Christian herself had initially been posted away from Wren HQ to Tilbury to oversee the process of degaussing merchant ships. 'Needless to say, as I left HQ for my new posting I had no idea what degaussing meant.'[16] Subsequently she became a Wren plotter, posted to Plymouth. Her job was to translate information from the various signal sources, which had been sent to Bletchley and decoded, into actual positions on a giant board from which tactics could be considered, threats ascertained and, ideally, support mustered. The interest she'd taken in ships since childhood – from an unforgettable day when she'd watched the Grand Fleet sail into Malta – would now stand her in good stead.

Jobs such as this brought women much closer to the reality of action at sea. Too close sometimes. In the early months of the war, cypher officers and coders in the port areas were usually Wrens from naval families (like Christian), as they were more immediately trusted by the men in command. It was hard when the reports the women were receiving, and the orders they were transmitting, involved people they knew, and some very dear to them. In a closely linked service like the Navy this was true for men as well. Christian was working in Belfast when she found herself having to plot the progress of HMS *Oribi*, her fiancé John's ship, as it headed into a U-boat wolfpack. Her fellow plotters tried to persuade her to leave the room but, just like Jane Austen's Mrs Croft, Christian was certain that ignorance would be agony: 'It was better for me to be there, in the thick of it.'[17]

Women's accuracy and conscientiousness ensured they were successful in these jobs. (In 2024 Christian was awarded the Légion d'honneur for her part in planning the D-Day landings.) Many Wrens also had civilian workplace experience as secretaries or administrators. They trained as wireless operatives, worked in the Y listening stations (wireless interception) and at Station X, Bletchley Park. They had far more direct knowledge of the actions of the war at sea than women had ever been trusted with before. The Wrens who worked with Gilbert Roberts at the Western Approaches Tactical Unit helped develop convoy defence tactics. The Wren attack teachers on the 'Perisher' course at HMS *Dolphin* challenged the officers of HMS *Taku* to take them to sea, secretly, in order to prove they could fire torpedoes with just as much accuracy as in the simulator. Other women, such as Ordnance Wrens, sometimes needed to go to sea to help test equipment. Christian's friend Elizabeth Scott, a cypher officer, was one of the few to use her skills on board ship. She was posted to the *Mauretania* – one of the 'monsters' that transported troops across the Atlantic, travelling at high speed, zigzagging incessantly and forbidden to stop.

While a significant number of Wrens did go to sea during the Second World War, probably the only one to fight afloat was the Frenchwoman Madeleine Bayard, aged 31. She and her lover, Claude Peri – alias Jack Langlais – had met in French Vietnam and worked together as sabotage experts. After the 1940 fall of France they had commandeered the former merchant vessel SS *le Rhin* and steamed from Marseilles to Gibraltar with a cargo of plastic explosive and other equipment that they had 'liberated'. Most of *le Rhin*'s crew (including her original captain) had not travelled with her. In Gibraltar, *le Rhin* attracted a group of refugee Belgian army officers who helped sail her to Barry Dock in South Wales, where she was renamed HMS *Fidelity* and taken into British naval service as a 'special service ship'. The foreign volunteers who stayed with her needed to adopt pseudonyms to protect their family members back home. Edward Marriott, author of *Claude and Madeleine* (2005), has seen the index entry for the document accepting Madeleine into the WRNS as 'Barclay M.V.' and conferring the rank of first officer (RN equivalent lieutenant commander), but the file itself has gone.

In 1941 HMS *Fidelity* was used by Special Operations Executive (SOE) to transport agents and equipment along the coast of southern France. During these clandestine missions she flew the flags of neutral Spain and Portugal. An additional idea was that she could enter neutral ports and commit acts of sabotage using Madeleine's expertise with explosives. In 1942 *Fidelity* was refitted as a commando carrier for duty in Southeast Asia. She was armed with four 4-inch guns, four 21-inch torpedo tubes, and carried two OS2U Kingfisher floatplanes, one motor torpedo boat *MTB-105*, and two landing craft, HMSs *LCV-752* and *LCV-754*. She was sent south as an additional escort for Convoy ONS 154 bound for Colombo but straggled due to engine trouble. On 30 December 1942 she was sunk by German U-boat *435*. As well as her regular crew, she was carrying a number of marines, commandos and 44 seamen who had been rescued after their ship (HMS *Shackleton)* had been sunk during a previous engagement.[18] Although most of the people on board may have survived the sinking, the U-boat captain followed the *Laconia* order, which forbade the rescue of Allied survivors. They were left to die in the water. Cruelly for their families, it was years before the truth could be told – possibly because of the embarrassment of having a woman on board. Madeleine's name is on the naval memorial at Portsmouth.

Vera does not mention this story and I have not been able to find either HMS *Fidelity* or Madeleine 'Barclay' in the Navy Lists. Perhaps this is not surprising? The inclusion of Wrens in the Navy List is disappointingly unmethodical. There is a non-alphabetical list of officers' names (after the list of Sea Cadets), with the ships (almost always 'stone frigates') to which they were posted bracketed next to their names. However, when one cross-checks to the vessels' names, the Wrens are not there. This is perhaps trivial, but given the official mindset, this simultaneous recognition that the women's service exists, coupled with a failure to include them in ships' companies (even 'stone frigates') sends a negative message – one that I assume would have saddened Vera. She believed passionately that women in the Navy should be fully respected and integrated, citing Francis Drake: 'The gentlemen shall haul with the mariners and the mariners shall haul with the gentlemen and we shall all be one ships company.' She may have misquoted Drake slightly but her vision was clear.

Early in 1941 the WRNS had been removed from the control of the Civil Establishment and became part of the Navy structure under the Second Sea Lord, as it had been in the First World War. As the numbers of women and their range of jobs expanded, the Admiralty found it necessary to issue an Admiralty Fleet Order (AFO) making it clear that men had to obey instructions issued by Wren officers, petty officers and leading Wrens in the course of their duty. Vera described this AFO as 'very useful', which seems something of an understatement when one considers the years of women's invisibility in Admiralty eyes. Nevertheless, her dream of full integration and equality would not be realised for another half century, when women were finally accepted as full members of RN ships crews in 1993.[19] And it is only in the second decade of this 21st century that all areas (including submarines, commandos and naval divers) have been opened equally to women.

The only Wrens to take direct charge of boats during the Second World War (rather than travel as passengers or carry out specialist work on board) were the Boat Crew Wrens, supported by other categories such as Wren Stokers. Their vessels were small. Boom Defence Wrens, for instance, worked on the drifters, tugs and motor vessels that opened and closed the defensive nets that protected harbour entrances but were not (as far as I know) employed on the large specialist vessels that had initially laid the nets. These Boom Defence Wrens undertook maintenance duties and received bosun-style training. Boat Crew Wrens were instructed in basic navigation, boat handling and the general duties of a coxswain. Wren Stokers were trained in engine maintenance.

When Vera had first visited Portsmouth in 1939 and looked at the variety of jobs being undertaken around the harbour by motor launches, picket boats and requisitioned yachts she had thought that there was no reason why women shouldn't run those boats. But she knew it was an idea ahead of its time. It took her until October 1941 to convince anyone else officially. Her friend Euphemia Welby – admiral's daughter and captain's widow – pioneered the use of Wrens for all harbour duties at Plymouth and the practice spread from there until the category was formalised. It was never large (little more than 500) and was always oversubscribed: 'everywhere was the wish to transfer from duties, however responsible, to become a real sailor.'[20] Many Wrens refused promotion to officer rank because they were afraid of being returned to the shore.

Women's pre-war yachting experience was usually overlooked when they volunteered. A naval captain told Vera of an occasion when he'd rather patronisingly congratulated a Wren bowman, 'You look as if you've seen a boat before', only to find she'd been sailing all her life and held a Yachtmaster Certificate. She may have been Dorothy Laird, who had worked for three years on Gustaf Erikson's *Penang* as a deckhand and ordinary seaman and was the first woman to be awarded the Board of Trade's Coastal Yachtmaster Certificate. But there were many other young women with practical seamanship skills. Again and again Vera fielded surprised comments about the excellence of Wrens' boat handling as well as their toughness and willingness to work in all weathers. The submarine captains on Loch Goil, for instance, were amazed by the skill of the Boat Crew Wrens from HMS *Forth*, who worked 16 hours a day and whose job frequently involved coming alongside small submarines in the dark to deliver scientists or engineers connected with the secret research work being carried out there.

As well as those Wrens who had arrived with knowledge and a love of boats, direct service on the water developed this in others. Rozelle Pierrepont had always hankered after the sea but her only previous experience had been gained from the deck of a cruise ship or a rowing boat on the Serpentine. She joined at the minimum age of 17 1/2 and by dint of looking plaintive and refusing all other categories, got herself taken on as a Wren Stoker. This did not mean shovelling coal but learning to maintain petrol engines and acting as a deckhand. She served for the final two years of the war in South Coast stations preparing for D-Day and realised she had found her vocation.

> *It was a black, stormy winter's night with the wind blowing, great guns from the southwest and an anti-aircraft gun on the end of the Ocean Dock firing at a lone German Raider somewhere up amongst the constellation of Orion. There was quite a sea running with the wind against the tide and clouds of solid spray burst across the bows of our boat from time to time causing a rivulet of icy water to funnel off the rim of my tin helmet into a small persistent channel which found its way inside my oilskin collar and eventually down the back of my neck. I leant over my beloved charge, an old 4-cylinder Kelvin engine to make sure that the pistons were still singing their rhythmic song despite the fury of the elements; and suddenly I realised that this was my ideal situation in life.[21]*

Although the WRNS remained a permanent part of the Navy after the war ended (and there was also formal recognition of the female Sea Rangers) the category of Boat Crew Wren was abolished, with many other specialisms, in December 1945. Many women were glad to return home and try to pick up their normal lives and peacetime careers; others, like Rozelle, were devastated. In 1934 Vera had given evidence to a committee considering whether women should be appointed to the diplomatic service – enabling them to become British consuls in foreign ports, for instance. It had been an unsuccessful and depressing experience. However, in 1945 she received a letter to say that the Admiralty, which had vetoed this as 'most unsuitable', had changed its mind. The committee chairman told Vera 'it was not a matter of deciding whether the door should be opened to women, but rather of recognition that they had crashed it open for themselves.'[22]

From left to right: Sue Huish, Joan Preece ('Winkle') and Rozelle Pierrepont in The Camel *(Thoresby Settlement Trustees)*

12

'Things will never be the same again'[1]
Women's lives disrupted by the war

Cecily Brent-Good (b. 1914); Gladys Newell (b. 1900); Margaret Bridges (b. 1913); Beryl Smeeton (b. 1908); Ann Davison (b. 1913)

'SAILING ALONE IS ONE of the most peaceful pastimes in the world. I learned to love it in those weeks of spring and early summer and was out on my own most days, keeping well within the restricted areas marked on the chart.'[2] It was April 1940. Cecily Brent-Good was on a week's notice for call-up as a Voluntary Aid Detachment (VAD) nurse in France. She'd resigned from her Air Raid Precautions (ARP) duties ready to go, but no call came. She felt dejected and useless. Instead, she went sailing, using an out-of-date fishing permit obtained in the early months of the war. The wind died, she was caught by a spring flood and was drifting helplessly towards a prohibited area between Yarmouth and Bouldnor Fort on the Isle of Wight. Her Yarmouth One Design keelboat was too heavy to row so she followed official instructions and threw out her anchor, intending to wait until the tide turned and she could avoid the prohibited area. The water was too deep. She added the only spare rope she had on board but still the anchor failed to bite. She drifted on until finally the anchor found the bottom and her small boat came to a halt under the guns of the fort. A naval boat hurried out and towed her ignominiously back to Yarmouth. The captain was furious, she was told. 'What won't I do to that son of a gun!' he had shouted, storming out on to the Solent YC balcony to stare at the little white racing boat. 'You can't do anything', his colleague had replied. 'It's a girl.'

Cecily had drifted through a minefield with her anchor down. 'It can't have been a very good one,' was all she found to say. Just a few weeks later she was back at the fort asking the captain for his permission to sail their family yacht *Gossip* to Dunkirk to take part in the evacuation. She felt perfectly capable of doing this alone if the captain could spare her an engineer. She was told to stock up the yacht and stand by – but the order never came. Soon afterwards she was called up for VAD nursing duty. Cecily recalled how she comforted herself in the bad days that followed, when bombs were falling all around her:

> *I would try and shut my ears to the noise and imagine I was lying in my bunk listening to the whispered gossip of the waves as they hurried past the ship's sides on their way to the open sea. I would imagine I could hear the call of the oystercatchers as they moved to new sandbanks at low water and the thrilling, rippling, bubbling notes of the curlews in the early morning as I had heard them so often on the Newtown River.*[3]

* * *

When men were called up for active service the disruption of women's lives could be extreme. Gladys and Eric Newell had been living on their 90ft yacht *Onda*, cruising the Essex and Kent coasts with the help of a season ticket that allowed Eric to commute to work in London from wherever the yacht happened to be. Gladys was a strong, independent personality. She had married at 18 to escape her father, whom she disliked, but later divorced her first husband, a wealthy businessman and Olympic ice hockey player, for his infidelity. She experienced the social ostracism of being a divorcee but developed her own career in the fashion industry. When she met Eric Newell, her life changed again as she turned her artistic flair and organising talent into making spectacular living spaces on board the yachts that were their homes. Their first, the barge yacht *Nancibelle*, was later a Dunkirk 'Little Ship'; their second, the impressive *Fortis*, was featured in *Yachting World*, then sold to an admiral. Gladys was careful to ensure that their homes also sailed well. She enabled *Fortis*, for instance, to sail to windward without her original leeboards. The family then moved to the 90ft *Onda*, where Gladys again created a functional and beautiful floating home. In September 1939 Eric, a Royal Naval Volunteer Supplementary Reserve (RNVSR) member was called up and *Onda* was requisitioned by the Navy. She was taken to a mooring on the Thames, where much of her interior was pulled out to enable tiered bunks to be installed, and she was used as a dormitory and training ship for naval cadets.[4]

Gladys and her young son, John, then faced an itinerant existence, usually living in boarding houses or rented accommodation as they traipsed around the country trying to keep in touch with Eric. John remembers that his mother's lovely auburn hair quickly turned white with the anxiety. 'Things will never be the same again,' she said. However, she was a woman of spirit and for part of the war made the best of her situation by running a boarding house. Eric remembered returning home on leave and meeting a Canadian serviceman who assumed he was a prospective lodger and heartily recommended its comfort and good cooking. After the war Gladys and Eric did have the opportunity to buy *Onda* back but decided she was no longer for them. They could not recapture their former life, either on the water or at work, and emigrated to Canada to make a new start in the early 1950s.

* * *

Margaret Townsend may have been the only woman to serve the British war effort under sail. She was born and grew up in County Clare, where she and her brother Richard sailed an 18ft dinghy from Queenstown (Cobh). She read French at St Anne's College Oxford, then began breaking in and training racehorses. After a particularly bad fall, in which she fractured her pelvis, she sold her saddle, bought *Mab*, a 6-ton gaff cutter and joined both the RORC and the Irish Cruising Club, where women members had always had equal rights. Her husband-to-be, Antony Bridges, claims that she'd sailed 20,000 miles in small boats before the outbreak of the Second World War. Their son, Richard, says that his father, a lawyer, was not prone to exaggeration.

Margaret and Antony met though the RORC. He had begun his career as a naval cadet at Dartmouth, but by the age of 16 he had contracted osteomyelitis and been invalided out. An only child he had loved fishing on the River Dart and took up ocean racing when so many other sports were denied him. He became a barrister but was even turned down by the RNVSR as war approached. By September 1939 Antony and Margaret were engaged, and she encouraged him in an unlikely scheme to volunteer their services as waterborne cargo-carriers. In October, to Antony's evident shock, they were offered a contract to deliver 60 tons of gelignite across the Pentland Firth to Orkney, where urgent work was in progress to improve the defences at Scapa Flow.

Margaret had already joined the AFS but was released when Antony bought *Mermaid*, a 15-ton former Kings Lynn pilot cutter, lying on the Hamble. All yacht movement was prohibited but Antony discovered a cousin, an Admiral at Portsmouth, who gave them 10 gallons of petrol, a vaguely worded permit and ordered the Hurst Castle forts not to shoot at them. They sailed to Teignmouth where Morgan Giles Ltd fitted a new mast, and Margaret joined the team renewing the rigging. Then, in early December, they set out for the small harbour of Scrabster, near Thurso in Caithness. In his book, *Scapa Ferry*, Antony details the very first gale they encountered, the cold heavy air and big seas that drove them to seek shelter in Brixham. After two days storm-bound, he and Margaret looked out over the harbour from the warm clubhouse as he secretly struggled with the temptation to give up on the Scapa Flow contract and go fishing. Then he looked at her 'dear face [...] so keen and happy'. 'Don't let's waste it', she said. 'Come on! An offshore wind and quiet water all the way to the Lizard. I believe we're going to get a break at last.'[5]

At Milford Haven she lost part of her finger in an accident involving tangled trawler anchor chains but wanted only to continue hurrying northwards.

Antony is a very good writer. His account of their trips across the notorious Pentland Firth during the harsh winter of 1939/40, deserves to be better known: he and Margaret stowing 4–5 ton loads of gelignite in *Mermaid*'s stripped out cabin, then sailing it from Scrabster to Lyness negotiating tide rips and standing seas, as well as heavy winds, freezing conditions and occasional brushes with officialdom. There's a tricky meeting with the Admiral Commanding Orkney and Shetland (ACOS) where Antony thanks God that: 'Margaret for once had decided to put some boots on'.[6] Usually she preferred to go barefoot. There's another memorable glimpse of her individuality when they are sheltering alongside a large salvage trawler. Margaret wants to fill a kettle, so climbs across to use the trawler's tap. The commander is rendered speechless. Antony comments: 'It was not a time for caring about appearances. Being barefooted, ragged and soaked was so common and necessary a condition of our job that she and anyone who knew her had long since ceased to think of it. But to an elderly commander, such an appearance on the deck of his ship in a gale in Scapa Flow at five o'clock in the morning was naturally unsettling.'[7]

They married at the end of the first year. Then, in 1942, their first child, Richard was born. Margaret went home to Cork for his birth and brought him back to Scotland in a basket. Another son, Meryon, was born in 1944, the cargo work changed and there is less to read about her nautical activity until the end of the book when *Mermaid* is fetched south to be sold in the autumn of 1945, 'an anxious journey through minefields and wreckage'. Margaret and Anthony moved to Ireland with their children in 1947. They were lost at sea in a gale off Castletownshend in June 1976.

* * *

The war began more slowly for Beryl and Miles Smeeton in India as Miles attended staff college in preparation for his unit's orders to mobilise. When he was not required for duty, they went rock climbing. 'These were golden days for Beryl and me [...] we lived so fully in the present and allowed no shadow of the coming separation, inevitable when I got my object and went to war, to cloud the horizon.'[8] They conceived their daughter Clio, who was born in Risalpur on 1 March 1941, and began writing a diary to her in case they were both killed. As Miles' departure grew closer, Beryl got rid of almost all their possessions, in order that they should travel light wherever they went next. When Miles finally left, expecting that his destination was North Africa, she and baby Clio began to search for a home where they would all live together when the war was over. Miles would have liked to go back to England but Beryl refused. They compromised on one of the Dominions – Canada, Australia, South Africa, possibly.

Motherhood is the most profound adjustment for an independent woman – arguably harder than marriage unless surrounded by nannies and other helping hands. Beryl had become opposed to the British-India status quo and was not keen on the *ayah* system. She didn't want to bring her daughter up in a society dependent on servants. Yet she craved her own space and frequently shocked people by leaving Clio alone or handing her to strangers to hold or to look after for an hour or two. They were further taken aback by her individual approaches to nutrition, hygiene and remedies. Clio wrote:

> *You have no idea how many people think I was a mistreated child. What a load of old rubbish, I had the happiest childhood and the only blot on my world was having to go to school. There was no school, and no kids, on the side of Saltspring island where our farm was, so I had to go to boarding school at Queen Margret's school in Duncan, where I wept from Monday to Wednesday and was uncontrollable Wednesday to Friday. Once we went to sea in Tzu Hang that blot was removed!*[9]

Anyone would find travelling alone with a very young first baby from India to the Australian Outback, then to Tasmania and back to India quite a challenge. Beryl achieved this during 1941–1943 but met with criticism along the way. Miles Clark quotes a few sentences from the diary Beryl wrote for Clio: 'One thing you must remember. If you travel with children of your own. They don't belong to you. They are PUBLIC PROPERTY. And anyone and everyone is entitled to, and usually does, interfere. If you remember that, you'll get along alright.'[10] This can't have been easy for her. One hundred years later, Dutch Olympic sailor Marit Bouwmeester writes for World Sailing about the challenges of new motherhood while training for the Paris Olympics – it's not the intrinsic problems of combining care for a baby with strenuous physical activity but the attitudes of others: 'people are coming at you with their own mindset about motherhood, bringing their own judgments.'[11] Miles Clark never met Beryl. He talked to many people who knew her and others who wrote about her – primarily of course her husband – but his choice of anecdotes presents her as an eccentric, indomitable figure, almost abnormal. A dangerous, irresponsible mother? Clio Smeeton would not agree, and other fragments quoted from the diaries suggest that Beryl found it just as hard to be a 'good mother', that she got as anxious, angry, lonely, emotional and miserable as anyone else. Then she dealt with it – rationally, sincerely and to the best of her ability. 'My highly independent sailing mother was the most loving woman imaginable and from my perspective, I was the apple of her eye.'[12]

After the biography of her parents was published in 1991, Clio remembers the amount of criticism levelled at her mother for her adventures and risk taking. She likens this to the criticism of outstanding climber Alison Hargreaves (b. 1962), mother of two, who died on K2 in 1995. Hargreaves had previously climbed the North Face of the Eiger when five-and-a-half months pregnant with her son, Tom. She had solo-climbed all the great north faces of the Alps in a single season, a first for any climber. In 1995 she had intended to climb the three highest mountains in the world – Mount Everest, K2 and Kangchenjunga – without the aid of guides or supplementary oxygen. She reached the summit of Everest unaided in May but died in a storm a few months later while descending from K2 in August. Her children Tom and Kate were aged six and four at the time, being cared for by their father. Tom also became an outstanding climber but died in 2019, on Nanga Parbat. I've been reading a Mumsnet discussion of the BBC Two film *The Last Mountain* made in 2021. The film is about Tom, yet all the criticism in the discussion is of Alison's 'selfishness' – as if she is somehow to blame for her son's death as well as her own.[13]

The double standard is at work of course – and the right (or not) of society to judge how individuals 'should' behave. It's a crucial problem for women ourselves. We each have to balance the exercise of our personal talents – or whatever is the essence of our identity – against the possible risk to people dependent on us, or the deprivation from the time we are not giving them. Time taken away from children to earn money may be accepted as essential. Taking time – or risks – for personal fulfilment is more problematic. Yet, like men, we only have one life each. If you don't grab a chance, it becomes a might-have-been. The thrilling thing about Beryl Smeeton is her refusal to live her life according to the doctrine of 'What if?' As Ella Maillart understood, Beryl lived fully 'in the moment'. Human experience is richer for people like this. Sailor, writer and former Royal Marine Ewen Southby-Tailyour put Beryl Smeeton first on his list of women personifying the spirit of independence. When I asked him for his view on mothers who take risks, his answer was clear: 'Well, I am all for adventure and if that adventurer is a young mother so be it. Opportunities lost are not often regained.' He remembered meeting solo circumnavigator Brigitte Oudry in the Falklands in 1978 and asking her about the husband and two-year-old daughter she had left behind. 'She had no regrets although she admitted that it looked selfish. She was certainly looking forward to getting home,' he wrote in an email.[14] Lucy Frost, sailing *Outlaw* in the 21st-century Ocean Globe Race, said that when she told people she was planning to race round the world they always asked her whether she had children. When she said no, their response was 'That's alright then.'

Beryl and Clio returned to India early in 1943 and managed some time together with Miles, who was on leave from North Africa. Beryl also bought them a smallholding in the west of Canada – sight unseen. The scope of her world view remains startling. Miles once told Miles Clark that there wasn't an inhabited page of the *Times Atlas of the World* that either he or Beryl hadn't visited. It's unsurprising that they would eventually begin to explore the seas as well. Meanwhile, Clio was a toddler, being taught to be brave. Miles Clark quotes a letter from the wife of one of Miles' fellow officers that describes Beryl as 'very alarming' and 'raving mad' and feeling 'outright compassion' for what Clio was 'being put through'.[15] Clio, on the other hand, describes her mother as 'fun, kind and empathetic'. She says she had a wonderful childhood and that growing up with her parents gave her confidence. Later, when they sailed as a family in *Tzu Hang* she was also given responsibility, which she relished:

> *My parents were immensely practical and their sailing was motivated just by the fun of it. I loved sailing beyond anything. When I was eight I stood my watch (daytime only) while they slept below. It was wonderful for a child and equally wonderful as I grew up and shared more of the responsibilities, though I was never particularly good at navigation.*[16]

She accepted that she would have to go to boarding school again and would not be on board *Tzu Hang* in 1956 when her parents and John Guzzwell followed the clipper route from Australia to England. She was twice close to being orphaned as they attempted to round Cape Horn but even after the first pitchpoling accident, which Beryl was extraordinarily lucky to survive, perhaps due to her exceptional swimming ability, and which left her with broken ribs and crushed vertebrae, the weekly letters kept coming without a pause, assuring Clio that she was loved.

* * *

'THINGS WILL NEVER BE THE SAME AGAIN'

For Ann and Frank Davison the coming of war had brought total – apparently senseless – disruption to their lives. Ann had been born Margaret Ann Longstaffe in Carshalton, Surrey. Her mother, Josephine, was an amateur artist, her father an accountant. Hers doesn't seem to have been a contented childhood. Perhaps she would have preferred itinerant parents, like the Smeetons. 'I was a misfit, a wanderer, a thoroughgoing cuckoo in the nest from the very start. If there was any devilment going, I was bound to be in it, not that I committed devilry with intent, so to speak. It just happened that way.' She felt that her appearance was against her: 'If I had been a lean brown child devilry would have been expected but as it happened, I was one of those chubby blue-eyed babies with long fair ringlets that make women quite imbecilic, and I looked so darn good it was easy to get away with almost anything.'[17] As soon as she was able to crawl, she had headed for the open road. She tells a story of being returned to her horrified young mother by the local milkman who had found her attempting to climb up his horse's legs. Ponies were Ann's passion as a child, though her mother hoped she would become an artist. She was a keen reader and although she did learn to draw well, words were her medium of choice.

Her mother died of septicaemia in 1928 when Ann was a young teenager. It may have been then that Ann went on an extended visit to relatives in New Jersey where, if photos give a true reflection, she had a wonderful outdoor holiday with horses, haymaking, river picnics on the Ramapo River, and friends her own age. A later trip to stay on a ranch in Argentina was even more significant, as it provided her first experience of flying. 'It changed the whole course of my life.'[18] When she returned to England her plans to work with horses or become a vet were all abandoned. It was flying lessons that she wanted. 'I don't see why you shouldn't,' said her father. Retrospectively, she was even more impressed by his tolerance and trust when he allowed her to fly to collect her younger sister Jo from school.

Ann gained her commercial licence in September 1936. She was based at Hanworth Air Park, which she described as 'interesting': 'All the aviation oddities seemed to gather there. It was full of queer aircraft and queerer characters.' Her first paid work was £5 to deliver a plane to Liverpool. She would fly anything she could lay her hands on. She would tow advertising banners, deliver parcels, deliver people. Although she later wrote that she felt almost guilty for being paid for doing something that she loved, she did need a steady income. She saw an advertisement from Hooton Airfield in north Cheshire and hurried 'to convince the advertiser that despite my sex, I was the man for the job'. Earning an independent living from flying was hard. Amy Mollison (Johnson) wrote, 'In England you can count on the fingers of one hand the number of women who are making a living directly from flying.'[19] That was in 1934, the year that entrepreneur Frank Davison had bought Hooton airport on the Wirral peninsula, with his wife, Canadian-born aviatrix Elsie Joy Muntz (b. Toronto 1910). They had married in 1933 and worked together to develop the airport facilities for use by local flying clubs while also building up a transport and charter business. Joy was an aerial photography specialist. Bank holiday pleasure flights and excursions to Blackpool were advertised and proved popular. By 1937 Joy and Frank could afford to hire more pilots.

Ann's first impression of her prospective employer was of his thinness, his yellow hair and his eyes: 'Clear, very blue eyes, that often look out of the faces of pioneers, aviators, sailors, restless practical men of imagination,' as she wrote later. Frank's eyes, unfortunately, were not the impeccable 20:20 vision required for pilots. His left eye had a serious defect so, while he had briefly managed to join the Royal Flying Corps (RFC) in the First World War, its weakness had soon been discovered after a crash and he'd had to transfer to the Royal Engineers. Ann got the job and learned more about Frank: he was meticulous and impulsive, had a passion for detail, was shrewd in business and romantic in outlook; hasty, yet with control over his temper. He was full of energy and versatility. 'The most interesting man I've ever known.' There was a sentimentally touching moment when they discovered they had kept identical miniature silver horseshoes as lucky mascots since childhood. They both had inquiring minds and were indefatigable talkers with many interests in common. 'He wrote poetry and I drew pictures.' They fell in love.

One interest that wasn't shared was sailing. Frank had grown up on the shores of Lake Windermere and attempted to take Ann sailing there. The first day they were caught by a line squall, the second soaked by incessant rain. She wasn't keen to try again.

> '*Well,*' *I said to Frank. 'I dare say if you like being frozen, battered, scared out of your wits, or just getting nowhere at all, sailing is a lot of fun. As for me, I'd rather fly and be frightened in comfort.*'

'THINGS WILL NEVER BE THE SAME AGAIN'

'You'll come to it,' said Frank, easily. 'You'll see sailing is the best fun in the world.'

Ann describes Frank's wife, Joy, as 'a highly intelligent, gifted and courageous woman, a brilliant pilot and as versatile and dominant as Frank.'[20] The difficult explanations, separations, divorce and new marriage happened, Ann says, as easily as possible between three civilised people.

How easy would this have been in fact? Divorce in the 1930s was governed by the Matrimonial Causes Act 1923. This had been intended to offer more fairness to women by enabling either party to petition for divorce on the grounds of adultery. Previously only men could use this as the sole ground for divorce; women additionally had to cite desertion or cruelty. Socially, adultery by a woman was viewed more harshly than by a man. This meant that 'amicable' divorce often relied on a mixture of lying and collusion, as in Beryl and Tom Peddie's case. To protect Beryl's reputation Tom had done the so-called 'gentlemanly' thing and set up a situation where he was discovered in bed with another woman, enabling Beryl to divorce him. This in effect meant that they were both breaking the law – first by making an arrangement between each other (collusion), second by Tom pretending to be unfaithful when he wasn't (perjury).

In 1934 the law reformer, writer, Independent MP and yachtsman AP Herbert had published the novel *Holy Deadlock*, which drew attention to the hypocrisies involved. He then prepared legislation that added desertion to the list of causes, and which was eventually passed as the Matrimonial Causes Act 1937. Might this have helped Joy, Frank and Ann manage their 'civilised' divorce? It seems more likely that Joy moved out of Hooton, Ann moved in, and they regularised the situation later. Writing to a friend, Joy states that she was no longer married from 20 November 1939.[21] It's obvious from Ann's writing that she and Frank had been living together and working as a partnership at Hooton for some significant time before they could marry. She talks of the business 'we' had built up. War brought it crashing down. All civilian aircraft had been grounded three days before war was declared and airfields such as Hooton were swiftly requisitioned. Ann and Frank offered their services to the war effort but were not required. 'We don't need pilots,' Ann was told. 'We've plenty of them.' An inexplicable fire in the old grandstand where their planes were housed meant that all their stock was gone – so there was no compensation payable by the government. Their house was taken. Ann and Frank had lost their home and their livelihood.

They felt 'thrust out, bitter and bewildered'. Frank had inherited some gravel pits. These were mortgaged but still provided a little income. They took over the near-derelict Mere Brook House on the Wirral with 5 acres of nettles, and tried to build up a smallholding – hens, ducks and goats. Ann's two old ponies came to live with them, as transport and to pull light implements. It was hard work but felt 'satisfyingly creative in a destructive world'. Freezing winter weather, however, meant that the gravel pits could not be worked. The amount owed to the mortgage lenders began to build up. When they foreclosed, the fledgling enterprise at Mere Brook House could not survive. In 1943 Ann and Frank packed up their goats, poultry, ponies and few basic possessions and went to live on an island in Loch Lomond. They hoped to develop their goat herd and also breed geese. The first island on which they settled as tenants, Inchmurrin, was inhabited by others and its connections to the mainland, while not frequent, were already established. The second, Inchfad, which they bought, was deserted. Once they and their livestock moved there in September 1944 they had to rely on transport by boat.

It was an extraordinarily tough three years during which Ann discovered her practical writing skill. 'In a moment of irritation, I wrote an article and it sold. In a moment of even greater irritation, I wrote another, and it sold.' These were sent to specialist publications such as *Goat Keepers' Journal* or *Farmers Weekly* and provided essential additional income. By autumn 1947 Ann and Frank felt that they had survived their island experience. They also felt wanderlust.

> *'Frank said, 'Two more years on this place and my roots will be down. I shan't want to leave.' [...]*
>
> *'Do you want to leave?' I asked and he nodded. I was vastly relieved. For I wanted to go. Not because I was tired of island life but because we had beaten it. Or at least it had not beaten us and, now we knew it never would, the old restlessness was on me again. The restlessness that has driven me on since the day I was born and will, I know, never cease its nagging until I am dead.'*[22]

It would take her further than she could have imagined – alone and by boat.

'THINGS WILL NEVER BE THE SAME AGAIN'

Clio, Beryl and Miles Smeeton with Poopa and Cully (Clio Smeeton)

From left to right: Richard Townsend, Antony Bridges, Margaret Bridges (showing her toes) and Captain Dundas RNR in Orkney (Richard Bridges)

13

'I wore the right shoes and didn't interfere'
Unexpected jobs in wartime

Susan Sclater (b. 1913); Kathleen Palmer (b. 1907);
Eileen Ramsey (b. 1915); Ingrid Holford (b. 1920);
Victoria Drummond (b. 1894); Elspeth Hallsmith/Emma Smith
(b. 1923)

SUSAN SCLATER DESCRIBES HERSELF as 'a girl with an Oxford accent'. She was the daughter of a long-serving science teacher and housemaster from Charterhouse school in Surrey. Both her parents had loved sailing. Her father's obituary in *The Carthusian* states: 'He was very fortunate in finding for his wife one who shared both his passion for astronomy and his love of the sea, and his talent as a yachtsman has been fully inherited by his daughter.' That was published in June 1933, long before Susan had met Eric Hiscock, the yachtsman she would marry in 1941. I take this to mean that Susan was already a skilful sailor in her own right before she became half of a partnership. Her own obituary states that she had owned a West Wight scow from the age of 17 and met Eric while sailing in the Solent.

After the outbreak of war, Susan volunteered to work on the land; up at six every morning to work in a freezing cold corrugated-iron cow shed, then out in the fields, carting muck and cutting kale. She was often cold and tired but always cheerful. Susan was someone (Eric said) who never lost her temper. When Eric was dismissed from the Navy as 'a danger to the service' because of his poor eyesight, he and Susan married and moved to a flea-infested cottage, which they renovated while working on a farm near Wantage in the Berkshire Downs. Susan's level-headed competence is always obvious. Also, her combination of vision and practicality: 'I can see it as it will be,' she had said of the cottage. When Eric took on the editorship of Adlard Coles' magazine *Yachting* in 1942 he shared the work with Susan and felt no hesitation in leaving her in sole charge when he seized any opportunities to join the Admiralty Ferry Crew Service, an organisation that employed yachtsmen for their expertise, disregarding age, eyesight or other medical issues.

* * *

In the offices of another magazine, *Yachting Monthly*, Maurice Griffiths and Norman Clackson, both RNVSR members, were called up promptly in 1939. GH Pinkard, the proprietor, assured readers that there would be no cessation of their regular service: 'It is my intention to carry on, as was done during the last war, with a skeleton staff and a determination to fulfil our obligations to readers.'[1] He didn't spell out precisely how this was to be achieved. One can scan every issue until Griffiths and Clackson returned in 1945 and find no hint at all that the magazine was being run, almost single-handedly, by a woman. It would be good to think that this was an example of gender-blindness: it is much more likely to have been fear of upsetting the readers.

Kathleen Palmer had joined *Yacht Sales and Charters* as a shorthand secretary in 1925. When Maurice Griffiths moved from there to *Yachting Monthly*, she had moved with him. She didn't even like boats; it was just a job. When Kathleen was left in charge of *Yachting Monthly* in 1939, she moved the magazine out of its offices in Clements Inn to her mother's home in New Barnet. Her nephew, Ian Palmer, remembers a large room in the rambling old house, entirely given over to stacks of *Yachting Monthly*. Presumably she was already in contact with many of the magazine's contributors and advertisers – and I can vouch from letters received by my father and uncle for the thoughtfulness she brought to her role. Now, she also had to deal with boatyards in transition to their new role as Admiralty suppliers, with advertisers needing to strike the right note promoting their products to an incompletely militarised world. She had to offer her readers hope for the future, escapism from the present and insight into the progress of the war as it affected the many thousands of male and female sailors who were serving. For this she developed the 'RNVR Journal', a section within the magazine where she mixed information from Admiralty bulletins with short stories, explanatory articles, deaths, marriages and births. Sometimes these included desperate pleas for news when a loved one was missing – or MBK, 'missing believed killed'. Usually MBK meant dead (bodies being elusive at sea) but there was always the hope that it might mean wounded-but-alive, perhaps a prisoner. Families could suffer months, sometimes years, of uncertainty, particularly if news was being officially suppressed for some reason.

Kathleen did have the part-time services of a young typist for the first couple of years but once this assistant had joined the Auxiliary Territorial Service (ATS) she was on her own. On her own and invisible. She put her initials to the occasional book review and to a particularly good series of articles about life in the WRNS – which later provided the text for *Wrens in Camera* (1945), a book of photographs by Lee Miller. Her editorials were unsigned and focussed on issues rather than personal opinion, though just occasionally she allowed herself a grumble about the difficulties of dealing with the censor's office.

From this distance and without direct testimony Kathleen seems to have taken on the role of editor with ease. This is sure to be a simplification. A story survives of a male contributor who asked for an article by Kathleen, then simply declined to acknowledge her as editor – 'I don't think we've been introduced have we?' – uncharmingly putting the 'presumptuous little typist' in her place. There will have been others. Her careful policy of anonymity bears its own witness to the potential hostility felt towards women in positions where they might have power over men. Even today women working in the nautical publishing industry say that they encounter unexpected prejudice and sometimes direct rudeness. After the war Kathleen wrote two books about sailing but used a male pseudonym ('Guy Pennant'), as she didn't think anyone would buy them otherwise.

What is certain is that Kathleen didn't want to hand back the editor's position when Maurice Griffiths returned. She knew she had to – her title was acting editor – but that didn't make it any easier. Ian explains that she thought out a strategy whereby she might keep a small part of the magazine her own by volunteering to cover yacht and dinghy racing, which were entering a period of great popularity. Maurice Griffiths, like several other *Yachting Monthly* editors after him, wasn't at all interested in racing – possibly almost disliked it. He accepted gladly, which left Kathleen with a problem of credibility. She may have had some sailing with Peter Gerard as a cadet on board *Juanita* but that was all. She'd never had a boat; there was no nautical tradition in her family. But her name was now on the *Yachting Monthly* masthead as an 'associate editor' with Griffiths and Clackson, and she wasn't going to slip back to being the secretary again.

One of the contributors who had not hurried away at the beginning of the war was Jack Jones. As an industrial engineer he was in a reserved occupation so wasn't called up until 1941, when the need for men at sea became acute. For the first two years of Kathleen's editorship, he helped fill the pages by writing contentious articles about yacht design under a pseudonym, then answering himself on the letters page and fanning any ensuing nerdy controversy until sometimes the editor had to announce 'This correspondence is now closed' or remind people that pseudonyms shouldn't be a cover for personal attack. Jack was quite badly wounded and was demobilised early, desperately keen to develop his career as a naval architect. Maurice Griffiths commissioned him to design a simple 'sharpie' for *Yachting Monthly* readers: the first one, *Willow Wren*, went to Kathleen, who was photographed sailing it in the relatively sheltered waters near Broxbourne.

As her confidence grew, Kathleen moved *Willow Wren* to the River Crouch, where she competed in handicap races. She then decided to focus on class racing, bought a Snipe named *Comet* (No. 7401) and moved on again to Medway YC at Upnor, where she raced with another lady member as her crew. Covering the male-only 1948 Olympic sailing events for the magazine was a significant advance and she kept a personal scrapbook of her time in Torquay. She also managed to express her outrage at the decision of the International Olympic Committee to exclude women sailors. No matter that they had competed in every games from 1900 to 1936, or that the French sailor Virginie Hériot had won gold in Amsterdam in 1928, the IOC president insisted that women sailors did not have 'permission'.[2]

In 1951/52 Kathleen had a new, lighter Snipe built (*Gallinago* No. 8856). By now she was not just competing but winning. Nephew Ian, now 18, regularly joined her as crew:

> *She was a very focussed skipper, and my problem was that another lady Snipe skipper always had young girl rangers as crew on her boat. So, on days of light winds, I was often chastised by my skipper for chatting to these*

young girls as we sailed gently past. I could not really complain though as we became 'the boat to beat' thanks to Kathleen's skill and determination.[3]

* * *

Post-war photographs of Kathleen sailing were frequently the work of Eileen Ramsey – 'the queen of British yachting photography'. Her story, as told by Barry Pickthall, is also one of wartime opportunity. Her career began in 1937 as a receptionist to the well-known photographer Gilbert Adams. His was a third-generation family business with studios in London, Reading and Southampton and an extensive staff. As war approached, Adams worried about the future. Rather than risk closing down, he gave each staff member a camera and told them to go out and take some 'interesting' photographs. The one to come back with the best pictures would take over the studio during the war.[4] Eileen won and duly took over. It wasn't easy. She had much to learn on the technical side and materials were hard to get. She developed her talent in portrait photography – men in uniform and wives left behind – and was well supported by Adams' chief technician, George Spiers, who became her partner.

After the war Eileen and George set up their own studio, first in Chelsea and then in Hamble as Eileen's flair for photography on the water became apparent. She had a little previous experience of sailing when she'd worked as a nanny after leaving school and developed an individual photography style that made impressionistic use of the reflections on the water. She used angles to convey a sense of movement, rather than the conventional side-on boat portrait style associated with companies such as Beken of Cowes. She and George bought a motor launch from which Eileen leant out dangerously to take water-level photographs of her subjects. Barry Pickthall reports that she lost a lot of cameras this way.[5]

People evidently liked Eileen. Some, like Uffa Fox and Max Aitken, tried hard to seduce her. Her friendship with the notoriously difficult Sheila Chichester ensured her unique access to Francis Chichester's *Gypsy Moth* yachts during the 1960s when his exploits were inspiring millions of people. Eileen was rare in becoming a household name within the male-dominated world of yachting. 'I don't know why,' she said. 'Perhaps it was because I wore the right shoes and didn't interfere.' She was also tough: 'Don't let anyone tell you that women can't make their own way in business. I always did and it got me to places that male photographers would have given their right arms to have been.'[6]

* * *

Ingrid Bianchi was another woman whose later career was shaped by her wartime experience. She graduated in 1941 with first class honours in economics from University College London (UCL), worked briefly as a statistician, then answered an advertisement from the WAAF to train as a meteorologist. She subsequently worked until 1946 as an officer-weather forecaster, lecturing and briefing aircrews. As so often, there seemed no opportunity for her to use her skills in peacetime, so she took a job in publicity. In 1948 she married Garth Holford, a member of the Thames SC. In a later booklet, written for the club, she thanks him for getting her interested in sailing 'against all the odds'.[7] Among the discouraging factors may have been the regulations of the club itself: only members could helm, and no ladies were admitted unless they could already sail.

It did not take very long after the war for women to obtain full club membership of the Thames SC, though Ingrid records 'considerable opposition from the traditionalists'. Once in, however, women were still restricted: central club areas, such as the bar, were out of bounds to them. Until 1952 they were served drinks through a separating hatch. But then children came too, 'because there were no nursemaids to leave them with'. The children began to sail cadet dinghies and the new availability of lightweight trailers and road transport meant that whole fleets and families could take to the roads at weekends to compete, or simply sail, in different areas. While her children were young, Ingrid managed to persuade *Yachting Monthly* to begin publishing her specialist articles on the weather. She also contributed more general articles such as ways of lifting to minimise back strain and on the importance of acknowledging fear, especially in young people. These add quite a new tone to the magazine. In the 1970s, her children a little older, she started writing books, beginning with *Interpreting the Weather* (1973), as well as weather guides for yachtsmen and pilots. She gave talks on BBC Radio and worked for Southern Television as a standby forecaster.

* * *

Even in wartime, however, there remained stupid wastage of women's skills solely on the grounds of gender. This was nothing new. Jo Stanley's book *From Cabin 'Boys' to Captains* (2016) has numerous examples of pioneering women failing to gain acceptance on British ships so either being forced to settle for less skilled work or join other nations. Suffragette Jessie Kenney (b. 1887), who qualified as a radio officer in 1923, could only find work as a stewardess.

Outstanding marine engineer Victoria Drummond had been able to follow her talent and complete an apprenticeship with the support of her well-connected family. She had worked in Clyde shipyards and had made four voyages to Australia and one to China as tenth engineer on the Blue Funnel line's *Anchises*. In 1926 she passed her second engineer exams to become Britain's first certificated woman engineer. She couldn't find work at this level so accepted a fifth engineer's job on the British India Company's steam turbine liner SS *Mulbera*, travelling to East Africa, India and Ceylon.

The real problems commenced when Victoria began sitting her Board of Trade Chief Engineer's exams in 1929. From then until 1936 she was repeatedly failed. Enquiry from a friend ascertained that this was solely because she was a woman. (The examiner said he always failed everyone else who took it at the same time – to make it fair!) Victoria lived ashore with her sisters but as war grew closer, she grew increasingly anxious to return to sea. Eventually she took the advice of a donkeyman friend, stopped trying for jobs on British ships and joined the Jewish-owned *Har Zion*. She was there until July 1940, working as second engineer with a multinational crew, mainly in the Mediterranean.

There seems to have been a pattern in Drummond's career that, while most of her workmates accepted her because they could see that her work was good – and some became her passionate advocates – there was always one who would do his best to make her life miserable. On this occasion it was the Greek third engineer who could not accept a woman senior to himself. Victoria left *Har Zion* a month before it was torpedoed and sunk with the loss of almost everyone on board. From there she joined the Panamanian *Bonita*, where her skill enabled the ship to dodge a 35-minute bombing attack by a Focke-Wulf Condor plane in the mid-Atlantic by increasing its speed beyond the theoretical maximum. The first mate wrote, 'She is about the most courageous woman I ever saw. She seems to be without fear or nerves, is very good at her job and has an uncanny power over engines, for which I once thanked God.'[8] She was awarded an MBE and the Lloyd's War Medal for Bravery at Sea. Her next ship, the Panamanian *Crixos*, was also bombed and machine-gunned from the air.

Finally, from 1942, Drummond began to gain employment on board British merchant ships, where she encountered drunkenness and hostility among the officers but loyalty and support from crew members, who at one point refused to sail without her when the ship's master was trying to have her discharged. She sailed on both Atlantic and Arctic convoys and her final wartime job was on a tanker, shuttling across the Channel to transport fuel to Normandy. Victoria, who was one of Queen Victoria's many godchildren, eventually made 49 sea voyages over a career of 40 years. Today she is commemorated by the Drummond building at Warsash Maritime Academy and the Victoria Drummond Award.

* * *

The overwhelming majority of the women in this book are those who had some money, education or social confidence to follow their dreams or grasp unexpected opportunities. Often, they were also able to write about their experiences. Emma Smith, author of *Maiden's Trip* (1948), offers her own fascinated glimpses of other, less well-educated women's lives, as she volunteered to work for the Grand Union Canal Carrying Company in 1943. Emma, born Elspeth Hallsmith, hated working as a War Office secretary in a hut in the grounds of Blenheim Palace. She felt confined, fuggy and that typing up long, dull letters was a completely inadequate contribution to the war effort. When her friend Eve learned that certain canal companies had a scheme to improve cargo-carrying efficiency by employing women, both girls applied at once, knowing nothing at all about canals or what they would be expected to do.

Emma's book is a creative compilation of her own and other girls' experiences over the two-year period that she worked on the Grand Union. They worked in teams of three, steering a 70ft canal boat and towing its engineless butty, typically carrying cargos of steel from Limehouse to Birmingham, then loading coal in Coventry for the return trip to London. Each circuit would take three weeks, the first two with a female trainer on board, after which they would be on their own: 'proper boaters'. Emma was young, uncertain, excited and on the threshold of experience. She felt a sense of liberation when she realised that none of her family knew where she was. Her childhood had been overshadowed by her father's post-First World War violent breakdown but she was supported by the courage of her mother, an ambulance driver from that war. *Maiden's Trip* details the hardship and challenge of volunteer war work on the canals and offers a rare glimpse of the indigenous canal folk.

The boaters of the Grand Union Canal were a self-contained community, to some extent insulated from the war, both by their inherent mobility and their general lack of literacy. Emma presents them as a dignified, uncommunicative people, where women in particular live a hard and limited life. They bloom as young girls, then exchange their father's boat for the boat of a husband. Their dowry is ornamental, 'lace curtains and brass knobs', but the rest of their lives will be spent in unremitting toil. Initially Emma found these women hard to differentiate – partly because the canal was like a street where the houses were always on the move so people could not be fixed by their location. Also the dark faces and plaited hair, earrings, black cotton skirts and leather belts of the canal women made individual identity 'perplexing' to outsiders. Emma found them frightening; they seemed so strong, so taciturn. She and her young companions assumed the women disliked them: in fact, the problem was complete mutual incomprehension. But this changed, mainly due to the surprising willingness of the boaters to accept and assist the newcomers.

Once they were working on the canals the young women experienced some of the racial hostility meted out by landspeople. They were spat on by children as they went under a bridge and pelted with stones, bricks, lumps of dung and rubbish. '"Gypsies," they yelled. "Dirty gypsies!"'[9] In fact, an overriding characteristic of many of the authentic canal women was how hard they worked to keep their boats clean. For some it was central to their self-respect and self-expression. Emma particularly remembered one of the families on the hard-running beer boats. These were usually crewed by men and boys because the work was so incessant that it was not conducive to a family life. The Foster family was different:

The children were always clean, the mother neatly dressed, the boats sparkling with brass and shining with scrubbed wood. She realised that the mother must have been an intensely self-respecting woman, self-proud, children-proud, house-proud and she understood how hard that mother must have worked to have kept them as they were.

Emma learned to understand that the deep frowns scored on many of the women's faces came from years of exposure to the sun and the wind. It did not mean they were all viragos, though some undoubtedly were. The young women had to learn to stand up for themselves as they made their way through the narrow cuts and tunnels and jostled for position in the locks and wharves. They needed to shout and swear and stand their ground if they wanted to earn respect. For the wartime volunteers, this experience was a rite of passage – they could move on; for the boater women, existence could be stifling. Emma's heart went out to 16-year-old Freda, highly skilled at boat handling, apple of her parents' eye but longing for the company of other girls and too ashamed to tell the young men she met that she lived on the canal.

Emma worked two years on the Grand Union, becoming a trainer herself, until she finally became tired of dungarees and foul weather, of the muscle-aching work of the paddles and locks, tired of always being tired. As the war drew to a close, she left the canal – as she had the freedom to do – and achieved her longstanding ambition to write.

Kathleen Palmer by Eileen Ramsey (Ian Palmer)

14

'I handed him a bundle of garments for a flare'[1]

Discovering courage

Ann Davison (b. 1913)

IN MAY 1949 ANN and Frank Davison put to sea in a hurry. They had sold Inchfad and most of its livestock, sent the ponies to live with Ann's sister and left, still with two goats and their dog. Deciding on their next step had been harder than they had expected until a chance conversation in a hotel with an ex-serviceman who was 'clearing out' of England encouraged them to do the same. They would buy a boat, live on board and explore the world. Leaving the island had been a joint decision: this next idea was mainly Frank's. 'I would stand by, suggesting, agreeing and hoping for the best as usual,'[2] wrote Ann. Her feeling for boats was still deeply ambivalent. On Inchfad they had chartered a small Clyde yacht, *Shireen*, for their general running to and from the shore. Loch Lomond sailing was made tricky by its multiplicity of rocks, shallows and islands and also by sudden, unpredictable weather changes. Frank had relished it; Ann had not. She hadn't learned to sail properly or built any confidence. *Shireen* had become 'a quarrelling point'. Yet when their year's charter was over Ann had discovered that she missed the little yacht: 'When she went, to my ineffable surprise, she took much of the fun of the island with her.'[3]

Finding the boat that would be their new home was not easy. In 1948 both boats and houses were in short supply and prices had risen dramatically. After six months' trailing around the country, they finally found a 70ft Fleetwood trawler, *Reliance*, built in 1903. It had been fished hard and was in a state of dilapidation but the surveyor, Humphrey Barton, thought they could make something of it. Most of their money

'I HANDED HIM A BUNDLE OF GARMENTS FOR A FLARE'

from the sale of the island went on its purchase, then the bills for repair and refitting mounted inexorably. This was Frank's project, and he was unwilling to compromise. Initially Ann stayed in their lodgings and was expected to get on with writing a book about their life on the island. She felt much happier when there was practical work to be done, though she was startled by the attitude of the local fishermen. She had thought she was used to working among men; the pre-war world of horses had been largely masculine, and aviation overwhelmingly so, yet she'd found no difficulty being accepted. Things were very different among the Morecambe Bay fishermen. 'A fishing port is almost monastic in its exclusive masculinity. A woman's place is in the home, in the net-making shops, in the fish-curers possibly but never aboard.'[4]

When Frank and Ann had realised that their capital wasn't sufficient to pay for all the work they needed to do on *Reliance*, they mortgaged her. There was then, inevitably, more to do and more expense than they had anticipated. By the time the work was almost complete they were failing to keep up the repayments. No one was interested in Ann's book proposal, and every scheme they devised to raise additional funds and ensure that *Reliance* would pay her way seemed to be jinxed. Eventually they were forced to take out a high-interest loan against a promissory note and try to sell *Reliance* privately. No buyers materialised. The mortgagees foreclosed and began legal proceedings. They found a skipper who was willing to take *Reliance* fishing, but they had been forced to give an undertaking that it would not be moved until the mortgage was settled.

Weeks dragged into months with no news and no opportunities. They became too disheartened to continue working, so *Reliance* remained unfinished. Finally they heard that the mortgagees had placed the yacht in the hands of a shipbroker. It might just make enough to pay off the mortgage and enable them to start again with nothing. Then the holders of the promissory note demanded immediate repayment of their loan and interest. If payment was not made, a writ announcing court proceedings would be nailed to the mast. This would end all chances of a successful sale. Ann wrote, 'It needed just this to push us over the edge of the abyss from which there is no return.'[5]

She remembered the moment that she was sitting, plugging away at a rewrite of her unwanted book, when Frank said: 'Ann, I cannot stand any more of this. Let's clear out.' She looked at his gaunt face and knew that he meant it. She realised she felt the same.

> *I thought of all that lay ahead: the grubby misery of the law courts; writs on the mast; brokers in the ship; the ignominies of a forced sale; vultures swarming over* Reliance; *losing her to someone to whom she would just be another ship.*
> *"And not even to have a had a sail out of her," Frank was saying.*[6]

When Ann came to write this crucial scene, she makes it clear that she was a willing accomplice; that Frank would have gone without her but that she insisted on sticking together. It's also obvious that he was the dominant partner. In practical terms, this was understandable – he knew how to sail; Ann didn't. But she also presents a man terrifyingly close to the edge; a man who wasn't going to listen to anyone else anyway. 'From now on the game is going to be played my way. According to my rules. And if anything goes adrift, it will be entirely my fault.'

Regrettably, Frank would be proved right.

Preparing to flit was difficult. They decided on Cuba – then an independent, non-communist republic – as their destination, so they needed to prepare and provision for an Atlantic crossing. They sold everything not wanted on the voyage to raise money for sailing necessities – including Ann's typewriter and the goats. 'We saw them off on the evening train, southward bound on the Friday night and returned to *Reliance*, silent and heavy-hearted, haunted by visions of their comic worried little faces when we had tied them up in the guard's van. They were the last link with the old life.'[7]

They had planned to leave at midday on the Sunday, expecting favourable tide and benign weather conditions. Belongings were stowed and farewell letters written (though fortunately not posted). Then the engine wouldn't start; a crucial component had cracked. It couldn't be replaced, so would need welding. More delay. Rumours had begun circulating that they were preparing to run. Officials arrived with questions. Their feeling of tension ratchetted up. The deception was harder on Frank than on herself, Ann wrote afterwards. 'His was a most forthright, downright nature. Subterfuge comes easier to women; it is part of their makeup and I had learned early on in life that ruthlessness is the only form of defence.'[8] This was a comment

'I HANDED HIM A BUNDLE OF GARMENTS FOR A FLARE'

that might bear out Ann's cousin, Ann Eaton's impression that her childhood relationships had not been easy.

There was a moment of joy when they finally left Fleetwood, but the good weather had passed, and the cloud ceiling was low. 'I'm glad I'm not flying today,' Ann thought. Then, soon, they were enduring their first Atlantic gale. Time began to blur; the steering jammed, and Frank was almost swept overboard while fixing it. They were frightened and exhausted. Frank began to worry about *Reliance*'s ability to stand up to the relentless pounding of the waves, and suggested they seek the shelter of a French port. All that this idea achieved was to put them off course and bewilder them. *Reliance* broached when Ann was steering and a liner hove-to, seeing they were in distress. They had no means of communicating with her and were still determined to go on.

Ann's account of their three-week battle with gales, gear failure and disorientation is one of the most powerful pieces of writing in sailing literature – which is nothing to what it must have been like to experience. Frank's judgement deteriorated and they quarrelled bitterly over their likely position. Although Ann had no chart-reading experience at sea, she had learned to navigate her plane, so began to recognise Frank's desperate mistakes. They came close to disaster off the rocks at Land's End but turned a lifeboat crew away. Ann took over the navigation but began to suffer blackouts from exhaustion. A new gale strengthened into a storm. *Reliance* started to take on water as they were blown helplessly up the Channel. Strain, exhaustion, lack of sleep and nourishment led Frank to a state of delirium in which he not only hallucinated his surroundings but saw Ann as the enemy. He was distressed and potentially dangerous.

Blessedly, this episode passed, and there was a moment when Ann slept, and Frank took charge again. He turned away an offer of help from a fisherman when they were off Plymouth. By some perverse logic, the experience of his period of insanity had made Ann additionally determined that they shouldn't give up and go ashore. She was convinced that the consequent legal troubles would put him out of his mind forever. The wind dropped and they drifted across the Channel, where an offer of a salvage tow from a French fishing boat was rejected three times.

Reliance's story ended in Lyme Bay, embayed and helpless, her engine failing at crucial moments, her sails blown out, finally driven on to the rocks of Portland Bill in the dark of another gale. It would take Ann more than a year before she could bring herself to write of their full experience. Her description of the final disaster, the end of all their struggle and hope, is agonising to read. She gave Frank a bundle of her clothes, which he soaked in paraffin and lit for a flare. *Reliance*'s mainmast came down, her bows buried into the rock. 'And above the roaring sea came the terrible sound of a dying ship.'[9]

By the lurid orange distress light, Frank and Ann scrambled for their Carly float, cast off and paddled for Weymouth. Soon they could see evidence of a search on shore, of a lifeboat coming round the Bill. But they were pushed out to sea in yet another storm, soaked, frozen and virtually invisible among the spray, even when dawn came. Finally, trapped in the maelstrom of Portland Race, they lost both paddles and suffered the first of several capsizes. 'Hours dragged out in inexplicable misery as the sea struck with a sledgehammer to kill a couple of gnats.'[10]

In the notebooks and loose pages of typescript where she struggled to describe these last helpless hours, Ann includes some scraps of conversation and interior monologue, including a final (I would say belated and inadequate) tribute from Frank:

'Ann, you are a good fellow. I don't know of anyone else who would have done this with me. Or stuck it like you have.' It was the most heartwarming thing that had ever been said to me in my life from one who mattered to me most. This thing was my reward, a tool to be kept closed, something forever.

In the final, published, version this and some other passages are not included. Frank's final slippage into hypothermia, delirium and death is written very simply. She is holding him, preventing him from attempting to climb out. She is rubbing his cold hands with her cold hands when a final monster wave crashes down on them. She is holding him as the float is engulfed by the wall of water. When it passes, he is dead. 'Nothing mattered any more. [...] The fight was over. I laid my head on my arms and closed my eyes, engulfed in a blessed darkness.'[11]

As she lay in the float with the body of her husband, Ann wanted to die. She seems to have wondered about cutting her wrists or her throat but had lost her knife. So she attempted passivity, lying on the raft, making no effort to help herself, waiting to die as Frank had died.

'I HANDED HIM A BUNDLE OF GARMENTS FOR A FLARE'

The seas moderated; no more waves broke over them. Ann noticed a puffin swimming around inquisitively; her mind began to work again as she imagined what might be said of her and Frank if she were not there to tell the truth and insist on the importance of carrying on: 'to strive, to seek, to find and not to yield' quoting Tennyson's *Ulysses*, a poem they had both loved. She made her life-changing decision: she would not die. She ripped a wooden handhold off the float and used it as a makeshift paddle to direct the float towards the shore. It was another long process.

When Ann came to begin writing the book that became *Last Voyage* (1951), she used blue school exercise books. One began with a numbered list of things that had happened since the moment they put to sea. The next started with the moment that was almost the end of the story in the final version – the moment they realised that there was no avoiding collision. She shies away from describing the death of *Reliance* and of Frank, to tell instead of her own landing on the rocks, of being flung face down with the float on top of her, of the absence of Frank's body. She details the various stages of her discovery of herself in a cave, the careful steps she took to find her way to safety, her refusal to look back or think of anything other than each large rock blocking her way. 'It seemed that life was nothing more than a series of physical problems to be surmounted slowly and with immense concentration.'[12]

Finally, bruised and bleeding, she reached the Coastguard station at the top of the 200ft cliffs. There, on Sunday 5 June 1949, *Reliance* became the property of the receiver of wrecks and the press was alerted. Ann gave one interview to the *Daily Mail* from the Coastguard station on Portland Bill. Then she vanished. Her father was no longer alive, but she had a stepmother, Grace, who hurried to collect her by car and take her to a safe place.

This was the Principal's House at the Royal Agricultural College, Cirencester. Here, Ann was unequivocally welcomed, protected and safe. Her uncle, Robert Boutflower, the college principal, had been her mother's especially close and beloved brother. The college was solidly all-male with predominantly titled patrons – possibly the last place that eager journalists would think to find her. Ann was right to know she could rely on her family.

Recovering from such trauma was not simply a matter of rest and shelter, however. Ann was determined that *Reliance*'s creditors should be paid off – as she had previously planned to do from Cuba – or wherever she and Frank might have reached. She had no boat to sell, only a story. But initially the story wouldn't come. She was also determined that she was going to fulfil the other part of their aborted adventure: she was going to sail across the Atlantic, alone. She was sufficiently businesslike to realise that if she could also be the first woman to do so – as Amelia Earhart had done by plane in May 1932 – her publicity appeal and earning power would be hugely increased. For now, she was in debt, had no boat and had confronted the lack of her own sailing experience in the most brutal fashion.

She contacted a literary agent and told him her plans. He showed interest but evidently she was still too close to the horror to write about it. After trying for several months, she took herself away from the comfort of the Principal's House and went to work in a boatyard where, as she put it, women were about 'as welcome as Beethoven at a jam session'. She lived aboard a hulk and did whatever jobs were put her way – usually following the instruction 'work it out for yourself'. The job ended when the boatyard owners left to live abroad, but it had given Ann sufficient reprieve to enable her to return to Cirencester, write *Last Voyage* with fluency and confidence, and send it off.[13]

In a letter to the agent, she explained that it had been 'an exceedingly difficult and painful book to write' and that she had had to scrap all her previous work, then write without interruption. 'It is an extraordinary story, but it is the truth as I know it.' She sets out details about copyright, available illustrations, mentions possible interest from connections in America and hints at her future plans. These are still uncertain but will include preparation for some single-handed voyaging. 'No woman has, remember.' She makes it clear that she intends 'to go on leading the kind of life I have always led and write more books.' Then, swiftly and confidently, she completed her second book, *Home was an Island* (1952), the story that had been crawling out all the time they had been in Fleetwood. AM Heath did well for Ann, finding good publishers in both Britain and America as well as selling lucrative serialisations. The debtors were repaid, and Ann earned sufficient money to buy a boat, which would enable her to embark on the next stage of her dream – much against her family's better judgement, though, as ever, with their support.

'I HANDED HIM A BUNDLE OF GARMENTS FOR A FLARE'

The story of Ann's record-setting Atlantic crossing in the 23ft wooden sloop *Felicity Ann*, built by Mashford Brothers at the Cremyll Shipyard in Cornwall, is well-known – and best told by herself, as she does in *My Ship is So Small* (1956). Richard King, author of *Sailing Alone* (2023), has described it as 'One of the most artistic and most thoughtful and surreptitiously poetic narratives ever penned by a solo sailor.' It's often very funny. The mistakes she makes early in the voyage are egregious. 'Ann, take in your jibsheet!' shouts Sid Mashford as she sails past the aircraft carrier HMS *Eagle* with her staysail flapping, not even seeing the enormous vessel. When her bilge pumps are blocked and her little yacht is slowly sinking, she is too frightened to unblock them – or even bail the water out of the cabin. Initially she is almost paralysed with fear: of the wind, of the sea, of the ship, of changing the sails, of stopping the engine and not being able to start it again. Ann is honest, even when she's not being honest. Assessing her own interview technique, she said, 'Although it pays to tell the truth, it rarely pays to tell the whole truth, so I went on giving the stock answers as convincingly as I could.'[14]

The whole truth was that, although she had put considerable thought into preparing and provisioning her boat, and had done her best to learn navigation, Ann had spent very little time improving her sailing skills. She needed people to believe that she was capable of undertaking the voyage, because she was going to have to do it anyway. Wonky logic persuaded her that she couldn't risk asking for help, because once anyone discovered the extent of her inexperience, her confidence would be dashed – but she would still have to go, because she had committed herself. Ann left Plymouth in May 1952 and ended her voyage in New York in November 1953. She was late arriving at almost all her stopping points and was deeply grateful for the help and friendship she encountered and for the fine qualities of her small ship.

My Ship is So Small is not a book she could have written if Frank had not died – and that doesn't just mean that she would have had no need to undertake this personal challenge. Sailing solo takes her a world away from the woman whom she previously portrayed 'suggesting, agreeing and hoping for the best as usual', to a person who has discovered 'courage as the key to living'.[15]

Reliance *finally breaks on the rocks near Portland Bill (Ann Eaton/Simon Kiln)*

Ann Davison and Felicity Ann *outside the New York Boat Show, January 1954 (Ann Eaton/Simon Kiln)*

15

'With my best suspender belt'[1]
Adapting to the post-war world

Rozelle Pierrepont/Beattie (b. 1925); Janet Rushbury/Bradford/
Vera-Sanso (b. 1928); Susan Hiscock (b. 1913); Mary Dixon (b. 1905)

DEMOBBED FROM THE WRENS in 1946 and returned either to her parents' home in Kensington or to Thoresby Hall, surrounded by the Nottinghamshire coal fields and Sherwood Forest, Rozelle Pierrepont, now aged 20, set herself to studying navigation and working for her Yachtmaster Coastal Certificate by correspondence. The rare occasions when she'd been allowed to take the helm of the various pinnaces or requisitioned motorboats running around Southampton Water had thrilled and inspired her. She needed to get back to sea as soon as possible. Her friends Sue and Winkle felt the same – as no doubt did many other reluctantly beached Wrens. An advertisement in the *Little Ship Club Journal* reads 'Ex-Wren member would greatly appreciate any opportunity of crewing or helping other members with fitting out etc. Able to cook.' Is there a note of desperation here? Such appeals were all very well when advertising in the Little Ship Club, when replies could be filtered through the secretary, but might be open to exploitation in the wider world. When Rozelle found a small ad in the back pages of *Yachting Monthly* asking for former Boat Crew Wrens to work for £1 a week as deckhands on a yacht heading for the Mediterranean, she and her friends assumed their dreams were coming true. They applied at once.

Rozelle's father, Gervase, Earl Manvers, was less impressed. He began investigating the yachtowners' background and discovered he was an undischarged bankrupt attempting to avoid his creditors. Rozelle, Sue and Winkle signed on anyway.

The three-week trial cruise to the Channel Islands was a miserable experience. The work was hard, the food poor, the owner dangerously incompetent, the atmosphere unpleasant. None of these things would have deterred Rozelle. Unfortunately Gervase had asked his friend, Sir Alexander Coutanche, the Governor of Jersey, to invite Rozelle to dine at Government House as soon as the yacht arrived, and to make her aware of the sordid, probably criminal, nature of her employer's past activities. Rozelle was so in love with the sea that she would have taken no notice. Her employers, not liking the attention, sacked her. Rozelle later wrote:

We had a calm grey voyage back to England, but for me it passed in a blurred haze of misery. I had gone to sea with my two certificates and a puffed-up opinion of my own value aboard a boat; and here was I three weeks later, the only one to get the sack. And it wasn't as if I hadn't tried ... [2]

The single positive outcome of the adventure was its effect on her parents – particularly her mother. "'If the child had a boat of her own," my mother suggested tentatively, "it might perhaps settle her and stop her going off on all those very undesirable voyages in other people's boats?"'[3]

For anyone who has read *Maid Matelot*, Rozelle's account of her Wren service, this volte-face seems astonishing. In the earlier book Rozelle portrays her mother as relentlessly concerned with ensuring she meets Nice Young Men and finds Suitable Partners and there are several incidents in that book where Rozelle, a naturally honest person, feels obliged to deceive the countess about the exact nature of her work and the company she keeps. Both Rozelle's older sister and brother had died as children (aged ten and four respectively) so it's easy to feel sympathy with her mother's protectiveness, though less so with the attitudes that led her to try to insist that Rozelle should be a part of the debutante social scene and upper-class marriage market. Rozelle successfully resisted a London Season but was frequently torn between her desperate need for independence and her duty as her parents' only surviving child and future inheritor of the Pierrepont estate. Time on the water was vital for her personal survival.

Though the family was rich in property, they were not well-off for spending money. The small, converted ship's lifeboat that Rozelle and her mother went to view in West Mersea – and bought just as soon as the owner could be persuaded to sell – was paid for by Rozelle herself from a small, lucky legacy and as a 21st birthday present from her parents. Its maintenance and management were her responsibility and her account of her naive adventures – despite her wartime experience and that coastal navigation certificate – makes alarming reading. One can only hope she kept the details secret from her parents.

She and her little motor yacht, *Imp*, started quietly enough, motoring on the upper reaches of the Thames and going for cruises in company with members of the Hurlingham YC, but Rozelle was soon attempting Channel crossings, either alone or with one of her ex-Wren friends or any trusting female relative she could persuade to accompany her. '*Ou est le capitaine?*' asked bewildered French fishermen as these cheerful young women arrived in their harbours, pumping their small and leaky boat. Arrival itself was a triumph. On Rozelle's first attempt to leave England she and Winkle were no sooner out of sight of land – with a brisk breeze steadily freshening – than they discovered they had lost the rudder blade. Winkle tipped them out a tot of rum each, then Rozelle swung into action:

Inspired by the sight of the bread knife rolling about on the cabin floor, I seized a section of the engine casing with trembling hands and sawed out a rectangular panel of wood: then I hung over the stern, with Winkle gripping my ankles, and after what seemed a very long time I succeeded in marrying the new piece of wood to the jagged remnants of the rudder with my best suspender belt, held rigidly in position by some strong codline lashings.[4]

Over the next few years Rozelle and her friends experienced fun and fear in varying proportions until finally *Imp* – which had an unreliable engine and only a rag of sail – was driven ashore in a gale and wrecked on the Belgian coast with Rozelle and Winkle unable to prevent disaster. Though *Imp* was eventually salvaged, and Rozelle brought her back to Dover (on her own in rough sea and poor visibility), the experience had been scarring. She was left with nightmares about being helpless in gale-force winds. Belatedly she realised that she should stop relying on an engine and learn to sail properly. She decided to buy a yacht.

It was about this time that her father died, and she inherited the Pierrepont estate. She also had a job in London. This time she could make a much more careful choice. She spent a year searching, then fell in love with the engineless folkboat *Martha McGilda*, built in 1953 and costing £950, owned by racing yachtsman Noel Jordan. He was looking for a larger vessel but had recently won the East Anglian Offshore Racing Championship with *Martha* and was prepared to teach Rozelle how to sail her. His advice on sail handling and general seamanship was invaluable. Jordan died unexpectedly soon from a heart attack, but Rozelle kept *Martha* for the rest of her life. She sometimes felt she could hear his voice in her head, warning her of danger or helping her make better decisions.

Meanwhile, she had also, somewhat inexplicably, married. Major Alexander Montgomerie Greaves Beattie had no interest in the sea but may initially have seemed to fulfil her mother's criteria as a Suitable Partner and a Nice Young Man. He had served in the Coldstream Guards during the Second World War and was now an artist. His nickname was 'Sweetie' and he was almost certainly gay, an uncomfortable identity then. Alexander is remembered as a kindly person. Friends who knew them both say Rozelle had remained sexually innocent, despite all the young men she'd danced and drunk rum with during the war, and was unlikely to have realised this fundamental incompatibility. She was probably hoping for someone to help her with the task of managing Thoresby Hall and its estates as her inheritance loomed.

Alexander decided that the house should be opened to the public. In 1957 he invited glamour model 'Sabrina' to stay overnight as a publicity stunt. Sabrina (Norma Sykes) was well-known as a dumb blonde with a large bust and tiny waist. Actors in the highly popular *Goon Show* often swore 'by the measurements of Sabrina'. At Thoresby, she dressed as Maid Marian and was photographed ostensibly showing off the features of the house – though judging from the cut of her costume these were not the main features on display. It's difficult to think of anything that Rozelle would have found less congenial. There's no hint of any public disagreement with Alexander. She just went sailing further and more frequently. She was usually alone, as most of her friends and cousins had also married and had families whom they were not quite so desperate to flee. She bought *Martha* an outboard motor, kept her at Dover, where she had a small lighthouse cottage, and left England for France or the Netherlands as often as possible, to escape what she referred to as the problems of the land.

She faced a different set of problems at sea. The outboard motor was kept in a locker and only brought out and attached for use when lack of wind or an adverse tide made sailing impossible. There was no self-steering equipment, so Rozelle spent long hours at the tiller. Halyards or furling gear were not led back to the cockpit as they might be in many yachts today, so all sail changes involved dashing back and forth to the mast or foredeck, which was obviously particularly hazardous in rough weather. On one occasion Rozelle was knocked unconscious by a blow on the head from the boom when she'd put in a reef over hastily and left the boom too low. She was lucky that she was sailing into Nieuwpoort at the time. 'When I came to, *Martha* had run aground on a neighbouring mudbank and a woman pushing a perambulator along the towpath was gaping at me with a look of astonishment in her eyes.'[5]

Managing her yacht alone with long hours at the helm was one thing ('complete peace and happiness or gibbering fright and wet freezing misery'): coping with public opinion – particularly female opinion – was another.

> *It was not long after I started single-handed sailing that I became aware of the severity of public opinion about a woman afloat on her own. It was all right, apparently, if you crossed the Atlantic or sailed round the world on a tea-tray, with plenty of Press coverage; then, at least, all the land women knew that you were out of harm's way for x number of months. But what they quite definitely did not approve of was a floating female at large off the North European seaboard, within easy reach of a number of popular harbours.*[6]

When she reached port at the end of the day, longing to eat a tin of baked beans then crawl into her sleeping bag, she was seldom left alone. She might find herself interrogated on her nautical ability from a 'pusser' fellow yachtie who had remembered to lower his ensign on the dot of sunset; propositioned by a man with an empty cabin; questioned by police made suspicious by the absence of any male on board; or whisked away to baths and dinners by well-intentioned people taking pity on her loneliness.

Rozelle was undeterred (or possibly desperate). In early summer 1959, she gave up her job and set out to sail to Russia. In an article for *Yachting Monthly* she presents this as a somewhat casual decision made at a tea party. "'Where would you most like to go?' 'Russia.' 'How would you get there?' 'By boat.'" In her memoir, *The Sea Bird* (1979), she never mentions Alexander or gives the slightest hint of his existence. She merely states that she was at 'a gloomy crossroads' in her life and needed time to think. Hence sailing 2,000 miles to the Gulf of Bothnia in a small yacht with a Seagull outboard engine.

She had hoped to do the whole voyage on her own, staying away for as long as possible, but her mother, now widowed and living alone, was so distressed by the idea that Rozelle compromised, agreeing to take a break in the middle of the voyage and fly home to prove she was all right. She also agreed to invite a female cousin or a friend to join her for occasional periods when they were able to take time away from their own families. She planned to be out of England for several months and would bring herself and her yacht back as cargo on a merchant ship.

When she reached the Baltic she found the navigation and sailing conditions far more complex than she'd anticipated. Rozelle often describes herself as a 'sea-mouse' cowering at an adverse weather forecast or making nervous little scurries from one harbour to the next. Keeping to her timetable, and not giving up on the challenge she'd set herself, took all the determination she possessed. Her final approach to the Åland Islands in the Gulf of Bothnia required a midnight departure in freezing cold rain after seven days of gales.

> *There was no sign of a light from any human habitation or passing vessel, and my little harbour seemed the loneliest and most desolate spot I had ever seen. Inside the cabin the warm glow of the stove and the oil lamp made the outside world seem infinitely remote. Presently the rain began to beat down on the deck with a steady persistence, and I found myself thinking 'Now or never, which is it to be?' But I knew, instinctively, that there was really no question of turning back, so I leapt into action, glad to be fully occupied at last.*[7]

Finally, she reached Mariehamn:

> *a place I had longed to visit since my earliest childhood. For years I had dreamt of all those glorious square-rigged ships sailing out of that very same harbour and had sensed the romance which attached to that proud group of islands where the women and children farmed the land while their menfolk wrested a living from the stormy seas.*[8]

'WITH MY BEST SUSPENDER BELT'

She had been denied a visa for Russian waters but had bought herself a courtesy flag anyway. Her friend Barbara joined her for the final leg. They visited Moscow and St Petersburg as land-based tourists, were given a suitably supervised Intourist experience and took photographs of major sights such as Red Square, the Kremlin etc. Then they returned to *Martha* and sailed through the skerries of Eastern Finland as far as the Russian island of Suursaari (Gogland), where Rozelle briefly raised her flag before joining the timber ship that carried them all home to England. It was not long afterwards that she divorced her husband, made her regular home in the cottage beneath the South Foreland lighthouse and spent a summer working as an assistant purser on a cross-Channel car ferry.

* * *

Janet Rushbury felt a similar longing for the sea. Born in Chelsea in 1928, growing up near Long Melford in Suffolk, she was the older daughter of artists Henry and 'Birdie' Rushbury. Although there was nothing in their family background to spark any nautical interest, Janet's sister Julia confirms that she was obsessed with sailing from earliest childhood, playing pirates in the garden of their country home and building rafts to venture on the nearby stream. The influence of *Swallows and Amazons* was particularly strong in that inter-war generation of children who could look forward to a new book from Mr Ransome every Christmas, taking them into a different world of self-reliance and freedom. There was no one in Janet's family to help her turn her dreams into reality but among her parents' friends was RORC member RA Bevan, joint owner of the racing yacht *Phryna*. He took the time to help her rig a model yacht and explain the various warps and their functions. She remained grateful to him for the rest of her life.

Janet was intellectually and artistically talented. She was accepted to study at the Ruskin School of Art in Oxford aged 16, then transferred to the Slade School of Fine Art and was still a student there when she met historian Ernle Bradford, recently demobbed from the Second World War RNVR and finding it hard to settle back into post-war London. They married and began to plan a different sort of life, away from the stifling city and the nine-to-five. Janet joined the Little Ship

Club to study seamanship and navigation. In 1950, aged 22, she caused some amazement by winning the Claud Worth trophy for the highest marks achieved in the Yachtmaster examination, the first woman to achieve this. She and Ernle left England in the spring of 1951, travelling through the French canals to the Mediterranean on their Dutch boier, *Mother Goose*.

They were not alone in their flight away from Britain. Dr Peter Pye had given up work as a GP in protest at the imposition of the NHS in 1946. Inspired by Weston Martyr's book *The £200 Millionaire* (1931), he and his wife Anne went to sea on *Moonraker* and achieved a low-cost cruising way of life, financed by writing books and articles (though also with the advantage of previously accrued capital in their boat and their cottage in Fambridge, Essex, which could be rented out to provide them with an income while they were away). Before the war Anne had been the person who wrote articles for the *LSC Journal*. She had described herself as 'Owner of *Moonraker*' and her husband as the 'Ship's Master' (in its specialist connotation of responsibility for ship handling and navigation). Once they changed their lifestyle, however, it was Peter who wrote the books and articles, though he used Anne's journals. In the immediate post-war period it seems possible to discern some handing back of power from women to men. Perhaps this was in emotional recognition of men's more active wartime role. Perhaps some men, still using their wartime officer ranks, continued to assume a habit of command. I notice that the language used in my parents' first joint logbook (they got married and bought their first boat together in 1950) retains a whiff of pseudo-naval hierarchy that they fairly soon lost as they discovered who they both were in this new world.

* * *

As soon as the war was over Susan and Eric Hiscock wanted to get to sea. *Wanderer II* had been laid up and needed too much work to be relaunched before the end of summer 1945, so their first post-war cruise was with Evelyn and Roger Pinckney of *Dyarchy II*. Eric described Evelyn as 'the youngest old lady that I had ever met. She was in her eighties when I first met her and continued cruising to the age of 91.' Eric continues: 'There are some who say that there is no room for women in small ships or large ones, either for that matter, but Mrs

Pinckney is a definite exception to any of the usual rules.'⁹ (So why say it? one wonders.) The following summer, Susan and Eric experienced the curse of yachting journalism that is remaining on land to write about sailing when others are afloat doing it. They had had the idea of producing an annual, *The Yachting Year 1946–47*, which kept them ashore until October. It was a joint publishing venture but only Eric's name was on the cover.

The Hiscocks appear to have enjoyed a particularly harmonious and equal partnership. His preferred pronoun is 'we'. Eric is sometimes quoted as saying that he found the perfect crew by marrying her – a remark that sets my teeth on edge – but Susan didn't use that label for herself: 'Crews argue, we don't,' was what she said. Their division of tasks was broadly traditional. When they set out on their first long cruise in May 1950 down the Atlantic coast of Spain and Portugal, Eric writes: 'I did the navigation and Susan did the cooking which was often a much more difficult and less rewarding occupation.'[10] He was also responsible for sail changes but still felt their division of labour was unfair, especially as she often had to do extra steering while he navigated. Their little boat – and Susan in particular – attracted attention in these very early post-war cruising days, as Janet Bradford did in the Mediterranean. Eric describes Spanish crabbers blowing her kisses off Cape Finisterre and French tunnymen coming to stare at this 'solitary auburn-haired woman out there in the wide Atlantic.' When Susan was on watch 'they came so close that the tips of their great fishing rods almost stroked our sails.'[11]

In May 1952 they set out on a three-year circumnavigation in their slightly larger yacht, *Wanderer III*. This caught the public imagination and Eric's account *Around the World in Wanderer III* (1956) became a bestseller and remains a classic of sailing literature. Books about sailing adventure sold well in the 1950s, responding to a thirst for adventure in a decade when personal travel was hard and TV adventure not ubiquitous. A new generation of women were inspired by Susan's quiet competence. Marcia Pirie wrote 'Here was a woman who played an equal part and without making a fuss of the fact.' Eric told Marcia, 'Yes, Susan does it while I just write about it.'[12]

It's noticeable that the best-known British sailing stories from this immediate post-war period, when couples went to sea together, were written by the man – Eric Hiscock, Miles Smeeton, Peter Pye, Ernle

Bradford, George Millar. Rupert Hart-Davis began publishing the Mariners Library in 1948 and continued until 1959. Of the 46 titles in that original series, only Elizabeth Linklater's *A Child Under Sail* (1938) and *Lis Sails the Atlantic* (1953) by Lis Andersen had female authors – both of them describing the experience of being children on their fathers' ships. This needn't have been inevitable: Anna Brassey's *A Voyage in the Sunbeam* could have been included; Mabel Stock's *The Log of a Woman Wanderer* (1923), Ella Maillart's *Gypsy Afloat* (1942), Winifred Brown's *Duffers on the Deep* (1939), Ann Davison's *Last Voyage* and *My Ship is So Small* were all available but were not chosen. The Mariners Library achieved canonical status and in books like the recently published *Sailing and Social Class* (2024) by Alan O'Connor, one can see it continuing to shape – and to skew – the idea of the cruising narrative.

Would it have been conceivable for Susan, not Eric, to have been the partner who wrote the book? Or Janet Bradford, Beryl Smeeton or Anne Pye? All of them intelligent, observant women perfectly able to put pen to paper, whether or not they had received equal formal education to their husbands. Belgian sailing wife Annie Van der Wiele, described her 'domestic circumnavigation' with her husband in *The West in My Eyes* (1955). Its French title, *Pénélope était du voyage*, neatly makes the point that, unlike Odysseus's wife, she had not remained at home. How would the British public have reacted to sailing adventures written by wives? Jane Russell tells of meeting Richard (his preferred name) and Mary Francis who had married in 1947 and began producing a hugely popular series of horse racing thrillers ten years later. When Mary was later revealed to have been integral to these novels, readers were shocked. In fact, they worked as an equal partnership – just as the best of the sailing couples did. Richard Francis said that he would always have liked to have seen Mary recognised as co-author but his publishers would not allow this. He compromised by privately considering 'Dick Francis' a pseudonym that covered them both. Looking at the shelves of books by men, and the overwhelmingly male nature of the yachting magazines where most of these writers first achieved publication, it seems that from a commercial point of view the publishers were right. Research into male/female reading habits, commissioned by Mary Ann Sieghart for her book *The Authority Gap* (2022), suggests that men have a clear preference for reading books by other men, whereas women will read either gender.[13] Yachting magazines of the 1950s and

1960s were directed at a male readership – even the increased number of pictures of women and children in the advertising columns was probably aimed at male rather than female purchasers as they were more likely to be making the financial decisions. Issue after issue of *Yachting Monthly* goes by with not an article, nor a letter, nor a review of a book by a woman. Kathleen Palmer is anonymous or hides behind her initials. Rozelle Beattie is a rare exception, as is Ingrid Holford, writing about weather. More female voices might have shaped the magazine differently. A surprising letter from an independently minded woman (Jean Barber, 1963) suggested that *Yachting Monthly* might run some profiles of well-known yachtsmen. She thought other women readers might enjoy these, since they were likely to be interested in people's personalities and motivations. She asked for comment. There was a crushing silence and, unsurprisingly, such articles never appeared.

* * *

A number of the men and women who left the UK in this immediate post-war period, either to explore the world by boat or to make new lives for themselves in other countries, did so because they were profoundly out of sympathy with the ideals of Clement Atlee's reforming Labour government of 1945–1951. Social services and the public sector were enlarged, the NHS was created, major industries and public utilities were nationalised, mass housing developments were planned and the new education act was partially implemented. For many people this establishment of a new welfare state promised new hope for Britain and an enactment of the spirit of fairness for which the war had been fought. Others – among them many lovers of life at sea – saw 'socialism' as restricting freedom, discouraging individual initiative and attacking liberty itself. The Atlee government also oversaw the withdrawal from Palestine, the creation of the state of Israel, the partition of India, and decolonisation of Pakistan, Ceylon and Burma. These were decisions that delighted some and shocked others. But not all those who disliked socialism and escaped to sea were old colonialists and not all colonialists disapproved of the transition from Empire to Commonwealth – Beryl Smeeton would be an immediate example. Suggestions that the increasing popularity of blue water cruising was nostalgia for the past days of empire are probably only convincing in an academic paper: adventurousness and an outward-looking attitude are more likely motivations.

* * *

Mary and Douglas Dixon are hard to categorise; politically right-wing, personally adventurous and also dedicated social reformers. Immediately before the war they had spent a winter living and skiing in Lapland (today Sápmi) above the Arctic Circle. Douglas had written *A Sail to Lapland* (1938) about their journey there and Mary would write her second novel, *Soft Falls the Snow* (1955), describing futuristic scientific experiment from the experience. She would not be on his title page, but he would be on hers. Lloyd's Register of Yachts shows *Dusmarie* slipping from joint possession to Douglas' alone. She was left laid up in Sweden during the war years. Mary had been 'immobilised' by a small baby (her daughter Astrid's words) while also working for the Ministry of Information and teaching history in prep schools. From 1945 she lectured in Economics for the Workers' Educational Associations (WEA) and the Cambridge Board of Extra-Mural Studies, then in 1946 was invited to join the Conservative RA Butler's Policy Committee, though Butler himself had just been ejected from power despite his ground-breaking Education Act.

This post didn't last long, since Douglas, who had worked as a defence correspondent at BBC Broadcasting House and as part of the Admiralty Ferry Service, was eager to revive his pre-war idea of offering British schoolboys sailing and skiing experience in Manno, near Luleå, northern Sweden. *Dusmarie* had been sadly neglected and Mary was needed in Sweden to help bring her back to sailing condition. Astrid, now six, came too, and the first expeditions – to train explorers of the future – took place as planned in the summer of 1947. Mary remained passionate about girls' education and girls' adventurousness. In 1950 she organised a girls-only ski trip in northern Sweden and in 1951 the two ventures were combined with ski trips for both girls and boys at Easter and sailing, for both, in Friesland during the summer. Occasional expeditions took place throughout most of the rest of the decade in Sápmi, Friesland, Yugoslavia and Greece.

Douglas achieved his personal ambition of a return to Gallipoli for Anzac Day 1958, sailing *Dusmarie* with Mary and Astrid as crew, then

Mary began the projects for girls' education that would occupy her for the rest of her life. She believed many girls were failing to achieve their true potential in the existing education system and they suffered from a lack of physical challenge. The sixth-form college she opened in 1959 from her home in Suffolk was only small but included ski instruction and sailing, often on *Dusmarie*. Douglas died in 1964, which left Mary free to follow her vision. A branch of her college was established near Montreal, Canada with expeditions to the Canadian Arctic. Then, in 1974, Mary began entering *Dusmarie* in the Sail Training Association Tall Ships Races, with all-girl crews and her daughter, Astrid, as skipper.

* * *

In *The Journeying Moon* (1958) and *The Wind off the Island* (1960), which describe their time together, Ernle Bradford makes it clear that Janet was the driving force in their post-war sailing partnership. His initial motive for leaving England was a disillusion with the dreary nine-to-five after the thrill and danger of his Second World War service: hers was a more visceral longing to be at sea. Exploring the Mediterranean and Aegean appealed to them both. The increasing difference between them was that he wanted to write about their experience whereas she was determined to live it.

Their first boat, *Mother Goose*, was an ex-racing boier, drawing just 2ft with traditional leeboards, curved gaff and an eye-catching tiller carved like a goose's head and neck. Her steel hull was painted blue, her sails a rich red. In the two-and-a-half years they spent exploring the Italian coast, Sicily and the Aegean, she'd proved both snug and capable, despite her shallow draft and leeboards. By the autumn of 1953 Janet and Ernle needed to get back to London, find work, earn money. They sold *Mother Goose* in Malta – but bought the former pilot cutter *Mischief* instead. 'She was my idea of a sturdy, seaworthy craft, built for work in any sea conditions. Her lines were sweet and utterly traditional,' wrote Janet later.[14] Bradford, too, was deeply attracted by *Mischief*'s obvious seakeeping qualities but claimed that the final goodbye to *Mother Goose* left him with a feeling of unease, 'as if we had sold our luck along with the boat.'[15]

Back in grimy London, Janet took jobs with the single-minded objective of getting back to sea again. Ernle, however, was discovering that he didn't hate London as much as he used to – he was glad to be near editors who liked his writing and paid him for it. He enjoyed going out and meeting people. Janet only wanted to return to their cruising life and begrudged every shilling of unnecessary expenditure that didn't get her closer to her aim. In the spring of 1954 she accepted an invitation to go sailing in Greece without him. She and Ernle then sold *Mischief* to the explorer HW Tilman, who was preparing to take an expedition to Patagonia.

Tilman had very little sailing experience at this point, so an arrangement was made whereby the Bradfords would remain with the boat, Ernle as skipper and Janet as bosun. She was the first and probably the only woman ever to sail with Tilman but even her love of sailing could not survive his inveterate misogyny. She and Ernle worked all summer to make *Mischief* ready for this new challenge. They found Tilman ignorant and opinionated but hoped they would get on better once they put to sea. Matters didn't improve. Tilman blanked Janet, despite her sailing skill and experience, and refused to eat food that she'd cooked, whilst ostentatiously praising Ernle's meals. They took longer than expected reaching Gibraltar from Majorca and ran out of bread. Janet found her friends Tom and Susan Worth there and borrowed a loaf from them. Tilman declared it stale and threw it into the water. That was the final insult. She told him, 'I was not a paid hand and went to sea for the love of sailing in good company', then walked off the yacht – followed by Ernle and the two other (male) crew members.

When Ernle felt he needed to spend more time ashore, developing his career as journalist and writer, Janet stayed at sea, where her bosun skills and general high standard of seamanship ensured her welcome on board other yachts, often with well-known skippers such as Bobby Somerset, Henry Denham and John Illingworth. Janet's career after she and Ernle parted has no public resonances but is perhaps the more extraordinary for the determination with which she continued to lead her chosen life. She helped found a yacht design and building company in Palma, Majorca and married an engineer, Juan Vera-Sanso, with whom she had two daughters. Neither the business nor the marriage succeeded, and Janet resumed her travelling existence. Now, if she was taken on as a crew member, she brought her small daughters with her.

Eventually she left the Mediterranean for America, where she used her gift for languages and her cultural knowledge to make a living

'WITH MY BEST SUSPENDER BELT'

for herself and her children as a travel agent and tour leader, also managing to purchase small vessels of her own. There was one magical year spent living in Greece, all of them speaking the language, until the two girls, Penny and Naomi, were old enough for boarding school in England, possibly at the insistence of their grandmother. This was hard for them, though postcards arrived from increasingly exotic parts of the world as Janet led specialised tours to explore different cultures. Both Penny and Naomi were intensely proud of their mother, but also knew that an independent life for a single parent comes with a cost for both her and her children.

As a sailor, the 1970s may have been Janet's happiest years when she bought a Vertue 100, *Return*, and took her back through the French canals to the Mediterranean. Her daughters often joined to sail with her. 'Where's the skipper?' was the bewildered question as people still struggled to come to terms with these adventurous all-female crews – just as they had in the previous decades. Some attitudes would prove very slow to change.

Janet Vera-Sanso on board Return, *Ionian Islands, 1979 (Anne Brownfield/ Naomi Vera-Sanso)*

16

'No experience necessary'[1]
Mixed-sex sailing, 1950s to 1970s

Marion Carr (b. 1932?); Jane Benham (b. 1943); Sally Hinchliffe (b. 1934); Penny Hughes (b. 1934); Julie Grainger (b. 1953)

MARION CARR DOESN'T SAY why she left her job as a secretary at the BBC and went travelling in 1950. She was just roving around, hitching lifts and finding work where she could. She ran out of money in Zurich, spent a night in prison and had to be returned home as a Distressed British Subject: 'defiant and not nearly as ashamed as I should have been for causing my long-suffering parents distress and worry. It says much for their forbearance that they allowed me without comment or criticism to return to the run-down little flat where they lived in the cold austerity of postwar England.'[2] She took a job as a secretary in a local factory and searched the situations vacant column in the *Evening News* for anything more interesting. Her eye was caught by this:

> *WANTED: female mate / cook for small coasting vessel. No experience necessary. Apply box...*

Marion wrote off immediately. She later discovered that she'd been just one of 74 other applicants. There was no interview. She was offered the job by post and told to arrive at a timber wharf in Essex, where she would find the sailing barge *Clara*. At that point Marion had no idea what a sailing barge was. She could, however, swim and had learned to row a dinghy as a child. She handed in her notice at the factory and went home to tell her parents.

Her father was horrified. In his opinion, bargemen were lower than street-sweepers. He told her she wouldn't last in the job six weeks.

'NO EXPERIENCE NECESSARY'

When she arrived in Maldon it was low water and the barge was deserted. She managed to get herself on board, broke the padlock into the living accommodation and made herself a meal before settling for the night. When the skipper arrived the following day, he found the decks scrubbed, the cabin spring-cleaned and Marion impatient to get on with whatever was scheduled to happen next. She would be a mate on *Clara* and other small coasting vessels for the next 14 years.

Clara had been built in 1896. She had no engine so was dependent on the wind and tide, on occasional tows from other vessels or on the use of warps, track lines and the timely deployment of its anchor. The sails and gear were heavy – the skipper would judge when they should be raised or lowered; Marion was expected to supply the muscle power. There was no wheelhouse to shelter the steersman from the weather and no lavatory. 'The method of relief was to draw half a bucket of water from over the side and retire with it to the fo'c'sle, afterwards returning all contents to the sea.'[3] She describes the physical toil, cold, discomfort and occasional stress of her new life – drifting downriver with no steerage way, then dropping and weighing the anchor just in time to swing the barge away from any obstacles in its path; entering a crowded dock under full sail with only her own quickness and strength to get the sails down and let the anchor go as the skipper spun the wheel to get them in position.

These were the last years of engineless trading barges. The 1950s dockers must have dreaded their approach. 'We were indeed an awkward customer with our towering mast and sprit between the two holds, and forehatchway inconveniently small; our great clutter of sails and ropes to be kept clear and the fact of having no engine obliging every movement of the craft to be made by the crew pushing and pulling by hand.' Nevertheless, the barge was met with cheerfulness and amused acceptance.

> *As soon as the dockers saw me on board they would yell 'Got the kettle on sailor?' We would bribe them with constant supplies of tea in the hope they would put their best effort into loading us as carefully and as quickly as they could. It would afford them great amusement to see me, with the skipper, wielding a sack hook, improving the stow in the wings of the hold, or on top of a stack of timber with a timber hook nonchalantly heaving baulks of timber, three inches thick and twenty feet long, into the required position.*[4]

Marion always worked in a skirt and jumper – plus duffle coat, woolly hat, scarves, gloves and mittens as necessary. She felt trousers would not have been considered decent for a woman in the 1950s coastal trade. (Emma Smith, working on the Grand Union Canal in the 1940s, had made a similar observation: while she and her middle-class friends wore trousers as a matter of course, the canal women never did.) Marion discovered how far an engineless barge could find its way up the shallowest creeks or lower its 40ft mast to slip under bridges. She learned the special smell of rat-infested paper mills, the maze of sandbanks and swatchways off the Essex coast, the inescapable dustiness of cement and the bliss of a roaring fire in a warm cabin when coming off watch. The sensation of being really wet, really tired and really cold helped her feel joy in being 'properly alive'.[5]

Captain Banyard, the skipper of *Clara*, was a well-read, independent-minded man with skill and a sense of humour, struggling to stay solvent as trading conditions changed. Not many years after Marion joined, he was forced to put an engine into the barge. This was a complicated and expensive undertaking, which, indirectly, finished *Clara*. It enabled them to take on a contract to deliver ballast into Leigh-on-Sea up a narrow, twisting creek. Marion's job was to stand forward with a boathook, marked in feet, feeling for the deepwater where the barge should turn with the channel. They fulfilled the contract for several months until one night the turn was missed and the barge grounded across the creek on a falling tide, dried out and broke her back.

Marion stayed with Captain Banyard through the ensuing workless period and continued when he signed them on to the *Olive May*, a large, converted barge carrying up to 200 tons of ballast, or sometimes coal, in and out of ports between Blyth in Northumberland and Par in Cornwall, where they loaded china clay. The *Olive May* was intended as a three-person vessel for long passages but, as the owners never supplied an extra hand, they took on young lads from various labour exchanges, most of whom found other work as soon as possible. Marion remembers one of them leaping ashore with his bag of belongings in his teeth and running for freedom as soon they'd touched the wharf at Redcar, at the mouth of the Tees.

Marion survived the hard conditions, rough seas, injury and near shipwreck for several more years until an accident in port – in which a dock worker was killed – put the *Olive May* out of action. Banyard then purchased the *Dingle*, a 'beetle barge' that had been built for the 1915 Dardanelles Campaign but was now lying mouse-infested and flea-ridden at the mouth of the Shannon. Marion helped bring it back from Ireland to Wivenhoe in Essex, where she worked on the complete disinfestation, cleaning and refurbishment of the vessel, including the installation of a marine toilet (this was now 1961). The *Dingle* then joined the ranks of the 'sandies', ploughing to and fro across the Thames estuary, carrying ballast from the Essex gravel pits, loading and unloading at 12-hour intervals as determined by high water. 'The sand and ballast quays of Essex are situated in awkward, hazardous and unreasonable places,' wrote Marion. 'There is not a lot to choose between them for dreadfulness, though each one is utterly different from the next.'[6] The berth at Alresford creek, off the River Colne, was apparently the worst of all and because the *Dingle* was skipper-owned and therefore in a weaker position than company-owned barges when bidding for cargo, the *Dingle* did most of the Alresford work. Marion remembers being trapped there for three weeks in the great freeze of 1962/63. Captain Banyard went home and left her to care for the barge.

> *There were always plenty of books on board and I had a radio. I usually had some knitting or sewing to do for I made most of my own clothes. Seeing the birds in dire straits, I used to scatter a bit of bread about though usually it was taken by the pigeons, those great survivors. Smaller birds had vanished and the ducks on the ice were dead.*[7]

The *Dingle* delivered ballast for the foundations of the M2 bridge across the Medway, and Bradwell nuclear power station in Essex. On one occasion she was loaded so deep that only her wheelhouse and mast were showing above the water. Marion expresses pride at the part she played in the construction of these (then) distinctively modern structures. When Captain Banyard retired in the mid-1960s she left the barging life and took no interest in the new, nostalgic barge restoration initiatives. In her memoir, published by a fellow bargeman in 1983, she mentions some of the new appliances, such as electronic depth sounders, radio transmitter and primitive automatic steering, which were introduced even on the *Dingle* – but laments the combination of increased regulation and the dying of the commercial trade. Perhaps in the new era she would have been able to apply for a mate's Certificate of Competency; she says she wouldn't have wanted one.

* * *

The foreword to Marion's book was written by another female mate of a Thames sailing barge, Jane Benham, daughter of Essex printer and newspaper proprietor Hervey Benham. Hervey was an enthusiastic amateur sailor who wrote about the working vessels of the English East Coast and was active in projects to preserve and repurpose them. Jane was Hervey and Barbara Benham's only child, and it's said that Hervey took little trouble to hide his permanent disappointment that she was not a boy. Jane was sent away to boarding school, which she hated, and failed to find a role either in her father's newspaper and printing businesses or in her mother's socially conventional female world. She struck some people as both unknowable and unhappy – except perhaps in her work with the young crews who replaced grain, gravel, paper, timber, hay, coal and (earlier) horse dung as the regular cargo for a working barge during the 1960s.

Jane went on to become co-founder of the East Coast Sail Trust (ECST) with barge skipper John Kemp and his wife Monica. From 1965 they took groups of a dozen children – ideally from the East End of London, where the former docklands were rapidly falling into disuse – sailing in the Thames estuary. The children slept in hammocks in what had been the main hold; adults had cabins. Facilities had improved since the old bucket-and-chuck-it days but remained distinctly spartan. The ECST concept was neither a straightforward sail-training, character-building exercise nor a school adventure holiday. Though it was all of those things, it also included study of the environment and awareness of the need to respect and protect the natural world. This was distinctively Jane's contribution.

Their first contract was with the London Borough of Redbridge, though later, when a second barge, the *Sir Alan Herbert*, was added to the Trust, cargos of children were accepted wherever they could be found – rather like the pragmatism that had compelled earlier barge skippers to take whatever loads were on offer if the money was there. The programme was called 'A Week in Another World' and it could be argued that this was as beneficial to the protected children of the middle classes as it was to those from the materially deprived London boroughs. Those children, however, were at the heart of the project as the reconstruction of the bombed East End and the effect of trading and social change on former dockland communities had flung families into unanticipated chaos.

From the mid-1970s, Rozelle (Pierrepont/Beattie) – by then happily remarried to GP Dick Raynes, medical officer for the London Borough of Newham, and living part of the time in Limehouse – would use *Martha McGilda* to give weekly sailing instruction, exploration and boat maintenance sessions to a group of troubled young boys living in care of Newham social services. These were her 'Tuesday Boys'. Perhaps this was some compensation for her own and Dick's childlessness; it was certainly a response to social conditions. Unlike the ECST project, Rozelle was able to build long-term relationships with some of these boys and know that she and Dick had made a positive difference to their lives. It was not all joy: one of the Tuesday Boys was murdered while sleeping rough; another went to prison; yet another had to be bailed by Rozelle and Dick to avoid this happening to him. Most were seen to have improved in personal happiness and attitude to life. A few sought jobs at sea or in boatbuilding.

Jane Benham's career as mate of a Thames barge had begun as Marion Carr's ended. They became friends and even took occasional holidays together with common interests such as art and music. Neither married nor had children. I accept I'm on completely speculative ground when I suggest that Jane, mate of a barge from the mid-1960s to 1980s, may have suffered much more innuendo about her private life, sailing with a male skipper, than Marion did in the early 1950s to mid-1960s. It's clear that Marion and Captain Banyard are congenial companions as well as workmates and she feels affection and loyalty towards him. It's also clear he has a home elsewhere. John Kemp's wife, Monica, another formidable personality, remained ashore with their four children but was fully involved with the practicalities of running the barge trust, as were Jane's parents. Yet from my perspective as a teenage observer in the early 1970s, helping at fundraising events and occasionally being given the opportunity to sail on board, the nudge-nudge speculation about Jane and John's relationship was incessant. Were they lovers? Was she hopelessly devoted to him but remaining chaste? Was he ruining her life by exploiting her devotion and running her as a second-string wife?

Or was she a secret 'lezzie'? The possibility that they were two adults of different genders working in a professional relationship – like Marion Carr and Captain Banyard – didn't seem to be considered.

Broadbrush social commentary would describe the 1960s as the decade of sexual revolution, starting with the 1959–1960 'Lady Chatterley' trial, where the issue was not the obscenity (or otherwise) of DH Lawrence's novel but the dissemination of it. 'Is it a book you would want even your wife or your servants to read?' asked Mr Mervyn Griffith-Jones, prosecuting.[8] The 'permissive society' may or may not have changed the way individuals chose to behave towards each other, privately, but it opened up many more areas to public discussion and speculation. This may have put additional difficulties in the way of women and men sailing together as friends. Some exceptionally confident women didn't care what people thought. Others may have felt irritated or humiliated by false assumptions.

The contraceptive pill had been available to unmarried women since 1967, but this didn't mean that all unmarried women were 'available'. Attitudes changed at different rates between different areas and social groups. In 1971 John and Marie-Christine Ridgway would insist that Nick and Julie Grainger (then aged 21 and 18) marry before they could come to work in their Scottish Adventure School as a couple. 'We can't have our school students going home and telling Mum and Dad that a couple of staff were just shacked up together.'[9] Looking back, 50 years later, Nick Grainger sees this as the gap between the north of Scotland and 'liberated London'. Yet in the 1950s Captain Banyard had felt able to advertise for a 'female mate / cook' for *Clara* and Marion had been accepted by fellow rivermen in her working role without, apparently, having to endure persistent innuendo.

* * *

Sally Hinchliffe and Penelope Hughes were reading Classics at Somerville College, Oxford in 1955 when they conceived the idea of buying a small open boat and exploring the Mediterranean and, potentially, the Aegean during their summer vacation. The world of their studies caught their imagination; they wanted to see the places whose ancient history they were reading. Penny had already worked in Greece as an au pair during her gap year and Sally had been one of Mary and Douglas Dixon's students, sailing in Friesland and the Zuyderzee.

'NO EXPERIENCE NECESSARY'

Holidaying abroad was difficult for many British people: exchange controls capped the amount of currency that could be taken out of the country and buying property abroad was officially forbidden. Sally and Penny calculated they could survive on very little if they lived on their boat and bought local produce. They also realised that Malta was still a British Crown colony so purchases could legally take place there. They wrote to the father of a friend, who was an RN officer, asking about the cost of redundant whalers. He suggested that a former ship's lifeboat would be a better buy. The two young women cycled eagerly around Oxford persuading friends to contribute £5 each, which would entitle them to a share in the boat and a fortnight's sailing in the summer.

Penny's parents were relaxed and supportive. She was one of five children of the painter Frances Bazley and novelist Richard Hughes. Much of her childhood had been spent in Wales, where she and her siblings were treated with 'benign neglect' and encouraged to explore the hills, ride, swim and sail the family dinghy when they were not being packed off to boarding school or to stay with other relatives. In many ways this childhood was idyllic, though Penny's youngest brother Owain writes of being stranded on Bardsey Island aged 12 for two weeks with a friend because his parents had forgotten about them. Penny said that being one of five meant that she felt 'dispensable'. Sally, on the other hand, was an only child and her parents were not at all keen on this new idea. They also wondered whether Somerville College would disapprove of the potentially mixed nature of the crew.

Fortunately, Sally managed to convince them that nothing improper could be expected to occur in a completely open boat with 18ft-wide side thwarts for sleeping accommodation. *Crab*, the double-ended former lifeboat they bought in Malta, was 17ft long, strong, shallow and somewhat reluctant to sail into the wind. She had two pairs of oars and a Seagull outboard, which Penny carried all the way from Wales. Everything they possessed had to be kept in the bottom of the boat and, as they usually sailed with four people on board, this meant very few possessions – one pair of trousers, one pair of shorts, a set of shore-going clothes and one pair of shoes – still leaving only minimal room to cook or move about. They had no sleeping bags. When it was time to go to bed they put on their extra clothes and lay down on the side thwarts, head to toe. Taller or broader crew members often found it more comfortable to sleep on the beach. There was no shelter from the sun or rain, apart from a couple of tarpaulins, and there was no privacy – which was especially tough when anyone was suffering from diarrhoea. In her account of their four summers on *Crab* (1955–1958) Penny doesn't mention how the female crew members coped with menstruation. Perhaps it wasn't an issue: stress, insufficient food and hard exercise are all factors that cause some women to miss their periods at sea.

Somerville College was not shocked. The then Principal, Janet Vaughan, was the first married woman to be appointed to lead a college and their tutor, Isabel Henderson, regularly spent her own summer vacations travelling to see the places about which she was teaching. Sally and Penny would have gone anyway. As Penny writes: 'In the Oxford crucible anyone who told young female students "you can't possibly do that on your own" was throwing down a challenge that simply had to be taken.'[10] In fact, the college gave them a small travel grant to assist research. Later, when Sally had graduated with First Class Honours and was working at the British School in Athens, she made a successful application to use *Crab* as part of a research project to investigate the feasibility of progressing against the north–south current in the Bosphorus in such a slow small boat in order to shed light on merchant travel in previous centuries.

Penny's father, 'Diccon' Hughes, joined their crew twice: once as a means of warding off official censure and once simply for his own pleasure and interest while he was slowly writing *The Fox in the Attic* (1961). Penny loved having him with them but was aware that he risked unbalancing not just the small boat (he was a big man) but also the delicate organisational structure that allowed them to make their own decisions and risk their own mistakes. This also happened occasionally when other crew members were young men with more experience and strong opinions. It was not until many years later that Penny and Sally read about the young women who had sailed that way before them.[11] Generally, the balance of confidence was maintained, leaving Penny and Sally free to make their own mistakes. They also benefitted from the generous help so often given to voyagers, especially to young people, and to women sailing alone. Richard Hughes commented:

> *This little boat is so unpretentious and friendly; people immediately react to you in a friendly way. They don't feel threatened. As they well might if you suddenly arrived in a gleaming yacht. I wonder whether when you get to the end of this four months of sailing, you'll find you are different people.*[12]

Robin, Penny's future husband, pays tribute to her skill as a helmswoman, which saw them through some frightening moments at sea.[13] Caught in a storm off the island of Lefkas, they were running before a strong following wind. Penny was steering, knowing that she must keep *Crab's* sternpost square to the waves or risk capsize. She was rigid with cold and nearing exhaustion. Robin was sitting beside her, singing to keep up her spirits; Sally was lying in the bottom of the boat; and Mags, their regular crewmate from Bristol University, was looking behind when she saw a fishing caique capsize and vanish. Penny knew that, by the law of the sea, they should turn round to help, but she also knew that they would almost certainly capsize themselves if they did and anyway, *Crab* would not be able to make any headway battling into such a violent wind. She held her course. It was a vast relief when they finally made port and discovered that the solitary fisherman who had been on board the capsized caique had reached the shore safely.

Robin had proposed marriage to Penny, but she was not sure this was what she wanted. She was seriously considering entering an Anglican convent and told him so in January 1958, though assuring him they would always remain friends. One final summer's sailing on *Crab* changed her mind. She and Robin became engaged, celebrating with wine, music and dancing in a cafe on Rhodes. Robin didn't have enough money to pay the bill, but the cafe owner wasn't worried. They'd put up all their prices in anticipation of a cruise ship full of American tourists. There was no expectation that the sailors in *Crab* would pay that much.

At the end of that 1958 summer *Crab* needed work and the Seagull outboard was finished. Penny and Sally sold the little boat to a fisherman then, in December, Penny married Robin and went to work as a teacher of Latin and Greek in a girls' high school. Sally became a highly respected Classics professor. Their love of sailing and of the Mediterranean proved lifelong.

* * *

In *The Voyage of the Aegre* (2023), Nick Grainger offers some inadvertent insights into 1970s gender expectations that he's too intelligent not to notice. He writes blithely of the sense of freedom he and his young wife Julie felt as 'children of the sixties'. He's complimentary about her intelligence and ability to learn – as well as the ease with which she made the decision to leave her university course and come adventuring with him.

He'd needed the encouragement of his landlady even to think of asking her.

> 'Why don't you ask Julie?' she said. Well, I couldn't imagine Julie wanting to do it. She'd never even been on a boat. And she's just starting a mathematics degree. There's no way she'd drop out to go off to sail the world,' I said. 'If you were Julie, would you?'
> She turned to me, smiling broadly. 'Like a shot!' she replied.

Nick continued worrying. Much of the planned voyage would be far offshore, well out of sight of land. For this he needed to master astro-navigation. He had bought the sextant, which was a start, but the overall process and calculations were still a mystery. 'Unfortunately, maths wasn't my strong point.'[14] It's one of those moments when you feel like shouting at the book. Some 100 pages and 18 months later, when they were crossing the eastern Pacific, Nick decides he should teach Julie how to use the sextant, work out the sights and plot the resulting position lines on the chart. 'She was good at it of course.'[15] The much older Nick, writing almost 50 years later, puts his readers' likely thoughts into words:

> Looking back now it seems extraordinary that from the beginning I had taken responsibility for learning how to use the sextant to take sights to calculate our position at sea. I had always been poor at maths at school. It would surely have been better if Julie who had recently studied mathematics at Warwick University, had taken this on. But this was the early seventies. Maybe this was just a man thing. I wanted to be competent at everything. Self-reliant as it were.

Julie, aged 18 when she'd agreed to join him, 19 when they left, was now 21. Some sections of her diary, included by Nick (with permission) show her feeling depressed and useless, crying in her bunk. There's an honesty about both the good and bad times in their relationship, which may be particularly appreciated by those of us who were young in that same decade, and who were perhaps also confused by the sun-warmed waters of liberation and the colder layers of unexplored assumptions below. Like all ocean voyagers, Julie and Nick were adventuring into their own depths as well as exploring the blue planet. She began to consider independent adventures; he dreamed dreams of his own. On the single issue of responsibility for the navigation, Nick's initially gendered assumption of responsibility was made sweetly more ironic as the teach-yourself book he had been relying on since before the beginning of their voyage, *Celestial Navigation for Yachtsmen* (first published in 1950), had been written by a woman, Mary Blewitt.

Marion Carr (Rob Kemp)

Sally Hinchliffe, Penny Hughes and Maggs Whitehead on board Crab
(Robin and Tom Minney)

17

'If I'm coming, I'm coming in my duffle coat'[1]

Women in offshore racing

Mary Blewitt (b. 1922); Janet Grosvenor (b. 1948)

ONE OF THE CRITERIA for the 2023–24 Ocean Globe Race (OGR) was its demand that navigation should be traditional. Rather than using GPS, competitors were bound to use a sextant, marine chronometer, almanac and sight reduction tables to fix their position. I was in Southampton, attending a taster tutorial for visitors, when I heard Mark Sinclair, skipper of the Australian yacht *Explorer*, give a simple answer to an audience member's question: 'I'd look it up in Blewitt.' Thousands of amateur sailors in the second half of the 20th century owe a debt of gratitude to Mary Blewitt, who applied her wartime RAF experience to simplifying navigation at sea.

Initially she had camouflaged her gender, following up an article in *Yachting World* in 1950 with a very small and simple pocket-sized volume, *Celestial Navigation for Yachtsmen* by M Blewitt. This was published by Iliffe at 5s. Now, almost a quarter of a century after her death, it's in its 13th edition and still selling well. Some of the younger OGR sailors learning celestial navigation for the first time welcomed it as 'a cool skill'; others commented that it made them feel in touch with the wider universe, giving a planetary dimension to their calculations. Mary's friend, master navigator and one-time novice monk Michael Richey, felt it had a spiritual sublimity. Mary's motivation was rather more prosaic: she was responding to a challenge from her father.

Mary was born and died at Boxted Hall, near Colchester in Essex. During her lifetime she travelled all over the world. After his First World War service Mary's father, Ralph, had qualified as a barrister, though he never practised. He was a keen sailor, a member of the Little Ship Club and the RORC, and founder of the Royal Artillery YC. Mary and her brother James grew up sailing dinghies at West Mersea and Burnham-on-Crouch, going on family cruising holidays to France and getting involved in Cowes week. Blewitt family life seems to have been intense, intellectual and argumentative. They also all – Denys, Ralph, James and Mary – produced intricate and beautiful tapestries.

Mary was educated at home by governesses until she was 13, then went away to Hayes Court, a progressive boarding school in Kent, where she eventually became head girl. Her closest friend there, Gabriele Ullstein, was the daughter of a German Jewish family and went on to study modern languages at Newnham College, Cambridge. She became a historian, author and film critic and married cultural historian Noel Annan. Mary, equally a bluestocking, did not go to university but directly into the WAAF. From June 1940 she served at RAF Duxford as a plotter. When she was 20, she qualified as a WAAF officer and was thus eligible to serve abroad. She worked as an intelligence officer in Alexandria, Cairo, Haifa, Algiers and Italy. (Her letters home are in the Imperial War Museum.) When the war was over, she shared a flat in London with Gabriele, qualified as a barrister at Lincoln's Inn and went sailing with her father.

'There's a much easier way of navigating than messing about with all these charts,' she told him, referring to the more straightforward RAF navigation techniques. 'It's no good just telling me. Write a book about it and tell everyone else,' came the typically blunt reply from her father, whose motto had always been, 'If you don't like the way I do it, do it your bloody self.'[2] The bookshelves at Boxted Hall contain a unique copy of the very first edition: *Navigation* by Mary Blewitt, rebound by Ralph for his personal use

Mary proved her navigation techniques in demanding company. She had taken part in the first post-war Harwich–Hook race in 1946 and joined the RORC having completed the requisite number of offshore miles. Very soon she had earned her place as navigator on top-class racing yachts, including John Illingworth's 'Malham' yachts, which set the post-war racing scene. Illingworth was an RN engineer officer, passionate about yacht design and offshore racing. He had been in Australia at the end of the war and had used the suggestion of a cruise to Tasmania to establish the Sydney–Hobart race, famous for its high winds and difficult seas. Jane Tate was the first woman to complete the race in 1946 and, as I write this chapter in January 2024, Irish-born navigator Adrienne Cahalane has just completed her 31st Sydney Hobart and has lifted the trophy as navigator of the winning yacht, *Alive*.

Illingworth won the inaugural race in his Australian-built yacht *Rani*. Then, on his return to England, he worked with the designer Jack Laurent Giles to develop *Myth of Malham* (1947), a shorter, lighter, differently rigged, essentially faster yacht than its contemporaries. It soon began winning races but meanwhile Illingworth had become commodore of the Royal Naval Sailing Association (RNSA) and turned his attention to developing a smaller yacht, *Minx of Malham* (1948), for class racing. As the 1949 Fastnet Race approached, he had left *Myth* laid up in order to concentrate on racing *Minx*. The smaller yacht had just won the Cowes–Dinard race and the crew were celebrating in the bar of the Dinard YC when Illingworth was tackled by an indignant Mary. 'My very dear friend Maria Blewitt, who had been crewing for me, said "You are a bloody fool to leave the best ocean racer in the world ashore with the Fastnet coming on us."'[3]

The race was only three weeks away. The champagne-fuelled evening continued with John agreeing to enter *Myth* for the Fastnet if American yachtsman Alf Loomis and Mary would sail with him. Loomis couldn't but Mary accepted his place as navigator, and by the end of the evening (or possibly the early hours of the morning) had collected a full crew for the race. Later there was a moment of confrontation when Illingworth, who was obsessional about weight on board his yachts, had suggested Mary shouldn't bring her large duffle coat. 'We had a bit of an up and downer about this for a second or two and she said, "All right, if you don't want me, you needn't have me but if I'm coming, I'm coming in my duffle coat," and so the duffle coat came too.'

She was sleeping in it as they approached the Scilly islands on the return leg when Illingworth felt uncertain of his position. 'Anyway, I shook Maria who turned out pretty promptly, with a few f's and b's for good measure. It was a lovely moon horizon and a brilliant night, and in about twenty minutes Maria had pulled down about five stars and we got a good fix.' With 100 miles to go they tore along with a fresh land breeze and won the race outright.

Illingworth often mentions Mary's straightforward, even confrontational attitude and also her bad language. He makes similar comments about Pam Ryan, another regular female crew member who had taken charge of the port watch for this successful Fastnet race. Swearing by watermen, bargees and other (male) sailors is accepted as a part of sea life, almost a convention. Women are assumed to be distressed or offended by this – which can then be used as a justification for excluding us – from alcohol-fuelled club events, for instance. Elizabeth Fairholme and Pamela Powell in their dinghy on the London River were grateful to the watermen for moderating their language when in their vicinity – and noticed that the gentlemen coaching the rowing teams didn't bother. Vera Laughton Mathews commented that the inclusion of Wrens on a naval base reduced bad language and improved behaviour. Traditionally it's felt to be additionally shocking when women swear but Emma Smith and her companions on the canals soon learned that shrieking abuse was an essential skill. Mary Blewitt and Pam Ryan swore as they pleased. Illingworth was also surprised that they showed no special aptitude for sail mending: 'Both were magnificent seaman and perfectly capable of skippering a yacht, and Maria of navigating it round the world. But they couldn't sew.'[4] Fortunately, there was a man on board who could.

It's hard, at this distance, to capture quite the flavour of this full-on offshore racing scene in the first decades after the war. Reaction to austerity was certainly a part of it; those with money were spending it, champagne flowed, and post-race celebrations were uninhibited. Gladness at being alive perhaps, a degree of triumphalism and a disregard of risk now that more obvious dangers had been survived. Post-war Britan is often considered to have been a bleak and tired environment but for these people and their new or newly fitted-out yachts, there was probably also a strong sense of release as they buffeted their way across the oceans to compete against each other. Illingworth once said that ocean racing makes people feel that 'everything matters desperately'. It's a good way of blotting out the more intractable problems of shore life. Mary Blewitt and Pam Ryan were praised as very good friends or jolly good hands and were expected to be resilient, tough, socially acceptable and possibly sexually robust. They may also have paid their own way, whereas Janet Bradford/Vera-Sanso would have been a paid crew member.

This offshore racing world was elitist and overwhelmingly male. Women like Mary with the skill and confidence to dictate terms for her own involvement were exceptional. The RORC, founded in 1925 after the inaugural Fastnet Race, had never included a specific ban on women members; nevertheless they remained rare, and rarer still in any position of power. Although Ray Pitt-Rivers (actress Mary Hinton 1896–1979), owner of the yacht *Foxhound* and first female skipper in the Newport–Bermuda race, became a rear commodore in 1957, it took almost 100 years (to 2023) for a woman to be voted RORC commodore. This was Dr Deborah Fish, a scientist from the Defence Science and Technology Laboratory at Porton Down. The first sailing of the Bermuda race, in 1906, had included 20-year-old Thora Robinson, crewing on board the 26ft sloop *Gauntlet*, determined to prove that if the sea was safe for amateur male sailors in seaworthy cruising yachts, it was safe for women as well.

Much of the impetus for the formation of yacht clubs came from masculine bonding. This brought the potential for informal but potentially high-level business deals. Pam Ryan had stormed off *Minx of Malham* after a row with Illingworth, then met and married Peter Green. Green was the commodore of RORC 1961–1964 and chairman of Lloyd's of London 1979–1983. He was immensely wealthy, implicated in some of Lloyd's' worst scandals and was fined and publicly censured in 1987, having been praised and knighted just five years earlier. Writing his obituary in 1996, journalist Godfrey Hodgson comments that 'the old Lloyd's in which Green grew up was riddled with casual favouritism and with a certain contempt for all forms of regulation'.[5] That somewhat swashbuckling approach is certainly the impression given by John Illingworth's memoir.

The RORC official history shows that the club became anxious about its reputation and the behaviour of some of its members after the war. It insisted that all candidates should be either proposed or seconded by a committee member (all male) – which would potentially increase its exclusivity – while also trying to make it easier for less wealthy people to accumulate the necessary sea miles by running a club yacht. It had the good fortune to appoint a really effective female secretary, former concert pianist Hope Kirkpatrick. 'If you stay here long enough,' Hope somewhat enigmatically told a younger successor, Janet Grosvenor, 'Your view of men will change completely.'[6]

Mary Blewitt's developing career would have the effect of opening up offshore racing to a wider, more multinational, more closely regulated fleet. Her books on navigation demystified the subject for less intellectual yachtsmen, and her later work both as secretary of the RORC and then chairman of the International Sailing Federation (ISAF, now World Sailing). The Racing Rules Committee brought greater clarity and honesty to the sport. Mary's intellect and personal fearlessness in the face of confrontation were essential qualities. There's a good anecdote of super-rich American entrepreneur Ted Turner striding towards the Protest room to lodge an objection after his yacht had done badly in a race. Turner was accompanied by a phalanx of supporters and lawyers, but when a junior official greeted them with the news, 'Mrs Pera's chairing the committee today,' he turned on his heel and left.

Mary's surname had changed, as she'd fallen in love with Italian racing sailor Gianni Pera. He had previously been married and, as a practising Catholic, was unable to obtain a divorce. So, Mary changed her name to his and lived as his wife, accepted and cherished by his family. Her cousin Charles states that it was a deep sadness for Mary that she and Gianni did not have children. They raced in the Mediterranean in his yacht, *La Meloria*, and helped develop Italian offshore racing until the nation was ready to compete in the Admiral's Cup series. This was a major competition, initiated between Britain and America, but extending every year to new teams and becoming rapidly more professional in boat design and management. When Gianni Pera died in 1969 with the Italian team almost ready to leave for England, Mary appointed herself captain and continued the challenge. She sailed as skipper of *La Meloria*, contributing to Italy's respectable fourth position behind the USA, Australia and Britain. Eleven countries competed.

Mary's sailing career was now over since she was suffering from rheumatoid arthritis, a painful, progressive, crippling disease. Her influence on the sport moved to a new level as she brought her mind to bear on its administration, working at the heart of organisations such as the Offshore Racing Congress (ORC), where she chaired the Special Regulations Committee. Her influence was crucial because she championed the development of the International Offshore Rule (IOR). This was a system enabling yachts of different sizes to race against each other. It had the knock-on effect that yachts from different countries could also compete against each other. At this point the ISAF had its first non-British president, the Italian Beppo Croce, while fluent-Italian-speaking Mary was head-hunted back to Britain to become secretary of the RORC. The new International Rule facilitated massive expansion of offshore racing, as worldwide certificates multiplied to thousands of boats racing round the world.[7]

Mary served as RORC secretary 1972–1978, published *Racing Rules for Sailors* (1997), then spent 20 years as chair of the Royal Yachting Association (RYA) Racing Rules Committee. From 1982 she also chaired the International Yacht Racing Union (IYRU) Racing Rules Committee and numerous top race juries and protest committees for the rest of her life. Large sums of money are invested in yacht racing, competitive passions run high, and the whole system of regulation encourages challenge and argument. Back in 1895, Barbara Hughes had commented that it was the job of designers to try to cheat the rules to gain maximum advantage. The racing mindset demands that every possible opportunity should be seized, sailing right up to the borderline of what is allowed. The legal mind needs to clarify these borders and enforce the rules. That was Mary's outstanding contribution.

* * *

Early in the 1970s, commercial sponsorship began making its way into offshore yacht racing. This posed an issue for an organisation like the RORC, still trying to maintain the balance between being a private members' club and a national representative organisation. It also challenged the ideal of amateurism – always something of a problem in the British upper-class psyche. As RORC secretary, seeing that this was about to become a complication for the flagship competition, the next (1971) Admiral's Cup, Mary took the neat, effective decision to bring in another woman.

Janet Grosvenor was in her early twenties. She'd lost her father when she was nine years old and had been brought up by her mother in Southampton. In common with many clever girls of her generation, university wasn't considered as an option and her career choices seemed limited to teacher training or secretarial work. Janet secretly longed to be a ballet dancer but once this idea was squashed, she chose secretarial training then went to work at Southampton University as a secretary. London seemed to offer so many more possibilities. In 1969 Janet saw an advertisement for a typist's job at the RORC and applied for it, even though she had never sailed in her life. A good reference

'IF I'M COMING, I'M COMING IN MY DUFFLE COAT'

from the university got her the position but her mother wouldn't speak to her for a week. She was appalled at the idea of her daughter going to live alone in the city and predicted she would never survive. 'I'll live in a bedsit and eat baked beans on toast every day if I have to,' said Janet, determined to gain her independence.[8]

The office was still being run by Hope Kirkpatrick, with Alan Paul as secretary. The atmosphere was intensely formal: 'You practically needed a chaperone to speak to a member,' Janet recalls. For many years lady members had not been allowed to stay overnight in the club, as the lavatories were at the end of the corridors and it was feared they might meet a gentleman member on the way. 'I think they forgot that these people might all have been sharing facilities on board a boat together.'

Janet worked there for two years before leaving to join the magazine *Which?*. It wasn't long, however, before Mary Pera was appointed secretary of the RORC and persuaded Janet to return on a project management basis to investigate the most appropriate ways for the Club – and the sport generally – to move into the new commercial area. Janet's desk was in Mary's office. Almost accidentally they discovered a shared sense of humour and became friends. Mary had a flat very near the office where she would invite Janet for a drink after work, where they could talk freely. She also invited Janet to Boxted Hall at weekends, advised her on her love life and insisted she should learn to sail and crew for the necessary amount of racing miles to become a RORC member in her own right. Mary invited Janet to travel with her and introduced her to other influential people in the racing world. This could be daunting, particularly when they entered spaces where women were prohibited. Mary took no notice of prohibitions: if she needed to be on the Royal Yacht Squadron balcony to start a race then that was where she went.

This was the era when women, even members' wives, had to enter the clubhouse by a separate door. Janet remembers how awkward she felt the first time Mary insisted that she accompany her into the forbidden space. It was the 1970s; Janet was in her fashion-conscious mid-twenties and had only brought two jumpsuits to wear, one red, one green. It would have been so much easier if she'd had a uniform or sponsor-logoed clothes. All she could do was dash back to her room and put on the cleaner jumpsuit, knowing how wildly inappropriate this was. Mary took a look and commented, 'I see you've changed from port to starboard.' The race was started; Mary remained on the balcony. Janet stood around feeling excruciatingly embarrassed, knowing no one and with nothing to do, until an elderly member took pity on her: 'Can I offer you a drink, my dear?' She packed more carefully in future.

When Mary moved on from the RORC secretaryship and was replaced by Alan Green, Janet remained as his deputy – which almost immediately made her part of the RORC response to the 1979 Fastnet Race disaster and one who helped facilitate the subsequent inquiry, report and recommendations. Later she became the RORC racing manager herself.

In 2019 she was presented with a Lifetime Achievement Award and made an Honorary Life Member for her immense contribution, both to the Club and the sport of yacht racing itself. 'I could not have imagined what a wonderful tapestry of a working life I would go on to have.' She's greatly respected, has travelled all over the world, knows that her work has made a difference, and is regularly, quietly consulted. It didn't always feel easy, particularly through the period when her contemporaries were getting engaged, marrying, having children – those conventional milestones of a woman's life. Janet was determined to continue her career but felt oddly uncomfortable that others outside the sailing world couldn't see that this was her deliberate choice, something of interest and value, not a second-best time-filler until she met Mr Right.

The crew on board Bloodhound. *Mary Blewitt in the front row, third from right, in her duffle coat (Janet Grosvenor/RORC)*

18

'Heather at the stemhead'[1]
Sailing from the Clyde

Emily Fazackerley (b. 1840); Seonaid Reid (b. 1972);
Elizabeth Todrick (b. 1914); Jean Wilson (b. 1914);
Irene MacLachlan (b. 1910); Katie Christie (b. 1938);
Anne Billard (b. 1964); Alison Chadwick (b. 1958)

FOR MOST PEOPLE IT'S not the sea but the particular coastline that shapes their sailing. Is it indented with rivers, fragmented into islands or stark with cliffs and jutting headlands? Does it have rocks or beaches? The land behind it matters too. Is it bare or populated? Are its people struggling for subsistence or do they have time to play? In the late 19th century Glasgow was the second city of the British Empire. The Clyde was crammed with shipyards, industry and innovation boomed, fortunes were made, artists flourished and yacht designers drew beautiful vessels for rich men while large numbers of people lived in overcrowded, insanitary conditions at risk of industrial injury and shortened lives. The healthier areas were to the west of the city and further west still were the lochs and islands of the west coast. Beyond them, around Ardnamurchan Point, the most westerly point on the Scottish mainland, lie the Hebrides and areas uncharted even today. Some sailors celebrate the first time they round Ardnamurchan by tying a bunch of heather to their stemhead.

Yachts were status symbols, as well as a means of getting away from the city. Some of the earliest female yachtowners listed in Lloyd's Register had their yachts built on the Clyde. Of the four women identified in 1878 (four out of approximately 1,225!), two (the

Countess of Cardigan and Miss EA Fazackerley) owned vessels built in Glasgow; yachts belonging to the other two (Mrs Hamilton and Mrs Leigh) were built on the south coast (at Cowes and Gosport). These were relatively large vessels: the countess owned *Sea Horse*, a 306-ton iron screw schooner and Miss Fazackerley (of Denbigh Castle, North Wales) owned *Fay*, a 65-ton wooden schooner as well as a steam-yacht. Emily Fazackerley was the first lady member of the Royal Mersey YC, to which she was elected in May 1877. There are plenty of stories about her personal eccentricities and her generosity to people in need, but little information about her interest in sailing, except for her club membership and the fact that she paid for one of her godchildren to attend HMS *Worcester* Naval Academy, which set him on course to become a master mariner.

The Coats family, textile magnates from Paisley, listed their company on the London Stock Exchange in 1890 for £5.7 million. Even before then, some of the women in the family had sufficient money and independence to enjoy yacht ownership – mainly of the large steam-yacht variety, in which they cruised the western isles with professional crews. In the late 19th century era, GL Watson of Glasgow and William Fife of Fairlie also designed small fast yachts for lady owners, such as Grace Schenley, some of which were sent south, others remaining to race in local waters. Despite these few examples, however, yachting in the Clyde area was still overwhelmingly masculine.

The Clyde Corinthian YC was founded in 1876 as a protest against the domination of yacht racing by large yachts with professional crews.[2] Its founders were a small group of men, several from the same family, and there's no information whether women were welcomed as members. From a somewhat awkward sentence in the 1976 club centenary history, one might guess they were not, though they were 'allowed' to race: 'If it was looked upon as bravado when the Club formed itself to provide races for amateurs; it must have appeared to onlookers in 1891 as madness when races were organised for ladies. Is this "women's-lib" really new?!!'[3] The first female commodore of the Clyde Corinthians in more than 140 years was Seonaid Reid in 2018. Seonaid was then in her forties, single and in possession of the 28ft wooden sloop *Malindi of Lorne*. These days she is married to fellow sailor Angus Spence, like Mr and Mrs Charles Pears, they maintain separate boats.

'HEATHER AT THE STEMHEAD'

Malindi was built by McGruer's yard at Clynder in 1964 and purchased by Seonaid's parents Ian and Millicent in 1974 for themselves and their four children. Millicent was Scottish; Ian was Northern Irish. They lived in Northern Ireland, so summer holidays were always spent sailing from one country to the other, which was a good way to gain respite from that period of Troubles. Seonaid remembers how surprised she was as a child to see police stations in Scotland without barbed wire.[4] Even local weekend sailing could take them across the border into Donegal, where her father was quietly advised to take down his red ensign but otherwise met with no hostility.

When Seonaid went to train and work as an accountant in London she didn't sail often, but her enthusiasm rekindled in 2003 when she crewed in the Round Britain and Ireland Challenge at her mother's suggestion. Her boat won. Soon afterwards she moved to Edinburgh, where sailing became more accessible. In 2007 she borrowed *Malindi* from her parents to compete in the West Highland Yachting Week with two women friends. They did well and Seonaid and *Malindi* have returned most years since, almost always with all-female crews, and very often being the only wooden yacht.

McGruer's was a family business, dating from the 18th century and probably earlier. In both world wars they switched from building pleasure yachts to naval vessels so needed to replace the male workers who left for active service. Elizabeth Todrick joined during the Second World War and never left. She had been educated at St Leonard's school (St Andrew's), founded as 'the Eton for girls' and previously attended by notably independent women such as Margaret Haig Thomas (Lady Rhondda) and Helen and Betty Archdale. She also became known for her 40-year ownership of the open cutter *Ayrshire Lass*, built by Fife's of Fairlie in 1897. McGruer's was a large yard in yachting terms. They generated their own electricity and developed a range of powered tools from early in the century. While this might have helped less muscular workers, Elizabeth is remembered as exceptionally strong. Local sailor Gordon Findlay saw her once, up to her chest in water with the bowsprit over her shoulder, pushing *Ayrshire Lass* off a rock while her two male companions watched from the cockpit.

She sailed engineless and very often alone. People remember her sitting, knitting, with the tiller tucked under her arm. Katie

Christie, first female commodore of the Clyde Cruising Club (more on her later), was returning from the Outer Hebrides one year and struggling to get round Ardnamurchan Point. There was no wind and their engine had failed. She noticed Elizabeth similarly becalmed on *Ayrshire Lass*. As the two yachts drew closer, Elizabeth held up an old-fashioned alarm clock and pointed to it questioningly. The clock was broken. It turned out that she'd had such a slow and solitary voyage, alone beyond the outer islands, that she'd not only lost track of the time but also of the day. As an employed worker she only had a fortnight's summer holiday, so this was a problem of some importance. Elizabeth had her last sail on *Ayrshire Lass* aged 94, and is commemorated via the Clyde Cruising Club's Todrick trophy. It's an impressive piece of silverware which is now awarded for 'an extraordinary feat of sailing of any kind' – but only when there is someone sufficiently remarkable to deserve it. Deaf circumnavigator, Gerry Hughes, is one such recipient.

* * *

The Clyde Cruising Club (CCC), founded in 1909, is not quite as old as the more racing-focussed clubs in the area. Cruising was (and for some of us still is) regarded as a solitary activity. However, not all cruising sailors are sociopaths; some like to cruise in company, some to race, more or less informally, and others enjoy the opportunity to swap tales in a fellow member's cockpit and share practical information about navigational hazards or sheltered anchoring places. The CCC is famed for its series of *Sailing Directions*. In 1937 Jean Wilson had been the first woman in Scotland to pass the chartered accountant final examinations with distinction – 'Women CAN count!' was a local newspaper headline. She lost her husband just a few days after D-Day. They had two young daughters and Jean was already fully involved in running his family textile business. However, she had enjoyed a happy childhood dinghy-sailing on Scotland's east coast and had continued as a member of the East Lothian YC at North Berwick. When the war was finally over Jean decided to commission a yacht for herself and her daughters.

Trefoil was launched in 1950 and named in acknowledgement of the Girl Guide badge. (Jean was a keen Guider who would become treasurer of the worldwide movement.) Jean and her daughters had much to learn: 'sail handling, mooring and anchoring, navigation, engines – all were complete mysteries'.[5] Later, when she looked back on her first season cruising, she realised that the weather had been really rough but, in her innocence of the Firth of Clyde conditions, she had assumed this was quite normal. She took other women friends with her and every time there was a crisis, she dashed below to consult *Sailing* (1949) by Peter Heaton. The following year she joined the CCC and went to their opening muster. As far as she could remember, she and her friend Margaret Monaghan were the only women there. She entered her first Tobermory race helped by former dinghy-sailing friends from East Lothian YC and won a bottle of whisky. 'The next year we achieved another ambition to earn our heather at the stemhead.' She remembered a long, wet beat to Ardnamurchan and then the feeling of triumph; 'James Cook had nothing on us!'[6]

Jean would sail many thousands of miles, anchoring in unusual places up and down the west coast and reporting on them for the CCC *Sailing Directions*. Her second husband, Peter Keppie, was also a keen sailor but died suddenly just five years later, at the helm of *Trefoil*, when he and Jean were approaching the start line of a race. Jean continued cruising and racing, often sailing with Girl Guide crews. Clive Reeves, archivist, former commodore, membership secretary and pretty-well-everything-else at the CCC, remembers Jean still undertaking *Trefoil*'s annual maintenance on her own until she was well into her eighties and sailing until she was 90. When she finally sold *Trefoil* in 2004, the new owner had to promise to always keep her hull painted blue, always sail her on the west coast, and never allow her to be sold to England!

* * *

Irene MacLachlan was born on the island of Luing. She didn't go to school but helped her parents on the farm and was educated by her mother. She's said to have been 'extremely well-read, articulate and with a rare sense of humour'. When the land was taken over by new tenants, after the death of her father, Irene had the job of rowing over to the nearby island of Torsa, in all weathers, to feed the cattle there.

She also became self-appointed guardian of the anchorage at Ardinamir, between Luing and Torsa islands.

> No one who has seen it could ever forget, after a hard sail, the sight of Irene standing on the shore on a driech July evening in full length oilskin and sou'wester, gesticulating wildly and imploring the entering yacht to 'keep over, keep over' to avoid the gravel patch on the port hand in a voice which could probably be heard in Loch Melfort. Should someone be too faint-hearted to do so and have the misfortune to run aground, she would leap into her huge heavy boat, with equally huge heavy oars and help the unfortunate into deeper water and a secure anchorage.[7]

She would also give them a good telling-off.

In 1949 a family from Dublin gave Irene a visitors' book and signed it. Soon it became a tradition for people to enter their signature and boat name whenever they visited the anchorage. By the time Irene was finally forced to leave the island to spend her last years in a care home, there were nine volumes of these books – a unique record of one small lagoon in the complexity of the islands. She had been made an honorary member of the CCC, the Royal Highland YC and the Royal Ulster YC and would wear the appropriate tie when certain yachts appeared. She also acted as an informal lookout for the Oban Coastguard. Many yachting people visited her in her last years in the care home or sent her letters and cards telling of their travels, but as the authors of *Cruising Scotland* (2015) state: 'visitors could not help but contrast the view from her window of a council housing estate with that from her little farmhouse at Ardinamir.'

* * *

Katie Christie is the only woman to have been commodore of the CCC in its 115-year history. Her grandparents had sailed on a square-rigger to Australia, where her grandfather Hugh McLean set up a boatbuilding yard in Brisbane before returning to Scotland, earning himself the nickname 'Boomerang'. *Myth of Malham* was just one of the famous and beautiful yachts that he built in his new yard at Gourock. His son David continued the business and Katie remembers many of the well-known yachtsmen and designers who worked with them there. It was a hard life – the yard still worked even on Christmas Day. In 1955 Hugh and David built themselves a Laurent Giles-designed Brittany class yacht, *Boomerang*, which took them on holiday every year. Katie's mother sat below, knitting – as Katie remembers most of the Clyde wives doing then. She wasn't at all interested in sailing, but it didn't seem to matter, as she was willing to cook, and the children were eager to help work the boat. However, when Clare Francis came to talk to the CCC in 1978, even Katie's mother was keen to attend.

Katie trained as a scientist and worked as a technician in the microbiology lab at Glasgow University. Her husband, Frank Christie, was artistic, running a decorating and furnishing business. After the death of Katie's father, they continued to sail and race *Boomerang* together. Then, after Frank's death in 2009, Katie kept the yacht for another five years, sailing with friends and family, until she realised that the time had come to sell. As for many people, watching a cherished yacht from a distance has not been an easy experience. Katie has never lacked invitations to sail with others and has continued to sail widely.

There were no other women on the CCC committee when she became commodore in 1996 and there are none currently. When asked why there is often such poor representation of women as flag officers in the more prestigious yacht clubs, her answer is immediate: 'male chauvinism' – though she quickly adds that she herself never encountered this during her period of office.

Anne Billard, only the second woman to be commodore of the Little Ship Club in London, despite its deliberate intention to welcome women as full members almost from its foundation, agrees with this.[8] Anne, who is French by birth, is a linguist who trained at the Sorbonne, and describes herself as 'very prickly' at any suggestion of gender-based patronage – 'Don't talk down to me!' – but has not found this when she has been working alongside men in her club. Perhaps the assumption is that once you're elected, you have proved yourself, though she also recognises the 'glass cliff' – a wider-industry habit of appointing women to senior positions when things are about to go wrong.

Anne is not from a sailing family but started sailing when her mother booked her on to a course when on holiday. She remembers the thrill of suddenly feeling why the wind direction mattered and thinking 'I could do this!' She begged for another week, then joined her university sailing club and made the most of those opportunities before moving to London in 1992. She has never owned a boat but has seized opportunities to sail wherever possible – that's one of the benefits of being part of a club.

So, why are there still so few women joining clubs independently? Or being elected to the top positions once they have joined? Is it still true, as Rozelle Raynes suggested in the early 1950s, that single women sailing may be regarded by other women as man-hunters? American cruiser Jean McKinney Long, writing in *Yachting* magazine in 1971, suggested that, to avoid hostility from other yacht club women, 'it's safer to cultivate a reputation for aloofness [...] rather than a lioness stalking all visible males.' She also tells a funny story of a yacht club manager on the Great Lakes completely unable to believe that she had come into a club by herself, urging her to tell him the name and club affiliation of the man she had come in with, but promising to keep it confidential. 'I've been a yacht club manager on these lakes for over 20 years and I know that no single woman is ever granted membership and I have yet to see a woman operate a cruiser.'[9]

Is it harder for a woman to penetrate a clubby atmosphere than it is for a man? Are the old stereotypes still invisibly reinforced by male-only features such as the club tie? On the water, there's now very little difference between men and women's sailing clothes (except that some women will say that their smaller sizes are harder to get – and relatively more expensive) but in a formal gathering the contrast between quasi-uniform blazers and frocks is very noticeable. Does this subliminally show the men as established and the women as decorative? We need equal but different says Anne. However, she is worried about the possible effect on women's opportunities by new understandings of equality where women claim the right to additional leniencies – paid time off for the menopause, for instance.

Captain Chris O'Flaherty RN, a diving specialist, faced the question whether equality should be a relative or an absolute concept. He was working to get the specialism 'clearance diving' opened equally to men and women. Candidates would need to pass a fitness test that included load-carrying. Should women be asked to carry a lesser weight?

The gender equality team advised that the test would need to be modified to give females a reasonable chance of passing, but I resisted that – each element of the test was designed to represent a practical element of diving that was not gender nor age related. For example, one load carry involves carrying 60kg for 200 metres in 2 minutes. The gender equality team told me that for females this needed to be reduced to 55kg. But a dive boat is 240kg and a dive team is four people, so if females could only lift 55kg, then three males would have to lift 62kg each. If a team had two females, then each male would have to lift 65kg etc. Against this explanation, the equality team, then realised what equality actually meant. [10]

The first time this selection test was run for a mixed group, two of the men failed and were returned to their ships. The two women passed. In 2010 Lieutenant Commander Catherine Ker (b. 1982) became the first woman to qualify as a Mine Warfare and Clearance Diving Officer. Only 5ft 2in tall, she wears the same equipment as her male diving colleagues, which is twice her bodyweight.

* * *

On the last night of our brief stay in Glasgow, Seonaid Reid invited Francis and me to the Clyde Corinthian's prize-giving dinner. She has completed five years as commodore and is continuing as secretary and treasurer, while her husband, Angus, is vice commodore. Our conversation during the meal with her and independent woman sailor Alison Chadwick was wide-ranging and fun. We clapped delightedly when Alison collected her large cup as best club performer in that year's Round Mull race. Alison isn't from a sailing family and didn't have any opportunity to get out on the water as a child, despite being brought up next to the sea. When she was offered the opportunity of crewing on a Sonata at her local sailing club, she grabbed it to try something new. The minute she stepped aboard she knew she had found her happy place. Forty-five years and three boats later, she loves every minute of sailing – the hard times ensure that she loves the good times even more. She's also a member of Oban SC and Royal Highland YC, the former being more race-oriented, the latter cruising – the best of both worlds. 'Being part of a club brings camaraderie, fun and a sense of belonging.' she said. 'It's a privilege to invite "newbies" (like I once was) and enthuse the next generation of sailors.'

Hazel Wiseman, current CEO of the Ocean Youth Trust (OYT) Scotland, accepted the generous raffle proceeds to help further their work with young sailors, especially those from disadvantaged backgrounds. This should surely matter to us all if sailing is to remain open to talent and enthusiasm. Heather Thomas, *Maiden*'s skipper, cites her early experience on the OYT's *James Cook* as a revelation after reservoir sailing in land-locked Yorkshire. Amid the general conviviality, however, I thought I noticed an expression of sour boredom on the face of one woman as the man next to her made his speech. Sailing can be a powerfully excluding passion for those who don't share its joy and I felt sympathy for all the 'plus-ones' who attend such events out of duty. It's still most usually a male hobby, which a female partner can either adopt or reject. Clare Allcard describes the jealousy that a boat can arouse in the excluded partner. 'I met one man who came back to his adored boat to find that his wife had filled the cabin with sticks of dynamite.'[11]

Millicent and Seonaid Reid sailing Malindi of Lorne
(Ron Cowan, Scottish Yachting Images)

19

'Nobody can find you'[1]
Families at sea

Di Beach (b. 1945); Jojo Pickering (b. 1965); Clare Thompson/
Allcard (b. 1946); Suzanne Cook (b. 1969); Rosie Swale (b. 1946)

DIANA BEACH'S TEENAGE YEARS felt stultifyingly conventional.[2] In her early childhood she'd crossed the Atlantic four times (by liner) as her father searched for work, which her mother's American family seemed to offer. Those opportunities had come to nothing and now she was at an English girls' grammar school in a middle-class stockbroker belt. Di was a rebel. She was a pretty, blonde girl with English rose complexion and no idea where her real interests or talents lay. She feared that her destiny was to wear pearls and marry some nice young man of her own social class and income bracket, live in a nice suburban house, and reproduce 2.2 nice children. Instead she met Rod Pickering.

Aged 18 in 1963, Di and her friend Lyn took a summer job in a hotel on Alderney. Rod and his fellow architects Colin, David and Manuel were enjoying a sailing holiday on his 22ft open boat, *Peggy*. When the girls decided to leave the hotel, as they weren't being paid, they asked the young men to take them back to England. 'For the first time I slept without a mattress under my body, without clean fresh linen against my skin,' wrote Di. When they reached Yarmouth, Isle of Wight, where Di and Lyn could catch the ferry and return home to their parents, they asked to stay on. Rod and his friends were off to work in Africa the following February, 'which didn't give him much time to decide he wanted to take me with him'.[3] When Di returned to college (Oxford Polytechnic) she grabbed every spare moment to hurry to London to see Rod or travel to Essex to sail with him in *Peggy*. Her parents didn't approve. Rod, though a qualified architect and then employed in a respectable job building undistinguished post-war houses, was obviously individualistic, with strong anti-authoritarian views; he came from Southend and was about to leave for another continent.

Di and Rod were convinced that they wanted to spend their lives together, but she was under 21 and needed her parents' consent if they were to marry. The Age of Marriage Act 1929, which had been supported by the National Union of Societies for Equal Citizenship (formerly the NUWSS) had established 16 as the legal minimum age for both men and women to marry (previously, marriages could take place from the legal age of puberty: 14 for boys, 12 for girls) but parental consent was required until age 21 (the age of majority then). In 1963, however, the right to marry freely was a live issue. The UN Commission on the Status of Women, which had been established in 1946, had drafted the Convention on Consent to Marriage, which reaffirmed the consensual nature of marriage in the context of human rights. It had been opened for signature and ratification by General Assembly in 1962 and was due to come into force in 1964.

Di took her parents to court to establish that she had the right to marry whoever she wished. The magistrates, though slightly bewildered by the case, were principally concerned to establish whether Rod had the means to support her – which he did. However, they also stipulated that she should finish her government-funded business course before leaving to marry and travel to Africa. Her parents considered this a win. They assumed that this enforced delay would mean that she'd come to her senses and fall in love with someone more suitable. Di disagreed: 'I had glimpsed a thrilling parallel existence. I wanted what Rod represented: freedom of thought and action, a rejection of Calvinistic notions of duty and suffering in favour of autonomy and self-reliance. And the chance to go to Africa.'[4] She was outraged by the magistrates' compromise and decided to get pregnant before Rod left – a traditionally acceptable way of evading laws on underage marriage. Her father offered to pay for her to have an abortion in Sweden. She refused.

Looking back, she expresses astonishment at her own boldness and also some sadness at the pain she gave, particularly to her father. 'These weighty life decisions of marriage and parenthood were unconsidered and precipitous. Such responsibilities tie some people down, but it didn't occur to us that we couldn't have everything. The Zeitgeist of the sixties spoke through us.'[5] She continued her battle until 'alone and unfrightened' she flew to Uganda, where she and Rod married. She was 19 and he was 24. Their daughter, Jojo, was born a few months later.

Life in Uganda was not perfect. Di took a part-time job but essentially had little to do, and Rod's work was frustrating. They began to bicker, until they were both swept along by the challenge of their next adventure: to build a boat and sail back to England. This was Rod's vision. He successfully inspired not only Di, but also his architect friends Colin and David. They moved from Kampala to the Islamic island of Lamu, which she described as 'a closed society to which we did not belong'. Unexpectedly, this offered her a degree of freedom:

> *It didn't seem to occur to them or to me that the demands of their religion might apply to me, and I continued wearing my shorts and sleeveless tops out of ignorance rather than any desire to be obstreperous. There was, at that time, in that place, a mutual acceptance across the cultural divide separating us.*[6]

There were no libraries on Lamu, no technical experts for Rod to consult. Materials were hard to source yet the local craftsmen built beautiful, strongly constructed boats. Di's description of the island, the people and the daily practical difficulties to be overcome is absorbing, and Rod's achievement, designing and building a beautiful seaworthy yacht under those circumstances, was truly impressive.

Finally, in the summer of 1967, they were ready to leave. Their yacht, *Mjojo*, would be their home for the next five years. She was 42ft long, engineless, a heavily constructed gaff cutter, striking to look at and with a surprising turn of speed. They had initially planned to travel up the Red Sea and had worried whether they should carry guns. Then, in June, the Suez Canal was closed after the Arab–Israeli Six-Day War, so their route would be via the Seychelles to Durban, where they would need to settle and find work. Jojo was not quite two when they set out and Di, still an inexperienced sailor, felt panic when it was finally time to go. She had been reading Eric Hiscock's early books, such as *Around the World in Wanderer III* and *Voyaging Under Sail* (1959), and Erling Tambs' *The Cruise of the Teddy* (1933) together with other cruising stories that Rod discovered in a second-hand bookshop in Kampala. But when the moment came, Di was terrified. She had stubbornly resisted official efforts to prevent her and Jojo from setting out. Fleetingly, she wished they had been successful. Her first night watch, alone at sea, was a crucial moment. She was feeling sick and was almost rigid with fear, yet once she felt the yacht responding to her touch on the wheel, 'the nausea subsided, and I no longer wished I was dead.'[7]

Many more families were taking their children, including babies, to sea in this post-war period. Leafing through issues of *Yachting Monthly* normally reveals very few letters from women (usually none), yet one subject that could stimulate debate was how best to cope with young children at sea. This, like cooking on board, was assumed to be the mother's responsibility. *Yachting Monthly* reader Beth Clackson wrote: 'As the mother of three sailors all afloat before they were ten weeks old, I can assure you it is hell for everybody.' Others were more constructive. An article entitled 'Neptune's Grandchildren' by Rosalind Elwood, a sailing nurse, published in January 1964, offered a range of sensible suggestions, including making good use of other adults: 'a husband-and-wife team who sail alone will be well advised to take a tolerant friend as extra crew for longer passages.'

Di and Rod in Africa wouldn't have read the article but in general terms Di was attracted by the communal idea for family living – groups of people supporting each other, rather than the isolated nuclear family with childcare and domestic work falling solely on the mother. Throughout the building of *Mjojo*, she, Rod, Colin and David had operated as a group of friends; now that their voyage had begun the cooking was shared – as were the watches – and Jojo benefitted from the vigilance and company of 'three daddies' as well as her mother. Once she had conquered her initial fear and sickness, Di fell in love with the ocean:

> *Every morning, every day, every evening the water was different. In my catalogue of memories, I still carry a picture of certain days, particular moods of the ocean and the sky and it does not surprise me to learn that some maritime cultures have a vocabulary to describe different aspects of the water. When you become intimate with it, you need more words.*[8]

By the time they reached Durban, Di and Rod were expecting their second child. The others moved off the boat at this time – they all needed to find work and the nature of the space on *Mjojo* changed as the boat became, temporarily, more like a domestic home – though without the isolation experienced by many young mothers. Durban was a port where members of the cruising community congregated. Di loved the feeling of being among other people who shared their attitude to life.

> *Since the 1950s an increasing number of people have escaped from the jail of modernity. People are heading for the hills, wilderness, seeking isolated nooks and crannies. With nostalgia, they pursue the crafts of a simpler world: pottery, spinning, weaving, horticulture. For those on the run possessed of the necessary attributes, the oceans are the obvious place to hide. They are last wilderness, where nobody can find you, tax you, make you wear disgusting stockings or throttle you with a tie, force you to conform, coerce you into living to work, or equate your time with money.*[9]

To get jobs and earn money for the next stage of their travels, they did, however, need to buy clothes, clean up and conform to some extent. Jojo, now three years old, went to a nursery school, which made Di aware of how important it was for children to socialise with their peers. Her daughter was precocious, wild and completely unused to other children. And, while Di loved the companionship of the fellow-cruisers, she did occasionally yearn for conversation that was not solely about boats. And living in Durban during the apartheid era – even within a congenial community – was not a comfortable experience, even more difficult than it had been being a white person in 1960s Uganda.

The new baby – Lulu ('pearl' in Swahili) – was five months old when they were ready to move on again. Di decided that she didn't want to take the two small girls round the Cape of Good Hope on board *Mjojo*, with notoriously strong winds in prospect. Instead, she travelled with them by train to Cape Town – which had its own perils, she discovered. She also resisted Rod's idea that they should head for the Magellan Straits and into the Pacific. It was time, she felt, that they should return to England, if only for a visit. As a teenager she had asserted her right to leave home, marry the man she loved and embrace the free, nomadic way of life. Now, as the mother of two young children, she asserted her need if not to stay in England, at least to settle somewhere her daughters could make friends and go to school. As Rod became more passionately determined to explore the wilder sea areas, Di's instincts were telling her to keep the risks for their children manageable and give them a basis of 'normality'.

Their arrival back in Falmouth was deeply emotional with both sets of parents coming out in a motorboat to meet them. For six months they tried to settle in England, almost buying a house in Essex, but it was cold and depressing. When a message came from their friend Manuel with an idea for a shared architectural business opportunity in southern Spain, they packed everything into their Fiat 600 and left immediately. Di never returned to living at sea and says she feels an imposter here in a book about women sailors: 'I was only a deckhand.' Yet she stood her watches, learned celestial navigation, and was an integral part of a remarkable voyage on a remarkable boat. Her independent, adventurous spirit can't be doubted as she continued to travel and live in different parts of the world, studying anthropology at University of California, Berkeley and finally realising her own passionate interest in understanding different cultures through their food. When she built her own boutique hotel in a deserted part of Andalucía, it was her version of the building of *Mjojo*.

Jojo, meanwhile, continued to sail with her father as often as she could. Aged ten she went with him to Tangiers to collect *Racundra*, Arthur Ransome's former yacht, which Rod had found abandoned there. They sailed it back to their home in Estepona, despite its dilapidation and opposition from customs officials. Rod restored *Racundra*, then gave up land life for the sea once again. Jojo was not with him when *Racundra* was wrecked off the coast of Venezuela, nor when Rod finally disappeared sailing a James Wharram catamaran across the Atlantic from Florida. Her career has been in the circus (stilt walking, juggling, acrobalance and unicycling) and at sea, sailing her 35ft traditional gaff cutter with her husband and family. Today she can describe herself as 'sailor, skipper, adventurer, traditional navigator, gaff rigged sailor, performer, mother, love life!' She is also a Yachtmaster instructor who feels passionately about the benefits of all-female crews learning sailing together.

* * *

In the mid-1960s Clare Thompson, an Army officer's daughter, made four attempts on her own life and was committed to a mental hospital. Clare had left school early to become an actress and had then trained as a nurse. In her sailing autobiography, *A Gypsy Life* (1992), she says only that she had failed at both 'and was fully occupied with being a wreck'.[10] Clare's full story is told in a currently unpublished manuscript, tentatively titled 'A Story of Hope'. She had been raped by a stranger, then her trauma had been compounded by misdiagnoses, including chronic pain from a trapped nerve being dismissed as psychosomatic.

She does now remember the terror of the attack and her conviction that the man was going to kill her. At the time she felt so ashamed that she told no one at all. She buried the assault so deep inside her that it was several years before she even remembered what had happened. Meanwhile, she developed what today would be called post-traumatic stress disorder (PTSD).

Mid-1960s psychiatric treatment for Clare included a cocktail of mind-numbing drugs and 26 sessions of electroconvulsive therapy (ECT) followed by 30 days of deep sleep treatment. Today the latter is banned pretty much globally and back then even the Soviet Union rejected it as barbaric. The idea was that it would completely wipe out the patient's memory. For Clare it did. And chillingly so. She woke to a totally unrecognisable world. She couldn't remember her name. Who she was. Where she was or why. Asked if she wanted cornflakes she couldn't answer because she didn't know what it was. She just knew that all the staff were her enemies. Out to destroy her. ECT was routinely prescribed from the mid-1950s, particularly for women, who comprised 70 per cent of the patient group.

Clare spent two years in a series of psychiatric hospitals as an involuntary patient. One day she happened to read a *Sunday Express* article 'Home is a Lone Boat for Edward Allcard'. It described the solo yachtsman's 12-year circumnavigation, following his dream. A throwaway remark leapt out at her. 'Of course the ideal would be to meet a girl who had the same idea.'

> *I sat down to write the first fan letter of my life. I told the man that I, too, could think of nothing more fabulous than to sail away into the pale blue yonder, but there was this one slight snag: I happened to be locked up in a loony bin. Would he mind waiting a couple of months until they set me free? Honesty further compelled me to point out that I couldn't actually sail or cook and wasn't much to look at either.*[11]

Clare wrote later, 'There is, in my opinion, only one person in the world who would have had the compassion and courage to answer that letter.'[12] They met in the spring of 1968. Edward had left his yacht *Sea Wanderer* in New Zealand, the halfway point of his solo circumnavigation, and flown back to the UK to see his mother, who was dying. Clare and Edward met and went for a picnic on the South Downs. They walked and talked and found they liked each other.

Edward was 31 years older than Clare and, at that point, had been separated from his wife and daughter for ten years. He was a naval architect who had been badly injured in the bombing of the London Docks; another member of the wartime generation who felt at odds with post-war society. Edward had become well-known as a single-handed sailor and writer and had made headlines when he discovered a beautiful stowaway, Otilia Frayao, hidden on his yacht *Temptress* on his return voyage from America in 1950. Twenty-three-year-old Otilia was not looking for love or marriage; she was a poet, seeking her personal freedom. Clare never discussed that part of Edward's life with him but thinks it's unlikely that they had a sexual relationship. Certainly the impression given by his writing is that he was more irritated by the awkwardness of the situation than eager for sexual advantage.

When he met Clare, Edward was preparing to return to New Zealand to continue his circumnavigation. He'd bought a Land Rover converted into a camper van and was planning to drive from Dover to Singapore. Clare, highly excited by the idea, volunteered to drive with him. They set out in July 1968, aged 22 and 53, and stayed together until Edward died, aged 102. They had a daughter, Katy, in 1969 and married in 1973. *A Gypsy Life*, Clare's account of their time together on the converted Baltic Trader *Johanne Regina*, shows her grateful and loving, inescapably conscious of Edward's far greater sailing experience and her own femininity.

If she had been reading *The Yachtswoman's Pocket Book* (1965) by Geoffrey Morgan and Pamela Tucker, she would have realised this was absolutely the correct attitude. Women were advised that it was better not to know too much, as that might risk challenging the authority of the skipper. The preface, written by Pamela Tucker's husband, states clearly: 'It is a wise woman who knows her place and contrives to leave the skipper's ego intact.' He explains that 'an intelligent woman aboard can be a very great asset to any skipper or crew, particularly in moments of stress or strain, provided she has taken the trouble to think through her true role. If she can be decorative and charming withal, she will be worth her weight in gold.'[13] Other respected sailing women, such as Joyce Sleightholme, felt it important to remind women not to challenge the skipper (usually their husband)'s authority. 'There can only be one person on board to make the decision. Wives should not undermine their skipper's authority, but they should help to influence him to do the right and safe thing at all times.'[14]

Joyce Sleightholme's *The Sea Wife's Handbook*, first published in 1971, expresses a way of thinking, 50 years past, which may seem more alien than some thoughts of a century ago. Joyce was a competent, experienced sailor who had worked as mate to her husband on charter vessels and had cooked on ocean racers, until they both came ashore at the birth of their daughter. From the early 1960s both she and her husband, Des, had been part of the editorial team at the magazine *Yachts & Yachting*, then in 1967 Des moved to *Yachting Monthly*, eventually succeeding Maurice Griffiths as editor. Joyce recognised the ability of women sailors who had tackled ocean crossings or cruised solo, but they are irrelevant to her book. She is writing 'for the woman/mate who is content to leave the command in male hands but would like to do a better job.'[15] She is eloquent about the joys of independence at sea, for men.

> *What we must try to understand is what sailing means to a man. In his workaday job he is often routine bound: he may have a dozen bosses and not much responsibility really, and no man worth being called male really enjoys this. His boat offers challenge, responsibility and the chance to be the absolute master [...] In fact at sea modern, urbanised, office-bound man becomes a male in his real element.*

But do women not have workaday, routine-bound, boss-ridden existences from which they might crave escape? Joyce's book was contemporary with the new magazine *Spare Rib*, which explicitly denied the woman-as-man's-helpmeet ideology. Second-wave feminism challenged people to consider the structures of personal life as political. Such 'women's lib' ideas caused irritation and offence but did, gradually, effect change, though it was slow to make a difference in the sailing world.

Clare Allcard embraced her new existence willingly, including its hardships. 'Are these the hands of an artist?' asked her friend Gail, displaying her small, delicate hands after helping to hoist *Johanne Regina*'s 750 sq feet of canvas mainsail, or struggling to turn the heavy winch handles that raised her massive anchor. 'I looked at hers and then at mine, larger but in the same state of interesting callouses and ingrained dirt. "And are these the hands of a nurse?" I wailed back, at which we promptly collapsed on the cabin top, overcome by helpless laughter.'[16]

She and Gail accepted the roles of cooks on board without feeling oppressed. The words 'sexism' and 'sexist' had become commonplace since their first introduction into English *c.*1965. Clare recognised that their cooking arrangements might be called 'sexist' but denied that this posed a problem. 'The way I see it is that there are jobs on boats that nobody particularly enjoys: fixing engines and cleaning bilges: cooking meals and scrubbing clothes. Such jobs should be allocated according to one's ability to do them. Neither Gail nor I could fix engines. Neither Gail nor I particularly wanted to learn to fix engines either.'[17] Clare also took main responsibility for Katy, worrying about her seasickness, recognising her need for fun, for the company of other children and for education.

Clare was determined that the restoration of *Johanne Regina*, their life on board and the sailing of this big ship should be her project as much as Edward's. When set against her instinctive care and protectiveness for Katy, it brought hard decisions – just as it had for Di Beach. Clare became convinced that they should not take Katy across the Atlantic when the time came to sail back to Europe. Her daughter's seasickness was chronic, though the child never once complained about it. Perhaps she thought all children were seasick? What if the sea was rough all the way? Might she not die of sickness and dehydration? Fortunately, Clare's parents were eager to help. They would come to the Caribbean, spend time getting to know their granddaughter, then, if she was willing, they would take her, aged five, back to England by plane. Clare would stay and sail on *Johanne Regina*. 'If I didn't, then she, like *Sea Wanderer* before her, would become nothing more than Edward's boat, a place Katy and I visited between his voyages. She would never be the family home I longed for, and that Katy and I both lacked.'[18]

As Katy grew up, other compromises were achieved to ensure she would have best chance to develop an independent future life, while knowing that she had the solid base of a happy family home. She could share the thrill of exploration but also find friends of her own age to whom she didn't need to say goodbye every time *Johanne Regina* left port. Clare educated Katy on board until she was 11 but then she was sent to school. Other boat daughters, such as Clio Smeeton and Astrid Dixon, became used to a way of life where they periodically had to leave their boat homes and return to Britain to grandparents or to boarding school, while their parents sailed on. This was not unique to the cruising community: other children of expatriate parents faced the same experience – and other parents (usually mothers) had the same difficult decisions to make.

* * *

Before he met Clare, Edward Allcard had considered the Norwegian sailor Peter ('Per') Tangvald as one of his greatest friends. In 1957 they had set out to race each other, singlehanded, across the Atlantic. Tangvald was already on his third marriage to then wife Lillemor, who was deeply uncertain about sailing. When she finally asked her husband to choose between her and his boat, he claimed that he felt no hesitation: 'Any sailor will know that it is a lot more difficult to get a new boat than a new wife.'[19]

Tangvald who published hubristic articles claiming all accidents were likely to be avoidable,[20] leapt to fame with his book *Sea Gypsy* (1966) and became evangelical about sailing without engines, safety equipment or any modern conveniences. He lost his second boat *Dorothea* on passage for Florida, but simply continued his current project designing and building an even more purist, stripped-down yacht, *L'Artemis*. Inexplicably he also continued to find women willing to marry him and submit to his uncompromising lifestyle. His record of seven marriages (with five divorces and two deaths of his wives at sea) perhaps says as much about the desperation of the women who were prepared to sail with him, serve him and earn money for him, as it does about his contempt for us.

After divorcing from Lillemor he married a resilient, independent Frenchwoman named Simonne before moving on to Lydia, a 17-year-old schoolgirl with whom he had a son, Thomas. Lydia was killed in an attack by pirates. Peter's next wife, Ann, was physically abusive to Thomas, had a daughter (Carmen) and died at sea when she was knocked overboard in an accident. Finally, Peter married another much younger woman, Florence, who had joined him to nanny the two children and experience engineless sailing. Another child, Virginia, was born. Peter was happy but Florence was not. Charles Doane quotes her as writing:

> *Simple pleasure like going out for an ice cream was absolutely forbidden and a jug of fresh milk was a rare luxury. But Peter believed this was the price to pay for some sort of elusive freedom. When I look back I strongly question this whole notion of 'freedom' and what it is worth.*[21]

Florence left, taking Virginia with her. Later she wished she had taken Carmen, too.

As Peter became more extreme, Edward Allcard became anxious about his recklessness, though not, apparently, about his attitude to the women and children who sailed with him. Perhaps he didn't see it. Sailing author and parent, Nigel Calder, was shocked by Tangvald's habit of locking his children in the forecabin – which he referred to, unashamedly, as a prison. His respect for Tangvald as a sailing icon was shaken.

In July 1991 Peter, with seven-year-old Carmen locked in the forecabin, attempted to tow 15-year-old Thomas across the Caribbean from Puerto Rico to Bonaire. By some unexplained misjudgement, *L'Artemis* was driven onto the rocks. Thomas leapt from his own small boat to escape on a surfboard, but witnessed the annihilation of *L'Artemis* and listened to Carmen's hysterical screams as she died. Peter also died. Clare and Edward had promised that they would care for his children if anything happened to him, so they stepped in to foster Thomas.

It seems, however, that the damage from his childhood had been too great and he was left prone to episodes of narcolepsy as well as later alcoholism. He was gifted and attractive, but his wife Christina eventually refused to sail with him – thus almost certainly saving herself and their two children from tragedy, when Thomas and his home-built yacht disappeared without a trace on a similarly risky expedition in 2014.

* * *

When Suzanne Cook (Heywood) was six years old, her father conceived a plan that they would buy a boat and sail round the world to commemorate the 200th anniversary of Captain Cook's third voyage in 1776. Suzanne was seven when they left, her parents intending to be away for at most three years. Nothing went quite according to plan (yacht cruises often don't) but the increasing problems for Suzanne were due to her longing for school education, her deteriorating relationship with her mother and the family expectation that, because she was a girl, she would constantly help her mother with galley and cabin chores, while her younger brother learned from their father on deck. She began to feel kidnapped by her parents, trapped inside someone else's dream. She longed for friends, and she longed to learn.

Suzanne's memoir, *Wavewalker* (2023), is an account of her struggle to break free of the cruising life, to gain a normal education and manage her own independent existence. This was finally achieved when she departed Vanuatu for Somerville College, Oxford, more than a decade after her family first left England. In a thoughtful final chapter, she touches on some of the deeper causes for the dysfunction. 'My mother didn't want to go to sea at all and only did so to be with my father. [...] My mother's decision placed my father in her debt – she'd sacrificed everything for his dream and in exchange he would take her side even when she set herself against their daughter.'[22] Suzanne also felt critical of her father's plans and tactics, and resented the extent to which she and her brother were expected to subjugate their requirements to their parents'.

She believes now that almost all of her childhood was taken from her, against her will, and that she was very lucky to escape. She acknowledges that her unusual upbringing gave her unexpected strengths and different types of knowledge. When she applied for entry to Somerville College, she knew she didn't fulfil their basic requirements:

I couldn't speak any foreign languages and had never studied chemistry [... but] I could tell from the movement of a deck under my feet or the shape of a sail when something on a boat was wrong. I could see a whale, a dolphin or a bird and understand how it fitted into the world. I could tie a knot, chop wood, change the oil in a car, knit and sew. I knew what it was like to come close to dying. I'd lived in places where a can of tuna or a fresh onion was an unbelievable luxury. And with grim determination I could achieve things against the odds.[23]

But it's not enough. Since the publication of *Wavewalker*, Suzanne has been contacted by many other people who have had challenging childhoods. Quite a few of them were at sea, and many of the people who suffered most are women. She writes:

There is a common theme coming out of these stories, which is a father (almost always the father) wanting to be seen as a hero, and wanting freedom, and not understanding that in achieving that by taking his family to sea, he is effectively subjugating them to his need and taking away their freedom. They would all say they learnt something from it, but many of them, if like me they were trapped at sea for extended periods with little access to friends or education, would say that what they lost was far greater.[24]

* * *

I wish I knew what Rosie Swale's children, Eve and James, thought of their earliest sailing adventures. In 1972 they were the first children to round Cape Horn in a catamaran with their parents Rosie and Colin. James had been born on board their catamaran, *Anneliese*, with his father Colin, sister Eve and *Reeds Nautical Almanac* as his delivery team. They were in Italy then, moored in Fiumicino, the port of Rome. Rosie balked at the cost of giving birth in an Italian hospital from which Colin and Eve would have been excluded. With no pain relief or professional support, she was in charge of her own labour – 'Keep calm and let Nature take its course' was apparently the advice from *Reeds* then. In her memoir *Rosie Darling* (1973) Rosie offers a vivid and personal description of her son's birth. Her description of her hard stomach at the height of breaking waves of pain as each contraction passed is masterly. Not long afterwards Rosie and Colin began planning their round-the-world adventure, seeking the towering waves of the Southern Ocean. Her subsequent book, *Children of Cape Horn* (1975), is filled with positivity, despite various near-death incidents. She writes of the comfort as well as the responsibility it was to have the children close to them.

> *We felt we owed the children so much. It was because of having Eve and needing a home that we bought* Anneliese *in the first place, now it was due to the cheerfulness of both children that we had been able to do the voyage. Having Eve and Jim with us had probably made the journey safer for* Anneliese. *We never took those little risks we might have been tempted to take if we had been by ourselves.*[25]

Rosie's own childhood had been marked by the death of her mother when she was two years old and other dramatic changes. Her life after the circumnavigation was also complex. She made *News of the World* headlines by leaving her family to live with a transgender woman in 1981, was divorced from Colin and later married Clive Pope. She sailed solo across the Atlantic in a 17ft cutter in 1983, rode 3,000 miles on horseback through Chile to revisit Cape Horn in 1984–1985, then began ultramarathon running. After Clive died of cancer in 2002, Rosie ran round the world in his memory. She shares Beryl Smeeton and Ella Maillart's belief that women travelling alone are less at risk than men and remains a beacon of positivity:

> *I believe that a woman travelling alone is safer. You have to obey the laws of the wild, certainly – to be polite and tidy, to pay your own way, to act unafraid. I've had murderers in Siberia teach me how to light fires. I've*

been to places far too dangerous for men to travel – they'd have been shot. But I'm not a threat, so again and again I have been OK. And I'm happy too – that radiates to people.[26]

David Mitchell and Di Beach on Mjojo *(Di Beach)*

Jojo Pickering (aged 2) on Mjojo *(Di Beach)*

20

'Enormous biceps, baggy jeans and a jolly, yo-ho manner'[1]

Femininity and determination

Sharon Sites Adams (b. 1930); Nicolette Milnes-Walker (b. 1943); Clare Francis (b. 1946)

MANY OLDER PEOPLE CAN remember exactly where they were on 20 July 1969 when astronaut Neil Armstrong first walked on the moon. Sharon Sites Adams had just sighted Point Arguello, California after sailing solo 74 days across the Pacific from Yokohama, Japan in *Sea Spray II*. She was close enough to the land to pick up Walter Cronkite's commentary and to reflect on the coincidence of making her first landfall at that historic moment:

> I wished then that my sailing had made some contribution to science or that I'd discovered something remarkable or invented something useful for humanity, but it didn't, and I hadn't. I hadn't done anything but bring an idea to fruition. The journey fulfilled my own wishes, and maybe I'd be setting a world record. But I wasn't charting new worlds. Or was I?[2]

Sharon had been born Phyllis Mae in a railroad line shack in Battleground, Washington. Her father was a dump-truck driver who lost his job in the Great Depression. The family moved to eastern Oregon, hoping for a subsistence living as sharecroppers. When Phyllis was two and her sister Elizabeth just a little older, their mother died. Their father struggled to care for them and in the end gave them away to a childless couple, who renamed them Sharon and Mariel. Sharon was a tomboy, hunting and fishing, swimming and camping, determined to do everything the boys of the neighbourhood did, though being constantly rejected by them. She remembers one group cutting off the lower branches of 'their' tree, confident that this would prevent her climbing it. It didn't. She was a good school student, gaining A grades in all her subjects and successfully insisting on taking mechanical drawing instead of domestic science – the first girl in her school to do so.

At home she was a different person, resentfully doing household chores, quarrelling with her adoptive mother, lonely and secretive. As soon as she graduated from school, she married her sister Mariel's brother-in-law to escape from home. She had no idea, until it was too late, that she could have gone to college and worked to support herself there. Her husband, Don, was a kind and decent man. They had children but Sharon could feel nothing for them. She stayed at home to cook and clean and care. 'The days began with ennui and ended with downright depression.'[3] She left. All ties were cut. Mariel's husband forbade the sisters from communicating any more; Don thought it best that Sharon didn't see their children. She moved to Los Angeles, found work, and eventually married again.

Aged 34, she was widowed with shocking suddenness when her husband died of stomach cancer just days after diagnosis. Sharon was working as a dental assistant and didn't really know what to do with herself. Almost by accident she found herself at Los Angeles' new project, the Marina del Rey. This is now North America's largest human-made small-craft harbour, home to approximately 5,000 boats and a popular tourism destination. Then, it was still very new, not yet officially open but already an attention-grabbing development. *Yachting Monthly* found it necessary to keep assuring its readers that the new marinas being proposed in Britain wouldn't be anything like this massive construction. One Sunday morning, after church, Sharon drove down to see what it was all about. It was a day that changed her life. She sat and watched the boats and wondered whether she too could learn to sail. Less than an hour after setting foot on the deck of a small boat during a brief one-on-one lesson, she was sailing alone. Her natural talent was immediately obvious, and she fell in love with this new world. She bought a 21ft fibreglass sloop and began to explore. One day, about two weeks after purchasing her boat, 'I was sitting in the cockpit, eating lunch and addressing Christmas cards, when I suddenly picked up my pen in mid-address and said to myself "I bet I could sail to Hawaii."'[4]

Hawaii was 2,500 miles into the Pacific. Sharon had only been sailing for a couple of months. She had, as she puts it, 'the muscles of an office clerk'; she would need to learn navigation (non-GPS), find a more suitable boat, plan, provision and cope with other people's disbelief, even their hostility. This was something no woman had previously attempted and there were many who poured scorn on this 'housewife's' dream. Others aided. The boatyard manager helped her find and adapt a 25ft clinker-built Folkboat (similar to Rozelle Raynes' *Martha McGilda*); author Hugh MacDonald, former spy plane pilot and OSS operative who was then in the Los Angeles County Sheriff's Department, offered to teach her navigation. Her doctor checked her physical fitness; her friends gave emotional support.

The Coast Guard was adamant that she shouldn't go. The project was completely irresponsible, they told her; she would simply be wasting public money when they had to come and rescue her. In June 1965, eight months after she first stepped on board a boat, Sharon set off for Hawaii. She 'didn't see why she shouldn't', she said. And she succeeded. Four years later, in May 1969, she sailed 6,000 miles, alone, from Yokohama to Los Angeles; 'I didn't see what there was about it that I couldn't do.'[5]

* * *

This was very close to the attitude of Nicolette Milnes-Walker when she conceived her plan to sail alone across the Atlantic in 1971. Her adventure had begun almost as a paper exercise. She was at the International Boat Show at Earl's Court, wandering around looking at the available equipment, thinking about the helpful lists often published in the back of cruising books, considering what she would choose to take were she ever to set out on a long voyage, then beginning a list of her own.

> *I was like someone whose eye has been caught by a new car. It looks rather nice, so you think you'll find out a bit more about it. Then you compare it with other cars and it's much more desirable. Then you happen to be passing the showroom. You might as well go in and have a proper look.*

Why shouldn't you have one? You can't get it out of your head, you just have to have that car so you buy it. I bought myself a transatlantic voyage.[...] I would go to sleep imagining the difficulties involved and wake up with the thoughts still chasing round my mind. I could find no reason for not going. So I decided to go.[6]

It was already mid-January. She needed to leave by mid-June to get the best chance of good weather. She would have to give at least three months' notice to her employer. Nicolette, aged 28, was then a research psychologist, living in Cardiff and working for University of Wales Institute of Science and Technology (UWIST) on the impact of stress and danger on people undertaking dangerous missions. When I asked her about her work, she made a joking reference to the Official Secrets Act and changed the subject. Her transatlantic voyage was a private experiment, testing the effects of loneliness and fear on herself.

Sharon Sites Adams had often experienced loneliness as terrifying and distressing – she writes about feeling desperation and screaming alone in her cabin – but her voyages were generally unnoticed beyond America. Nicolette, who was reading all the solo sailor books she could find and following press reports, cannot remember ever hearing of Sharon. Few people reading the British yachting press would hear much about her achievement either. There was, however, general interest in the psychological effects of loneliness on single-handed sailors, particularly after the suicide of Donald Crowhurst in July 1969 while competing in the first *Sunday Times* Golden Globe race. The only finisher, Robin Knox-Johnston, was examined by a psychologist and pronounced 'distressingly normal'.

Nicolette had very little sailing experience other than in a Mirror dinghy, which she had built for herself, and a sail to the Azores and back with an experienced skipper. She was the third of four daughters of a Cheshire surgeon. Her mother was an active local councillor; her oldest sister was married with children. Nicolette was a self-questioning person, trying to develop her own philosophy of life. She had endured a period of unhappiness at school, an unsuccessful relationship at university and had stopped being a Christian. However, she also had a naturally lively personality, was well able to make friends and 'couldn't resist a dare'. This voyage was a dare to herself, and she was also excited by the concept of being 'first'. One reason that she decided not to wait until the next running of the Observer Single-Handed Trans-Atlantic Race (OSTAR) scheduled for 1972 was that she knew she didn't have enough money to buy a boat with any chance of winning and wasn't really interested in struggling along towards the back of the fleet.[7] A race, even undertaken single-handed and scattered across an ocean, is, to some extent, a communal experience: Nicolette wanted to be truly alone and self-reliant. She did not expect to be rescued if she ran into trouble, though she did carry flares and a liferaft. She knew she was a poor swimmer but with no one on board to rescue her if she did go over the side, she almost counted this as an advantage. She imagined what it would be like to be in the waters watching her yacht sailing on for America. She promised herself (and her mother) that she would wear a safety harness and would remain clipped on for all work on deck.

Her yacht, *Aziz*, a Pioneer 9, was as robust and well prepared as possible. She knew there was a danger of being run down. Although single-handed sailing had caught the popular imagination, there were many who disapproved, on the grounds that a proper lookout could not be kept at all times, as required by the collision regulations. Vessels at sea had always been expected to maintain vigilance, but these Safety of Life at Sea (SOLAS) rules had been formalised by the International Maritime Organization (IMO) in 1960, at the same time that the development of self-steering systems was making it easier for yachtsmen not to spend long hours on deck. The Second World War had accelerated the use of radar to assist lookout on naval and merchant ships but sets small enough for use on sailing vessels were not yet available. Neither wood nor glass fibre made a good radar target; all that the seagoing yachtsmen could do was hang metallic reflectors in their rigging and hope this would make them visible to larger vessels – and that there was someone keeping a lookout on board those larger vessels. Sally Hinchliffe and Penny Hughes hoisted a flattened aluminium saucepan up *Crab*'s short mast. Nicolette had a radar reflector mounted between the shrouds near the crosstrees. She had to wrap a tea towel round it to stop the mainsail chafing. Did she really believe it would be effective? Probably not; 'But one had to hope.'

Nicolette's interest was in psychology. Would she be able to complete the crossing without 'disturbing her personality'? She wasn't afraid of the loneliness but wondered how she would react to being frightened. Privately, she believed that women were likely to be more resilient than men.

> *I think this is because women are less self-centred than men, for a woman's life is usually centred on her husband and/or children and so she has a motive for fighting on when all is lost. Of course I could not claim to be in this position, being unencumbered by family responsibilities, but if there is any truth in the argument of evolved innate sex differences, which I think there is, I could expect to have this survival capability.*[8]

The first Women's Liberation march in the UK took place in March 1971. Nicolette didn't go on it and would probably have denied she was a 'women's libber', then a phrase heavily charged with antagonism, frequently arousing overt hostility or silly remarks about bra-burners. She got on well with men, was glad of their help and was determined to live her life in her own way. She didn't feel personally oppressed but was ready to challenge the status quo, while remaining well aware of her own femininity as well as her intelligence and competence.

She wrote to Ann Davison asking for advice and received a sensible letter back emphasising the importance of good nutrition. Ann had stayed in America and remarried – once mistakenly, once well. She had survived cancer treatment, then undertaken a solo powerboat exploration of America's lakes and inland waterways, where discovery and understanding were her main aims and her gender an additional asset. She was shrewd enough to know that travelling on her own as a woman would attract more interest – thus making the trip financially viable – but her personal motivation was to gain more insight into a country where, as she had discovered, they 'put marshmallows in the salad'.[9]

Nicolette's adventure tested her spirit, her resilience, her courage and her practicality. It made her think about Life and her life while facing the daily challenges of staying alive in a small boat crossing an ocean. Early in the voyage she made the discovery, which Clare Francis would also make, that the act of speaking into her tape recorder made her more emotional and aware of loneliness than writing her diary or the daily activities of thinking and doing. She has kept her tapes but doesn't share them. When she arrived at her destination – Newport, Rhode Island – just over six weeks after leaving Dale (near Milford Haven), she changed into a minidress, brought for that moment.

The Coast Guards who came to tow her in joked that they'd expected hot pants. Hot pants (tiny, bottom-hugging shorts, best worn with high-heeled, knee-high boots) were then a vivid challenge to expectations of suitability and propriety. Nicolette was bubbling over with joy but also soaking wet from a heavy rain shower. She was barefoot as she hoisted signal flags, prepared warps and fenders and looked out for her parents, who were waiting to greet her.

When she wrote her book (delivered to the publisher ten weeks after her return to England) she deliberately included the fact that she'd sailed naked whenever the weather allowed. This was quite a normal fact of male or married cruising life, mentioned by writers such as Edward Allcard. Di Beach commented how unnecessary clothes began to feel and how soon the voyagers on board *Mjojo* got used to each other's naked bodies. Both Nicolette and Sharon spoke of nakedness as an aspect of the extraordinary freedom they experienced when far out to sea in good weather. They were also sufficiently sophisticated to guess that such information would cause more of a frisson when the nude sailor was a pretty young woman instead of some bearded old salt. Sure enough, Nicolette's revelation made tabloid headlines when she and her minidress came home. She was unperturbed, as she had written the book with the advice and support of her future husband. Bruce Coward, first introduced to readers as her 'literary agent', was a distant cousin and an experienced publisher and publicist. He had negotiated the book deal that would make it possible for her to repay her father the money he'd loaned her to buy *Aziz*. Bruce had also rented a cottage where she could settle and write in relative peace once she had returned to England. By the time the book was complete, they were engaged.

Too much emphasis on minidresses and media management shouldn't be allowed to get in the way of Nicolette's practical skills as a navigator, engineer and problem-solver. Behind the pretty figure and the sweet, shy smile was a trained, analytical mind. Her understanding of navigation by RAF wireless tables is very clever. When puzzling over the absolute silence with which her achievement was treated by the British yachting establishment, I have begun to think that she fooled or offended them by making it all look too easy. They forgot she was a scientist.

Sharon Sites Adams had also taken great care over her appearance on both her arrivals – into Honolulu in 1965 and Los Angeles in 1969.

She washed her hair, painted her nails, applied make-up and wore attractively feminine outfits. Both she and Nicolette (and Clare Francis after them) were aware that they were contributing to a new public image of the woman sailor. Nicolette wrote, 'I took great delight in the surprised reaction of people meeting me. Clearly they expected a large, strong, horsey faced English girl, long in tooth. Instead I was a small, apparently frail, round-faced girl, a teenage imposter.'[10] She had fun, enjoyed the media attention, accepted invitations, married Bruce and spent the next two years giving talks and living this new life. Then she became pregnant with their twin daughters. Bruce was increasingly disillusioned with newspaper life in London. (This was a period of conflict as technology changed, printers went on strike and papers were forcibly moved out of Fleet Street to new, un-unionised premises in the former London Docklands). Nicolette, Bruce and their children moved to the Harbour Bookshop in Dartmouth, which they ran with success until their joint retirement. She packed away her photos, tapes and newspaper cuttings and didn't mention her achievement to her new neighbours.

It was quickly forgotten. *Aziz* had been put on display at the 1972 Boat Show, alongside Chay Blyth's *British Steel*. Nicolette was also given a special award as Yachtswoman of the Year but the award list, managed by the Yachting Journalists' Association, did not include Nicolette's name. When I came to ask them about this, while republishing her book for her 80th birthday in 2023, they had not heard of her. Nicolette agreed that the record should be corrected but was essentially untroubled. She felt she had had her moment of fame and moved on. The enduring legacy of her 1971 transatlantic voyage was personal; it was in her head and she 'didn't have to prove anything anymore' – a mental and emotional independence that has lasted the rest of her life.

* * *

Commercial sponsorship had the potential to affect individual adventure. It opened new opportunities to some sailors who weren't independently rich or couldn't count on family help, but it also raised the overall cost of participation. Boats and equipment that were going to advertise a sponsor's brand to the world were likely to cost more than boats and equipment selected for their ability to do a job and remain within a personal budget. The increasing competition to achieve sponsorship threatened to shut out some sailors whose faces didn't fit the corporate profile. It might prove a mixed blessing for women with a dream. Nicolette was fortunate that her father had been able to offer her a loan to buy a relatively modest small boat. Bruce's expertise and contacts had negotiated the book deal that would ensure the loan could be repaid (as long as she achieved her objective). She also needed to sell the boat on her return. Ann Davison's writing had earned the money to buy *Felicity Ann* and she was also supported by media interest. Eventually she too had to sell the yacht to finance her *Gemini* adventure. Sharon Sites Adams' Pacific crossing had been made possible by a yacht builder agreeing to supply her with a yacht, newly built in Yokohama, to deliver to Los Angeles. She chose its name and felt as if it was hers, then handed it back ten days after her return. Fewer women than men had significant fortunes of their own and this has always been a limiting factor in sports where participation requires something additional to the individual human body – a horse, a car, a plane, a boat.

Occasionally this may work in a woman's favour – 'this boat is so simple even a woman can sail it' – but more often feminine gender introduces uncertainty. Should sponsors be seen to be encouraging a woman to put herself in danger? If a woman is not the 'normal' face of a sport, considerations other than her essential skill come into play. Her appearance, for instance – something women are judged on more frequently than men. 'What's she wearing?' was the first question Sharon heard as commentators spotted her approaching Marina del Rey from Yokohama. Janet Grosvenor describes it as a relief when sponsor-logoed shirts and corporate jackets came in, as it removed a layer of problems. It's why Vera Laughton Mathews took so much trouble over uniform for the WRNS.

The 1970s was a decade when more women began to demand equal pay for equal work and an end to automatic resignation from the workplace on marriage. Women wanted their own money – not an 'allowance' from their husband. They wanted to finance themselves and compete for themselves. Costs were rising, due to inflation and the increased material inventiveness of the period. There was more to buy, more competition among producers, more advertising – and sponsorship on behalf of products not for people. Clare Francis was the first woman in post-war British sailing to be successful in attracting commercial sponsorship to achieve her individual challenges and will point out that she worked hard for it: both to earn the sponsorship, and then in giving her sponsors good value. She had (still has) a poise and star quality that is a gift to interviewers and cameramen.

Clare was born in Surbiton, Surrey and was educated at the Royal Ballet School. It seems to me that the Royal Ballet School education may have been a significant factor in enabling her to meet the physical challenges of sailing, as well as finding essential resilience and eventually being able to project her achievement in the public sphere.

After school, Clare studied economics at University College London, then worked in the marketing department of Robertson's jam and marmalade. This was a good job, as she describes it: 'with grad. pension, comp. car and fringe benefits', but after three years, she quit. A legacy enabled her to buy and fit out a Nicholson 32, *Gulliver G*, then she too sailed across the Atlantic alone. Looking back now she can see that this was a possible practice for taking part in the next OSTAR, but at the time she could barely acknowledge this, even to herself.

Clare crossed from Falmouth to Newport in 37 days. She then sailed to the West Indies, where she lived on board, wrote articles, earned money from day charters, and enjoyed friendships. She realised that she didn't want to spend her life as a single-handed cruising sailor; she liked the company of others and also sought a range of experiences and challenges. The Round Britain & Ireland Race (RB&I) had been established in 1966 and was rapidly growing in popularity, despite criticism from some of the 'rules-based' racers who described these open-entry races as 'stunts'. The RB&I race could be sailed by any type of boat, with crews of two, starting from Plymouth and pausing, compulsorily, for 48 hours each at Crosshaven (Ireland), Castlebay (Hebrides), Lerwick (Shetland) and Lowestoft (Suffolk) before returning to Plymouth. The constant presence of the coast made the race tactically difficult, but the stopping points developed a sense of togetherness, even when the disparity of vessels meant that the fleet was widely strung out.

The overwhelming majority of the competitors were men, but some male/female couples also raced together. In 1970 Mary Bevan had become the first female skipper to compete, sailing *Myth of Malham* with her husband as crew – but there had not been a team of two women. While Clare was in the West Indies, she was approached by Trish, a girl she didn't know, who had some sponsorship for the RB&I

but no boat. She persuaded Clare to enter *Gulliver G*, then persuaded Cherry Blossom shoe polish to sponsor the boat when Clare objected that *Gulliver G* would need new sails. Trish dropped out before the race and her place was taken by Clare's lifelong friend, Eve Bonham. In a race dominated by fast multihulls and high winds they came 22nd overall and third on handicap. Of the 61 starters, 39 finished.[11] Clare and Eve developed their lifelong friendship during the race and Clare met Jacques Redon, the man she would later marry.

As Clare wondered what to do next, she felt increasingly tempted by the OSTAR – a challenge from the same Corinthian stable as the RB&I. She was also tempted to stay at home and 'look after' Jacques. If she entered the OSTAR she would be the first British woman to take part and 'while I am no Women's Lib-er out to beat the men' she also wanted to do well. Though the OSTAR had been conceptualised as a race for amateurs, competitiveness had raised the stakes. Clare would need a larger, faster, lighter boat to have any chance of achieving success, and that boat would also need expensive equipment and provisioning. Joan Green, married to Ron, had been one of many women who had admired Clare and Eve as they sailed the RB&I race. She and Ron owned a fast Ohlson 38, which they offered to lend Clare for the OSTAR.

This was the sort of generosity from which Barbara Hughes, Marian Wyllie, Mary Bevan and Sharon Sites Adams had benefitted, but in the higher-tech racing of the 1970s, even the loan of a boat was not enough. Clare needed sponsors to help her with travel and equipment costs. The UK was in recession and many advertising budgets had been cut. Looking back, she suspected that the designedly glamorous photo of herself, which she'd included in her begging letters, had been a mistake. She had assumed she needed to counter what she believed to be a general preconception of single-handed sailing women as having 'enormous biceps, baggy jeans and a jolly, yo-ho manner'. Perhaps she was anxious about a general hostility towards 'mannishness' and the accusations that women who wanted to compete in men's arenas weren't proper women.

Clare's feminine photo, regrettably, tended to bring out the protective instincts in too many controllers of advertising budgets. One company wrote to say they 'couldn't believe a little thing like me could possibly manage to cross the Atlantic alone and they would not like to encourage me to do so.'[12] Setting aside the fact that she had already achieved a solo Atlantic crossing in *Gulliver G*, Clare herself was worried about the weight of the sails in the Ohlson 38. Winch design had improved significantly in the 1950s and 1960s, with power-multiplying winches making it easier for both women and men to raise large Bermudian mainsails and powerful genoas,[13] but only individual muscle and determination could help with sail changes. Typically, sails had to be brought up from below, through the forehatch, then manipulated on a potentially highly unstable foredeck. Retrieving headsails that had gone over the side and become waterlogged was a serious challenge for the single-hander of either sex. Clare was taking on a fast, responsive yacht with heavy sails that would need frequent changes. She and Jacques simplified systems until she was certain she could manage everything if she accepted it was going to take her very much longer than it would the gorillas of Cowes week. Determination (or stubbornness) was Clare's strong suit. She was also competitive. For the OSTAR, she chose navigational options that she considered gave her the best chance of making good time, even if this might lead her close to icebergs.

Clare finished the race 13th overall and set a new women's single-handed transatlantic record of 29 days. She had felt spurred on, she said, by the enthusiasm and support of other women. Despite her own ambivalence about 'women's lib' she knew that other 'ordinary' women really wanted her to beat the men.[14] Her 13th place was an impressive achievement for a relatively inexperienced sailor of either gender. The 1976 OSTAR was big, controversial and sailed in difficult weather conditions. Two other women in the race (Ida Castiglione and Elie Labourgade) came 42nd and 43rd and another (Aline Marchand) retired when her boat was damaged. Clare weighed only 43kg (6st 11lb) on arrival.

Essential sponsorship had come from Clare's former employers, Robertson's, and other help had followed. Marconi lent Clare a radio telephone – a huge step forward for someone sailing alone. It enabled her to contact Jacques, or her family, thus lifting the weight of guilt felt, for example, by Nicolette. She might know that she was alive and well but was aware that her parents could have no such assurance unless some passing merchant ship with better equipment recognised her yacht and reported the sighting. Clare could both give and receive reassurance using the Marconi equipment. She could also send reports back to the *Daily Express*. A more complex requirement was from the BBC, who loaned equipment and asked her to film herself for *The World About Us*. As she listened to the instructions from the technician Clare had wondered if he had any idea what he was asking her to do. She coped. The resulting film, like the footage brought home by Francis Chichester after sailing round the world in 1967, proved hugely inspiring to the viewing public, as did her book, *Come Hell or High Water* (1977). Clare, unsurprisingly, was a good communicator – though she discovered that when she announced boldly to the camera that she wasn't lonely, the act of articulation would bring her close to realising that she was. 'I'd have a bit of a job not to shed a tear,' she told a later interviewer. She didn't always succeed, and the viewers' hearts went out to her.

In 1977–1978 Clare became the first woman skipper on the Whitbread Round the World Race, sailing the Swan 65 ADC *Accutrac* (which competed in the 2023/24 Ocean Globe Race as *Translated 9*). She sailed with her husband Jacques and a mixed crew, containing two other women: her friend, Eve Bonham, and the ship's cook, Bumble Ogilvy-Wedderburn. In her subsequent book *Come Wind or Weather* (1978) Clare is quite scathing about all-female crews and also (again) about 'women's lib'.

> *The idea that the mainspring of a talented woman's achievements is a desire to get even with men or even to beat them into the ground is a demeaning notion put about by the popular press with their love of out-of-date clichés. Any mention of Women's Lib is guaranteed to make my blood boil.*[15]

She was motivated by her appetite for challenge, excitement, achievement; she did not see that her gender should prevent her having an equal opportunity to sail fast across an ocean or round the world, but it was the goal, not the ideology, that excited her – mainly.

The reaction of other women to what she was doing was different. The women who had followed her progress round Britain or rushed up to wish her well in Plymouth before the OSTAR *did* want her to beat the men. It would be felt as a victory for women against injustice. The popular press may use cliché but it's popular because it understands its core readers. Many women did feel oppressed; many people would never have the same opportunities as Clare (or Robin Knox-Johnston or Francis Chichester) to achieve ambitious individual goals. Clare carried their hopes. As skipper of *ADC Accutrac*, Clare says that she felt her gender disadvantaged her on a physical level. If she needed to lift the large spinnaker boom, for instance, she had to ask one of the men to help her. She felt lesser because she was asking others to do things that she couldn't do herself. Yet on that reckoning, only large, strong people should take command. What Clare achieved was to run a happy ship, to ensure disparate characters would work together and create an environment where everyone's talents were used to best effect. This may or may not be a female characteristic; it's certainly a good form of leadership.

Nicolette Milnes-Walker and Aziz arriving at Newport (Nicolette Coward)

Clare Francis (Clare Francis)

21

'Hiring leaky oilskins from the charter company'[1]
Women making their own way

Claudia Myatt (b. 1956); Miranda Delmar-Morgan (b. 1954); Jill Kernick (b. 1958); Lesley Marsh (b. 1947); Jo Adey (b. 1974)

CLAUDIA MYATT WAS ONE of many women inspired by Clare Francis. She remembers reading *Come Hell or High Water* on the train as she headed to her own first charter holiday in Cornwall. It was 1976; she was living in a London bedsit, working as a secretary. Her flatmate, Frances, had calculated that it was cheaper to hire a boat than a cottage, especially if you were prepared to go out of season – in March, for instance. They had found a couple of friends: John, who came from Cornwall and was believed to know something about sailing, and Nick, who knew about knots. Claudia knew nothing. She didn't think she'd ever seen a yacht before.

She had, however, been to sea. Her father was an RAF meteorologist, which meant that the family moved about regularly according to his postings. These were often on islands: Malta, Anglesey, Singapore. The six-week voyage home from Singapore made an enduring impression. Claudia was 12, too old for the ship's nursery, too young for adult company. Her mother made a couple of attempts to persuade her to keep up with schoolwork, but the impact of the journey came from hours spent standing at the ship's rail, looking out at the flying fish, and beginning to sense the special magic of the deep ocean. She experienced seasickness and felt the dichotomy of sensation – the ocean was either the worst place in the world or the place that made her certain that she'd never really lived until then.

'HIRING LEAKY OILSKINS FROM THE CHARTER COMPANY'

Return to England was an inland posting to RAF Wattisham and a land-based life that included the break-up of her parents' marriage and a purely mechanical application to university: 'just put down the subject where you got best marks at school,'[2] she was told. Any tentative hopes that she might study art were discounted, so she soon put her energies into ice-skating and partying, dropped out of her Modern Languages course and went to work in a burger bar.

The defining moment on that first charter holiday was the moment they turned off the engine. They had only a tiny jib up but the change in motion was like opening a new door in her mind. Everything was thrilling. Yes, she got seasick, cold and scared but she was hooked. From then on, Claudia and her friends went twice a year, out of season, which was the most they could afford, hiring leaky oilskins from the charter company and gradually extending their cruising range as the company learned to trust them. They read everything they could to gain new skills and felt the same intense seriousness about their responsibilities as Arthur Ransome's *Swallows and Amazons* children, who seemed to sail with them. She also read the Hornblower novels and all the cruising accounts she could find. Independent voyages by women fired her imagination. Some of the cruising couples could occasionally sound just the slightest bit contentedly ... smug (though never Beryl Smeeton).

Everything connected with sailing was thrilling, especially when she and her friends could afford slightly larger boats and kinder times of year and could venture a little further – to the Scillies or the Channel Islands. She relished every moment – the sleeping on board, the cooking, the daily routines as well as the sailing – and has never forgotten her horror at the misplaced generosity of a male crew member when they arrived in Jersey. As soon as they'd tied up, he slipped away and returned looking pleased with himself. 'You see that Grand Hotel there,' he said to her and the other woman sailor on board. 'I've booked you two ladies in there for the night.'[3]

They built up their roles: John was the skipper; Claudia was the first mate (in charge of ropes and sail handling and agreeing with the skipper); Frances, the second mate, did logistics and food and keeping them all within budget. They were consciously working according to aptitude and experience, not gender, but it nevertheless meant that by the time Claudia bought a boat of her own, she'd only been part of a team, never actually in charge. Her passion for sailing – plus the increasing cost and instability of living in London during a period of mortgage chaos and negative equity – began to change her outlook in unexpected ways. She gave up trying to conform and live in a house and work a nine-to-five job. She moved to Suffolk, bought a boat, lived on board and began the hard task of trying to make her living as a marine artist. 'Now that I was on my own and in charge,' Claudia remembers, 'I was almost too terrified to get off the mooring.'[4] But she took responsibility and did it – with the help of her friends. This first boat was *Kitty*, a Tamarisk 24, tiny gaff cutter with 21ft waterline length, yet tough enough for cruising at sea as well as river sailing and exploring estuaries.

Knot guru Des Pawson, a friend of Claudia's, suggested she might like to come to a festival at Brixham to sell boat portraits. She and *Kitty* struggled there from Suffolk, battling incessant south-westerly winds. 'How the hell did you get here?' asked Des. 'I didn't know I couldn't', she answered. So many sailors, looking back to their younger selves say, 'It was amazing. We just went.' They feel sailing has become more regulated and risk-adverse, less spontaneous now – or perhaps that's the creeping timidity of age.

During a live-ashore period in the early 1990s Claudia became part of an informal group of women dinghy sailors in Burnham-on-Crouch. It had been founded by a few club wives from the Royal Burnham YC who'd decided they'd had enough of being sandwich makers or fender holders and wanted to sail. Club member Lizzie Brown, who had been a top-class competitive sailor before having children, offered to teach them in scows. These simple, relatively inexpensive sailing dinghies are usually about 11ft long, with a single lugsail and wide beam, originally designed to be seaworthy in a Solent chop. The men coined the term 'cows in scows' for the group, meaning it to be derogatory, but the women turned it round and adopted it. That would be the mildly defiant, self-mocking spirit of much female below-deck humour. Claudia began drawing cartoons for club newsletters then, later, she was commissioned by the RYA to write and draw the cartoon-style *Go Sailing!* series for young sailors – full of her characteristically clever, wince-able puns. In the early noughties, the magazine *Practical Boat Owner* asked her to stand in for the great cartoonist and sailor Mike Peyton, whose eyesight was failing. She may have been the first female cartoonist working in a sailing magazine. She's been there ever since.

Claudia agrees that there is sometimes a female perspective to her cartoons – when she reverses the expected roles, or a woman gets her own back on a bossy skipper. This sort of underdog humour forms a perceptible stream in the sparsely populated shelves of sailing books by women. With varying degrees of resentment and sarcasm, women writers point to the self-important, even bullying behaviour that some male 'Masters under God' display as soon as they step aboard their floating kingdoms. Sometimes this makes a whole comic book – such as *Adventures of a Reluctant Boating Wife* (2013) by Angela Rice (*Motor Boat & Yachting* columnist). Sometimes this only lasts for the first few chapters, until the woman venturing on board has got over her culture shock – arriving in the wrong clothes, getting baffled by jargon, astounded by swearing or by being shouted at – and has either left or found a way to cope.

* * *

When Miranda Delmar-Morgan became skipper of the 1939 Alden schooner *Yankee*, running charter trips between Newport Rhode Island and the Caribbean in the early 1980s, it was generally assumed that she'd got the job by sleeping with the owner. Not true. Miranda had been 'in a relationship' on board, but that was with the previous West Indian skipper. She'd ended it and left, but the owner had realised her ability. When he needed a new skipper and called Miranda back, it was on merit. In retrospect perhaps this was not surprising: on her father's side Miranda came from a long line of naval personalities – her three-times great-grandfather, William Locker, had been Nelson's mentor and friend – yet her personal journey to work on charter yachts hadn't been easy. Her father, Edward, a naval engineer, had left his first wife for Miranda's mother, a younger woman. His family were shocked; her family disowned her. For the first three-and-a-half years of Miranda's life, she and her mother lived on an old prawning boat out in the anchorage at Burnham-on-Crouch, swinging with the tide, while her father commuted to work for Shell. They had a charcoal stove and no running water. Once a week they had a bath in one of the Burnham yacht clubs. Only when Miranda's younger sister was born were they able to move ashore.

It wasn't an easy childhood. Although weekends and holidays were spent sailing while her father was writing pilotage notes for the French, Dutch and Belgian coasts, Miranda's mother suffered seriously from depression. When Miranda was 12 her father had a stroke and sold the boat. Her education stopped before she reached A-levels – 'If I'd been a boy I'd have gone to Eton,' she says. Then her father died. When Miranda was 21 she applied for a cooking job in the Caribbean and left home. This was her salvation, though she soon realised that she wanted to work on deck, not in the galley – handling sails, not cleaning and laundering. The years went by as she moved from one boat to another, sailing on beautiful classic yachts, gaining her Yachtmaster Offshore qualification, and undertaking interesting deliveries, including three transatlantic crossings. She sometimes wonders whether she got the jobs because she didn't have the confidence to ask for much money but remains ever grateful to the owner of *Yankee* for his leap of faith appointing her as skipper. 'I knew I could sail her, I was less sure about manoeuvring an 80 ton boat under power in close quarters, but we both survived.'[5]

After a decade of Caribbean sailing Miranda returned to England, where she made a serious attempt to put together an all-female team for the Whitbread race, potentially chartering the 1973 French entrant *Kriter* and searching unsuccessfully for sponsors who wanted to do any more than simply rename the yacht. She got plenty of publicity but very little actual money. In the midst of what she calls 'this failing endeavour', Miranda met her future husband, Edward Sprot, a landscape gardener. They married, moved inland and had two daughters, Rachael and Arabella.

Away from the water Miranda experienced deep depression. She felt she could scarcely get her daughters on the bus to school. Finally, a lucky financial windfall enabled her to seek psychoanalysis. She came off the blurred welter of medications she'd been prescribed, had the chance to disentangle her difficult childhood relationship with her mother and was given the blindingly simple, liberating advice that she should return to her own specialism, the thing she did best, which made her who she was – sailing. The family moved to Hampshire, where they bought the 34ft *Polar Bear* and Miranda taught Edward and her daughters to sail. She remembers a magical moment when they were exploring the river above Lézardrieux one summer:

> *I put the girls on the bow and told them to tell us what they could see around the bends and told both of them to shout if they saw any rocks. I gave Arabella the lead line and showed her how to swing it. At some point Rachael called back and shouted, 'Oh, this is a whole other world!' Arabella nodded in agreement. I was delighted that they had both understood the magic of adventure and exploration that sailing gives you.*[6]

Teaching her family to sail and owning a wooden boat gave Miranda something to write about. *Yachting Monthly* liked her articles and her academic confidence grew. She began proofreading and editing for Allan Brunton Reed, then took on *Reeds Handbook of Maritime Flags* and *Reeds Marine Distance Tables*. 'Think of every distance as a voyage,' she says. She became involved with the RCC Pilotage Foundation, responsible for north Germany and Poland, exploring their inland waterways and the Hanseatic ports. They cruised to St Kilda, to Great Skellig off the west coast of Ireland, and explored Basque harbours in Euskadi and along the difficult north coast of Spain.

> *The unwritten understanding was that Edward was prepared to put up with all the discomfort, banging his head, cramped living quarters, providing I took him to interesting places. So that's what we did [...] we didn't have firmly fixed destinations because those just add a layer of stress, expectation or frustration. Since I am happy on a boat wherever I am I never minded this approach.*[7]

Today Miranda is still writing and sailing and supports her daughters in their own maritime careers.

* * *

When Jill Kernick, aged 16, went to her school careers fair in 1974, she headed straight for the General Council of British Shipping stand to ask about becoming a navigation officer in the Merchant Navy.[8] She wanted to follow her Master Mariner father. He had been a deck officer for the Union Castle line working between Europe and Africa.

That was how her parents had met, when her mother (from the Transvaal) was travelling to a nursing position in America. Instead, she had fallen in love and settled on the Isle of Wight to bring up their family: three boys and Jill. By the time Jill, the third child, was born her father had come ashore and was a licensed Trinity House pilot in Southampton. When she was four, he bought his first small cruising yacht and from then on family summer holidays were usually to France or the Channel Islands.

Jill loved sailing, her brothers, not so much. When she was 11, her father built her a Mirror dinghy in their kitchen. He taught her navigation and a love of the sea, which they lived next to in Cowes. The dinghy could be trailed across the road and launched from a little slipway. It gave her freedom.

None of this counted at the careers fair. 'We don't have women at sea,' was the crushing reply from the General Council of British Shipping. There was nothing else Jill wanted to do so she remained at school and took A-levels. Her best O-level grades were in French and German, so that's what she studied. Then, in 1975, the Sex Discrimination Act was passed. Jill applied to Ocean Fleets Ltd, along with several other shipping companies, for a cadetship, and this time she was successful. After an introductory course at the company's building, Aulis in Liverpool, she and another girl, Pam Cripps, joined the cargo ship MV *Glenlyon* at London's Royal Albert Dock for a trip to the Far East. In those days the girls were always sent in pairs and were taken at 18, rather than 16, as was the case for the boys. Much later in life, when Jill was a lecturer at Warsash Maritime Academy, she listened to the experiences of some more recent female cadets and was saddened by the lack of care shown to some of them.

Jill's first trip on the *Glenlyon* was for four months from London to Europe through the Suez Canal to Singapore, Jakarta, Brunei, Manila, Hong Kong, Taiwan and Japan, then back to Singapore and Port Kelan, followed by the Suez, to commence discharging cargo at Lisbon, Leixões, Bilbao and Dublin. In the latter, she was relieved for one month's vacation, before joining ship for another four months. Jill loved every moment of it. The sense of adventure, seeing the world and getting paid for it all thrilled her and she didn't mind the hard work on deck. The cadets were under the care of the bosun, a Scouser who took his lower set of false teeth out as soon as they were at sea and therefore wasn't always easy to understand. Work on deck was sweeping, scrubbing, painting, overhauling the blocks and greasing the wire runners. There was one occasion when the bosun offered to excuse Jill from the deck work if she'd sew his buttons on for him, but she refused.

On their second six-month voyage the cadets shadowed the ship's officers. This meant standing their watches with them on the bridge and understudying as they supervised the loading and discharging of the ship's cargo. Jill took her sailing chances too – helping a friend bring a yacht back across the Atlantic pre-GPS, getting involved in Cowes week, and acting as navigator for the Belgian yacht *Incisif* in the 1979 Fastnet race.

The late 1970s were the last years before containerisation. Cargo handling was a specialised skill, soon to become redundant. Initially, the general hold cargo on ships like the *Glenlyon* was supplemented by containers carried on deck, and then the ships themselves began to be sold off as the new system made them outmoded. After her apprenticeship, Jill qualified as a second mate and continued working for the company and improving her qualifications until she was made redundant in 1983. Now her enforced extra time at school studying A-levels suddenly became useful. Trinity House, the 500-year-old corporation charged with overseeing all the lights and navigation markers around the British Isles, had a contract to provide guardships for a large barge lying anchored and immobile in the middle of the English Channel, acting as a central point for a cable-laying operation between Sangatte and Folkestone. They hired two disused trawlers and their crew but also needed their own officers, including French-speaking mates. The lads, who had left school and taken up their Merchant Navy cadetships at 16, had not usually studied languages to any high level. Jill, with her mate's certificate and her language A-levels, became the first woman to be employed by the corporation as a seagoing officer.

Sitting in the middle of the Channel watching the traffic go by was dull. The conditions were easy – four hours on, eight hours off, two weeks on, two weeks off – but Jill longed to join the buoy tenders, where the real work was done. She was told women weren't physically strong enough. She disagreed; it wasn't strength that was needed, but agility and courage. The lights on the navigation buoys in those days were powered by acetylene burners. If a light was reported as being out, the buoy tender would hurry to the spot, then the junior second mate would jump from the vessel on to the buoy, whatever the weather conditions, with matches in the top pocket of their boiler suits to relight it. Jill was certain she would be able to do this but, time and again, young men who had joined the service more recently were preferred for transfer. Eventually she challenged the corporation and obtained her posting. As she'd expected, the job was interesting and great fun. Toilets and showers were shared but this caused no problems.

Jill met her future husband, an engineering officer, at sea. He was also made redundant when the British Merchant Navy fell into decline. While she worked at Trinity House, they lived in Penarth and he studied for a degree. When Jill became pregnant with their first child, she kept it secret for as long as she could but was eventually forced to leave. She was given three months' maternity leave and three months' sick pay, on the understanding that she would work a further three months for Trinity House in the first year after her baby was born or pay the money back. Jill managed this, with her mother's help, but everyone told her that her seagoing career was over – and she believed them.

The family moved to Liverpool when her husband got a new job and Jill became full-time mum to their now four children, meaning she couldn't revalidate her Chief Officer Certificate of Competency. Then, almost ten years after she'd left Trinity House, her husband suggested she begin volunteering with the Sail Training Association (now Sail Training International). This would be unpaid work but would help towards regaining her Certificate of Competency. She also started teaching RYA Yachtmaster courses (shore-based). The Maritime and Coastguard Agency (MCA) agreed to consider her case on an individual basis and revalidated her Chief Officer Certificate. She later gained a job locally on the high-speed ferries across from Liverpool to Dublin and the Isle of Man, returning to Liverpool each night, working one week on, one week off. Getting home at the end of the day made it possible to combine the work with care for her children and to gain the required sea time required to sit for her Master Mariner Unlimited Certificate of Competency. The wage was good enough to enable her to pay her mortgage but there wasn't anything extra – for instance, to buy a dinghy for her son when he seemed keen on sailing. The service was withdrawn for the winter and then cutbacks meant that this job was also gone. Jill's experience and her Master's Ticket got her a job with Wightlink Ferries and she and her family moved back to the Isle of Wight, where house prices were cheaper. Her final job was as a senior lecturer at Warsash Maritime Academy (later Solent University). For 15 years she was the only woman on the full-time staff.

* * *

Lesley Marsh is a member of the Not Under Command club – a phrase I'd like to have stolen for the title of this book. In fact the club is (or was) an association for school staff members who also volunteer to help with their school's Combined Cadet Force (CCF). They have an official rank, learn to instruct young people in Navy, Army or Air Force skills and go with them on training exercises. When they're away, they're working alongside professional sailors, soldiers and air crew so are sometimes made to feel slightly second class. The Not Under Command club brings all such volunteers together for pleasure and mutual support. Women are, as usual, in a minority.

Lesley was a speech and language therapist, but her husband was chaplain of Hereford Cathedral School, which had a Royal Navy CCF and wanted to offer its female students a chance to take part in activities on the water. The girls were keen but none of the women teachers wanted to go away on the training exercises. Lesley volunteered in 1988 and served until 2012, becoming only the second woman to achieve lieutenant commander rank. Her service began before 1993, when the Wrens were formally integrated with the Navy and women could serve at sea. This made Lesley a second-class member (female) of a second-class group (reservists). Arrival at a naval base in the early days of her volunteer service was daunting. She found she had to summon up her courage just to walk into the wardroom.

She was also shocked by some of the active misogyny she and her female pupils encountered, both from certain male CCF officers from all-male schools and occasionally from junior RN officers – though never, and she stresses this, from the non-commissioned officers (NCOs) who were the main professional hands-on instructors for the training exercises. They were older men, experienced and kind, nearing the end of their careers. They didn't have much patience with 'the silly little woman act' but they were the people she would have wanted to be alongside in a crisis. Elsewhere, she learned that the girls she was looking after had to work twice as hard as the boys, and there were still men who would deliberately mark them down because of their gender. This didn't change quickly.

Proportions were usually about 3–4 girls in groups of 20–30 people. Some girls wouldn't attend when certain men were in charge because they were sarcastic, rude and likely to demean them. In the early to mid-1990s this was still commonplace. Lesley coped because she'd chosen to be there; she enjoyed the small boat sailing and adventurous outdoor activities. Her involvement increased until she was spending several weeks a year away on such exercises. As she became more senior, she found it hard to have the NCOs, the older men whom she admired, saluting her. She needed to remind herself that they were saluting her Commission from the Queen, not her as a person. She also got used to dealing with advances from certain male colleagues who were 'off the leash' away from their wives and assumed this was what women were 'for'. 'It wasn't for the faint-hearted. You had to stand your ground.'[9]

* * *

Jo Adey, a generation younger than Jill Kernick and Lesley Marsh, also had a father who had been in the Merchant Navy.[10] He told her not to join. Her initial ambition was to qualify as a dentist, then sign up with a seagoing service. She was a keen Girl Guide and had no difficulty deciding that the Royal Navy would be her career (she'd also discovered that the Merchant Navy didn't employ dentists). But her A-levels weren't good enough. Today, Jo says that although your gender must never stop you doing what you want to do, your lack of qualifications or competencies might.

Instead, she went to study agriculture at Newcastle and joined the RN reserve there, thinking it would be an interesting hobby. After university she worked in retail, studied management and took whatever naval opportunities she was offered: a week on a frigate, time on fishery protection patrol vessels. Then, in 2000, she was asked to represent the Navy in Bosnia for seven months as part of Operation 'Palatine', the NATO-led multinational stabilisation force established after the Bosnian war of 1992–1995. By the time she returned home she had accepted that the RN wasn't just a part-time interest for her; it was where she wanted to work.

'HIRING LEAKY OILSKINS FROM THE CHARTER COMPANY'

After four years as a full-time reservist Jo transferred to the regular service in 2004. Today, she is a commodore, one of the most senior officers in the RN, commanding the men and women of the maritime reserve and also with responsibility for almost 30,000 young people who are members of the Royal Navy's cadet forces. Women now comprise 15 per cent of the entire Navy and there are no areas that are not open to us, including the Royal Marines and the submarine service. This represents quite a change from the attitudes of the 1970s, when a woman discovered on a submarine at sea could provoke something close to panic, as Sue Eagles recalls:

> *I first went to sea by accident in 1975, in a diesel submarine, day-running out of Gosport. I was a Wren Photographer and was onboard on a photographic job, taking pictures of hairline cracks in a piece of equipment for a defect report, when instead of returning to HMS Dolphin, we dived and set off down the Channel into the Southwest Approaches. When I appeared in the Ops Room there was an outcry onboard, and I was told to keep out of sight and get my head down in the Midshipman's bunk in the wardroom. In those days it was very superstitious, especially in submarines, to have a woman onboard!*[11]

Although Jo's career has been shore-based it has included many challenging assignments, such as being a woman in charge of the education of marine commandos when these were still all men. She has never personally experienced bullying though she accepts, with regret, that it seems to be a characteristic of human interactions that those who are perceived as different are vulnerable to being picked on.

Sarah West, the first woman to command an RN warship, is now the civilian CEO of Harwich Haven Authority (HHA), responsible for the safety of navigation in 150 sq miles of water extending 12 miles out to sea, including Felixstowe, Britain's largest container port. This year (2024) she announced that 50 per cent of HHA's marine apprentices are female. 'I would hate people to miss out on the opportunities I've had because of the myth that the industry isn't open to women.'[12]

Jill Kernick driving a high-speed ferry (Jill Kernick)

Duet (Claudia Myatt)

22

'Who wore the pants?'[1]
The role of skipper

Liz and Anne Hammick (b. 1951, 1953); Mary Danby/Barton
(b. 1920); Jane Russell (b. 1966); Annie Hill (b. 1955)

Liz and Anne Hammick experienced the unexpected benefits of having parents whose young adult lives had been disrupted by the Second World War.[2] Their father, Mick, had left university to serve in the RNVR; Eleanor, their mother, had been a Wren. 'When I was their age, I was crossing the ocean on a troop ship,' Eleanor remarked to a friend who asked if she wasn't worried when Liz and Anne sailed two-handed for the first time. Travel, either for work or in the services, was considered normal and three of their grandparents were born aboard, as was Liz, and their early years were spent in Iraq until the Suez Crisis (1956) forced the family home. They settled in Lymington, where Mick built boats. Eleanor came from a naval family, though she didn't learn to sail until she met fellow Wren Mary Danby (later Mary Barton) in what was then Ceylon, where they sailed dinghies on Trincomalee harbour. Mick had learned to sail in his teens aboard his father's gaff 28-footer. So when, in 1974 and after reading Eric and Susan Hiscock's *Beyond the West Horizon* (1963), Liz announced that she was planning to join three others to sail round the world in a 40ft ketch, no barriers were put in her way.

Anne was inspired by the blue airmail letters that arrived from her mother's friend. After the war, Mary had spent many holidays crewing on a yacht in Malta, then in 1969, she gave up her job as a secretary in London and signed on as crew on a yacht sailing from Gibraltar to the West Indies. This was the first of her seven Atlantic crossings.

She jumped ship in Grenada, married Humphrey Barton, founder of the Ocean Cruising Club (OCC), and sailed with him.

After Humphrey's death in 1980, Mary moved ashore to live near her stepdaughter Pat Pocock, herself an intrepid long-distance sailor with her husband Mike. In 1981 Mary travelled to the Azores to present the first Barton Cup. This went to Wendy Moore, who had sailed there non-stop from Northern Ireland in a 27ft sloop with her two children, aged ten and eight, and another crew member. Mary sailed back to England with Rachael Hayward in *Loiwing*. This was a family boat. Rachael's husband, Roger, had sailed her out while Rachael was crewing for Kitty Hampton in the inaugural TWOSTAR Atlantic race, then Rachael skippered her home.

Reading information like this in the Ocean Cruising Club's 50th anniversary volume gives a reassuring impression of the extent to which women sailing alone or with other women were not regarded as extraordinary within that club by that time. Intrepid, yes – the minimum qualification was (and still is) a voyage of 1,000 miles, after which people could, if necessary, apply for membership rather than waiting for their name to be put forward by an existing member. As most members were (as usual) men, this more open entry system may have helped women. The OCC had been inaugurated by Humphrey Barton in 1954 with both Ann Davison and Mary Blewitt among its founder members. After Humphrey's death Mary Barton joined the OCC committee, becoming commodore in 1988 to bring 'peace and leadership' after a difficult period. In 1994 she was appointed the OCC admiral and continued to travel widely and to sail until she was 90.

Liz and Anne Hammick had also raced in that first 1981 TWOSTAR and, many years later, Anne would also become OCC commodore and win some of its awards. After leaving school she completed a secretarial course (which she remembers as possibly the worst year of her life), but it landed her a job with *Yachting Monthly*. After three office years she seized the opportunity to make the first of her Atlantic crossings by signing on as sailing secretary for the well-known yachtsman Don Street in his classic yawl *Iolaire*.

After her return from the Caribbean, Anne took a temporary job in the press office during the 1980 OSTAR. She used the quiet periods on night duty to write a sponsorship proposal for her and Liz to compete together in the 1981 TWOSTAR, and to their considerable surprise her former employers, the Alfred Marks secretarial agency, agreed. The weather that year was wild; more than a quarter of the entries were forced to retire but Anne and Liz, sailing a Freedom 35 called *Miss Alfred Marks*, reached Newport, Rhode Island without serious incident. Both sisters were eager to do more ocean sailing, preferably as free agents, and the following year their father agreed to lend them the money to buy their own boat, a Rustler 31 named *Wrestler of Leigh*, stipulating that they must not take her out of home waters until they had paid for her. *Wrestler* proved a tough and trustworthy boat, taking them on two Atlantic circuits in the 1980s and being sufficiently handy for Anne to sail by herself when Liz married an American fellow sailor. She has remained Anne's home ever since.

The sisters developed their own techniques for sailing together. Anne had a more mathematical mind so took responsibility for the navigation, though she insisted that Liz should also learn to work out sextant sights. Liz was responsible for the 'domestic' side. They bought *Loiwing*'s Hasler wind-vane steering gear when Roger and Rachael Hayward decided to upgrade, and adopted a watch routine that rotated their duties every two days. When, ahead of their second circuit, an insurance company tried to insist they should have a third crew member 'for safety', they pointed out that this would actually be less safe, as they'd never find someone who knew their boat as well as they did.

When Liz married and moved to America (she later sailed round Africa with her husband and their young daughter) it wasn't easy for Anne to combine sailing, OCC involvement, earning a living and (later) caring for her parents as they grew older, but she managed these complex priorities. It had long been her ambition to write a book, and the first (1989) edition of the cruising guide *Atlantic Islands* was researched and largely written (on a rusty portable typewriter) during their second Atlantic circuit in 1986/87. *Ocean Cruising on a Budget* (1990) was published next, based on Anne's first-hand experience of sailing 'on the cheap'. That done, the RCC Pilotage Foundation asked her to update *The Atlantic Crossing Guide*, then *Atlantic Spain and Portugal*, *Islas Baleares* and *The Baltic Sea and Approaches*. In 1990 she took over as editor of the OCC's journal *Flying Fish* – a post she still holds after more than 30 years. She is proud to be a Fellow of the Royal Institute of Navigation as well as an Honorary Member of the Ocean

Cruising Club, the latter defined as a 'distinguished and respected person who has given significant service to offshore cruising'.[3]

* * *

When Jane MacVicker was a child, her parents, Katherine and David, raced National 12s in Torbay.[4] They had been brought together by Katherine's love of sailing. As a young doctor and talented helmswoman, she had visited Shaldon to sail in a dinghy open meeting and had fallen in love with the area. Shortly afterwards Katherine saw a job advertised with a GP practice at nearby Kingskerswell and applied immediately. The practice belonged to David's father. David was younger than Katherine, an engineer and not then a sailor. Katherine taught him to sail, then handed over the helm and sailed as his crew in Merlin Rockets and Flying Fifteens for as long as Jane could remember. When Jane and her brother had a Mirror dinghy, he was the older child, so was automatically the helm while she crewed.

When the family moved to Cheshire, opportunities for sailing were limited, so Jane went riding instead. She relished the freedom of being out alone for hours at a time, exploring the countryside, enjoying her private adventures, scaring or thrilling herself sometimes. For many years I felt faintly guilty that I'd loved riding more than sailing as a child. Going to the boat was a family activity, where my parents were in charge; riding was just the pony and me. Researching this book has taught me how many other girls and women found their initial independence and adventure with horses or turned to them when sailing was not available.

Once Jane went to university she returned to sailing, first at Salford, then in London, where she became commodore of the sailing club while she was doing a PhD in biology at Imperial College. University students raced dinghies – Fireflies and Larks. Jane met David Russell, a London University engineering student, and they began going out together. Although Jane knew nothing about cruising yachts, David had had the thrilling experience of crewing on board the famous and beautiful *Sunstone*, owned by Vicky and Tom Jackson. Twenty years later Vicky and Tom would be awarded the Blue Water Medal by the Cruising Club of America for a lifetime of cruising and racing adventure. By then (2015) they would have covered 200,000 nautical miles, cruised every ocean and visited over 40 countries.

'WHO WORE THE PANTS?'

The Blue Water Medal list is an instructive read. Although it was instituted in 1923, no woman was awarded it in her own right until 1994, when the sisters Jacqueline and Christiane Dardé were honoured for their five-year circumnavigation in 1978–1983 and their subsequent circumnavigation of the Pacific basin, 'All accomplished with competence, grace and humour.' The first solo woman honoured was American Karen Thorndike in 1999. She had completed a circumnavigation during which 'She inspired school children with her daily reports and encouraged them to make adventurous use of the sea.' Perhaps it's a bit chip-on-the-shoulder to wonder whether these women had needed to do just a little more than the equivalent men to be considered for the award? Grumpiness aside, the language of too many pre-1970s citations (before second-wave feminism persuaded some people to choose their words more carefully) abounds with the property-privileged phrase 'owner and wife'. Often, when men and women sailed together, the medal was awarded only to the man. 'And wife' may not even be named yet she presumably made her own choice to participate in the voyage, contributed her effort, stood her watches and had an equal chance of drowning.

* * *

Vicky and Tom Jackson had their own distinctive approach to sailing, combining cruising and racing. When David Russell first knew them, they were teachers, living on board their boat in Brighton. Vicky was assistant dean in the Faculty of Social Science at Southampton Institute (now Southampton Solent University) and Tom was principal of Portsmouth College. When they needed to strip *Sunstone* down to race, they took their extraneous domestic possessions ashore and stored them in a container, putting them back when the race was done. Today they live in New Zealand, and sail a different yacht, but maintain the website www.sunstonesailing.com to share some of their experiences. They have this to say about cruising couples:

> *Among many cruising couples, one person will be more experienced and probably more confident than the other. We think it is the duty of* **both** *persons to ensure that the less experienced person gains the expertise, experience and most importantly the confidence to carry out all the normal evolutions of*

a watch keeper alone. This should include reefing, changing sail, pilotage and navigation. There have been numerous accounts of voyages in which the more experienced person in a two-member crew has been incapacitated and the less experienced has had to work the boat alone to the next port. It is neither sensible nor safe to maintain a tacit conspiracy of superiority for one person and convenient incompetence in the other. Each person must be able to trust the other to work and navigate the ship.[5]

David Russell had looked at the Jacksons' way of life and had read many of the classics of cruising literature, given to him by his grandfather. This was the life he wanted for himself. When he'd known Jane for about two months, he asked her if she thought she'd like to make her home on a boat. Jane said yes at once. She knew nothing at all about yacht cruising but did know that the detached suburban house, the Ford car in the drive and 2.2 children was not what she wanted. She and David began searching for a yacht that would also be their home – 'it was kind of nuts, but that was what we did'. They found *Tinfish*, a 34-year-old, 37ft Dutch design built in rolled steel. After they were married, they moved on board and began to realise the scale of the task they had set themselves. Much of *Tinfish*'s hull below the waterline had decayed and needed replating. Jane was working as a teacher and lecturer by day, earning her teaching qualification and also studying Yachtmaster theory in the evenings, then returning home to *Tinfish* to continue to graft on the hull on top of which they lived. It got worse when they realised that they also needed to take out all of the concrete that successive owners had tipped in. The concrete had flexed, saltwater had got in, and all the various compounds had reacted with each other to make what Jane describes as an 'acidic soup'. At one point they hired a Kango demolition hammer to help break up the concrete. Then, when it was all out and the exterior welding complete, they rebedded the ballast pigs in bitumen. This meant boiling the bitumen in a large drum on the quay, then hauling it up a ladder to tip into the bilge. It must have been quite a challenge for Jane to arrive looking suitably clean and tidy to teach each day.

When they finally got to sea, intending an Atlantic circuit, Jane was hopelessly sick – even when she'd been racing a dinghy, she'd been likely to throw up. She also discovered that she loved being at sea, even when she was incapacitated almost all the way from Penarth to Bayona. She could understand that her level of sickness – to the point of dehydration

– was a worry for David but her own enthusiasm was undiminished. It was a huge relief when she discovered scopolamine patches, yet she remains adamant that sickness would never have put her off. The joy of being at sea – however cold, wet, frightened or nauseous she felt – was something completely separate from its discomforts or inconveniences.

Jo Stanley quotes research by Samson C Stevens and Michael Parsons, *The Effects of motion sickness on crew performance*, which gives a figure of 1.7 women to every 1 man affected by seasickness.[6] The impression given by sailing literature is that women are even more susceptible than this. I wonder whether this is in part because this has historically been written by men, who may already expect women to feel sick? The way women may be treated when on board – sent below for a precautionary lie-down, or expected to remain below, either to cook or keep out of the way – may be more likely to precipitate nausea than remaining in the fresh air on deck, preferably on the helm. There are many theories, including the different balance within women's bodies makes us sway differently. There may be a hormonal element in seasickness, as some women report the problem reducing post-menopause. (On the other hand, older women may have become more confident and better able to manage their sickness.) People who feel nervous in an unfamiliar environment might be more susceptible. But Jane's sickness happened anyway. She and David confronted it as a practical issue and continued to make all decisions jointly.

'So, who's the skipper?' Couples who sail as an equal partnership may resent this question – though possibly it's one better than *'Ou est le capitaine?'*, often asked of women sailing without men. Historically there has been an assumption that the man will take the lead, and the woman will provide support, almost irrespective of their actual talents and experience. Remember Katherine, Jane's mother, a more experienced sailor than her husband, teaching him to sail, then handing over the tiller? Blue Water medallist Annie Hill says that when she sailed with her first husband, she had to ask that he write her down as 'mate' rather than 'crew' on their clearance papers: 'A request he didn't seem to understand.' He was sufficiently 'feminist' to expect her to enjoy being cold, wet and uncomfortable and to learn practical skills like painting and splicing but had no inclination to treat her as an equal. 'I once suggested that occasionally I should be skipper for the day,' Annie recalls. 'But he refused point blank. "Why not?" I asked. "Because I want to be skipper" was his reply.'

It would be good to think of this title 'skipper' purely as a job role, like 'navigator' or 'sailing master' or 'ship's husband', and it may be so on yachts when the owner is on board and the skipper is a paid professional. This can bring its own problems if the owner is female. Mike Bender in *A New History of Yachting* (2017) quotes an anecdote concerning Lady Margaret Crichton-Stuart (b. 1875) who had such trouble getting the crew of her steam-yacht to obey her orders that she took and passed her Board of Trade Master Mariners exam, which made disobeying her an act of mutiny.[7] More usually, however, the word 'skipper' is understood as a substitute word for captain. Many people who go sailing accept as axiomatic that there can only be one skipper/captain and that when men and women are sailing together, this will usually be the man. But why? Quick, important decisions will need to be taken, and they are best taken by the person with most all-round knowledge of the situation at the time, whatever their gender. On board *Tinfish*, if Jane was on watch, she would take immediate decisions. If David had the responsibility, he would. Decisions that were not instantaneous would be discussed, and the better for it. They describe themselves as co-skippers, respecting each other's knowledge and points of view and compensating for each other's weaknesses. If this is still a rare approach, sailing is the poorer for it.

Cruising yachts are small worlds in which humans commit themselves to an alien element. All are at equal risk. The hierarchy of esteem that assumes that navigation is a higher-order skill than provisioning, for instance, needs some reconsideration in the context of a boat offshore. One of the wisest moments in Arthur Ransome's book *Peter Duck* (1932) is when Captain Flint, attempting to accede to a request from his crew to go 'foreign', first asks Mate Susan how much food and water they have on board. It is her answer that sets the parameters of what is possible. Yes, skilful navigation matters hugely in the unmarked ocean – but so does sufficient provision of drinking water. They are interdependent – as Tom and Anna Brassey had demonstrated, back in 1876.

On a small family cruiser, the rational approach to best management can be curdled by unexamined emotional issues and unacknowledged power struggles. In the case of Miles and Beryl Smeeton, Miles willingly acknowledged that Beryl was the motivator in their adventures, yet Miles Clark reports an incident where a friend joked that Beryl 'wore the pants in the Smeeton family ... Miles went absolutely puce and just stopped short of hitting him.'[8] Sailing wives Joyce Sleightholme and Hilary Wickham stress the importance of upholding the man's ego. Yet many people will have noticed that it is usually a woman who is being shouted at by a man at the helm. Too many women on small vessels have suffered belittlement of their skills and attacks on their self-esteem, which are hard to shrug off in the confined space of a saltwater home. Annie Hill writes:

> *My second, unhappy, marriage was probably influenced by the fact that [...] I had started to find my feet and think for myself. It was my bad luck and/ or bad judgement that I discovered somewhat too late, that this man didn't take kindly to having his decisions or judgement questioned. As time went by, his attacks on my self-confidence and self-esteem finally hit something in me that refused to back off anymore, so I jumped ship and started – somewhat terrified at the prospect – to live on my own and on my own terms.*[9]

Annie was married twice: once to Peter Hill, once to Trevor Robertson. Now, when she looks back she sees her single life as tough but a relief:

> *Once I was on my own, I came to realise that while living with Pete and trying to keep him happy, and likewise with Trevor, things had been ticking away in my subconscious and, once I'd got past the stage of feeling a failure because I Didn't Have A Man, I realised that I had a very clear idea of how I wanted to live.*

Her friend Shirley Carter agrees:

> *I enjoy the independence that sailing on my own gives me. The ability to choose where and when I want to go (weather permitting of course), where and when I want to eat, etc. is a wonderful luxury. This may make more sense to other women as most men take these things for granted anyway. Naturally there are times when it would be nice if there was someone else to fix whatever has just broken, or help with keeping watch, but it is a very satisfying feeling when you arrive at a safe anchorage after what may have been a difficult passage and you have done it on your own.*[10]

Annie Hill had met Pete when she was 18 and he was 23. Initially they sailed together on Pete's 28ft Wharram catamaran *Stormalong*. They set out for the West Indies with Annie having no idea at all what to expect, therefore feeling no fear. (She had needed to look in her father's atlas to have any idea where the West Indies were.) They returned determined to continue this way of life but also realising that they would need more space. After various false starts they began building the 34ft junk-rigged sailing dory *Badger*. They lived on a boat, worked full time to earn money and also built *Badger* full time. Annie even managed to save some money. With that and the proceeds from selling their liveaboard boat they eventually accrued sufficient capital to give them an income of £15 a week, on which they could be 'poor and free rather than wage slaves.' Then they set out voyaging.

Many sailors, even those for whom passage making is not a full-time way of life, feel indebted to Annie for her book *Voyaging on a Small Income* (1993), which takes a consumerist technique of comparison and evaluation to underpin a way of living that is an escape from consumerism. Prices and products have changed since the book was first published but her thinking retains its value: 'Because we live on so little, we are in fact wealthy. Poverty is having insufficient money to buy the necessities and comforts of life. Wealth is having more money than you need to live on at your chosen standard.'[11] Twenty-first-century sailor Susan Smillie sets out this same equation very simply: 'The longer my money lasted, the longer I'd be at sea and there's nothing as motivating as that.'[12]

Setting off in 1983, Annie and Pete spent most of the next two decades exploring the North and South Atlantic oceans – as far north as Greenland and Baffin Island, as far south as South Georgia. From the outside they were an inspirational couple but as Annie grew more confident and knowledgeable, she found it harder to live with Pete's assumption of superiority.

> *Pete decided where we would go, when we would go, the way in which we'd sail and what we'd sail. I was allowed some input, but he made the final decisions. A typical example of Pete's idea of letting me have a say in things, was to tell me that he couldn't decide between one of two choices, and which would I prefer! I don't think he ever asked me what I would like to do.*

She accepted this because she loved Pete and was impressed by his confidence. However, when he insisted on selling *Badger* against her wishes, their marriage came to an end. During the first decade of the 21st century Annie sailed with Trevor Robertson in *Iron Bark*

II, including spending a winter frozen in the ice in Greenland. Their explorations inspired others, and they were awarded a Blue Water Medal in 2009, but Annie had had enough of an existence that she found increasingly controlling. She left.

Since then, Annie has developed her own way of life in New Zealand, first on board the 26ft fibreglass boat *Fantail*, which she converted to junk rig, and now on the junk-style plywood boat *FanShi*, which she designed and built herself. She undertakes slow coastal cruises rather than piling on the miles long-distance voyaging. Her interest in vegetarianism and minimalist living has moved on from personal thrift into a conscious care for the environment. Like Shirley Carter (who also sailed with Pete Hill for a while) she enjoys managing life on her own. The most important thing for her today is to 'tread lightly on the planet'.

Annie Hill on FanShi, *the boat she designed and built (Annie Hill)*

23

Trouser suits

Married teamwork

Sheila Chichester (b. 1905); Naomi James (b. 1949)

DO EQUAL, INTERDEPENDENT COUPLES have a place in this book? Jane Russell, co-skipper with David on *Tinfish II*, says, 'We have always been a team. Neither as good on their own without each other.' Rozelle Beattie found a happy second marriage to Dr Dick Raynes and wrote 'I can safely say that single-handed sailing has absolutely nothing to offer compared with double-handed sailing with the right man!'[1] Yet interdependent people also remain themselves with their individual talents and possibilities. One of the truest accolades that can be offered is when one partner is able to say to the other, 'I could never have been so much myself without you.' Jane and David's cruising together resulted in Jane developing her navigation and pilotage skills, while David developed his skills in boatbuilding and ships' husbandry. In 2008 Jane took responsibility for *The Atlantic Crossing Guide* (6th edition). She then served ten years as editor-in-chief for the Royal Cruising Club Pilotage Foundation (RCCPF), overseeing its extraordinary range of pilot guides covering (it seems) almost all the navigable areas of the globe. Rozelle's happy second marriage gave her the confidence to write her first books, and also to undertake projects such as the 'Tuesday Boys' initiative in East London, which Dick supported, but where the leadership was hers.

Sheila Chichester fulfilled a more conventional wifely role of supporter, onshore organiser and publicist for her husband but did this on her own terms. Her assertive, individual style antagonised some people but made a tangible difference to Francis' ability to achieve. It gave her personal satisfaction and growth, while almost incidentally spurring on other sailors, including women. When Sheila wore a red trouser suit in 1967 to attend her husband's knighting at Greenwich by Queen Elizabeth II it made headlines – not friendly ones. Her stated reasoning was that she had sailed up the Thames with her husband on *Gipsy Moth IV*, and trousers were more practical for scrambling off boats. Essentially, she just liked trousers. In 1960, when the competitors left Plymouth at the start of the first OSTAR and she was preparing to return to London before travelling to America herself, she held a dinner party where all the ladies were asked to come in trousers. 'I have always liked them and was taking several pairs with me to America, so I thought it would be rather fun to wear them on this occasion.'[2] Although this first single-handed transatlantic race was an all-male affair, Sheila was a convinced supporter of Blondie Hasler's ideas to simplify sailing, as she believed this would help women.

> *I've always thought there were far too many chores in sailing. I don't mean below – that is pretty simple because it's all so small. No, I mean on deck where in the past they had these terribly heavy warps and sheets, stiff canvas sails and ghastly great boat hooks and so on. One of the most valuable things the Solo race did for sailing was advance a lot of very necessary ideas which have been a help to crews, ocean racers and in fact all sailing people. Above all, of course, the wind vane. This self-steering device really developed from the race. There had been a few before but nothing like the number now in use, and this is of immense benefit to women. One can often take a watch quite easily but it's very tiring to take the helm for hours on end.*[3]

She tested her belief directly by sailing back from New York with Francis after he had won that first race. It was one of their happiest times. 'Miranda', the self-steering vane, could take charge while she and her husband had time together. Sheila's autobiography, *Two Lives, Two Worlds* (1969) is full of strong personal views – on clothes, veganism/vegetarianism, alternative medicine, the power of prayer – yet her whole *raison d'être* (as she saw it) was to support Francis. Looking back at her younger self when they first married (1937) and were struggling financially she wrote, 'The strange thing is that I never thought of taking a job then. Married women didn't. I just lived for Francis and planned everything for him.'⁴

Later, when Francis' sailing exploits meant that he was often away, she did take a hands-on interest in their map business. She enrolled on a salesmanship course – the first woman the training company had ever seen – and announced herself as managing director of Francis Chichester Ltd. Unsurprisingly, she attracted some hostility. She's perhaps a little in the mould of Evgenia Ransome – a woman of great energy and forcefulness, guarding her husband and his health like a dragon, thus allowing anyone with a potential gripe against the husband to project their dislike on to her. She was also someone who had been denied the opportunity to develop her own career. In her memoir she describes a difficult and tightly restricted upbringing, a poor relation within a rich and snobbish family, with the additional taint of being a child whose father killed himself within three months of her birth. As a young woman she showed clear gifts as a dress designer or portrait painter but the idea of her earning her own living 'seemed quite wrong to my mother':

> *When I was 17, a friend offered to finance me in a dress shop, but my mother refused this just as she did the opening for me as a designer in Paris. If I have a regret in life. I regret that I didn't have a proper métier, as the French say. I could have been a successful dress designer, I am certain of that. I could also have been a good portrait painter. But I was devoted to my mother and it never entered my head to leave her and strike out on my own.*⁵

When Sheila's mother died in 1932, Sheila was 27. Her grandfather's lawyer told her that she might never marry so should take out insurance. At this point Sheila lost her temper and said that she didn't care whether she married or not; she wanted to travel and she was going to India. When she agreed to marry Francis, all she knew was that he had no money and wanted her to come with him to New Zealand. She had no idea that he was already famous as an aviator. It was a defining moment when Amy Johnson came to a party in Sheila's flat and told her she was also marrying one of the best navigators in the world. Yet, without Sheila as motivator, communicator, organiser and dragon, it's unlikely Francis would have achieved his extraordinary post-war fame as a sailor. They both believed she'd saved his life from cancer. She was absolutely right to go for that red trouser suit.

* * *

Once records are set, they inspire others to challenge them. In 1966–1967 Francis Chichester had sailed *Gipsy Moth IV* 29,360 miles round the world via five great capes in 266 days, with a single stop at Sydney. In 1977 Naomi James left Dartmouth, determined to do this more quickly. Her husband Rob was already at sea, crewing on board Chay Blyth's *Great Britain II* in the 1977/78 Whitbread Round the World Race. Chay had lent Naomi his yacht (renamed *Express Crusader*) for her attempt. His wife Maureen was a tower of strength helping Naomi prepare and provision it. They – and above all Rob – had transformed her life.

Naomi had been born Naomi Power on a remote farm in New Zealand. Her childhood had been spent at a remove from other people – and from the sea. She was 23 before she learned to swim. As children, she and her brother and sisters spent most of their days on horseback, making up in courage and determination for what they lacked in equipment and quality animals. They could ride for miles and see no one. They also read and acted out their books, and Naomi dreamed of heroic deeds. She says she dreamed her way through school as well, to such an extent that she was advised to leave when she was 16, to avoid failing all her exams. The family had moved from Hawkes Bay to the Bay of Plenty, where there were more people and social life. Naomi went to train as a hairdresser, which she says cured her of her shyness but left her with a lasting dislike of tittle-tattle and provincial gossip. 'There was much that I wanted to know about people, what made them tick, what made the world go round, but none of the women I met seemed interested in those subjects. I had to turn back to books and try to find out at second hand.'[6] She went to night classes and obtained some O-levels, and learned German, but otherwise spent her time at home, reading and riding and saving for her chance to travel. 'I wanted to have control of my own future; I wanted to choose, not just accept.'[7]

Although her sister Juliet travelled to Europe with her, Naomi's account of her adventures is essentially solitary – she almost relished being alone in a crowd. She also felt frustrated. Where was the great adventure of life? She felt that all she'd learned so far was what she didn't want. Perhaps she should move to England and find a job working with animals. In St Malo, by the merest chance, she met Rob James, then skippering *British Steel*. This was the yacht in which Chay Blyth had completed his 'wrong way' circumnavigation of the globe in 1970/71. It was then being used as a charter yacht, with Rob in charge. In little more than a week Naomi was signed on as deckhand/cook. 'It was an ambitious title since I didn't know one end of the boat from another; and in addition, I couldn't cook.'[8] At first she was horribly seasick and profoundly grateful for Rob's encouragement to spend as much time as possible on deck. She worked on *British Steel* all summer and learned from listening to Rob's patient instructions to each new charter crew. It was hard when he had to take the yacht away for six months on the 1975/76 Atlantic Triangle Race and she was not able to go with him.

Naomi returned to New Zealand, to her family and to horses. She earned money as a 'fleecer' (part of a sheep-shearing team) and read an article about Brigitte Oudry's plan to sail solo round the world. Might she attempt something similar? It was 1975 – International Women's Year, which helped inspire such ambitious projects. Polish shipbuilding engineer Krystyna Chojnowska-Liskiewicz (b. 1936) had the same idea and set out on her circumnavigation in February 1976. Naomi and Rob married as soon as they were reunited and spent another summer working together on a new charter yacht, also belonging to Blyth. It was a while before Naomi told Rob about her dream of circumnavigating single-handed. As soon as he realised she was serious he gave her his full support – as did Chay Blyth. Yet despite their best professional efforts, no sponsor could be found. It took a party, several cocktails, an unexpected offer from a former *British Steel* charter crew member together with the loan of Chay Blyth's *Spirit of the Cutty Sark* to turn Naomi's dream into a reality. They had only a month to prepare and she'd never sailed alone before. No insurance company would accept the risk, but three private individuals (all men) pledged the money that would compensate Chay if his yacht was lost.

Naomi and the newly renamed *Express Crusader* left Dartmouth on 9 September 1977 to sail 30,000 miles round the world via the 'Clipper Route' – the Cape of Good Hope, Cape Leeuwin and Cape Horn. She was accompanied by a kitten, but her real encouragement came from the knowledge that Rob in *Great Britain II* was circumnavigating not so far ahead and one day they would be able to continue their life together. Despite the jobs to be done, the weather changes and problems arising, Naomi found she had time to think at sea. As long as Rob was somewhere in the world, she didn't need anyone else. She also discovered that the risk in sailing was integral to her pleasure. Her skills improved as she continued tackling maintenance tasks and planning ahead for heavy weather. She tightened her engine alternator belt and was 'happy to do something I'd never have attempted if there was a man around'.[9] Her radio failed. Six weeks would pass before damage to the self-steering forced her to make landfall at Cape Town, at which point she realised how worrying her silence had been for her family: 'When I read their letters it nagged me that I was being very selfish and unkind. However, it had to be and anyone making this sort of journey has to be a little hard-hearted.'[10]

She lost the kitten. It was a struggle not to allow grief to overwhelm her. Instead, she redoubled her own safety precautions against an inadvertent slip. She hung trailing lifelines over the side and a rope ladder to assist her scrambling back on board. The fear of going over the side had been a major worry since first she challenged herself with this big 'dare'. The loss of small items overboard distressed her disproportionately: it reminded her of 'the finality at the edge of the boat'.[11]

As she approached the South Island of New Zealand she spoke to her family, who were living on the North Island, their minds taken up with their own concerns – the price of wool, the weather, a scone recipe. Once again, she asked herself what had driven her to make this trip: Was it her slight fear of other people? Was it a wish to prove that one's life didn't need to be determined by one's background? 'If you want to do something different, you can.'[12] What had persuaded Rob and Chay to support her wish to sail alone round the world? She saw it as an expression of faith: 'They believe I can do it because I believe I can.' She knew that if she failed and died, they would be blamed by the public. On the stretch from New Zealand to Cape Horn, her starboard lower shrouds came down, leaving the mast swaying, only semi-supported, putting her in real peril. She dropped the mainsail and rigged temporary rope supports, knowing they were not enough. After two days spent battling to free a jammed nut, extract the crucial through-mast bolt, drill new holes in cracked metal plates and reattach the shrouds, she was bruised and exhausted. The barometer was falling fast, the sky looked ominous, and she knew there was a storm coming. Some 2,800 miles onwards to Cape Horn or 2,200 miles back to New Zealand? She took the decision to turn back, then complete her circumnavigation via the Panama Canal, not the Cape. That was the route taken by Krystyna Chojnowska-Liskiewicz, who started and ended her voyage in the Caribbean, taking 401 days but becoming the first woman to sail alone round the world on 20 March 1978, 39 days before Naomi's eventual arrival in Dartmouth.

This decision marked the lowest point of the voyage. The wind blew up beyond storm force, a wave hit *Crusader* with a crash, she capsized and began taking on water. Naomi found the hole and plugged it with a T-shirt. She went on deck, strapped herself on to the binnacle, faced the waves and began to steer by hand, returning below at intervals to continue to pump. The waves were mountainous, a combination of 20ft swells with 20–30ft waves on top. If one of them toppled on to her, she would be crushed. *Crusader* began surfing wildly. Naomi knew she had to keep the yacht's stern absolutely square to avoid being whirled around and overturned. Yet through all of this, the mast stayed up. Once the wind had moderated sufficiently to enable her to think again about her situation, she realised that her decision to turn back had been based on fear. She resumed her original course.

She passed Cape Horn on 19 March 1978 without setting eyes on it and (somewhat miraculously) without realising quite how close she had been to icebergs. She found help with her mast and radio in the Falkland Islands and achieved a rendezvous with Rob off the Azores. Towards the end of the final stretch to Dartmouth, arriving too early for the official reception, she had time to drift and reflect on all she'd learned. She compared herself to other circumnavigators: Robin Knox-Johnston, Francis Chichester, her friend Chay Blyth. She thought about faith – which for her lay in Rob, her family and friends; she was never alone when she could think of them. Yet being alone had given her additional strength. When she had been up the mast, struggling to free the jammed nut, it was the knowledge that there was no one else that had enabled her to succeed.

In a purely physical sense, she, like Clare Francis, realised that her arms had changed. She had muscles where there had been none before.

She arrived on 8 June 1978, wearing a white trouser suit, chosen by her sister Juliet and transported on board by Rob, who was allowed to join her once she had crossed the official finishing line. She had beaten Francis Chichester's record, though only if time spent ashore is added to both totals. Brigitte Oudry, who also circumnavigated via Cape Horn, arrived home that same year.

Naomi had not expected to write a book about her experience, but she had kept personal journals. These formed the basis for *At One with the Sea* (1979). She joked later about her 'weekness' in spelling and grammar but the book was her own, with the assistance of an editor, not a ghost-writer. Writing it was hard, even with her journals for reference. She became aware that the 'me' who had lived through the voyage and written the journals was a different person from the one who had set out, and different also from that same person she discovered again as soon as she returned. 'As I wrote I was drawn back to a life that had closed its doors on me and had become the past as soon as I had come within reach of the English coast.'[13] Her experience may be understood by other people who experience periods of near-absolute solitude together with the active pressure of ensuring survival in an alien element. Ellen MacArthur expresses a sense of dread on her first moment of return from solo circumnavigation. The example of Bernard Moitessier, who turned away from the first Golden Globe race and sailed on, is well-known and probably even understood by others who simply take themselves away alone on their boat for a weekend and feel reluctance to go home. It is as if, as well as a 'different world', there is a different person living in your body when you are on the water and out of contact with others. Naomi's first book ended thoughtfully:

> *In attempting this voyage I risked losing a life that had at last become fulfilling; but in carrying it out I experienced a second life, a life so separate and complete it appeared to have little relation to the old one that went before. I feel I am still much the same person now, but I know that the total accumulation of hours and days of this voyage have enriched my life immeasurably.*[14]

Finding that Rob was still the same and that he recognised her as 'herself' (the one he had loved and married before the voyage) helped immeasurably. What she hadn't anticipated was the way that celebrity – and indeed the book itself – would threaten to deprive her of just the autonomy of experience she had learned to value so highly. Other people's attitudes to her changed. She realised that she had brought this on herself, so had to accept the unwelcome consequence. Her second book, *At Sea on Land* (1981), is an account of the difficulties of this new life, where she discovers herself lost in a straitjacket of public expectations, publicity schedules and interviewers trying to present her as someone different again. In Canada, for instance, she appeared with Krystyna Chojnowska-Liskiewicz, Betty Cook (the first woman to win the world powerboat championship) and two young Canadian dinghy champions. She was surprised to discover that few women in Canada participated in sailing – there were virtually no women-only dinghy or keelboat races – but resented being interviewed on behalf of a 'woman's cause'. 'I sailed for myself for my own particular reasons which had nothing whatsoever to do with women's lib.'[15] In Spain, she found herself used as an example for and against feminism; in Germany (Hamburg) she had tried to retell (in German) her story against herself of the occasion she discovered she had mixed up latitude and longitude. It didn't go down well:

> *Next day at the boat show I was confronted by a trio of incensed middle-aged Sunday sailors who demanded to know what I thought I was doing by saying such rubbish on television. 'Don't you realise that this sort of irresponsible remark could entice half the women in Germany into sailing off around the world tomorrow?'*[16]

Again and again, she expresses her gratitude for the part Rob played in ensuring she could cope with an existence she found so alien. Sometimes he needed to remind her of the financial difference this was making to their lives – a new room in the Irish home for which they both longed, for instance. In 1980 they both competed in the OSTAR: Rob finished 16th and Naomi 24th (the only woman who completed the race that year). A glimpse of the internal dynamic of their relationship comes when Naomi admits that most of their joint activities – windsurfing, skiing, sailing – turned into competitions that Rob invariably won (except for chess, at which she beat him). She says she was glad that he was 'the stronger member' of their team; 'Rob would not have liked to be the loser too often.'[17] In 1982 they sailed together to win the Round Britain race in the trimaran *Colt Cars*. Naomi's seasickness on that voyage was so bad that she announced that that was the end of her sailing career. She was also in the early stages of pregnancy. In March 1983, ten days before their daughter's expected birth date, Rob fell overboard while stowing *Colt Car GB*'s sails approaching Salcombe harbour and died of hypothermia. 'Finality at the edge of the boat' indeed.

This most cruel irony may not be the most sensitive moment to point out the significant difference in the survival rates between men and women in the water, something Ann Davison discovered as she and Frank endured being alternately soaked and frozen while exposed on their cork float in the seas off Portland Bill. Women often 'feel the cold' more than men – it's connected with the relative quantities and distribution of muscle and body fat. Body fat protects the inner organs but can block the flow of blood leading to the skin and the body extremities (hence our pleasure in gloves, bed socks and hot-water bottles) – but the comparative risk rates for death from hypothermia show men at a definite disadvantage. For many years women's superficial responses to heat and cold were used as justification for denying participation in military combat roles, for example. Those decisions were frequently underpinned by using tests designed for male bodies, where sweating and shivering reflexes, for example, often work differently. An early indication of women's ability in cold water came in 1926 when Gertrude Ederle, aged 20, swam the English Channel, then considered one of the toughest endurance tests in the world. She took two hours off the previous male record. Sailing is often an endurance sport: many women, as well as men, have proved that they have outstanding capacity to endure.

There are, of course, many other factors affecting personal survival rates, mental attitude being one of them. Nicolette Milnes-Walker's conjecture concerning the likelihood of superior female resilience, due to an innate, inherited habit of centring thoughts on husband or children, receives an unexpected endorsement from Miles Smeeton's account of his and Beryl's differing reactions when *Tzu Hang* was pitchpoled off Cape Horn. Beryl was steering and had been thrown out of the yacht, briefly losing consciousness. She had then succeeded in swimming back, even with a broken shoulder. Miles and their fellow crew member, John Guzzwell, had helped her on board, both believing that the end had come. *Tzu Hang* seemed to be on the verge of sinking. Miles wrote:

> *After this first action. I went through a blank patch. Thinking that it was only a few moments, a few minutes of waiting, thinking despondently that I had let Clio down. Beryl's bright, unquenchable spirit, thought of no such thing. 'I know where the buckets are!' she said. 'I'll get them.' This set us working to save* Tzu Hang.[18]

Today Naomi James lives quietly in the cottage in Currabinny, which she and Rob had bought. She is a graduate of University College Cork, studies Wittgenstein and has spent the last few years writing a life review, which she describes as 'an essential exercise in understanding the paths we (often unconsciously) follow'. Her view of feminism has changed from the 1970s and 1980s. Then, she was trying to separate herself from male/female stereotypes that didn't feel relevant to her life. Now, she sees it as one of the ongoing battles for equality that are relevant to us all.

Sheila Chichester in her red trouser suit, on Gypsy Moth IV *with husband Francis, after his record-breaking singlehanded circumnavigation, May 1967 (Getty Images)*

24

'I pinned a smile on my face'[1]
Winners

Tracy Edwards (b. 1962); Ellen MacArthur (b. 1976)

ON 29 FEBRUARY 1980, Tracy Edwards, aged 17, left home and headed to Greece with her boyfriend. She'd been suspended from school 26 times, then expelled, had a court appearance for joyriding against her, a reputation for drinking and snogging, and had fallen out irreparably with her stepfather. She'd also been bereaved and bullied. Until her father's death, when she was ten, Tracy's childhood had been a happy one. Her mother was a dancer and her father's electrical business kept the family in modest comfort in the village of Purley, near Reading in Berkshire. Tracy went to stage school and loved ponies. When her father died suddenly of a heart attack, her mother struggled to carry on but found there was little support for a woman in business then. She remarried two years later and moved to Llanmadoc on the Gower Peninsula. The scenery and the animals were wonderful but life for an English, private-school-educated girl in a Welsh comprehensive school was 'hell'. Tracy became tough to survive. In her autobiography she writes: 'All these years later I still can't explain why I ran so far off the rails [...] Perhaps I never got over Dad's death.'[2] Possibly this developed a fighting spirit and a degree of social understanding that she might never had discovered in Purley.

Less than ten years after her arrival in Greece, Tracy was the best-known woman sailor in the world. She had been awarded the MBE and voted Yachtsman of the Year by the yachting journalists who had previously reviled her. It's often said that she was the first to be honoured thus. Technically that's true – when Nicolette Milnes-Walker was given her award as 'Yachtswoman of the Year' alongside Chay

Blyth, it was described as a 'special' award; perhaps it wasn't thought to count? It might also show how quickly women's achievements can be forgotten. In Nicolette's case, the yachting media had simply blanked her from their pages. Tracy had aroused active hostility – just as she did when she arrived at Gowerton comprehensive school.

Tracy's struggle and success with *Maiden* and an all-female crew in the 1989/90 Whitbread Round the World Race is well-known, not least because of Alex Holmes' award-winning documentary *Maiden* (2018). The ending of this film regularly moves hard people to tears as the yacht makes her entrance to the Solent, and to Ocean Marina, and Tracy and her crew realise that the boats massing around, the horns blowing and the crowds waiting, are for *them*. 'No one cared that we hadn't won, we had done something we'd been told we couldn't do.' These women were Tracy Edwards, Amanda Swan, Mikaela Von Koskull, Claire Warren, Michele Paret, Tanja Visser, Sally Creaser, Dawn Riley, Nancy Hill, Jeni Mundy, Jo Gooding, Sarah Davies and Angela Farrell, plus Marie-Claude Kieffer, whom Tracy had sacked two weeks before the start. Tracy has said that watching the closing sequence of the film, 27 years after they'd actually crossed the finish line, was the moment that the women fully realised their achievement. They'd come together for the premiere, several of them bringing their children. People had gone their separate ways after the race, but motherhood had become another shared experience for some. When Tracy had given birth to her daughter Mackenna, Jo Gooding sent her a set of baby clothes that had been passed to her from Claire Warren, who had inherited it from Sally Creaser. Watching their past triumph through the eyes of the next generation gave it a new dimension. Tracy remembers Jeni Mundy's boys turning to their mother and saying, 'Mum you're really cool!' Finally, the women could allow themselves to be proud.

The forgettability of women's achievements may also dampen ambition, particularly for girls who already feel at odds with society. Tracy describes her younger self as reactive, not a thinker or planner. She sees it as a disadvantage to her sailing career that she'd not grown up in the dinghy racing, yacht club environment – though frankly that sounds about as realistic as a cat wishing it had grown up as a dog. Instead, when she went to Greece as a teenager, she was very much on her own, despite the boyfriend. She needed to rely on herself to survive,

'I PINNED A SMILE ON MY FACE'

even occasionally in the most basic terms of food and shelter. She was an adventurer – someone who habitually said yes to opportunities. That led her to her first job as a stewardess on board a charter yacht. Her first transatlantic crossing gave her a sense of the freedom of the sea – a feeling that she was leaving behind all the bad things that had happened since her father died. When fellow crew members or skippers took time to teach Tracy anything, like steering or navigation, she was quick to learn.

After her first experience of racing (in 1984 on board *White Quailo* at the Swan Regatta in Sardinia) she felt she'd found a reason for living. She began to mend family relationships and to plan. She read *Cape Horn to Port* (1978) by Erroll Bruce and became obsessed by the idea of the Whitbread Round the World race. 'No other event put competitors at such risk for so long and so far from help.'[3] It appeared to be a virtual no-go area for women. Despite Clare Francis' successful skippering of *ADC Accutrac* in 1979/80 and Miranda Delmar-Morgan's attempt to gather an all-female team, there were only about five women out of 250 sailors in the 1985/86 race and most of them were cooks. Tracy found herself a place as a cook on *Norsk Data* (formerly Chay Blyth's *Great Britain II*). Journalists asked them questions 'about how we were going to keep "our men" fed and watered on the voyage. I sounded like the little woman baking below decks while the serious business went on above.'[4]

When Tracy left *Norsk Data* at Cape Town and joined the more serious racer *Atlantic Privateer* for the next leg to Auckland, she was treated in much the same way that Elizabeth Young and her mother Sarah had been treated almost 100 years before, sailing that same clipper route. 'In heavy weather I was a liability. If I went on deck to help, someone always kept an eye on me. This put undue pressure on the crew which they didn't need.' She remembered a stormy night when the call went out for all hands. 'I dragged on my wet weather gear and scrambled through the hatch. As my head emerged, Paul put his hand firmly on top of it and pushed me down. The hatch slammed shut. I hammered on the inside, screaming at them, "Let me out, let me help!"'[5] Afterwards, when she tried to explain that as she was a member of the crew, she had wanted to help, her friend Paul had looked surprised. He explained that he was only thinking of her; he hadn't wanted her to get hurt. Her relationship with the crew had improved from initial hostility to an affectionate big brothers/little sister dynamic. Not a partnership of equals with different skills.

When the race was over Tracy felt a sense of loss and a longing to do it again, but as a deckhand, not as a cook. Despite the example of the few other high-profile women sailors of the 1970s and 1980s, she was convinced that that no man was ever going to let her navigate round the world. That made her the more determined. With no public profile and only relatively recent sailing experience, Tracy set out to raise the £1.8 million she thought she needed to get an all-female team to the starting line. For an unknown 23-year-old this was ambitious. Krystyna Chojnowska-Liskiewicz had sailed from Poland to England with an all-female crew before the Polish Sailing Association had sponsored her to become the first woman to sail alone round the world in 1975. Naomi James, lucky in her relationships, had already been offered a place on Chay Blyth's *Great Britain II* for the 1977/78 Whitbread with the title of navigator, but Tracy probably didn't know that.

Tracy has said that she felt she had found her 'tribe' in the hand-to-mouth 'boat bum' sailing – other adventurous spirits taking their chances where they could. The yachting establishment is a stark contrast and can present a forbidding aspect to the outsider, especially if that outsider is a woman without money of her own. Tracy has described herself as someone who almost instinctively sets herself the most demanding challenges and takes the most difficult route to achieve them. It may be that one of her most outstanding qualities is financial courage – how far she is prepared to go out on a limb to raise money. She mortgaged her house to buy *Maiden*, then mortgaged the boat to pay for the fitting out. I wonder whether some of the hostility she evoked was because of these independent forays into the financial world. Women raising their own money for their own projects presented a challenge to the status quo. Tracy remembers one potential sponsor's answer: 'I don't want to be rude, Miss Edwards, but the thought of twelve of my wife sailing round the world is so horrifying I simply couldn't contemplate it.'[6]

She had to learn to deal with disappointment, with sexist comments, with accusations of irresponsibility, with anonymous phone calls. 'You should be chained up at home, you stupid bitch.'[7] However, she found others who shared her passion. The project became a 'magnet' for women who'd been told no. She became more and more determined to see this through, not to let down the people who believed in her. Getting *Maiden* and her crew to the start line was a remarkable achievement. Many people doubted that the 'tinful of tarts'[8] would survive the Bay of Biscay. Whether commentators supported or criticised the project, *Maiden*'s participation was only seen as a human-interest story, not as a contender for racing success. When Tracy and her team not only survived the first leg but finished third in their class, then went on to win the Southern Ocean leg to Freemantle, too many people still thought – and said – it was a fluke. A close-won victory over *Rucanor* – match-racing the final miles of the third leg to Auckland, which revealed tactical skill as well as endurance – quietened the critics, ensured additional funding to finish the race and allowed Tracy to begin to dream of winning overall.

This didn't happen. The glorious procession into the Solent, so movingly recreated in the film, celebrated a triumph but not a win. They had nearly lost the yacht when a serious leak developed coming up the Atlantic and Tracy had felt the reality of her responsibility for 11 other lives. She was left with many unresolved issues concerning decisions both before and during the voyage that she could have taken differently. She had been working as both skipper and navigator after sacking Marie-Claude, and was drained. The impact of celebrity was overwhelming. She drove herself to exhaustion saying yes to all requests, her very new marriage collapsed, the media interest became toxic and she finally suffered a breakdown, withdrew from competitive sailing and retired to breed horses on the Gower.

Although she had not always managed internal relationships successfully – she would continue to feel guilt over her treatment of Marie-Claude – she now knew that the people who had asserted that 12 women sailing round the world together would inevitably quarrel, were wrong. Tracy had loved working with other women; 'they allowed me to be who I was.' Heather Thomas, *Maiden*'s 2023 skipper and navigator (sharing day-to-day responsibility with first mate Rachel Burgess) goes further and suggests that one reason that an all-female crew may be more resilient than an all-male crew is that they are better at supporting one another. Tracy's crisis came only when her crew had dispersed, and she had no new project to carry her forward. She disappeared, but not forever. 'Once the sea has wormed its way into your heart and soul, there's no escape,'[9] she wrote.

Eventually her new project crystallised: she wanted to win the Jules Verne Trophy – the round-the-world speed record – with an all-female crew. In January 1998 she began sailing the 110ft maxi catamaran *Royal & Sun Alliance*. Her crew were Adrienne Cahalane, Miki von Koskull, Helena Darvelid, Emma Westmacott, Sam Davis, Emma Richards, Sharon Ferris, Hannah Harwood, Miranda Merron and Frédérique Brulé. Their record attempt took place in the year 2000. The pressure was relentless as they raced their invisible adversary, the current record holder Olivier de Kersauson, and the times he'd posted. They needed to maintain a speed of 450 miles a day. The weather was wild, Tracy injured her back, then, finally, the catamaran's rig came down as they approached Cape Horn. The experience of failure was devastating. A friend sent her the poem 'The Quitter' by Robert Service, '*Just have one more try / It's so easy to die / It's keeping on living that's hard'*.[10]

Finally, the catamaran was towed into Puerto Montt in Chile. Everyone on board *Royal & Sun Alliance* was dreading this moment.

> *The dock was packed with people waving and cheering. Chilean dancers dipped and whirled as a band played. The tug had come alongside us. Its crew were all wearing T-shirts we'd given them.*
>
> *Untying the ropes we drifted the last few feet. I took a deep breath, pinned a smile on my face and turned towards the crowd.*[11]

* * *

'There were boats of all sizes heading towards us and helicopters with searchlights sweeping as if looking to pinpoint an escaping prisoner.'[12] It was February 2001 and Ellen MacArthur was approaching Les Sables d'Olonne, sailing *Kingfisher* into second place in the Vendée Globe race. She didn't consider washing her hair or putting on a special outfit. 'I stood there in my boots, thermals and oilskin trousers.' Her problem at that moment was whether she could cope with returning to the land. She knew her life was about to change; she didn't want to leave her boat.

Other people – 'the guys' – came on board and took control. They dropped *Kingfisher*'s mainsail without consulting her, gave her flares to brandish, a champagne bottle to shake. In similar photos, taken four years later when Ellen had broken the solo non-stop round-the-world record, she looks like a Formula One racing driver. In an *Independent* article, Naomi James is quoted as saying 'What I did was completely different. Ellen is a professional racer; I was an adventurer.'[13] She is not dismissing Ellen's outstanding achievements, just saying they are different. However, there are some in the yachting world who cleave to the amateur ideal and dislike Ellen for this reason. There are others of us for whom her achievements are unforgettable and glorious.

Ellen, like Rozelle Pierrepont and Janet Rushbury, was born many miles inland, yet with an overwhelming passion for the sea. Later she wondered whether this was something genetic, connected with her father's family's Scottish seafaring ancestry, but that wasn't something she knew about at the time. She was one of so many 20th-century children whose longing for adventure was fuelled by the *Swallows and Amazons* series. She was also fortunate to grow up in a family where women made their own choices. Her Aunt Thea (Cynthia Lewis) had bought and restored a near derelict boat and regularly invited her mother and her sister's family to sail with her. Irene Lewis, Ellen's 'Nan', had loved learning and worked hard at school to earn a further education place, which she was forbidden to take up. She helped Ellen buy her first boat. Ellen's mother, Avril, was a woman who devoted herself to supporting others; her husband with a back injury; her mother, her mother-in-law and sister all with significant health problems; her older son with difficult life decisions. She refused Ellen's offer to remain at home and help when her father had suffered a serious accident. Ellen later wrote, 'Although I decided to carry on sailing, it wasn't a comfortable decision to make and was one I still look back on with unease.'[14]

While writing this book I have been thinking about the 'spirit of independence' that Barbara Hughes considered was 'so often denied to our sex'. What are its opposites? There is 'dependence' – when women must depend on other people for permissions or the means of existence – but there is also 'care', the curtailment of independence when other people depend on us. Caring – whether for children, a disabled partner or a frail parent – dramatically restricts individual freedom of action. Historically, and probably also currently, caring has usually been seen as a woman's responsibility. The word 'care' in English has twisted semantic roots. It comes from the Latin *carus* meaning 'dear', in the sense of beloved. It also contains the Angle-Saxon *cearu* meaning 'sorrow'. Women and men both know that it feels hard to leave people you love, and who depend on you, just to go sailing, even when it feels like your vocation. Ellen made a difficult choice: Ellen's mother – crucially – released her from a sense of obligation.

Making her own way was tough. Perceptive working people like Maureen and Dave King, who ran a sailing school in Hull, recognised her quality and offered opportunities and introductions but no feather bedding. She squeezed in courses between school exams or camped out on their radio-room floor to get more time to learn about boats. Those who (rightly) worry about the elitist nature of sailing can take some comfort from Ellen's early career. Her determination and capacity to endure hardship is comparable to Beryl Smeeton's but her wealth was in talent, not money. It was difficult when she first moved from Hull to the Hamble and found herself in a world of weekend racers, expensive cars and loud voices that never seemed to say hello. Janet Grosvenor remembers that when the equally determined but more socially confident Ashley Perrin, the youngest-ever elected member of the RORC, reached out and brought Ellen into the club with her, people had the impression that Ashley, not Ellen, was the person who would be making a name for herself.

Aged 18, small, apparently shy, Ellen was nominated by her friends in Hull as Young Sailor of the Year. Senior RYA Cruising Coach James Stevens had initially withheld Ellen's Yachtmaster Instructor certificate on the grounds of her lack of experience. He and fellow examiner John Goode presented her with it as she and her Corribee, *Iduna*, arrived in the Solent, before setting out on the final section of their anticlockwise journey back to Hull. She had sailed *Iduna* round Britain solo. By then Ellen had decided that work as an RYA instructor, or a steady job as a skipper with the Sea Cadets, was not what she wanted. She wanted to race.

This decision for anyone, male or female, who was not from a wealthy family or part of a prestigious club, meant two things: instant readiness to grab opportunities, however tough or ill-paid; and many hours devoted to the search for sponsorship. People who want to win in any sport where high-quality equipment is crucial and costs are always rising, must find money. For someone as young and talented as Ellen, it might have seemed likely that there would have been RYA studentships or support grants, but somehow she didn't qualify.

She'd not arrived through the dinghy sailing pathway; she didn't much enjoy sailing 'round the buoys'. Although the success of Scottish sailor Shirley Robertson, who won the first of her Olympic gold medals in 2000, would be one of the factors that would channel significant 21st-century money into developing talented women racers, it's hard to see that a 20-year-old Ellen would qualify for RYA funding even now. She certainly didn't when she was living in a Portakabin, limiting herself to £10 a week on food and struggling to find the money to enable her to enter her first Mini-Transat in 1997. 'I had been an RYA member since I first went on my first dinghy training course on Rutland Water ten years before and I had trained up through their scheme to Yachtmaster Instructor. I couldn't help but feel disappointed.'[15]

The Foundation for Sport and the Arts was more generous with a grant towards equipment but there was no commercial sponsorship forthcoming. A loan from the Bank of Mum and Dad enabled her to buy a specialist small boat to compete in the Mini-Transat. Her parents were using vital compensation money from her father's accident so would need to be repaid from the sale of the boat as soon as the race was done. When the entrants assembled in Brest, Ellen and Mark Turner were the only two British competitors. More than 70 per cent of their fellow competitors were French – she was coming to love the French for their enthusiasm for short-handed offshore racing – but she was naively surprised to find herself the subject of constant media attention: 'What was it like being the youngest competitor and the only girl in the race?' The only answer she could give was that she couldn't answer – she had no idea what it felt like to be ten years older or a man.

Although Ellen has said that when she was a child, she had sometimes wished she were a boy, she generally seems untroubled by her gender, except perhaps in that difficult period following her father's accident in 1995. Historically, many families have been more protective of their daughters than their sons, and more anxious to keep them at home. Ellen has repeatedly thanked her parents for giving her the freedom to follow her dreams. In 2009 the parents of 14-year-old Laura Dekker in the Netherlands were widely criticised – and, for a while, legally prevented – from supporting her in her ambition to be the youngest person to sail solo round the world. Britain does not have minimum age requirements for taking charge of a boat, though, illogically, it currently does for achieving RYA Day Skipper or Yachtmaster qualifications. Laura's eventual departure therefore was from the British Overseas Territory of Gibraltar. Laura's parents were divorced and the support for her sailing had mainly been given by her father. In a society where men are generally richer and more powerful than women – such as the 20th-century sailing world – male support is often crucial in practical terms. It can also make a significant emotional difference. Tracy Edwards, who had endured so much public belittlement, described herself as 'gobsmacked' when Peter Blake, 1989 Whitbread race leader in *Steinlager II*, congratulated her on 'some great sailing'.[16]

Although Ellen didn't lack self-belief, she too needed affirmation and could become distressed if she thought that someone close to her secretly believed her opponent to be better than her. People in the sailing world, as in any other, can be spiteful. Back on land, after her success in the Vendée Globe, Michel Desjoyeaux needed to apologise for having added fuel to the rumours that Ellen's success had been due to outside assistance – very similar to the charges from which Vendée Globe sailor Clarisse Crémer (b. 1989) has recently been cleared.[17] He did so sincerely, but Ellen's friend Ashley has heard a similar false rumour repeated by a senior woman in the sailing world.

Is it perhaps hard for people to accept that outstanding women sailors succeed on merit? Is there still the suspicion that brilliant female athletes (or film stars or singers) are being managed by malign male forces? Occasionally we discover that they are, but the regularity of such suspicion is belittling, and should never be allowed to tarnish admiration for sheer talent and determination. Hard things have been said about Sheila Chichester's influence over her husband – or Evgenia Ransome, indeed – but never to the extent that it diminishes the actual achievements of Francis or Arthur. Such smears against women are not only spread by men. Some of the very few women who reach the top in sailing have battled so hard to smash the glass ceiling that they have attempted to pull the ladder up behind them by casting doubt on others' achievement. Not all have Mary Blewitt's practical generosity and thought for the future.

Ellen's writing spares the reader little of her emotional insecurities or of the physical hardship that accompanied her racing in the stripped-out boat shells that took her over or through waves at such high velocity. Her style, especially in her second book *Race Against Time* (2005), was

'I PINNED A SMILE ON MY FACE'

something of a gift to parodists. Those who know her best explain that her success is inextricably connected with her total personal dedication. 'She would continue asking questions until she made your ears bleed,' says Merfyn Owen, Ellen's former partner and co-designer of her Vendée Globe yacht *Kingfisher*. 'Every breathing moment was focussed on the race,'[18] adds Ashley Perrin, remembering Ellen tipping bread mix into a panini machine to make herself the cheapest, quickest meals when she was living in that container in Hamble.

Ellen's brilliance made her a record breaker: she came second in the 2000/01 Vendee Globe and in 2005 she took the solo non-stop round the world record. While life could be tough for her most intimate male friends (she has the candour to describe a scene where she attacked her sailing partner Mark Turner), women like Anne Hammick and Helen Tew also describe her sweetness and interest in individuals. Helen wrote, 'One day, when she's outgrown all this high-powered sailing, I hope she'll find time to go cruising and get as much fun as I've had.'[19]

Helen Tew Transatlantic at Last *(Tew Family)*

25

'Dressed like I wanted it'
Changing priorities

Elaine Bunting (b. 1967); Carla Stanley (b. 1958); Abbey Molyneux (b. 1991); Elaine Penhaul (b. 1963); Ashley Perrin (b. 1978); Heather Thomas (b. 1997); Vuyisile Jaca (b. 1998)

THE QUOTE CHOSEN FOR the back cover of Ellen's first book *Taking on the World* (2002) describes her as 'The first true heroine of the 21st century.'[1] In both of her triumphal returns she captured the imagination of millions of people by her small stature in large boats, by her defiance and determination in conditions of physical hardship, by her professionalism and her success. By the end of the first decade of the new millennium, however, she had decided record-breaking racing was no longer for her. Other things had begun to matter more. She may now have a stable, supportive relationship and a small, simple boat of which Helen Tew might approve, but her passion is poured into non-personal causes: she enables children with cancer to experience sailing and campaigns for global sustainability. 'When you sail on a boat you take with you the minimum of resources. You don't waste anything. You don't leave the light on; you don't leave a computer screen on. And I realised that on land we take what we want. You'd never do that on a boat.'[2]

Many other 21st-century women sailors have continued to set records and achieve inspiring 'firsts', highlighting women's capacity for endurance, ingenuity, technical skill, negotiation with the elements, determination and courage. Female firsts open up these qualities across all people rather than confining them only to the male half of humankind. In 2006 Dee Caffari (b. 1973) was the first woman to sail west round the world, against the prevailing winds and currents. Completing the Vendée Globe in 2009 made her the first woman to have sailed non-stop and unassisted both ways round the world. Then she went one better as she sailed round again non-stop and became the only woman to have circumnavigated three times non-stop (and six times in all). She is currently working with Alexia Barrier (b. 1979) of France on the Famous Project, another all-female attempt on the Jules Verne record. But it's more than that, at least according to its website: it has a human and social commitment, an environmental commitment, an educational commitment, a sporting commitment – a Mission. There is something very 21st century about that approach. Dee is also an ambassador for several charities, including United Kingdom Sailing Academy (UKSA) where she started her career and where she now champions mental health and resilience. She's chair of the World Sailing Trust, which aims to promote inclusivity in sailing and greater awareness of the health of the oceans. The anxieties of the 21st century mean that many of the highest profile races and individual challenges include environmental pledges. Many sailors are sailing for additional causes. In 2017 Lisa Blair (b. 1980), sailing in the cause of Climate Action Now, made the first of her solo circumnavigations of Antarctica. In 2018 Nikki Henderson (b. 1993), aged 25, became the youngest-ever skipper to lead a team in the Clipper Round the World yacht race. Then, in 2019 she joined *La Vagabonde* to sail 16-year-old climate activist Greta Thunberg back across the Atlantic to speak at COP25 in Madrid.

In 2020 Hannah Mills (b. 1988) became the world's most successful female Olympic sailor. In the past there have been fewer Olympic sailing events open to women than to men, but the 2024 Paris games offered gender parity. Also, in 2024, the America's Cup offered a (separate) women's event. Hannah led the British team. In 2023, high-latitude sailor Kirsten Neuschäfer (b. 1982) became the first woman to win the Golden Globe Race (established 1968) – and the first South African sailor to win any round-the-world event. In 2024, 5ft 2in tall Cole Brauer (b. 1994) became the first American woman to sail solo round the world. She came second in the Global Solo challenge, in which she was the youngest skipper and the only woman. Dinghy-sailor Eve McMahon (b. 2004) from Howth in Ireland was the first person (male or female) to win three Laser world championships in a single season.

Jeanne Socrates (b. 1942), continuing to cruise on her own after the death of her husband, showed immense tenacity to become, firstly, the oldest woman to sail round the world (at her third attempt in 2013), and secondly, the oldest person in 2019.[3] As the global population ages, such records may not stand for long. Jeanne's title as 'oldest person' was overtaken by a male sailor, Australian Bill Hatfield (aged 81) within less than two months. Considering material and technical barriers to female participation, Elaine Bunting writes: 'Round the world sailors proved beyond doubt that there is no physical barrier that cannot be overcome or designed out.' Many male and female sailors who dread the dependency and diminished horizons of old age may now be hoping that 21st-century designers will focus their skills on overcoming the aspects of yacht (and marina) design that exclude the less nimble from continuing to experience the freedom of sailing for as long as possible. We look to the undimmed spirits of 'granny sailors', such as Helen Tew who crossed the Atlantic in the year of the millennium, having been left behind by her father, Ralph Graham, long ago in 1934. Having lived through both world wars and past the millennium, Helen said she had come to believe that uncertainly is the only certain state. 'Don't listen to the pessimists. Whatever you want to do, someone will tell you you can't. It's too difficult or dangerous, you're either too young or too old. In fact, the time is never right unless you make it so. My advice, therefore, is simple; just get on and do it.'[4]

But is inclusive design for older or less physically able people actually a priority, even today? Or is it go faster, go further, go harder, as usual? In Cowes, in April 2024 (the month *Maiden* came home) I walked past the RORC office. Almost the entire front window was covered by a dramatic photograph showing a team of beefy white men hurtling through the spray. The advent of AC40 foiling yachts (used for the America's Cup) saw the first generation sailed only by men. In 2024 these were passed to women for their separate event, while the main race moved on with even more powerful AC75s. But, as Elaine points out, not all the roles even on these most powerful and demanding boats demand brute strength. 'There are big physical roles such as grinders and cyclors, but there are roles for helm, trimming, strategy, weather, design, organisational command. Where are all the women?'[5] In a sideshow, some would say.

Many 21st-century race organisers will try to promote mixed-gender teams either by imposing a quota system or offering inducements via the handicapping system. Sponsors are said to be keen to be seen supporting mixed teams, and women 'play well' on social media platforms. The situation highlighted by the World Sailing Trust's Strategic Review into Women in Sailing in 2019, however, identified major issues of discrimination against women and concluded that the sport was gender-biased at every level. Perhaps Deborah Fish, the RORC's recently appointed female commodore – or Janet Grosvenor as their new admiral – will make a difference to the window-dressing. There have been female firsts in some of the oldest yacht clubs: the Royal Mersey YC has recently appointed Carys Jarvis its first woman commodore since 1844. Annamarie Fegan, a former coastal rower as well as a Fastnet sailor, is the new admiral at the Royal Cork YC, founded in 1720. Like a football lioness she comments that she stands, 'on the shoulders of outstanding female members who worked tirelessly for the club but were not given this opportunity'.[6] Janet Grosvenor's appointment as the RORC's first female admiral as it enters its centenary year, sends a racon beam to the next generation. In the Royal Navy, Jude Terry became the first female rear admiral in 2022, the same year that all four RN training bases had women commanding officers (Jo Deakin, Sarah Oakley, Suzi Nielsen, Catherine Jordan).

Jane Russell is now rear commodore of the Royal Cruising Club, which has not yet succeeded in electing a woman as commodore, though women have been eligible for membership almost throughout its history. We looked together at the millennium membership records and discovered – not entirely to our surprise – that in the year 2000, members with voting rights were overwhelmingly men.[7] The RCC is not a misogynistic club. It has never had the insulting conventions that have tended to mar too many 'gentlemen's clubs' (its host, the Royal Thames YC, for instance, for many years enforced a regulation where women members were not allowed to use the front staircase.) The disproportion seems more likely to be caused by the simple human factor that members proposing other members for a club where congeniality matters, are most likely to suggest people like themselves, either in gender, race or social background. This will make any initial imbalance cumulative unless some radical solution is adopted.

Does it matter? The RCC is not a club with material resources that are being unfairly withheld, and I must say loudly that its members have been exceptionally helpful in researching this book. Its Pilotage

Foundation is a largely separate entity (though overseen by RCC Trustees) and has recently achieved equity in male and female authors, editors and contributors. That is important: if new generations of women are to continue to use RCCPF guides to explore unfamiliar places, the insights of those who have gone before will help. The problem of gender imbalance among the membership is one of perception and status. During the 20th century it was considered an honour to be asked to join the RCC. If so many more men than women were considered worthy of this honour, what message does this send? That women are not interested in cruising, or that cruising is not interested in them?.

Carla Stanley, until recently chair of the RYA youth racing committee, believes that the challenge for sailing now is less to attract girls but to keep them as they feel the pressure of other responsibilities.[8] Carla has worked in advocacy, notably for the Equalities and Human Rights Commission. When her three daughters were growing up, she and her husband Richard, a farmer, poured their energy into the junior section of their local sailing club in Gloucestershire. From this inland setting Carla began taking UK teams all over the world, first for the International Optimist Class Association and then for 420s. She set the Youth Racing Committee a target to achieve gender equality and attempted to tackle inclusivity equality issues across other RYA committees. Some old attitudes die hard, she found. Carla believes that girls coming through the dinghy racing system are likely to begin to plan ahead and consider their future sailing options earlier than the more opportunistic boys, who tend to assume that something will turn up. If young women don't see a future, they are likely to leave. 'Subtle signals from society' will reinforce this if they also become mothers.

Experienced financial consultant Seonaid Reid points out that many women, perhaps subconsciously realising that they are likely to earn less than men over a lifetime, are more likely to do a cost-benefit analysis of the financial implications of boat ownership. Do I want a tin of antifouling or a new pair of shoes? She's quick to add that she's not following her own advice – her attachment to *Malindi of Lorne* is such that she'll keep her anyway, despite the financial reckoning. (I feel the same about *Peter Duck*.) Heather Thomas, better-grounded in the reality of making a living in the sailing world, says that opportunities for women, particularly as instructors and within the sail-training world, are better than they've ever been – though it may still be more difficult in professional racing. Thinking about the voluntary sector, Carla suggests that the style of management for organisations such as sailing clubs may need to change for women to remain involved with committees and to consider becoming flag officers. These are often roles for older club members and can be very demanding. The demarcation between working life and retirement today is a blurred one, particularly for women. We are still busy, often with continuing careers and complex caring responsibilities. Meetings need to be brisk and focussed and to have clear purpose, not perpetuating unnecessary ritual. Perhaps we need to reconsider the 21st-century expectations of flag officers *per se*.

* * *

Abbey Molyneux ('Abbey Boat Builder'), a shipwright running her own yard in Norfolk, thinks British social attitudes need to change. She says there is no reason for women not to have a career in boatbuilding, if that's what they want. Traditional wooden boatbuilding need not be an endangered craft. Yards have work, need staff and should be growing the next generation of boatbuilders, irrespective of gender. Part of the problem is the way in which boatbuilding is taught in Britain, as a hobby, rather than as a way to earn a living. The range of skills is narrow and the importance of deadlines and the ability to work at pace and with focus is overlooked. Lack of money is a considerable barrier:

> *I didn't come from anything. I was raised at home and taught at home, we had no money to our name, my Dad worked days and night shifts and my Ma raised me and my sister. I wiggled my way into an apprenticeship, I won't say which one coz I don't have much good to say about 'em but with no money and no formal education I had to move counties, away from all my family and feed and house myself on £4.50 an hour to get a foot in the door as a boat builder. There were local courses and colleges but they weren't obtainable for kids like me and they still aren't.*
>
> *And I'd like to tell you all that it was HARD. There wasn't an ounce of support from anyone. In my apprenticeship I was held back for being small/not strong enough. The chap training me said I couldn't drill off keel bolts because my hands were too small to hold the drill, but I can tell you now, I've built more boats with these tiny hands in 10 years than he has in his entire career.*[9]

In retrospect, she says, her real learning came with her first proper job, at Dennett's yard in Chertsey. Again, she was the only female but now whatever skill she wanted to learn was open to her. It was tough, she got shouted at, she had to live 'like a ragamuffin' but she knew that this was what she could do. She discovered her ability to work by eye and by touch: also using visualisation, making shapes in an empty space. 'With restorations you are building backwards, and you have to figure out a new way of doing it each time.'[10] When she had finished her apprenticeship she had been told, 'Obviously you'll only ever be able to build small boats,' but 5ft-tall Abbey loves the largest boats and sees no problem with this.

After eight years at work, she left to set up her own business. Her first major restoration, the 42ft Broads cruiser *Queen of Light* (1932) was completed in 102 days, working 14 hours a day. It earned her the Young Boatbuilder of the Year title and 'muscles like Popeye'. There's more, of course, to owning a business.

> In the last 10 years my skill set has gone from making a £500 overdraft last four weeks to balancing big numbers on big projects, learning to do spreadsheets, file VAT returns and the inevitable cash flow issues of every boatyard. Boat building isn't for the faint hearted. But it's not just a job, it's a lifestyle.[11]

Visiting the Northwest School of Wooden Boatbuilding in Port Townsend WA in 2024 offered Abbey a glimpse of a community where she was a boatbuilder first and a female second. 'It was a feeling that I've never had before.' It was perhaps ironic that she was there with the UK's Women in Boatbuilding group, a supportive network founded by Belinda Joslin. It gave her an idea of the scale of change that still lies ahead, for both men and women, in Britain.

* * *

Elaine Bunting started sailing as a child, raced dinghies, qualified as an RYA Instructor, cruised and raced extensively. She joined *Yachting World* in 1990 and became the first female editor in its 117-year history in 2014. She wrote:

> There have been massive changes in the years I have been actively involved as a sailor and journalist. Almost all for the good. It was a real old boys'

> club. Many yacht clubs were old boys' clubs too, even if they didn't recognise it. Groups of mates sailed with their mates. There was a strong drinking culture. Matey nicknames.[12]

Elaine speaks of 'the active exclusion of women' from the social side of racing and the difficulties women faced gaining the requisite experience to break into professional racing, where a living might be made. 'Participation sailing' – by which she means non-professional sailing – is ahead of the industry in its attitudes and opportunities.

> But still men steered and navigated while women scurried around with the lines and did galley work – and to an extent still do, despite it clearly being physically sensible to swap some of these roles. However, there are many, many couples cruising round the world today with equal roles, skills and ambitions.

In Elaine's early years as a journalist, when the *Yachting World* team went off to do a group test, she was expected to assess the galley and interior facilities, despite her own active sailing experience. 'That was quite normal and not remarkable. I couldn't object then. Gen Z definitely would, and good for them.' Gen Z women are (loosely) those born between 1997 and 2010. Before them come Millennials (1981–1996) and Gen X (1965–1980). Such categorisations offer only broad generalisations as to the circumstances and likely attitudes of people born at different times. Individuals will still make their own choices. It's good to remember Jill Kernick as a Merchant Navy cadet in the 1970s refusing to do the bosun's sewing chores as a means of avoiding deck duties. Discussing past experience with other women of my own 'boomer' generation (1946–1964) sometimes leaves us amazed at the gender stereotyping and casual sexism that we took for granted. Carla pointed me to a relatively recent scandal reported in Scuttlebutt news from the Etchells World Championship in Florida in 2023. An unnamed female sailor – presumably a Millennial or from Gen Z – wrote a stinging letter to 'Dear Men of the Sailing World' complaining vigorously about the degree of unwanted groping and propositioning to which she was subjected as soon as she took off her team sailing uniform and dressed for a post-regatta party.

> I rarely dress up, because I'm just not that kind of girl, but I certainly like to on occasion. And I figured a World Championship awards party was

such an occasion. I traded my Patagonia shorts for a skirt and sunblock for mascara. It's fun to look pretty! But apparently that meant I was no longer your equal, but your prey. No less than half a dozen men harassed me, beginning at the awards dinner and continually throughout the evening up until I had to fight past one just to get home.[...] the sad thing is, a lot of people already know who you are, and they allow you to continue on, and I will just be called out as a drama-starter. Because 'boys will be boys.' And I was 'dressed like I wanted it'.[13]

It wasn't the complaint itself that prompted Carla to refer to this story but the fact that the Etchells Class Association responded so seriously:

The International Etchells Class Association leadership is dismayed to learn of the experience of our competitor at and following the 2023 Etchells World Championship awards party and condemns the behaviour reported. This type of conduct is not unique to the Etchells class, sailing, or sport. Women face such behaviour in all aspects of their lives. We applaud the courageousness of the author for speaking out. Indeed, these types of actions need to be called out, discussed, and eliminated. This is incumbent on all of us, not just the victims.[14]

It's hard to imagine that Barbara Hughes or other early women racers had to put up with this sort of behaviour. Perhaps this is why 'ladies' needed to be kept out of the 'gentlemen's' clubs – because the men couldn't trust themselves? Alongside a rethinking of gender roles through the 20th century, there was also an increased sexualisation of relationships, which now causes offence. As society's rules relaxed, particularly in the later 20th-century decades, women and men of the same classes were more frequently in each other's company – in education and at work as well as socially. Women seemed increasingly 'available', particularly as more reliable contraception lowered the sexual stakes. Harassment became more blatant. It could be confusing for women to be challenging gender stereotypes, insisting on our right to manage our own lives and to enjoy sex, while also redrawing boundaries as to what was and wasn't acceptable.

Women afloat in yachts usually felt safe. Libby Purves, looking back at the blithe confidence with which she placed crew advertisements in the back pages of *Yachting Monthly* in the early 1970s, is amazed that she never considered they might be answered 'by the likes of Jack the Ripper and Dr Hannibal Lecter'.[15] When 25-year-old Elaine Penhaul was working as an instructor in the 1980s, providing boat-handling practice to groups of novice sailors (usually men) before their flotilla holidays, she might decide to take her crew back into the marina for the night rather than stay out at anchor if she felt at all uneasy about her male crew members. But she never really encountered a problem – except for the first-timers asking her what time she expected the skipper to arrive in the morning.[16]

Elaine was not from a sailing family but, as a teenager, had successfully exploited divisions between her parents (her father hated water) to get herself booked in to a sailing course on the Norfolk Broads. She was yet another woman from a non-sailing background to fall in love with life on the water. Another to use sailing as her means of escape. In 1985 she was training as an actuary in Scotland, desperately bored, when she spotted an advertisement for someone to help set up a flotilla holiday centre in Greece. She remembers her boss turning white with horror when she told him she was leaving, and why. Her decision led to happy and adventurous years earning her living as an itinerant instructor – learning as she went – and proved no hindrance to a subsequent successful business career on land.

Twenty-first-century anxieties differ from 20th-century ones. For women, currently, the very concept of gender can rapidly whip up a storm. Is it innate or a matter of choice? When Elaine became a mother, she was fully involved with her children's sailing progress and was elected commodore at their local club. One of the youngsters who had been sailing as a girl took the decision to become a boy. His peers had little problem accepting the new identity. For the club committee it was considerably harder. The junior racing was mixed – no separated girls' cups and boys' cups. Sailing, as Barbara Hughes commented so long ago, is (or should be) a sport where male and female can compete on equal terms, as long as they have equal access to money and facilities; equal access to boats, to equipment, to coaching. There were no hindrances of that sort in Elaine's sailing club. The issue was lavatories – just as it had been when Vera Laughton arrived at Crystal Palace in 1917, seeking accommodation for her first contingent of Wrens, or when the female 'dilution' workers arrived for their first shifts at Fairfield shipyard in

Govan. Also, the club's junior changing rooms were without cubicles. The transitioning youngster needed some privacy.

As far as Elaine was concerned the issue was simple. The club had a disabled toilet. Designate that a gender-neutral space. Problem solved. But not as far as some of the older committee members were concerned. Adopting this apparently straightforward solution was a battle that lasted many months, though it did conclude successfully. Commodore Jo Adey, with responsibility for 30,000 young people in the Royal Navy's cadet forces says that, in the end, if long-serving volunteers are unable to reconcile their own ethical codes with the complex choices of the new generation, then it is the adult volunteers who must finally be asked to step aside.

* * *

A salty sailor, home from a lifetime at sea, might find herself running a riverside pub. Visiting Hamble-le-Rice, where Barbara Hughes and her family had lived in 1891, I found that the landlady of the King & Queen pub was Janet Bradley, a former professional yacht racer from South Africa's Eastern Cape. Janet's pub is a welcoming place, much used by local sailors. Eileen Ramsey and George Spiers based themselves there when they first moved out of London, and it's twice been voted the world's best yachting pub. For much of Janet's own sailing career she was the only woman in a crew of men and while she was personally untroubled by this, she's a strong advocate of women in sailing, for their own pleasure and the sake of the sport she loves. She introduced me to Ashley Perrin and her husband Merfyn Owen as they came to order their Sunday lunch.

Ashley has an impressive career as an offshore racer, sailmaker, rigger, delivery skipper and boat captain. She was the first woman to become Senior Boating officer with the British Antarctic Survey and now runs a Racing Yacht Management and, separately, an Ice Pilot company for high latitude superyachts. Hers is a thoroughly professional career. She describes Merfyn (Merf) as the 'chick designer'. He's designed yachts for Ellen MacArthur, Miranda Merron and Emma Richards. I asked him about female yacht designers. Yes, they do exist, but they are few and not generally well-known. He mentioned Liz Tier, from LTDesign Southampton, working as a consultant, and Alex Phillips, who trained as a naval architect, made her name in high-performance racing, then developed her interests in psychology to work as a one-to-one coach and team-builder.

Ashley and Merfyn had plenty of tales to tell of sailing sexism – the male deck officer who steadfastly refused to speak to Ashley when she needed to check that the Oyster 82 she was having transported from Rotterdam to Long Beach was strapped down correctly; the female French journalist in Halifax who interviewed Merfyn, when Ashley was preparing to race her boat from Halifax to Saint-Pierre-et-Miquelon, at the start of a circumnavigation of Newfoundland via Greenland and Labrador and presented him as 'taking his wife on an adventure on the family boat'.

Ashley remembered being asked to race in Florida when she was about 19. The crew member meeting her on arrival looked shocked: 'Oh, there's a problem.' 'What?' 'You're a girl.' 'Yes.' 'You can't sail with us.' '?' What he meant was that she wouldn't be allowed to sail on the yacht of the immensely rich owner, because his wife (who wasn't sailing) couldn't accept a woman on board. After some thought, however, a crew member decided to tell the owner that he was having an affair with Ashley – which persuaded the wife that she could safely be allowed to join the yacht. What does this say about professional racing, so in thrall to the power and prejudice of the very rich?

Despite these pub yarns, Ashley, Janet and Merf were adamant that we are living in a period of tangible change in the opportunities available to women in sailing. Britain (and France) lead the world in the numbers and the achievement of the women involved. Ashley quoted a figure of 40 per cent female participation in the offshore double-handed racing classes. 'I never had to queue for the Ladies before!'

There were photos of *Maiden* on the wall of Janet's pub. The all-female, ethnically diverse crew, whom I'd first met in St Katherine's Dock all those months ago, had won the 2023/24 Ocean Globe Race. Marie Tabarly (b. 1984) in *Pen Duik VI* had been first home with a mixed, mainly French, team that included British professional sailor Tom Napper as first mate. Their achievement had been impressive in every leg of the race. Heather Thomas and Rachel Burgess, with *Maiden*, had always been consistent, never out of the leading group and, as they were sailing a significantly smaller, lighter yacht, had gained overall victory on handicap. This was a glorious success for British sailing, for women, and for the shared attitudes that had enabled them to work so well together and bring *Maiden* home safely. I thought of Clare Francis' summary of her achievement 40 years earlier. 'The boat stayed in one piece, and we stayed in one piece.'[17] Clare's former yacht, *ADC Accutrac*, sailing this time as *Translated 9*, had finally to withdraw from the 2023/24 Ocean Globe Race, damaged. She had sailed fast and well but had been pushed very hard. Too hard? It reminded me of a conversation I'd had with Lesley Marsh when we'd talked about a possible difference in competitive riders' attitudes to their horses: push to the maximum and then a little more; the horse may win — or it may break. Or push to the limits but not beyond. We'd designated these 'male' and 'female' attitudes, though they may be more closely linked to personality than to gender. 'To finish first, you have first to finish,' said Heather. Marie Tabarly, so closely attuned to *Pen Duik VI*, which had previously been sailed by her father, spoke of the tensions she had felt, all the time, knowing how hard she was pushing the boat, aware of the potential crisis, were anything to fail.

I'd come to Hamble to take a last chance to talk to Vuyisile Jaca, the young woman who had welcomed me with such warmth and sensitivity when I'd arrived in St Katherine's Dock that evening eight months ago.

Vuyie was born in uMzinto, KwaZulu-Natal in 1998 and grew up in eMgangeni, an inland village where children were taught to fear the water. The adults had never learned to swim so could not teach their children. This made rivers dangerous, so they told their children stories about monsters in the water to ensure they kept well away and didn't risk drowning. Vuyie's mother, Thandiwe, died when Vuyie was seven. When she was 14 her father also died and she and her brother were sent to KwaMashu, a township north of Durban, to live with relatives. The transition from the village to the township wasn't easy. Vuyie doesn't talk about it much. Fortunately she's a quick learner. She discovered that she was ahead of her new classmates in some subjects and won awards in her new school. When the time came to choose specialist subjects, she chose science. This, in JG Zuma High School, included nautical science as an option. It was a new subject, the teacher was ex-Navy, and the 15 students learned about chartwork, meteorology and ship stability. In their second year they were taken to the charity Sail Africa for a practical introduction to the water. As none of the young people could swim, safety instructions needed to be rigorous.

Vuyie attended Sail Africa weekly for the last year of school, loving the sailing, and hoping to study science at university. However, her maths grade wasn't good enough and she had no money to study further. She hung around with nothing to do, feeling lonely and depressed. She went back to the charity asking whether there was anything she could do to assist, in return for some more sailing. She became a volunteer, attending once a week to help kit out the new students with lifejackets and take any chances to get out on the water. When she first asked to go offshore, the organisers were sceptical. Other girls had tried a single offshore session, had been frightened and had not returned. The charity had to explain this to funders as their failure. They took a chance on Vuyie and another girl formerly from the JG Zuma school – and succeeded. (Vuyie's companion is now third mate on an Oldendorff bulk carrier.)

The charity developed an all-girls team to take part in regattas, then found support and sponsorship to upgrade their L34 yacht, *Spirit of Anna Wardley*, to qualify for the 2021 Vasco da Gama race from Durban to East London, Eastern Cape. This is a tough race, including overnight sailing with strong south-westerly winds, the Agulhas Current potentially creating huge swells down a wild stretch of coast. The team of four girls and four boys was the first all-Black team to compete in the 50-year history of the race and won a trophy for the first L34 yacht to finish. Jackie de Fin, operations director at Sail Africa, then put Vuyie's name forward for possible selection as part of the Maiden Foundation's educational tour. Vuyie almost felt too nervous to fill out the application form: 'There's no way I'm going to get onto that boat. It's from England and I've got few qualifications. But at least if I do, they'll know there's a girl from South Africa who would like to have a try.'[18]

When she googled *Maiden* and read about Tracy and the achievements of the first team, Vuyie felt even more overawed. When she heard she'd been selected for a place sailing from Dakar in Senegal to Cape Town, she couldn't allow herself to believe it. There were delays. She prepared herself for disappointment, but Sail Africa helped her get a passport then, finally, in December 2022 she left for Dakar to join the yacht for the trip to Cape Town. Heather Thomas recognised Vuyie's quality and kept her on as *Maiden* sailed home from Cape Town to Hamble Point Marina, where they prepared for the Ocean Globe Race. She began working with British engineer Ami Hopkins and discovered a talent and a passion for this aspect of sailing. When Ami was unable to sail legs three and four of the race, due to health issues, Vuyie took over responsibility for the generator, the water maker and the electrical systems. Heather has also paid tribute to Vuyie's contribution to the spirit of the team, helping to keep morale high even when there were problems.

As we talked, Vuyie remembered her feeling of responsibility and thrill at the start of the race, approaching the line off the Royal Yacht Squadron at Cowes and knowing they were sailing for Britain. She was at the helm of *Maiden* when they sailed into Cape Town at the end of the first leg, then, when they arrived back in Cowes she was holding her own South African national flag as one of the three crew members – with Junella King (Antigua) and Maryama Seck (France) – to be the first Black women to race round the world. There was sadness as well as joy for Vuyie. When I met her on the pontoon at Cowes harbour marina, just an hour after *Maiden*'s triumphal arrival, she was thinking of her parents and wishing they had been able to know what she had done. But like Nicolette Milnes-Walker, she also realises that this experience is something that will stay with her for the rest of her life. 'As much as I don't have a varsity qualification, to sail around the world is not something you wake up one morning and do. It will remain my lifelong memory, it's like I've achieved a degree, and nobody can take that from me.'[19]

Now Vuyie was ready to return to Durban, after more than a year away, to try to find the money to get her Coastal Skipper qualification, to study as a marine engineer, but most of all to try to inspire other young women to believe in themselves and be the best that they can be. We said goodbye and I walked to Hamble Point Marina, where *Maiden* was lying, now officially retired from her global sailing career. There wasn't anyone at the gate to let me in, but I was happy to sit on a bench in the sunshine, looking at the river and the Sunday sailors, and thinking about the power and beauty of the wind and the water, which is so completely other. It has no intrinsic connection with the human constructions of gender, sexuality, money, property and power with which we pattern it. It can facilitate trade and empire, oppression and freedom, innovation and initiative, collective achievement or personal independence. It can kill or it can save.

Then it was time to go home to my own river and plan my summer's sailing, 'with no-one to say me nay'.

'DRESSED LIKE I WANTED IT'

2023/24 crew of Maiden, *winners of the Ocean Globe Race (Maiden Factor Foundation)*

Vuyisile Jaca outside the King & Queen pub (Julia Jones)

Abbey 'Boat Builder' Molyneux (Abbey Molyneux)

Jill Kernick working on navigational marker for Trinity House (Jill Kernick)

BIBLIOGRAPHY

Abrams, Lynn, *Myth and Materiality in a Woman's World* (Manchester University Press, 2005)
Alexander, Ted and Verishnikova, Tatiana, *Ransome in Russia* (Portchester Publishing, 2003). Reproduced with the permission of Special Collection Leeds University Library BC MS 20c Ransome/3/13 and the Arthur Ransome Literary Executors
Allcard, Clare, *A Gypsy Life* (WW Norton & Co., 1992)
Allcard, Clare, *The Intricate Art of Living Afloat* (WW Norton & Co., 1990)
Allcard, Edward, *Temptress Returns* (Putnam, 1951)
Andersen, Lis, *Lis Sails the Atlantic* (Rupert Hart-Davis, 1953)
Austen, Jane, *Persuasion* (Penguin, 2012)
Balmforth, Mike and Mason, Edward, *Cruising Scotland* (Imray Lorie Norie & Wilson, 2015)
Beach, Diana, *Mjojo na Lamu* (YouTube)
Beach, Diana, *The Ocean Voyager and Me* (Independently published, 2014)
Bender, Michael, *A New History of Yachting* (Boydell & Brewer, 2017)
Berry, John, *Discovering Swallows and Amazons* (Sigma, 2004)
Blewitt, Mary, *Celestial Navigation for Yachtsmen* (Adlard Coles, 2011)
Bourne Eriksson, Pamela, *The Life and Death of the Duchess* (Houghton Mifflin, 1959)
Bradford, Ernle, *The Journeying Moon* (Jarrolds, 1958)
Bradford, Ernle, *The Wind off the Island* (Hutchinson, 1960)
Brassey, Anna, *A Voyage in the Sunbeam* (Century, 1984)
Brassey, Anna and Lady Mary Broome (Ed.), *The Last Voyage, to India and Australia, in The 'Sunbeam'* (Project Gutenberg, www.gutenberg.org/files/29778/29778-h/29778-h.htm)
Bridges, Antony, *Scapa Ferry* (Peter Davies, 1957)
Brown, Winifred, *Duffers on the Deep* (Pitchpole Books, 1939)
Calder, Nigel, *Shakedown Cruise* (Adlard Coles, 2018)
Carr, Marion, *The Call of the Running Tide* (Sailtrust Books, 1983)
Chambers, Anne, *Grace O'Malley* (Gill Books Anniversary Edition, 2019)
Chambers, Roland, *The Last Englishman* (Faber, 2010)
Chichester, Sheila, *Two Lives, Two Worlds* (Hodder & Stoughton, 1969)

Childers, Erskine, *The Riddle of the Sands* (Smith, Elder & Co, 1903)
Chivers, David, *An Eye for Innovation: the life of Austin 'Clarence' Farrar* (Independently published, 2016)
Clark, Michael, *The Sailing History of Lough Erne* (Clogher Historical Society, 2005)
Clark, Miles, *High Endeavours* (Hugh Douglas & Co., 1991)
Clyde Cruising Club, *Cruising Scotland* (Imray, 2023)
Collis, Rose, *A Trouser-Wearing Character: The Life and Times of Nancy Spain* (UNKNO, 1997)
Criado-Perez, Caroline, *Invisible Women* (Vintage, 2020)
Crossman, John, *Dusmarie: The story of the Colchester smack Daisy and Douglas Dixon* (privately published)
Dalzel-Job, Patrick, *Arctic Snow to Dust of Normandy* (Pen and Sword Military, 2007)
Dalzel-Job, Patrick (writing as Peter Dalzel), *The Settlers* (Constable and Company, 1957)
Davison, Ann, *By Gemini* (Peter Davies, 1962)
Davison, Ann, *Home was an Island* (Peter Davies, 1952)
Davison, Ann, *Last Voyage* (Peter Davies, 1951)
Davison, Ann, *My Ship is So Small* (Golden Duck, 2024)
Deane, Shirley, *The Expectant Mariner* (Murray, 1962)
Dear, Ian, *The Royal Ocean Racing Club: the first 75 years* (Adlard Coles, 2000)
Delany, Vincent, *The North Shannon Yacht Club* (Afloat.ie, 2020)
Dixon, Douglas and Mary, *Seagull and Sea-Power* (William Blackwood and Sons, 1937)
Dixon, Douglas, *A Sail to Gallipoli* (East Anglian Magazine Ltd., 1965)
Dixon, Douglas, *A Sail to Lapland* (William Blackwood and Sons, 1938)
Dixon, Mary and Douglas, *Soft Falls the Snow* (Hodder & Stoughton, 1955)
Doane, Charles J, *The Boy Who Fell to Shore* (Latah Books, 2022)
Drummond, Maldwin, *The Riddle* (Unicorn, 2016)
Edwards, Tracy, *Living Every Second* (Hodder & Stoughton, 2001)
Edwards, Tracy (with Tim Madge), *Maiden* (Simon & Schuster, 1990)
Fairholme, Elizabeth and Powell, Pamela, *A Dinghy on the London River* (Peter Davies, 1937)
Findlay, Gordon, *My Hand on the Tiller* (Author House UK, 2005)
Francis, Clare, *Come Hell or High Water* (Sphere Books, 1977)
Francis, Clare, *Come Wind or Weather* (Sphere Books, 1978)
Gerard, Peter, *Who Hath Desired the Sea* (Arthur Baker, 1962)
Gould, Cecily, *Gossip* (Gentry Books Ltd, 1972)
Grainger, Nicholas, *The Voyage of the Aegre* (Vinycomb Press, 2023)
Griffiths, Maurice, *Ten Small Yachts* (Edward Arnold & Co., 1949)

BIBLIOGRAPHY

Griffiths, Maurice, *The Magic of the Swatchways* (A&C Black, 1932)
Griffiths, Maurice, *Yachting on a Small Income* (Hutchinson & Co., 1930)
Hammick, Anne, *Ocean Cruising on a Budget* (Adlard Coles, 1990)
Harcourt, Keith and Edwards, Roy, 'Engineering and the Family in Business: Blanche Coules Thornycroft: Naval Architecture and Engineering Design', *Science Museum Group Journal* 10(10), November 2018
Harcourt, Keith, '24. Eily Marguerite Leifchild Smith Keary', Magnificent Women, 21 March 2019 (www.magnificentwomen.co.uk/engineer-of-the-week/24-eily-marguerite-leifchild-smith-keary)
Hardyment, Christina, *The World of Arthur Ransome* (Frances Lincoln, 2012)
Heald, Henrietta, 'What was a girl to do? Rachel Parsons (1885–1956): engineer and feminist campaigner', Blue Stocking, 23 May 2014 (www.blue-stocking.org.uk/2014/05/23/what-was-a-girl-to-do-rachel-parsons-1885-1956-engineer-and-feminist-campaigner)
Heckstall-Smith, B, *Yachts and Yachting in Contemporary Art* (The Studio Ltd, 1925)
Herbert, AP, *Holy Deadlock* (Methuen, 1934)
Heywood, Suzanne, *Wavewalker* (William Collins, 2023)
Hichens, Robert, *We Fought Them in Gunboats* (Golden Duck, 2023)
Hill, Annie, *Voyaging on a Small Income* (Tiller Publishing, 1993)
Hill, Judith, *In Search of Islands: a Life of Conor O'Brien* (The Collins Press, 2009)
Hiscock, Eric, *Around the World in Wanderer III* (Oxford University Press, 1956)
Hiscock, Eric, *I Left the Navy* (Edward Arnold, 1945)
Hiscock, Eric, *Voyaging Under Sail* (Oxford University Press, 1959)
Hiscock, Eric, *Wandering Under Sail Third Edition* (Oxford University Press, 1948)
Holford, Ingrid, *Interpreting the Weather* (David and Charles, 1973)
Hubbuck, John H and Edith C, *Jane Austen's Sailor Brothers* (Cambridge University Press, 2015)
Hughes, Barbara, 'Cruising and Small Yacht Racing on the Solent', *The Sportswoman's Library, Vol. 2*, (Archibald Constable & Co., 1898)
Hughes, Owain, *Everything I've Always Forgotten* (Seren, 2013)
Hughes, Richard, *The Fox in the Attic* (Chatto & Windus, 1961)
Humphreys, Steve, *The Call of the Sea: Britain's Maritime Past* (BBC Books, 1997)
Illingworth, John, *The Malham Story* (Nautical Publishing Co., 1972)
Ipcar, Charles and Saville, James (Eds.) *The Complete Poetry of Cicely Fox Smith* (Little Red Tree, 2015)

Isbester, Jack, *Hard Down! Hard Down!* (Whittles Publishing, 2019)
Jacobsen, Betty, *A Girl Before the Mast* (Charles Scribner's Sons, 1934)
James, Naomi, *At One with the Sea* (Hutchinson, 1979)
James, Naomi, *At Sea on Land* (Hutchinson, 1981)
Kemp, John, *A Fair Wind for London* (SailTrust Books, 1983)
King, Richard, *Sailing Alone* (Particular Books, 2023)
Lacy, Mary, *The Female Shipwright* (Caird Library Reprints, 2008)
Lamb, Christian, *Beyond the Sea: A Wren at War* (Mardle Books, 2021)
Lance, Kate, *Alan Villiers: Voyager of the Winds* (National Maritime Museum Greenwich, 2009)
Le Faye, Deirdre, *Jane Austen's Letters Fourth Edition* (Oxford University Press, 2011)
Levitt, Dorothy, *The Woman and the Car: A Chatty Little Handbook for all Who Motor or who Want to Motor* (HardPress, 2019)
Linklater, Elizabeth, *A Child Under Sail* (Jonathan Cape, 1938)
Loeffler, Frank, *Against the Elements: Aldeburgh Yacht Club, the first 100 years* (Aldeburgh Yacht Club, 1997)
MacArthur, Ellen, *Race Against Time* (Michael Joseph, 2005)
MacArthur, Ellen, *Taking on the World* (Michael Joseph, 2002)
McDermid, Dr Jane, review *of Myth and Materiality in a Woman's World: Shetland, 1800–2000*, (review no. 595), www.reviews.history.ac.uk/review/595, Date accessed: 18 September 2024
Maillart, Ella, *Forbidden Journey* (H. Holt, 1937)
Maillart, Ella, *Gypsy Afloat* (Heinemann, 1942)
Marriott, Edward, *Claude and Madeleine* (Picador, 2005)
Mathews, Vera Laughton, *Blue Tapestry* (Hollis & Carter, 1948)
Meggitt, Geoff, *Winifred Brown Britain's Adventure Girl No 1* (Pitchpole Books, 2013)
Miller, Lee, *Wrens in Camera* (Hollis & Carter, 1945)
Milnes-Walker, Nicolette, *When I Put Out to Sea* (Golden Duck, 2022)
Monsarrat, Nicholas, *Life is a Four Letter Word* (Cassell, 1970)
Morgan, Geoffrey and Tucker, Pamela, *The Yachtswoman's Pocket Book* (Max Parrish & Co.,1965)
Mortimer, Molly, 'Scillonian Great-Aunts', *Marine Quarterly, Vol. 1* (2011)
Myatt, Claudia, *Sketchbook Sailor* (Golden Duck, 2020)
Neville, Sophie, *The Making of Swallows and Amazons* (Classic TV Press, 2014)
O'Connor, Alan, *Sailing and Social Class* (Routledge, 2024)
Parkin, Simon, *A Game of Birds and Wolves* (Sceptre, 2019)
Pera, Mary, *Racing Rules for Sailors* (Adlard Coles, 1997)
Pickthall, Barry, *Eileen Ramsey* (Adlard Coles, 2012)

Pirie, Marcia, *Travellers on a Trade Wind* (Frontier Publishing, 1992)
Price, Nancy, *The Gull's Way* (Victor Gollancz Ltd., 1937)
Purves, Libby, *This Cruising Life* (Adlard Coles, 2001)
Randall, Cassidy, 'Alone at the edge of the world', *The Atavist Magazine*, No. 131, September 2024 (www.magazine.atavist.com/alone-at-the-edge-of-the-world-susie-goodall-sailing-golden-globe-race)
Ransome, Arthur, *Racundra's First Cruise* (G. Allen & Unwin, 1923)
Ransome Arthur, *Racundra's Third Cruise* (Jonathan Cape, 1924)
Ransome, Arthur, *Swallows and Amazons* (Jonathan Cape, 1930)
Ransome, Evgenia (Ed. Ratcliffe, Margaret), *No Holds Barred: Evgenia Ransome's Diaries 1927-1933* (Amazon Publications, 2022)
Raynes, Rozelle, *Maid Matelot* (Golden Duck, 2022)
Raynes, Rozelle, *The Sea Bird* (Golden Duck, 2024)
Rice, Angela, *Adventures of a Reluctant Boating Wife* (Adlard Coles, 2013)
Ring, Jim, *Erskine Childers* (Faber, 2011)
Robertson, E Arnot, *Ordinary Families* (Virago, 1982)
Scott, Peter, *The Eye of the Wind* (Hodder & Stoughton, 1961)
Shaddick, Jane, *Ivy's Journal* (Morgan Giles Heritage Foundation, 2018)
Sieghart, Mary Ann, *The Authority Gap* (Black Swan, 2022)
Sites Adams, Sharon, *Pacific Lady* (University of Nebraska Press, 2008)
Sleightholme, Joyce, *The Sea Wife's Handbook* (Regnery, 1971)
Slocum, Joshua, *Sailing Alone Around the World* (The Century Company, 1900)
Smeeton, Beryl, *Winter Shoes in Springtime* (Rupert Hart-Davis, 1961)
Smeeton, Miles, *Once is Enough* (McGraw Hill, 2001)
Smillie, Susan, *The Half Bird* (Michael Joseph, 2024)
Smith, Emma, *As Green as Grass* (Bloomsbury, 2013)
Smith, Emma, *Maiden's Trip* (Bloomsbury, 2009)
Smith, Victoria, *Hags* (Fleet, 2023)
Somerville, Edith and Ross, Martin, *Some Experiences of an Irish RM* (Abacus, 1989)
Speed, Maude, *A Yachtswoman's Cruises* (Longmans Green, 1911)
Stanley, Jo, *From Cabin 'Boys' to Captains: 250 years of women at sea* (The History Press, 2016)
Stark, Suzanne J, *British Women in the Age of Sail* (Pimlico, 1998)
Stephens, William P, 'The Development of the Small Cruiser Part 53', *Motorboating*, October 1943
Stock, Mabel, *The Log of a Woman Wanderer* (Heinemann, 1923)
Stock, Mabel (Ed. Wilson, Linus), *Sailing the Ogre: A Log of a Woman Wanderer* (annotated) (Independently published, 2019)
Stock, Ralph, *The Chequered Cruise* (T Werner Laurie,1916)

Stock, Ralph, *The Cruise of the Dream Ship* (Heinemann, 1921)
Stopes, Marie, *Married Love* (AC Fifield, 1918)
Swale, Rosie, *Children of Cape Horn* (Macmillan, 1975)
Swale, Rosie, *Rosie Darling* (Pelham Books, 1973)
Swale-Pope, Rosie, *Just a Little Run Around the World* (Harper Collins, 2009)
Swinstead, David, *The Bembridge Redwings* (Cross Publishing, 1997)
Tambs, Erling, *The Cruise of the Teddy* (Jonathan Cape, 1933)
Tew, Helen, *Transatlantic at Last* (Seafarer Books, 2004)
Tilman, HW, *Mischief Goes South* (Lodestar, 2016)
Underhill, Arthur, *A Short History of the Royal Cruising Club 1880–1930* (Privately published, 1930)
Van der Wiele, Annie, *The West in My Eyes* (Rupert Hart-Davis, 1955)
Vasey, Tony, *The Ocean Cruising Club: the first 50 years* (Chalvington Press, 2004)
Villiers, Alan, *Falmouth for Orders* (Jonathan Cape, 1952)
Villiers, Alan, *Grain Race* (C Scribner's Sons, 1933)
Wickham, Hilary, *Sea Wisdom for Small Craft* (S Paul, 1964)
Wyllie, MA and WL, *London to the Nore* (A&C Black, 1905)
Wyllie, MA, 'Punt Racing', *The Sportswoman's Library, Vol. 2* (Archibald Constable & Co., 1898)
Wyllie, MA, *We Were One: A Biography of WL Wyllie* (G Bell, 1935)

ENDNOTES

INTRODUCTION

1 Jane Austen, *Persuasion*, p.69
2 Barbara Hughes, *The Sportswoman's Library, Vol. 2*, p.23
3 Peter Gerard, *Who Hath Desired the Sea*, p.48
4 Barry Pickthall and Susie Goodall, quoted in 'Alone at the edge of the world' by Cassidy Randall, *The Atavist Magazine*

CHAPTER 1

1 Anna Brassey, *A Voyage in the Sunbeam*, p.31
2 Anna Brassey, *A Voyage in the Sunbeam*, p.31
3 Anna Brassey, *A Voyage in the Sunbeam*, p.31
4 Anna Brassey, *A Voyage in the Sunbeam*, p.290
5 Anna Brassey, *A Voyage in the Sunbeam*, p.332
6 Anna Brassey, *A Voyage in the Sunbeam*, p.407
7 Anna Brassey, *A Voyage in the Sunbeam*, p.ix
8 Anna Brassey, *A Voyage in the Sunbeam*, p.147
9 Anna Brassey, *A Voyage in the Sunbeam*, p.27
10 Anna Brassey, *A Voyage in the Sunbeam*, p.32
11 Anna Brassey, *A Voyage in the Sunbeam*, pp.34–35
12 Anna Brassey, *A Voyage in the Sunbeam*, p.363
13 Quoted in 'Doings of the Sunbeam: Contextualising the Collections of Lady Annie Brassey (1839–1887), 1870s–1880s' (www.doingsofthesunbeam.wordpress.com)
14 Anna Brassey, *A Voyage in the Sunbeam*, p.217
15 Anna Brassey and Lady Mary Broome, *The Last Voyage*
16 Anna Brassey, *A Voyage in the Sunbeam*, p.202
17 Anna Brassey, *A Voyage in the Sunbeam*, p.191
18 Anna Brassey, *A Voyage in the Sunbeam*, p.414
19 Anna Brassey and Lady Mary Broome, *The Last Voyage*
20 Anna Brassey and Lady Mary Broome, *The Last Voyage*

CHAPTER 2

1. Elizabeth Linklater, *A Child Under Sail*, p.18
2. Jo Stanley, *From Cabin 'Boys' to Captains*, p.50
3. Deidre le Faye, *Jane Austen's Letters*, p.250
4. Jane Austen, *Persuasion*, p.70
5. Elizabeth Linklater, *A Child Under Sail*, p.15
6. Elizabeth Linklater, *A Child Under Sail*, p.18
7. Elizabeth Linklater, *A Child Under Sail*, p.194
8. Elizabeth Linklater, *A Child Under Sail*, p.225
9. Elizabeth Linklater, *A Child Under Sail*, p.176
10. Elizabeth Linklater, *A Child Under Sail*, p.vii
11. Dr Jane McDermid, review of *Myth and Materiality in a Woman's World*
12. Jack Isbester, *Hard Down! Hard Down!*, p.36

CHAPTER 3

1. Barbara Hughes, *The Sportswoman's Library, Vol. 2*, p.15
2. Barbara Hughes, *The Sportswoman's Library, Vol. 2*, p.23
3. Barbara Hughes, *The Sportswoman's Library, Vol. 2*, p.24
4. Barbara Hughes, *The Sportswoman's Library, Vol. 2*, p.11
5. Barbara Hughes, *The Sportswoman's Library, Vol. 2*, p.13
6. Barbara Hughes, *The Sportswoman's Library, Vol. 2*, p.15
7. *The Yachtsman* magazine (Summer No. 1900)
8. Barbara Hughes, *The Sportswoman's Library, Vol. 2*, p.14
9. Barbara Hughes, *The Sportswoman's Library, Vol. 2*, p.27
10. https://sailcraftblog.wordpress.com/2016/09/08/1-12 (Chris Thompson, *Sail Craft Blog*, 8 September 2016)
11. Email correspondence with David Swinstead (14 February 2024)
12. The first female gold medallist, American-born Hélène de Pourtalès, also sailed for Switzerland, winning in 1900
13. https://sailcraftblog.wordpress.com/2016/09/08/1-12 (Chris Thompson, *Sail Craft Blog*, 8 September 2016)
14. Barbara Hughes, *The Sportswoman's Library, Vol. 2*, p.58
15. Barbara Hughes, *The Sportswoman's Library, Vol. 2*, p.32
16. Barbara Hughes, *The Sportswoman's Library, Vol. 2*, p.23
17. David Swinstead 'Early Women Sailors in Bembridge SC' email (14 February 2024)
18. Though women were not able to jump-race professionally until the 1970s, they had been able to hunt and to compete in point-to point steeplechases with no impediment other than their own levels of skill and courage
19. Dorothy Levitt, *The Woman and the Car*, p.87

ENDNOTES

CHAPTER 4

1. Maude Speed, *A Yachtswoman's Cruises*, p.14
2. Interview with Charlotte Dorrien-Smith by Molly Mortimer, *Marine Quarterly*, No.1, p.84
3. Interview with Charlotte Dorrien-Smith by Molly Mortimer, *Marine Quarterly*, No.1, p.86
4. Personal reminiscence email correspondence with Sam Llewellyn (11 March 2024)
5. Maude Speed, *A Yachtswoman's Cruises*
6. Maude Speed, *A Yachtswoman's Cruises*, p.10
7. Maude Speed, *A Yachtswoman's Cruises*, p.67
8. Maude Speed, *A Yachtswoman's Cruises*, p.7
9. Maude Speed, *A Yachtswoman's Cruises*, p.192
10. Arthur Underhill (early history of RCC)
11. RCC membership records
12. MA Wyllie, *We Were One*
13. MA Wyllie, *We Were One*, p.61
14. MA Wylie, *The Sportswoman's Library, Vol. 2*, p.81
15. MA Wyllie, *We Were One*, ch.4
16. MA Wyllie, *We Were One*, p.158
17. MA Wyllie, *We Were One*, ch.8
18. MA Wyllie, *We Were One*, p.55
19. MA Wyllie, *We Were One*, p.217
20. Jane Shaddick, *Ivy's Journal*, p.22
21. Jane Shaddick, *Ivy's Journal*
22. Jane Shaddick, *Ivy's Journal*
23. Jane Shaddick, *Ivy's Journal*, p.41
24. Jane Shaddick, *Ivy's Journal*, p.31
25. Jane Shaddick, *Ivy's Journal*, p.32
26. Jane Shaddick, *Ivy's Journal*, p.48
27. Jane Shaddick, *Ivy's Journal*, p.81

CHAPTER 5

1. www.anphoblacht.com/contents/24233 (Mary Spring Rice, *An Phoblacht*, 27 July 2014)
2. Email correspondence (20 October 2023)
3. www.youtube.com/watch?v=bldV8_d2KMw (Shannon One Design Association, 17 April, 2021)
4. www.historyireland.com/every-delicacy-of-the-season-conspicuous-consumption-during-the-great-hunger (*History Ireland*, May/June, 2018)

5   Email correspondence with Vincent Delany (24 September 2024), citing William Frederick Wakeman, *Three Days On the Shannon* (Dublin, 1852)
6   Somerville and Ross, *Some Experiences of an Irish RM*, p.79
7   Maldwin Drummond, *The Riddle*, p.217
8   Mary Spring Rice, *Diary of the Asgard*, 12 July 1914

CHAPTER 6

1   Vera Laughton Mathews, *Blue Tapestry*, p.12
2   Jim Ring, *Erskine Childers*, p.148
3   Judith Hill, *In Search of Islands*, p.42
4   Vera Laughton Mathews, *Blue Tapestry*, p.17
5   Vera Laughton Mathews, *Blue Tapestry*, p.11
6   Vera Laughton Mathews, *Blue Tapestry*, p.29
7   Vera Laughton Mathews, *Blue Tapestry*, p.15
8   Vera Laughton Mathews, *Blue Tapestry*, p.20
9   Vera Laughton Mathews, *Blue Tapestry*, p.7
10 Vera Laughton Mathews, *Blue Tapestry*, p.47
11 Charles Ipcar and James Saville (Eds.), *The Complete Poetry of Cicely Fox Smith* (Little Red Tree, 2015), quoting: Martha Plaisted, 'Sea Songs by a Woman', *The Bookman Vol. 60*
12 'The Dust of the Way' from *Wings of the Morning* (1904) Ipcar and Saville, p.144
13 Charles Ipcar and James Saville (Eds.), *Complete Poetry of Cicely Fox Smith*, p.240
14 Charles Ipcar and James Saville (Eds.), *Complete Poetry of Cicely Fox Smith*, p.738
15 Mark Barton RINA editorial, 'The Legacy of Eily Keary 1892–1973'
16 Harcourt and Edwards, 'Engineering and the family in business', p29

CHAPTER 7

1   Beryl Smeeton, *Winter Shoes in Springtime*
2   Quoted by David Swinstead
3   Patrick Dalzel-Job, *The Settlers*, p.2
4   Patrick Dalzel-Job, *The Settlers*, p.4–5
5   Miles Clark, *High Endeavours*, p.15
6   Beryl Smeeton, *Winter Shoes in Springtime*, p.15
7   Beryl Smeeton, *Winter Shoes in Springtime*, p.123
8   Beryl Smeeton, *Winter Shoes in Springtime*, p.226
9   Email correspondence
10 Beryl Smeeton, *Winter Shoes in Springtime*, p.193

ENDNOTES

11 Beryl Smeeton, *Winter Shoes in Springtime*, p.12
12 Beryl Smeeton, *Winter Shoes in Springtime*, p.13
13 Douglas and Mary Dixon, *Seagull and Sea-Power*, p.12
14 Douglas Dixon, *A Sail to Lapland*, p.x

CHAPTER 8

1 Peter Gerard, *Who Hath Desired the Sea*, p.219
2 Ralph Stock, *The Cruise of the Dream Ship*
3 Ralph Stock, *The Chequered Cruise*
4 Mabel Stock, *Log of a Woman Wanderer*
5 Mabel Stock, *Log of a Woman Wanderer*, p.14
6 Mabel Stock, *Log of a Woman Wanderer*, p.7
7 Arthur Ransome, *Racundra's First Cruise*, p.76
8 Roger Wardale, *Ransome at Sea*, p.6
9 John Berry, *Discovering Swallows and Ransomes*, p.23
10 Quoted Ted Alexander, *Ransome in Russia*, p153
11 Arthur Ransome, *Racundra's Third Cruise*
12 Roland Chambers *The Last Englishman*, p.294
13 Evgenia Ransome, *No Holds Barred*, p.117
14 Evgenia Ransome, *No Holds Barred*, p.70
15 *Little Ship Club Journal, Vol. 2*, No. 2
16 Peter Gerard, *Who Hath Desired the Sea*, p.13
17 Peter Gerard, *Who Hath Desired the Sea*, p.28
18 Peter Gerard, *Who Hath Desired the Sea*, p.38
19 Muriel Wiles, *Little Ship Club Journal, Vol. X*, 1936
20 Sophie Neville, *The Making of Swallows and Amazons*
21 Christina Hardyment, *The World of Arthur Ransome*, pp.76 & 83
22 Peter Gerard, *Who Hath Desired the Sea*, p.76
23 Peter Gerard, *Who Hath Desired the Sea*, pp.76–77
24 Peter Gerard, *Who Hath Desired the Sea*, pp.76–77
25 Maurice Griffiths, *The Magic of the Swatchways*, p.67
26 Maurice Griffiths, *The Magic of the Swatchways*, ch.9
27 Peter Gerard, *Who Hath Desired the Sea*, p.35
28 Peter Gerard, *Who Hath Desired the Sea*, p.73
29 Maurice Griffiths, *The Magic of the Swatchways*, p.234
30 Peter Gerard, *Who Hath Desired the Sea*, p.192

CHAPTER 9

1 Quoted by Kate Lance, *Alan Villiers*, p.42
2 Kate Lance, *Alan Villiers*, p.ii

3 Kate Lance, *Alan Villiers*, p.42
4 Alan Villiers, *Grain Race*, p.48
5 Betty Jacobsen, *A Girl Before the Mast*, p.1
6 Betty Jacobsen, *A Girl Before the Mast*, p.5
7 Pamela Bourne Eriksson, *The Life and Death of the Duchess*, p.77
8 Pamela Bourne Eriksson, *The Life and Death of the Duchess*, p.66
9 Pamela Bourne Eriksson, *The Life and Death of the Duchess*, p.82
10 Pamela Bourne Eriksson, *The Life and Death of the Duchess*, p.66
11 Pamela Bourne Eriksson, *The Life and Death of the Duchess*, p.73
12 Pamela Bourne Eriksson, *The Life and Death of the Duchess*, p.75
13 Pamela Bourne Eriksson, *The Life and Death of the Duchess*, p.64
14 Pamela Bourne Eriksson, *The Life and Death of the Duchess*, p.88
15 Pamela Bourne Eriksson, *The Life and Death of the Duchess*, p.184
16 Pamela Bourne Eriksson, *The Life and Death of the Duchess*, p.241

CHAPTER 10

1 Elizabeth Fairholme and Pamela Powell, *A Dinghy on the London River*, p.14
2 *Little Ship Club Journal* (Jan 1929), p21
3 Elizabeth Fairholme and Pamela Powell, *A Dinghy on the London River*, p.14
4 Elizabeth Fairholme and Pamela Powell, *A Dinghy on the London River*, p.213
5 Elizabeth Fairholme and Pamela Powell, *A Dinghy on the London River*, p.222
6 Peter Scott, *The Eye of the Wind*, p.221
7 Michael Clarke, *The Sailing History of Lough Erne*
8 www.britishpathe.com/asset/39710/ (British Pathé, 11 March 2022)
9 Winifred Brown, *Duffers on the Deep*, p.9
10 *Yachting Monthly* (April 1938), p.509
11 *Little Ship Club Journal* (February 1933)
12 E Arnot Robertson, *Ordinary Families*, p.115
13 *Yachting Monthly* (May 1938), p22
14 *Little Ship Club Journal* (November 1934)
15 *Little Ship Club Journal* (1936)
16 *Little Ship Club Journal* (February 1937)

CHAPTER 11

1 Original title of Christian Lamb's book, *I Only Joined for the Hat*
2 Vera Laughton Mathews, *Blue Tapestry*, p.51

ENDNOTES

3 Vera Laughton Mathews, *Blue Tapestry*, p.76
4 Vera Laughton Mathews, *Blue Tapestry*, p.135
5 Vera Laughton Mathews, *Blue Tapestry*, p.98
6 Robert Hichens, *We Fought Them in Gunboats*, p.297
7 www.linkedin.com/pulse/meet-one-only-two-female-commerical-marine-pilots-uk-john-ferguson- (John Ferguson, LinkedIn, 1 February 2020)
8 Nicholas Monsarrat, *Life is a Four Letter Word*, p.114
9 Rose Collis, *A Trouser-Wearing Character*, p.56
10 Robert Hichens, *We Fought Them in Gunboats*, p.291
11 Vera Laughton Mathews, *Blue Tapestry*, p.118
12 Vera Laughton Mathews, *Blue Tapestry*, p.121
13 Vera Laughton Mathews, *Blue Tapestry*, p.117
14 Vera Laughton Mathews, *Blue Tapestry*, p.131
15 Vera Laughton Mathews, *Blue Tapestry*, p.134
16 Christian Lamb, *Beyond the Sea*, p.52. Degaussing was the process of placing electric cables round a ship to 'wipe' its magnetic field thus reducing danger from magnetic mines
17 Christian Lamb, *Beyond the Sea*, p.184
18 www.wrecksite.eu/wreck.aspx?17199 (Wreck Site)
19 First women to serve officially on operational warship HMS *Brilliant* October 1990, during the Gulf War
20 Vera Laughton Mathews, *Blue Tapestry*, p.201
21 Rozelle Raynes, *Maid Matelot*, p.14
22 Vera Laughton Mathews, *Blue Tapestry*, p.177

CHAPTER 12

1 Gladys Newell, quoted in email correspondence with John Newell (26 March 2024)
2 Cecily, Gould, *Gossip*
3 Cecily, Gould, *Gossip*, p.22
4 Email correspondence with John Newell (26 March 2024)
5 Antony Bridges, *Scapa Ferry*, p.35
6 Antony Bridges, *Scapa Ferry*, p.75
7 Antony Bridges, *Scapa Ferry*, p.144
8 Miles Smeeton, *Change of Jungles* quoting *High Endeavours*, p.175
9 Email correspondence with Clio Smeeton (22 November 2023)
10 Beryl Smeeton, diary 11 July 1942, quoting *High Endeavours*, p.192
11 www.sailingscuttlebutt.com/2024/04/30/motherhood-and-olympic-goals/ (*Scuttlebutt Sailing News*, 30 April 2024)
12 Email correspondence with Clio Smeeton (22 November 2023)

13 www.mumsnet.com/talk/telly_addicts/4359812-Alison-Hargreaves-and-her-son (Mumsnet, 26 September 2021)
14 Email correspondence with Ewen Southby-Tailyour (6 December 2023)
15 Miles Clark, *High Endeavours*, p.212
16 www.yachtingmonthly.com/cruising-life/beryl-and-miles-smeeton-high-endeavours-81598 (Theo Stocker, *Yachting Monthly*, 27 September 2021)
17 Ann Davison
18 Unless otherwise credited, almost all the information in this section is from the box of papers which Ann's cousin, Ann Eaton, keeps safe
19 www.afleetingpeace.org/index.php/pioneering-women/gower-pauline-mary-de-peauly?highlight=WyJkb3JvdGh5Iiwic3BpY2VyIl0= (Terry Mace, A Fleeting Peace)
20 Ann Davison, *Last Voyage*, p.14
21 www.ata-ferry-pilots.org/index.php/category-blog-1940/171-davison-elsie-joy?highlight=WyJkYXZpc29uIl0= (Terry Mace, Ferry pilots of the ATA)
22 Ann Davison, *Home was an Island*, pp.235-236

CHAPTER 13

1 *Yachting Monthly* (October 1939)
2 Letter from Peter Scott, *Yachting Monthly* (December 1948)
3 Email correspondence with Ian Palmer (29 November 2023)
4 www.classicboat.co.uk/articles/the-queen-of-british-yachting-photography (Barry Pickthall, *Classic Boat*, 13 July 2011)
5 www.theguardian.com/artanddesign/2017/feb/21/eileen-ramsay-obituary (Barry Pickthall, *The Guardian*, 21 February 2021)
6 www.theguardian.com/artanddesign/2017/feb/21/eileen-ramsay-obituary (Barry Pickthall, *The Guardian*, 21 February 2021)
7 www.thamessailingclub.co.uk/history/TSC-and-its-Sailing-History (Thames Sailing Club)
8 Wikipedia, quoting Cherry Drummond, *The Remarkable Life of Victoria Drummond*, p.94
9 Emma Smith, *Maiden's Trip*, p.29

CHAPTER 14

1 Ann Davison, *Last Voyage*, p.228
2 Ann Davison, *Last Voyage*
3 Ann Davison, *Last Voyage*, p.44
4 Ann Davison, *Last Voyage*, p.74
5 Ann Davison, *Last Voyage*, p.131
6 Ann Davison, *Last Voyage*, p.132

ENDNOTES

7 Ann Davison, *Last Voyage*, p.139
8 Ann Davison, *Last Voyage*, p.150
9 Ann Davison, *Last Voyage*, p.229
10 Ann Davison, *Last Voyage*, p.233
11 Ann Davison, *Last Voyage*, p.234
12 Exercise book, pp.4–5
13 Letter dated 23 October 1950. The agent was CH Brooks at AM Heath Ltd
14 Ann Davison, *My Ship is So Small*, p.12
15 Ann Davison, *My Ship is So Small*

CHAPTER 15

1 Rozelle Raynes, *The Sea Bird*, p.30
2 Rozelle Raynes, *The Sea Bird*, p.20
3 Rozelle Raynes, *The Sea Bird*, p.18
4 Rozelle Raynes, *The Sea Bird*, p.30
5 Rozelle Raynes, *The Sea Bird*, p.88
6 Rozelle Raynes, *The Sea Bird*
7 Rozelle Raynes, *The Sea Bird*, p.120
8 Rozelle Raynes, *The Sea Bird*, p.114
9 Eric Hiscock, *Wandering Under Sail*, p.13
10 Eric Hiscock, *Wandering Under Sail*, p.214
11 Eric Hiscock, *Wandering Under Sail*, p.237
12 Marcia Pirie, *Travellers on a Trade Wind*, p.123
13 www.theguardian.com/books/2021/jul/09/why-do-so-few-men-read-books-by-women (MA Sieghart, *The Guardian*, 9 July 2021)
14 Janet Vera Sanso, *Mischief Goes South*, Afterword
15 Ernle Bradford, *The Journeying Moon*

CHAPTER 16

1 Marion Carr, *The Call of the Running Tide*
2 Marion Carr, *The Call of the Running Tide*, p.1
3 Marion Carr, *The Call of the Running Tide*, p.5
4 Marion Carr, *The Call of the Running Tide*, p.5
5 Marion Carr, *The Call of the Running Tide*, p.15
6 Marion Carr, *The Call of the Running Tide*, p.64
7 Marion Carr, *The Call of the Running Tide*, p.66
8 Quoted Francis Wheen, *The Sixties*, p.90
9 Nicholas Grainger, *The Voyage of the Aegre*, p.29
10 Penny Minney, *Crab's Odyssey*, p.12

11 Marthe Oulié, *Cinq Filles en Méditerannée*
12 Penny Minney, *Crab's Odyssey*, p.208
13 Interview with Robin Minney (11 February 2024)
14 Nicholas, Grainger, *The Voyage of the Aegre*, p.60
15 Nicholas, Grainger, *The Voyage of the Aegre*, p.162

CHAPTER 17

1 John Illingworth, *The Malham Story*, p.96
2 Interview and email correspondence with Charles Bazeley
3 John Illingworth, *The Malham Story*, p.94
4 John Illingworth, *The Malham Story*, p.96
5 www.independent.co.uk/news/people/obituary-sir-peter-green-1331349.html (Godfrey Hodgson, *The Independent*, 30 July 1996)
6 Interview with Janet Grosvenor, RORC (13 August 2023)
7 www.giornaledellavela.com/2023/04/13/do-you-want-to-know-what-the-ior-is-the-people-who-gave-birth-to-him-tell-you-about-it/?lang=en (Nicola Sironi, *Vela*, 13 April 2023)
8 All quotes from interview and email correspondence with Janet Grosvenor (13 August 2023)

CHAPTER 18

1 Jean Keppie, 'Forty Years of Trefoil', *Clyde Cruising Club Journal* (1990)
2 The Mudhook YC and Royal Western YC were formed around the same time for similar reasons
3 www.clydecorinthian.org/about-ccyc/history-of-the-club (Clyde Corinthian Yacht Club, 16 April 2024)
4 Interview (11 February 2024)
5 Jean Keppie, 'Forty Years of Trefoil', *Clyde Cruising Club Journal* (1990)
6 Jean Keppie, 'Forty Years of Trefoil', *Clyde Cruising Club Journal* (1990)
7 *Cruising Scotland*, p.85
8 Interview with Anne Billard (23 January 2024)
9 Kean Mackinney Long, 'When a Lady Cruises Solo', *Yachting* (September 1971)
10 Email correspondence with Chris O'Flaherty (28 March 2024)
11 Clare Allcard, *The Intricate Art of Living Afloat*, p.176

CHAPTER 19

1 Diana Beach, *The Ocean Voyager and Me*, p.234
2 Interview with Diana Beach (19 February 2024)
3 Diana Beach, *The Ocean Voyager and Me*, p.10

ENDNOTES

4   Diana Beach, *The Ocean Voyager and Me*, p.13
5   Diana Beach, *The Ocean Voyager and Me*, p.14
6   Diana Beach, *The Ocean Voyager and Me*, p.55
7   Diana Beach, *The Ocean Voyager and Me*, p.149
8   Diana Beach, *The Ocean Voyager and Me*, p.166
9   Diana Beach, *The Ocean Voyager and Me*, p.234
10 Clare Allcard, *A Gypsy Life*, p.49
11 Clare Allcard, *A Gypsy Life*, p.49
12 Clare Allcard, 'Serendipity'
13 *The Yachtswoman's Pocket Book*, p.13
14 Joyce Sleightholme, *The Sea Wife's Handbook*, p.10
15 Joyce Sleightholme, *The Sea Wife's Handbook*, p.3
16 Clare Allcard, *A Gypsy Life*, p.51
17 Clare Allcard, *A Gypsy Life*, p.40
18 Clare Allcard, *A Gypsy Life*, p.58
19 Charles Doane, *The Boy Who Fell to Shore*, p.126
20 *Yachting Monthly* (February 1964)
21 Charles Doane, *The Boy Who Fell to Shore*, p.126
22 Suzanne Heywood, *Wavewalker: Breaking Free*, pp.394–395
23 Suzanne Heywood, *Wavewalker: Breaking Free*, p.349
24 Email correspondence with Suzanne Heywood (5 July 2024)
25 Rosie Swale, *Children of Cape Horn*, p.239
26 www.alastairhumphreys.com/rosie-swalepope (Alistair Humphreys, 17 March 2016)

CHAPTER 20

1   Clare Francis, *Come Hell or High Water*, p.19
2   Sharon Sites Adams, *Pacific Lady*, p.174
3   Sharon Sites Adams, *Pacific Lady*, p.63
4   Sharon Sites Adams, *Pacific Lady*, p.18
5   Sharon Sites Adams, *Pacific Lady*, p.xviii
6   Nicolette Milnes-Walker, *When I Put out to Sea*, p.16
7   The West German sailor, Edith Baumann, was the first woman entrant in 1968, but did not finish. Marie-Claude Faroux (France), Teresa Remiszewska (Poland) and Anne Mikailof (France) entered and completed in 1972
8   Nicolette Milnes-Walker, *When I Put out to Sea*, p.36
9   Ann Davison, *By Gemini*
10 Nicolette Milnes-Walker, *When I Put out to Sea*, p.127
11 www.rwyc.org/club-history/rbi-history/rbi-1974 (Royal Western Yacht Club, 9 April 2024)

12 Clare Francis, *Come Hell or High Water*, p.19
13 https://www.yachtingmonthly.com/archive/the-history-of-winches-6545# (*Yachting Monthly*, 28 July 2010)
14 Clare Francis interview with Paddy Feany, 'Intrepid Women'
15 Clare Francis, *Come Wind or Weather*, p.21

CHAPTER 21

1 Interview with Claudia Myatt
2 Interview with Claudia Myatt
3 Interview with Claudia Myatt
4 Interview with Claudia Myatt
5 Phone interview and email correspondence with Miranda Delmar-Morgan (April 2024)
6 Phone interview and email correspondence with Miranda Delmar-Morgan (April 2024)
7 Email correspondence with Miranda Delmar-Morgan (22 April 2024)
8 Interview with Jill Kernick (24 November 2023)
9 Interview with Lesley Marsh (17 August 2023)
10 Interview with Jo Adey (12 April 2024)
11 www.navywings.org.uk/30th-anniversary-of-wrns-at-sea
12 www.eadt.co.uk/news/24325081.harwich-haven-authority-ceo-need-women-going-sea (*East Anglian Daily Times*, 18 May 2024)

CHAPTER 22

1 Miles Clark, *High Endeavours*, p.335
2 Interview and email correspondence with Anne Hammick (15 March 2024)
3 www.oceancruisingclub.org/Honorary-Members (Ocean Cruising Club, 2024)
4 Interview with Jane Russell, RCC (2 February 2024)
5 www.sunstonesailing.com/tips/tipsc.html (Tom & Vicky Jackson, Sunstone Sailing)
6 Jo Stanley, *From Cabin Boys to Captains*, p.37
7 Michael Bender, *A New History of Yachting*, p.209
8 Miles Clark, *High Endeavours*, p.335
9 Email correspondence with Annie Hill (January 2024)
10 www.speedwelladventures.com/me.html (Shirley Carter, *Speedwell Adventures*)
11 Annie Hill, *Voyaging on a Small Income*, p.122
12 Susan Smillie, *The Half Bird*, p.106

ENDNOTES

CHAPTER 23

1. Rozelle Raynes, *The Sea Bird*, p.188
2. Sheila Chichester, *Two Lives, Two Worlds*, p.89
3. Sheila Chichester, *Two Lives, Two Worlds*, p.87
4. Sheila Chichester, *Two Lives, Two Worlds*, p.44
5. Sheila Chichester, *Two Lives, Two Worlds*, p.21
6. Naomi James, *At One with the Sea*, p.17
7. Naomi James, *At One with the Sea*, p.18
8. Naomi James, *At One with the Sea*, p.24
9. Naomi James, *At One with the Sea*, p.87
10. Naomi James, *At One with the Sea*, p.103
11. Naomi James, *At One with the Sea*, p.97
12. Naomi James, *At One with the Sea*, p.136
13. Naomi James, *At Sea on Land*, p.75
14. Naomi James, *At One with the Sea*, p.185
15. Naomi James, *At Sea on Land*, p.61
16. Naomi James, *At Sea on Land*, p.107
17. Naomi James, *At Sea on Land*, p.148
18. Miles Smeeton, *Once is Enough*, p.74

CHAPTER 24

1. Tracy Edwards, *Living Every Second*
2. Tracy Edwards, *Living Every Second*, p.43
3. Tracy Edwards, *Living Every Second*, p.102
4. Tracy Edwards, *Living Every Second*, p.115
5. Tracy Edwards, *Living Every Second*, p.122
6. Tracy Edwards, *Living Every Second*, p.137
7. Tracy Edwards, *Living Every Second*, p.153
8. Term used by yachting journalist Bob Fisher, later amended by him to 'a tinful of smart fast tarts'
9. Tracy Edwards, *Living Every Second*, p.258
10. Tracy Edwards, *Living Every Second*, p.390
11. Tracy Edwards, *Living Every Second*, p.403
12. Ellen MacArthur, *Taking on the World*, p.2
13. www.independent.co.uk/news/the-forgotten-dame-who-sailed-round-the-world-1530210.html (Chris Redman, *The Independent*, 12 February 2005)
14. Ellen MacArthur, *Taking on the World*, p.87
15. Ellen MacArthur, *Taking on the World*, p.125
16. Tracy Edwards, *Living Every Second*, p.194
17. Ellen MacArthur's Vendée Globe record stood until Clarisse Crémer beat it in the 2020/21 Vendée

18 Conversations with Merfyn Owen and Ashley Perrin (28 April 2024)
19 Helen Tew, *Transatlantic at Last*, p.174

CHAPTER 25

1 www.theguardian.com/uk/2001/feb/11/sport.theobserver (*The Guardian*, 11 February 2001)
2 Ellen MacArthur announcing her retirement from competitive sailing http://news.bbc.co.uk/1/hi/uk/8289226.stm (BBC News, 4 October 2009). Cf Ellen MacArthur, Full Circle (Michael Joseph, 2010) p.261
3 www.yachtingmonthly.com/cruising-life/jeanne-socrates-77-and-solo-non-stop-around-the-world-72022 (Katy Stickland, *Yachting Monthly*, 17 May 2020)
4 www.thetimes.com/article/helen-tew-jcqhrkps87f (*The Times*, 20 November 2004)
5 Email correspondence with Elaine Bunting (May 2024)
6 www.rte.ie/news/munster/2024/0123/1428154-yacht-cork/ (Jennie O'Sullivan, *Raidió Teilifís Éireann*, 24 January 2024)
7 45 women of 557 total members with voting rights: 116 women of 118 associates without voting rights. Cadet members 21 men:11 women. This was in 2000
8 Interview with Carla Stanley (30 January 2024)
9 'Fight or Float' speech at Wooden Boat Festival, Port Townsend (7 September 2024)
10 Interview by Catherine Larner, *Classic Boat Magazine* (1 September 2022)
11 Introduction from 'Fight or Float' speech at Wooden Boat Festival, Port Townsend (7 September 2024)
12 Email correspondence with Elaine Bunting (May 2024)
13 www.sailingscuttlebutt.com/2023/04/24/dear-men-of-the-sailing-world (*Scuttlebutt Sailing News*, 24 April 2003)
14 www.etchells.org/news/article/statement-regarding-dear-men-of-sailing (Etchells Class, 25 April 2023)
15 Libby Purves, *This Cruising Life*, p.2
16 Interview with Elaine Penhaul (30 April 2024)
17 Francis Wheen, p.90
18 This and other quotations from interview and email correspondence with Vuyisile Jaca (28 April 2024)
19 www.iol.co.za/ios/news/brave-durban-woman-makes-around-the-world-sailing-history-413f4928-092b-42fb-a6cc-ba57848 11dfb?fbclid=IwZXh0bgNhZW0CMTEAAR0SncgqvGjardgVv9kfETfnJ3SnDLMxXAaVv-w-X1IvvWdHJGniUEQFOPQ_aem_AfiUzNjdj9B8YoM0CN5cukv8k84rizLSspOtOLCkQ8h4df02ueRz_l9VPThmdK2gGrsd2jTcvce8tJlIA6I69rES (Mervyn Naidoo, *Independent Online*, 28 April 2024)

INDEX

Adams, Gilbert 148
Adams, Ron 110, 111
Adams, Sharon Sites 224–226, 227, 230, 232, 234, 305, 317
Adey, Commodore Jo vii, 238, 248–249, 294, 318
Agar, Augustus 69
Aitken, Max 148
Allcard, Clare (née Thompson) vii, 208, 209–214, 215, 216, 217, 218, 219, 220, 301, 316, 317
Allcard, Edward 215, 216, 218, 219, 220, 230, 301
Allcard, Katy 216, 218
Andersen, Lis 172
Annan, Gabriele (née Ullstein) 191
Annan, Noel 191
Archer, Colin 58, 85
Archdale, Betty 120, 201
Archdale, Helen 120
Armstrong, Sheelagh 52
Atlee, Clement 63, 173
Austen, Cassy 20, 21
Austen, Cassandra 20, 21
Austen, Charles 20, 21
Austen, Fanny (née Palmer) 20, 21
Austen, Francis 20
Austen, Harriet 21
Austen, Jane 3, 20, 21, 125, 301, 303, 304, 307, 308
Austen, Martha, (née Lloyd) 20
Austen, Mary (née Gibson) 20

Baden-Powell, Robert 51
Bangsund, Bjørg 74

Banyard, Captain 180, 181, 183, 184
Barker, Colonel Barrington 42
Barrier, Alexia 285
Barton, Humphrey 154, 252
Barton, Mary (née Danby) 251, 252
Barton, Robert 57
Baumann, Edith 317
Bayard, Madeliene (alias MV Barclay) 116, 126
Bazley, Frances 185
Beach, Diana vii, 209–214, 218, 223, 230, 30, 316, 317
Beattie, Alexander 166, 168
Beattie, Rozelle see Raynes, Rozelle
Bender, Mike 258, 301, 318
Benham, Barbara 182
Benham, Hervey 182
Benham, Jane 178, 182, 183
Berry, John 87, 301, 311
Bevan, Mary 233, 234
Bevan, RA 169
Billard, Anne vii, 199, 205–206, 316
Bingham, George 12, 18
Blake, Sir Peter 282
Blair, Lisa 285
Blewitt, Denys (née Henderson) 191
Blewitt, James 191
Blewitt, Mary see Pera, Mary
Blewitt, Ralph 191, 192
Blyth, Chay 231, 265, 266, 268, 275, 276
Blyth, Maureen 265
Bodichon, Barbara 17
Bonham, Eve 234, 236

Bourne, Sir Henry 101
Bourne, Pamela see Eriksson, Pamela
Boutflower, Robert 159
Bouwmeester, Marit 136
Boxer, Beryl see Smeeton, Beryl
Boxer, Charles 75
Boxer, Hugh 74
Boxer, Myles 75
Boxer, Jeannie 75
Bradford, Ernle 169, 170, 171, 175, 176, 301, 315
Bradford, Janet see Vera-Sanso, Janet
Bradley, Janet vii, 294, 295
Brassey, Anna (née Allnutt) 4, 5, 9–18, 19, 22, 35, 51, 172, 258, 301, 307
Brassey, Helen 35
Brassey, Marie 16
Brassey, Muriel 14, 15, 35
Brassey Mabelle 14, 15
Brassey, Sybil 35
Brassey, Thomas 9, 10, 11, 13, 14, 15, 16, 17, 18, 35
Brassey, Thomas Allnutt 15, 19
Bratby, Michael 109
Brauer, Cole 285
Brent-Good, Cecily see Gould, Cecily
Bridges, Antony 133, 134, 143, 313
Bridges, Margaret 131, 133–135, 143
Bridges, Richard vii, 143
Brocklehurst, Sir Philip 77
Brown, Lizzie 240
Brown, Elsie 110
Brown, Winifred 95, 106, 110, 111, 112, 172, 301, 304, 312

Brutton, Mrs 47
Buckmaster, Hilda 116, 118
Bunting, Elaine vii, 284, 286, 290, 291, 320
Burgess, Rachel 277, 295
Bruce, Erroll 278
Brulé, Frédérique 278
Byrne, Aisling 54

Caffari, Dee 284, 285
Cahalane, Adrienne 192, 278
Carew, Marian *see* Wyllie, Marian
Cardigan, Countess of 200
Carr, Marion 178–182, 183, 184, 189, 301, 315
Carson, Beryl (RCC member) 43
Carter, Shirley 261
Carus-Wilson, Fanny 47, 49
Carus-Wilson, Ivy *see* Morgan Giles, Ivy
Castiglione, Ida 235
Catherwood, Irwin 109
Chadwick, Alison vii, 199, 207
Chichester, Francis 1, 148, 236, 264, 265, 268, 269, 272, 282
Chichester, Sheila 148, 262– 265, 272, 282, 301, 319
Childers, Erskine 43, 51, 57, 58, 61, 81, 302, 305, 310
Childers, Molly (née Osgood) 51, 58–60, 61, 81
Christie, Frank 205
Christie, Katie (née McLean) vii, 199, 201, 204, 205,
Chojnowska-Liskiewicz, Krystyna 266, 268, 270, 276
Clark, Miles 75, 136, 138, 258, 310, 314, 318
Clackson, Beth 212
Clackson, Norman 145
Coats Family (industrialists) 200

Cochrane, Blair 33
Cochrane, Jeannie 33, 35
Cochrane, Mary (née Sutton) 33
Coles, Adlard 89, 145
Coles, Mamie 89
Collins, Bunny (Elspeth Marion Towers-Clark) 71
Collis, Rose vii, 122, 313
Cook, Betty 270, 33
Cornwallis West, Constance *see* Westminster, Duchess of
Coutanche, Sir Alexander 164
Cox, the Misses 31
Coward, Bruce 230, 231, 232
Coward, Nicolette (née Milnes-Walker) vii, 224, 226–232, 235, 237, 271, 272, 274, 298, 304, 317
Criado-Perez, Caroline 6, 302
Crémer, Clarisse 282, 319
Crichton, Lady Mabel 57
Crichton-Stuart, Lady Margaret 258
Cripps, Pam 244
Crowhurst, Donald 227
Croce, Beppo 195
Croghan, Mary 31
Cronkite, Walter 224

Dalzel-Job, Ernest 73
Dalzel-Job, Ethel 71, 73, 74
Dalzel-Job, Patrick 73, 74, 302, 310
Danby, Mary *see* Barton, Mary
Dardé, Christine 255
Dardé, Jacqueline 255
Darvelid, Helena 278
Darwin, Charles 22
Davies, Sarah 274
Davis, Sam 278
Davison, Ann (née Longstaffe) 131, 139–142, 154–162, 172, 229, 232, 252, 271, 302, 314, 315

Davison, Frank 140, 141, 142, 154, 155, 156, 157, 158, 159, 271
Davison, Elsie Joy (née Muntz) 140, 141
Day, Jeanne 98, 99
Deakin, Captain Jo 14
De Cloux, Ruben 99, 100
De Kersauson, Olivier 278
De La Warr, Gilbert 35
De La Warr, Muriel (née Brassey) 35
De Horsey, Admiral 42
De Horsey, Louisa *see* Phillips, Louisa
Dekker, Laura 281
Delany, Alf 53
Delany, Vincent vii, 32, 51, 52, 55, 56, 302, 310
Delmar-Morgan, Miranda vii, 238, 241–243, 275, 318
Delmar-Morgan, Edward 241
Denham, Henry 176
Denny, Mr 48
Desjoyeaux, Michel 282
Dick, Mrs Aitken 94
Dixon, Astrid *see* Llewellyn, Astrid Dixon
Dixon, Douglas 79, 80, 82, 83, 81, 174, 175, 184, 302, 311
Dixon, Marjorie (née Brown) 80
Dixon, Mary (née Turner) 71, 79, 80, 81, 163, 174, 175, 184, 302, 311
Dixon, Shirley 80
Doane, Charles vii, 219, 302, 317
Dodge, Mary 35
Dorrien-Smith, Cicely 38, 39
Dorrien-Smith, Charlotte ('Babs') 38, 39, 40, 309
Dorrien-Smith, Gwendolin 38, 39
Dorrien-Smith, Innis 38, 39
Dorrien-Smith, Mary 38, 39
Dorrien-Smith, Teona 39

INDEX

Doyle, Anne 52
Doyle, James 52
Doyle, Mamie 51, 52, 57
Drake, Francis 127
Drummond, Victoria 144, 150, 151, 314
Du Boulay, Helen (née Sutton) 33
Du Boulay, Ernest 33, 35
Dudley, Earl of 57
Dundas, Captain 143

Eagles, Sue 249
Eales, Frances 238, 239
Earhart, Amelia 160
Ederle, Gertrude 271
Edge, Selwyn 36, 37
Edwards, Mackenna 274
Edwards, Tracy vii, 1, 5, 6, 8, 273–278, 282, 297, 302, 319
Elwood, Rosalind 212
Eriksson, Pamela (née Bourne) 98, 101–105, 301, 312
Eriksson, Sven 101, 102, 103, 104, 105
Eriksson, Sven-Cecilie 105
Erikson, Gustaf 98, 99, 100, 118, 128

Fairholme, Elizabeth (Liz) 106, 107–108, 113, 193, 302, 312
Farrar, Alfred 72
Farrar, Austin 302
Farrar, Celia (née Packard) 71–73
Farrell, Angela 274
Farrar, Norman 72
Fazackerley, Emily 199, 200
Faroux, Marie-Claude 317
Fegan, Annamarie 287
Ferris, Sharon 278
Fife, William 200, 201
Findlay, Gordon 201, 302
De Fin, Jackie vii, 297
Fish, Dr Deborah 194
Foster family 152
Fox, Uffa 109, 148

Fox Smith, Cicely ii, viii, 61, 66–68, 303, 310
Foy, Mark 45, 46
Francis, Clare vii, 205, 224, 229, 231–238, 268, 275, 296, 302, 317, 318
Francis, Mary 172
Francis, Richard ('Dick Francis') 172
Frank, Colin 209, 211, 212
Frayao, Otilia 216
Freda (canal daughter) 153
Frost, Lucy 138
Furey, Jimmy 54

Gann, Mr 49
Garbo, Greta 103
Gartside-Tipping, Henry 108
Gartside-Tipping, Mary 108
George (friend of Liz & Poo) 108
'Gerard, Peter' (Dulcie Kennard) 7, 84, 91–97, 147, 302, 307, 311
Goodall, Susie 7, 307
Goode, John 280
Gooding, Jo 274
Gore-Booth, Constance see Markievicz, Constance
Gore-Boothe, Sir Henry 66
Gould, Cecily (née Brent-Good) 93, 131–132, 302, 310
Grainger, Julie viii, 178, 184, 187, 188
Grainger, Nick viii, 184, 187, 188, 189, 302, 315, 316
Graham, Ralph 285
'Grand, Sarah' (Frances Bellenden Clarke) 28
Green, Alan 198
Green, Joan 234
Green, Pam (née Ryan) 193, 194
Green, Peter 194, 316
Green, Ron 234
Grey, Sir Edward 61
Griffiths, Maurice 91, 93, 94, 95, 96, 97, 113, 145, 146, 147, 217, 302, 303, 311

Griffths-Jones, Mervyn 184
Grosvenor, Janet vii, 190, 194, 196–198, 232, 260, 287
Guzzwell, John 138, 271

Haig Thomas, Margaret (Lady Rhondda) 65, 201
Hamilton, Mrs 200
Hammersley, the Misses 31
Hammick, Anne vii, 251, 252–254, 283, 303, 318
Hammick, Eleanor 251
Hammick, Liz vii, 251, 252, 253
Hammick, Mick 251, 253
Hampton, Kitty 252
Hargreaves, Alison 137, 314
Hargreaves, Kate 137
Hargreaves, Tom 137
Harwood, Hannah 278
Hatfield, Bill 286
Hasler, Blondie 253, 263
Hayward, Rachael 252, 253
Hayward, Roger 253
Heaton, Peter 203
Henderson, Isabel 186
Henderson, Nikki 285
Herbert, Alan P 141
Herreshoff, Nathaniel 22
Heywood, Suzanne (née Cook) vii, 209, 220, 221, 303, 317
Hill, Annie vii, 257, 259–261, 303, 318
Hill, Nancy 274
Hill, Pete 257, 259, 260, 261
Hinchliffe, Sally 178, 184–187, 189, 228
Hiscock, Eric 144, 170, 171, 211, 315
Hiscock, Susan (née Schlater) 144, 145, 163, 170–172, 251
Hlongwa, Thandiwe 296
Hodgson, Godfrey 194, 316
Holford, Ingrid (née Bianchi) 144, 149, 173, 303

Holmes, Alex 45
Hope, Linton 45
Hopkins, Ami 297
Hughes, Barbara viii, 5, 28–35, 37, 51, 196, 234, 303, 307, 308
Hughes, Edith 31
Hughes, Evangeline 29
Hughes, Grace *see* Schenley, Grace
Hughes, Gerry 302
Hughes, John St John 28, 30
Hughes, Owain 185, 302
Hughes, Penny *see* Minney, Penny
Hughes, Richard 185, 186, 303
Huish, Sue 130, 163
Hunt, Mr and Mrs 94

Illingworth, John 176, 191, 194, 316
Irvine, Arthur 25
Isbester, Allan 25
Isbester, Arthur 25, 26
Isbester, Eric 26
Isbester, Jack 25, 26, 27, 304, 308
Isbester, Kathleen 25, 26
Isbester, Norman 27
Isbester, Susie (née Irvine) 19, 25, 26, 27
Isbester, Thyra 26

Jaca, Vuyisile vii, 1, 284, 296–299 320
Jackson, Tom 254, 255
Jackson, Vicky 254, 255
Jacobsen, Betty 98, 100, 312
James, Naomi (née Power) vii, 262, 265–272, 276, 279, 304, 319
James, Rob 265, 266, 267, 268, 270, 271 272,
Jarvis, Carys 287
Jenkins, Horatio 38
Jessop, Mr 32
Johnson, Amy *see* Mollison, Amy
Jones, Jack 147
Jones, June 87

Jordan, Commodore Catherine 287
Jordan, Noel 166

Keary, Eily 61, 69, 70, 303, 310
Kemp, John 182, 183
Kemp, Monica 182, 183
Kenney, Jessie 150
Keppie, Jean (née Wilson) 202–203, 300, 316
Keppie, Peter 203
Kennedy, Miss 43
Kernick, Jill vii, 238, 243–247, 250, 291, 300
Kerr, Lt-Cmdr Catherine 207
Kieffer, Marie-Claude 274
King, Dave 280
King, Junella 298
King, Maureen 280
King, Richard 161, 304
Kirkpatrick, Hope 194, 197
Kipling, Carrie 36
Kipling, Rudyard 36, 68
Knox-Johnston, Robin 1, 98, 227, 236, 268

Labourgade, Elie 235
Laird, Dorothy 128
Lamb, Christian (née Oldham) 116, 118, 125, 126, 304, 312, 313
Lance, Kate vii, 98, 99, 304, 311, 312
Laughton, Sir John 63
Laughton, Vera *see* Mathews, Vera Laughton
Laurent Giles, Jack 192, 205
Layard, Nina 72
Leigh, Mrs 200
'Levitt, Dorothy' (Elizabeth Levi) 28, 36, 304, 308
Lewis, Cynthia ('Aunt Thea') 279
Lewis, Irene 279
Linklater, Elizabeth (née Young) 19, 22–24, 92, 172, 275, 304, 308
Linklater, Eric 24
Linklater, Robert 24

Llewellyn, Astrid Dixon (née Dixon) vii, 82, 83, 174, 175, 218
Llewellyn, Betty 106
Llewellyn, Margaret 106–107
Llewellyn, Sam vii, 40, 309
Locker, William 241
Loomis, Alf 192
Long, Jean McKinney 206

MacAleavey, Cathy *see* Murphy, Cathy
MacArthur, Avril 279
MacArthur, Ellen 269, 273, 278–283, 24, 294, 304, 319, 320
MacDonald, Hugh 266
MacDonald Moreton, Anna (née Sutton) 33, 35
MacPherson, Florence 121
MacPherson, Hugh 121
MacVicker, David 254
MacVicker, Jane *see* Russell, Jane
MacVicker, Katherine 254, 257
McMahon, Eve 285
Maillart, Ella 78, 137, 172, 222, 304
Marchand, Aline 235
Markievicz, Countess (née Gore-Booth) 66
Marriott, Edward 126, 304
Marsh, David 42
Marsh, Lesley vii, 238, 247–248, 296, 318
Martin, Violet ('Martin Ross') 56, 305, 310
Martinez, Mr 12, 13
Mary, Princess 122
Mashford, Sid 161
Mathews, Elvira Laughton 124
Mathews, Gordon Laughton 60, 124
Mathews, Vera Laughton 61–65, 116–124, 127–130, 193, 232, 293, 304, 310, 312, 313
Maturin, Maude *see* Speed, Maude

INDEX

McLachlan, Irene 199, 204, 205
McLean, David 204, 205
McLean, Hugh 204, 205
Meggett, Geoff 110, 304
Merron, Miranda 278, 294
Millar, George 172
Miller, Lee 146
Mills, Hannah 285
Milnes-Walker, Nicolette *see* Coward, Nicolette
Minney, Penny (née Hughes) 178, 184–187, 189, 228, 315, 316
Minney, Robin vii, 187, 189, 316
Mitchell, David 209, 211, 212, 223
Moitessier, Bernard 269
Mollison, Amy (née Johnson) 140, 264
Molyneux, Edward 117
Monaghan, Margaret 203
Moreton, Evelyn 35
Moreton, Colonel MacDonald 33
Moreton, Margaret *see* Phillips, Margaret
Morgan, Geoffrey 216, 304
Morgan Giles, Frank viii, 48, 49, 134
Morgan Giles, Ivy (née Carus-Wilson) 38, 47–50, 305
Morgan Giles, Admiral Morgan 50
Moore, Wendy 252
Morris, Stewart 109
Mortimer, Molly 38, 304, 309
Mundy, Jeni 274
Muntz, Elsie Joy *see* Davison, Elsie Joy
Murphy, Cathy (née MacAleavey) vii, 51, 53, 54
Murphy, Conor 54
Myatt, Claudia vii, 238–241, 250, 304, 318

Napier, Miss 43
Napper, Tom 295
Nelson, Horatio 241
Newell, Eric 131 132 133
Newell, Gladys 131, 132–133, 313
Newell, John vii, 133, 313
Neville, Sophie 93, 311
Neuschäfer, Kirsten 285
Nicholson, Charles 35
Nielson, Captain Suzi 287
Nixon, WM vii, 51, 52
North, Admiral Sir Dudley 121

Oakley, Captain Sarah 287
O'Brien, Charlotte 58
O'Brien, Conor 57, 58, 59, 94
O'Brien, Kitty (Kate) 57, 58, 59, 61, 94
O'Brien, Margaret 57, 58, 61
O'Brien, Nellie 58
O'Callaghan, Jeremiah 55
O'Connor, Alan 57, 172, 304
O'Flaherty, Chris vii, 206, 316
Ogilvy-Wedderburn, Bumble 236
Oldham, Christian *see* Lamb, Christian
Osgood, Molly *see* Childers, Molly
Owen, Merfyn 283
Oudry, Brigitte 137, 266, 269

Packard, Celia *see* Farrar, Celia
Packard, Edward 72
Packard, Ellen 72
Packard, Nina 72
Palmer, Kathleen ('Guy Pennant') 144–148, 153, 173
Palmer, Ian vii, 145, 147, 314
Pankhurst, Christabel 63
Pankhurst, Emmeline 120
Paret, Michele 274
Parsons, Charles 70
Parsons, Katherine 70
Parsons, Rachel 61, 70, 303

Paul (Tracy Edwards' fellow crew) 275
Pawson, Des 240
Payne, Arthur Edward 33
Paul, Alan 197
Pears, Charles 97
Peddie, Tom 75, 76
Penhaul, Elaine vii, 284, 293, 294, 320
Pera, Gianni 195
Pera, Mary (née Blewitt) 189, 190–194, 197, 198, 252, 282, 301, 304
Percival, Mr 33
Peri, Claude ('Jack Langlais') 126
Perrin, Ashley vii, 280, 282, 283, 284, 294, 295, 320
Peyton, Mike 241
Phillimore, Miranda 40
Phillips, Alex 294
Phillips, Admiral Tom 42, 121
Phillips Louisa (née De Horsey) 42, 121
Phillips, Margaret (née Moreton) 35
Phillips, Norman 35
Phillips, Vaughan 42
Pickering, Jojo vii, 209, 211, 212, 223
Pickering, Lulu 213
Pickering, Rod 209, 210, 211, 212, 213, 214
Pickthall, Barry 7, 148, 307, 314
Pierrepont, Gervase (Earl Manvers) 163, 164, 165
Pierrepont, Rozelle *see* Raynes, Rozelle
Pinkard, GH 145
Pinckney, Evelyn 170, 171
Pinckney, Roger 170
Pirie, Marcia 171
Pitt-Rivers, Ray ('Mary Hinton') 194
Pocock, Mike 252
Pocock, Pat 252
Powell, Pamela (Poo) 106, 107–108, 113, 193, 302, 312
Power, Juliet 265, 269

Power, Naomi *see* James, Naomi
Pope, Clive 222
Poyser, Nancy 92
Preece, Joan ('Winkle') 130, 163, 165
Purves, Libby 292
Putnam, George 100
Pye, Anne 170, 172
Pye, Peter 170, 172

Quin, May 19

Radek, Karl 88
Radek, Rosa 88
Ramos, Julia (née Rushbury) vii, 169
Ramsey, Eileen 144, 148–149, 153, 294, 304, 314
Ransome, Arthur viii, 48, 86, 87, 88, 89, 90, 114, 214, 239, 258, 282, 301, 303, 305, 311
Ransome, Evgenia (née Schelepina) viii, 84, 87–90, 264, 282, 305
Ransome, Ivy 89
Raynes, Dick 183, 262
Raynes, Rozelle (née Pierrepont, also Beattie) viii, 116, 129, 130, 163–169, 173, 183, 206, 226, 262, 279, 305, 313, 315, 319
Read, Bil 72
Redon, Jacques 234, 235, 236
Reed, Allan Brunton 243
Reeves, Clive vii, 203
Reid, Ian 201
Reid, Millicent viii, 201, 208
Reid, Seonaid vii, 199, 200–201, 207, 208
Rhodes, Beatrice (née Sutton) 33
Rhodes, John 33
Rice, Angela 241
Richards, Emma 278, 294
Richardson, Henry 109
Richardson, Phyllis (née Gartside-Tipping) 106, 108, 109

Ridgway, John 184
Ridgway, Marie-Christine 184
Riley, Dawn 274
Roberts, Gilbert 125
Robertson, E Arnot 113, 312
Robertson, Shirley 281
Robertson, Trevor 259
Robinson, Thora 194
Rushbury, Birdie 169
Rushbury, Sir Henry 169
Rushbury, Janet *see* Vera-Sanso, Janet
Russell, David 163, 169, 171, 172, 175, 176, 177, 193, 279
Russell, Jane (née MacVicker) vii, 172, 251, 254, 256–258, 262, 287
Ryan, Pam *see* Green, Pam

'Sabrina' (Norma Sykes) 166
Sandys, Diana (née Churchill) 118
Schlater, Susan *see* Hiscock, Susan
Schenley, Grace (née Hughes) 28, 31, 33, 35, 72, 200
Schelpina, Evgenia *see* Ransome, Evgenia
Schelepina, Iroida 88
Schiottz, Eyvin 53
Scott, Alex 2
Scott, Elizabeth 126
Scott, Peter 109, 305, 312, 314
Seck, Maryama 298
Service, Robert 278
Seymour, Admiral Sir Michael 39
Shepherd, Gordon 59, 60
Sieghart, Mary-Anne 172, 305
Sinclair, Mark 190
Sleightholme, Des 257
Sleightholme, Joyce 216, 217, 259, 305, 317
Smeeton, Beryl (née Boxer) 71, 74–78, 131, 135–138, 141, 143, 172,

173, 222, 239, 258, 271, 272, 280, 305, 310, 311, 313, 314
Smeeton, Clio vii, 77, 78, 135, 136, 137, 138, 143, 171, 258, 271, 272, 305, 313, 314, 319
Smeeton, Miles 75, 76, 78, 135, 138, 143, 171, 258, 271, 272, 313, 314, 319
Smillie, Susan 260, 305, 318
Smith, David 38
Smith, Emma (Elspeth Hallsmith) 144, 151–153, 180, 193, 305, 314
Smith-Dorrien, Edith (née Tower) 38
Smith-Dorrien, Thomas 38
Smith, H 72
Smith, Victoria 6, 305
Smithwick, Captain 56
Socrates, Jeanne 286, 320
Somerset, Bobby 176
Somerville, Edith 56, 305
Southby-Tailyour, Ewen vii, 137, 314
Spain, Nancy 116, 122, 302
Speed, Henry 40, 41
Speed, Maude (née Maturin) 38, 40–42, 305, 309
Spence, Angus 200
Spiers, George 148, 294
Spring Rice, Mary 51, 58, 59, 60, 66, 309, 310
Sprot, Arabella 242
Sprot, Edward 242, 243
Sprot, Rachael 242
Stanley, Lady Carla vii, 284, 288, 289, 291, 320
Stanley, Lord Richard 288
Stanley, Jo 19, 150, 257, 308, 318
Stark, Suzanne 20
Steve (crew of *Ogre*) 85, 86
Stevens, James 280
Stevenson, Robert Louis 107
Stickland, Katy vii, 320
Stock, Mabel (aka Peter) 84, 85, 97, 172, 305, 311

INDEX

Stock, Ralph 84, 85, 86, 305, 306, 311
Stone, Jane 120
Stopes, Marie 90
Street, Don 252
Sutton, Anna *see* MacDonald Moreton, Anna
Sutton, Beatrice *see* Rhodes, Beatrice
Sutton, Helen *see* Du Boulay, Helen
Sutton, Sir Richard 32
Sutton, Lionel 33
Sutton, Mary *see* Cochrane, Mary
Sutton, Maud 28, 33, 35
Sutton, Winnie 28, 33, 35, 51
Swale, Colin 222
Swale, Eve 221
Swale, James 221, 222
Swale, Rosie (Swale Pope) 209, 221, 222, 306, 317
Swan, Amanda 274
Swinstead, David vii, 32, 35, 308, 310
Symons, Jim 48, 49

Tabarly, Marie 295, 296
Tambs, Erling 211
Tangvald, Ann 219
Tangvald, Carmen 219, 220
Tangvald, Florence 219
Tangvald, Lillemor 219
Tangvald, Lydia 219
Tangvald, Per/Peter 219, 220
Tangvald, Simonne 219
Tangvald, Thomas 219, 220
Tangvald, Virginia 219
Tate, Jane 192
Tenison, Edward King 55
Tenison, Lady Louisa 55
Terry, Rear-Admiral Jude 287
Tew, Helen 283, 284, 286, 320
Thomas, Heather vii, 2, 208, 277, 284, 288, 295, 296

Thompson, Clare *see* Allcard, Clare
Thompson, Chris vii, viii, 34, 308
Thorndike, Karen 255
Thornycroft, Blanche (née Coules) 69
Thornycroft, Blanche Coules 61, 69–70, 303, 336
Thornycroft, John 69
Thunberg, Greta 285
Thurstan, Violetta 116, 119
Tier, Liz 294
Tilman, HW 176, 306
Todrick, Elizabeth 199, 201, 202
Tower, Edith *see* Smith-Dorrien, Edith
Townsend, Margaret *see* Bridges, Margaret
Townsend, Richard 143
Trelawny, Ian 120, 123
Tucker, Pamela 216, 304
Turner, Mark 281, 283
Turner, Mary *see* Dixon, Mary
Turner, Rev Henry 81
Turner, Ted 195

Ullstein, Gabriele *see* Annan, Gabriele
Underhill, Arthur 42, 306, 309

Vallance, Mr 49
Van der Wiele, Annie 172, 306
Vaughan, Janet 186
Vera-Sanso, Janet (née Rushbury, also Bradford) 163, 169–170, 171, 172, 175–177, 193, 279
Vera-Sanso, Juan 176
Vera-Sanso, Naomi vii, 176, 177
Vera-Sanso, Penny vii, 176, 177
Victoria, Queen 14, 41, 51, 151

Villiers, Alan 98, 99, 100, 304, 30, 311, 312
Villiers, Daphne 100
Visser, Tanja 274
Von Koskull, Mikaela 274, 278
Vyvyan, Clara Coltman Rogers 39

Waldron, Mrs 48
Wallace, Mick 54
Warren, Claire 274
Watson, GL 34, 200
Welby, Euphemia 128
Wellington, Duchess of 39
West, Sarah 249
Westmacott, Emma 278
Westminster, Duchess of 33
Wharram, James 214, 259
Whitehead, Mags 187, 189
Wickham, Hilary 259
Wiles, Muriel 93, 114–115, 106, 311
Wilkinson, June 123
Wilson, Jean *see* Keppie, Jean
Wiseman, Hazel 207
'Winkle' *see* Preece, Joan
Wittgenstein, Ludwig 272
Wood, Mr 31
Worth, Claude 43
Worth, Janet 43
Worth, Susan 176
Worth, Tom 176
Wyllie, Bill 43, 44, 45, 46, 306
Wyllie, Dick 46
Wyllie, Eva 46, 47
Wyllie, Harold 65
Wyllie, Marian (née Carew) 6, 38, 43–47, 51, 65, 234, 306, 309

Yarrow, Sir Alfred 69
Young, Elizabeth *see* Linklater, Elizabeth
Young, James 22, 24
Young, Sarah 22, 23, 275